Acknowledgments

We wish to thank the Middle Tennessee State University Faculty Research Committee and the Middle Tennessee State University English Department Research Committee for grants that made possible our editing of this volume; Kevin J. Donovan, John T. Shawcross, and Donald Peter McDonough for their help in organizing the 1997 Conference on John Milton, the Virginia Peck Foundation Trust Fund for financial support, and all the participants for their contributions to an event both stimulating and convivial; new friends at Valdosta State University and time-honored colleagues at Christian Brothers University and Middle Tennessee State University who have supported and encouraged us; Carrie and Chris, Janie and Anton, Elliott, and Andrew, "more hands" who lighten our "labors"; and, most especially, the sixteen contributors, whose "progeny" are the "pretious life-blood" of this collection.

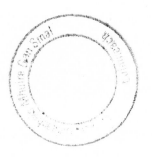

LIVING TEXTS

LIVING TEXTS

Interpreting Milton

Edited by
Kristin A. Pruitt and
Charles W. Durham

SUP

Selinsgrove: Susquehanna University Press
London: Associated University Presses

Associated University Presses
440 Forsgate Drive
Cranbury, NJ 08512

Associated University Presses
16 Barter Street
London WC1A 2AH, England

Associated University Presses
P.O. Box 338, Port Credit
Mississauga, Ontario
Canada L5G 4L8

Library of Congress Cataloging-in-Publication Data

Living texts : interpreting Milton / edited by Kristin A. Pruitt and Charles W. Durham.
    p.   cm.
    Includes bibliographical references and index.
    ISBN 1-57591-042-X (alk. paper)
    1. Milton, John, 1608–1674—Criticism and interpretation—
Congresses.   I. Pruitt, Kristin A., 1945–   . II. Durham, Charles, 1939–
    PR3588.L59   2000
    821'.4—dc21   00-034442

To Michael Lieb and Albert C. Labriola,

"complete" in their "own Perfections,"
for "Shedding sweet influence" on the field
of Milton studies

Contents

Introduction

> For Books are not absolutely dead things, but doe contain a potencie of life in them to be as active as that soule was whose progeny they are; nay they do preserve as in a viall the purest efficacie and extraction of that living intellect that bred them. . . . [A] good Booke is the pretious life-blood of a master spirit, imbalm'd and treasur'd up on purpose to a life beyond life.
>
> —*Areopagitica*

John Milton's justifiably famous defense of books as possessing the intelligence, the potency, and, indeed, the very blood and marrow of their creators is, of course, the inspiration for *Living Texts: Interpreting Milton*. No other writer of the seventeenth century bequeathed to the twentieth century such vigorous progeny, offspring themselves capable of begetting living texts and thus destined to sustained "life beyond life." And so it is that "generations" of readers, including those represented in the present collection, have "come / From all the ends of th' Earth, to celebrate / And reverence . . . thir great Progenitor" (*Paradise Lost*, 11.345–47).[1]

Michael Lieb, in the opening essay, describes Adam's story in book 8 of *Paradise Lost* as "structured with a consummate sense of artistry and skill. Adam is a superb storyteller. More than that, he is both a poet and an orator." Adam, then, might well be seen as the image of his "master sprit" Milton, whose renderings of biblical narratives in *Paradise Lost, Paradise Regained*, and *Samson Agonistes* are, to use the phrase Lieb applies to Adam's account, "triumph[s] of poetic art." But as the essays in this volume demonstrate, Milton's accomplishments extend beyond those of storyteller, poet, and orator. His "living intellect," "preserve[d] as in a viall," drew sustenance from human concerns as diverse as politics and obstetrics, and later centuries in turn have drawn sustenance from Milton's real or presumed roles as cultural icon and commentator on Christian doctrine.

The sixteen essays that follow were originally presented at the

1997 Conference on John Milton, and because they were judged particularly significant for Milton studies through a rigorous selection process, their authors were invited to expand and revise them for this volume. Despite their diverse subjects and approaches, these essays nonetheless exhibit certain themes and issues in Milton studies on the cusp of the millennium. For example, several identify and examine sources—in the classics, among the church fathers, in the Hebrew Bible and lexicons, in religious controversies. Others address issues of relationship—between Adam and Eve, humankind and God, Father and Son; still others investigate the portrayal of Chaos in *Paradise Lost*, and a number consider the controversy regarding the authorship of *De Doctrina Christiana*. In their "dialogue" with each other and with Milton, they demonstrate how truly alive are the texts of "thir great Progenitor."

Lieb, in "Adam's Story: Testimony and Transition in *Paradise Lost*," views Adam's narration of his creation to Raphael as a reflection of diverse literary genres, especially that of spiritual autobiography. For, as Lieb argues, "To engage Adam's account . . . is to involve oneself in the phenomenon of personal experience, the narrative of selfhood 'writ large.' " Adam herein "maps the course of his spiritual awakening from the point of his coming to consciousness to his union with Eve, a journey that involves an ascent to ever higher realms of enlightenment" and documents "a remarkable 'conversion' " to awareness of God's providential design. As such, "Adam's story not only brings to the fore some of the most important themes" of *Paradise Lost*; "it also provides insight into the transformation of biblical source into poetic text."

In response to Lieb, J. Martin Evans devotes his "Afterthoughts on Adam's Story" to "Adam's afterthoughts on the same subject," focusing on the psychological and moral implications of Adam's narrative in contrast to Eve's critique of that narrative. According to Evans, "If we follow Lieb's advice and view Adam's story 'within the context of Eve's reflections on her own coming to awareness of self and other,' then we can hardly escape the conclusion that Eve's portrayal of her encounter with her husband not only 'contains additional details that supplement the story that Adam tells' but also contains additional details that totally subvert the story that Adam tells." Evans concludes that "Adam's romanticized misrepresentation of his wife's behavior" is both "a pathetic exercise in self-deception" and "an ominous foreshadowing of 'the vehemence of love' that will lead him to eat the forbidden fruit in the next book."

The "vehemence of love" accorded Milton among Victorian readers is the subject of Anna K. Nardo's "John Milton, Object of the Erotic Gaze?" Despite their veneration of the author of *Paradise Lost* "as a kind of Protestant saint," Victorian writers were "prone to sensationalize the life stories of their idols," and hence Milton's imagined erotic life became the topic of popular writing. Nardo offers "a cultural history of Victorian representations of Milton as a lover . . . to demonstrate how some of these fictions gratified the Milton idolaters by reversing Adam's love story . . . in order to create a love story for the young Milton" and "to show how George Eliot's epic novel *Middlemarch* exposes the excesses of the cult of Milton by testing its folly against the truths of Milton's own epic vision."

Using seventeenth-century obstetrical theories and practices as her springboard, Susan McDonald, in " 'Wide Was the Wound': Cesarean Section and the Birth of Eve," focuses on Adam's story of Eve's creation to argue that her emergence from Adam's left side suggests procedures for cesarean childbirth in Milton's time, by means of which the poet "invokes a variety of associations—medical, gender, iconographic—that expressed and engendered professional and personal anxieties." Milton's purpose, she claims, is not "to displace woman from" her role in childbearing but rather "to suggest the possibility, and perhaps to intensify our understanding of the loss, of unfallen procreation."

Approaching Eve's role in *Paradise Lost* from a feminist and legal perspective in "A Preliminary Study of Informed Consent and Free Will in the Garden of Eden: John Milton's Social Contract," Lynne Greenberg explores the conflicting views "of patriarchal obedience and subordination" and an emerging "contract-based, egalitarian society." Whereas "Adam's relationship with God is framed as a contract," a "mutual, free, and informed arrangement," Eve, Greenberg believes, does not "covenant directly with God"; her " 'acceptance' of her marriage to Adam functions as her only opportunity to an agreement in the poem" and that, Greenberg indicates, "despite its rhetoric of voluntarism, does not provide the paradigm of a free agreement but rather one of coerced participation." As such, the situation "parallels a married woman's relationship to seventeenth-century law" and reveals that "[s]ocial contract theory has not replaced patriarchal theory, but rather it has subversively reappropriated and subsumed it within its own ideology."

Using historical research and textual analysis to document Satan's visual fixation on Eve, Cheryl H. Fresch, in " 'Aside the Devil Turned / For Envy': The Evil Eye in *Paradise Lost*, Book 4," maintains "that Satan is not so much an epithalamic choragus, an epithalamic Chorus, or a voyeur . . . as he is what the classical writers of marriage songs—among a significant body of other authorities—identified as the *fascinum*, 'the evil eye,' and furthermore, that Milton's blind bard, insofar as he shares Satan's perspective, also participates in that role within the fourth book of *Paradise Lost*." Satan hopes to "destroy the happiness of the young couple" as he "peers at their naked embrace." However, as the bard envisions the sleeping pair in the nuptial bower, "Milton may be evoking . . . the concept that the rabbis called the Good Eye, as opposed to the Evil Eye."

Also focusing on Satan, sources, and analogues, Raphael Falco, in "Satan and Servius: Milton's Use of the Helen Episode (*Aeneid*, 2.567–88)," mines the early neo-Latin poetic and biblical commentaries and their vernacular counterparts to posit that the controversial and possibly spurious Helen episode that Milton presumably used in books 1 and 2 of *Paradise Lost* may actually have been an adaptation of Pontanus's commentary on the *Aeneid*, commentary that itself relied on readings by Servius and Scaliger. Falco states: "I think that Milton—like every other learned author—read Vergil, Ovid, and Horace, maybe even Homer, against the background of a lively and voluminous tradition of commentary. Thus what we often regard as a direct response to a passage in, say, Vergil, is very possibly a response to a commentator's exegesis of Vergil, and moreover to the marginal debate surrounding a particular canonical passage in Renaissance editions of the classical works." Although he emphasizes that "Satan has numerous textual origins" that he is not seeking to displace, Falco sees the possible source of the Helen episode as "a witty exculpation," for "if the text Milton imitated is itself spurious, then how can he be blamed that his character turned out to be such a liar?"

Claude N. Stulting Jr. also turns to commentary, that of a church father, as a gloss on the unfallen Adam and Eve in "*Theosis* and *Paideia* in the Writings of Gregory of Nyssa and the Prelapsarian Books of Milton's *Paradise Lost*." Stulting asserts that Gregory's concept of *theosis*, the deification of humankind through divine *paideia* (education), "illuminate[s] our understanding of . . . humankind's prelapsarian condition." Raphael, in his discourse with the unfallen couple in book 5, clearly "articulates Adam's and Eve's prelapsarian spirituality," suggesting that they "are created primarily for participation in and communion with God" and that "[f]rom the moment of their creation, they undertake an educational venture." Through obedience, "they become more complete and perfect." In closing, Stulting observes: "It is an intriguing possibility that Milton's poetics of deification represent a partial solution to [the] 'unexplored' and 'unsolved' Latin transformation of the ideal of divine *paideia* first articulated by Gregory of Nyssa."

In "Riding the Hebrew Word Web," Peggy Samuels explores the importance of Hebrew lexicons and concordances for "negotiating the Hebrew Bible" in the seventeenth century, especially for a writer such as Milton, who brought languages other than Latin and English to scriptural interpretation. Samuels claims that "Milton certainly believed that all doctrinal points were easily enough understood through vernacular translations of the Bible. . . . But to render the fullness of the Hebrew into English required a means of opening and presenting the rich web of associations locked inside the Hebrew roots," and she cites numerous examples in *Paradise Lost* of the way "in which Milton plays a word or a concept over and over in varying contexts, allowing the word to be used with such wildly varying intents and meanings, and frequently causing the word to turn into its opposite," which is, she explains, "a use of language that closely resembles the reading of the Bible in Hebrew, especially as it was facilitated by lexicons and concordances."

In "When Worlds Collide: The Central Naturalistic Narrative and the Allegorical Dimension to *Paradise Lost*," Sarah R. Morrison points out that "[t]here is considerable disagreement about the precise nature and extent of the allegory Milton employs in his grand epic." She goes on to contend that the poet "allows the allegorical elements of *Paradise Lost* to undercut the central naturalistic narrative because to do otherwise would be to appear to endorse parascriptural elements of doubtful authority that go well beyond the bare and self-contradictory scriptural account of creation and the Fall: his highly fictionalized interpretation of sacred history must necessarily contain within itself subtle indications of its nature as an accommodated version of scriptural truth." Through "freedom of invention," Morrison believes, Milton "provides the means for readers to ascertain that *Paradise Lost* is ultimately more allegory than history."

John Leonard's "Milton, Lucretius, and 'the Void Profound of Unessential Night' " argues for Milton's indebtedness to Lucretius's *De Rerum Natura* for his conceptions of Chaos and Night in *Paradise Lost*. Despite "the doctrinal gulf that separates the two poets," both present a "model of a finite, spherical universe surrounded by an infinite void in which atoms randomly collide," and "Milton (in a line borrowed from Lucretius) calls his abyss 'the womb of Nature and perhaps her grave' (2.911) and boldly conjectures that God might draw on the 'dark materials' of Chaos 'to create more worlds' (2.916)." Contending that "Night is in some ways . . . more sinister" than Chaos, Leonard engages fellow critics, John Rumrich and Dennis Danielson in particular, to advance his argument, concluding that " 'Satan's view' of the abyss reveals Milton's fear of what our universe might be. Milton does his best to confine Night to outer darkness, but she still casts her shadow over us and him. Milton's pale dominion only partly checks the Night."

"Of Chaos and Nightingales," Rumrich's rebuttal to Leonard's essay, is another look at Chaos, in which Rumrich "respond[s] to Leonard's pregnant meditation on possibly infertile Night." Referring to his earlier considerations of Chaos, Rumrich insists that "my main argument has long been, in a critical context roundly condemnatory of Chaos as hostile to God, that Chaos is not evil or God's enemy, that indeed, Chaos is, after its fashion, good." Because it "lacks God's creative and moral goodness," he continues, "the realm of Chaos is good only in the sense that it is materially sufficient for God's creative purposes." As for Night, Rumrich states that "Milton does not uniformly or predominantly present Night and darkness as threatening, dreadful, or terrifying" and offers evidence from *Paradise Lost* that Leonard "neglects to mention." Although "Milton wrote in a poetic culture with a strong antipathy to . . . Night," Rumrich finds his "deviation from" this "cultural predisposition" especially telling.

In his consideration of "The Confounded Confusion of Chaos," William B. Hunter provides yet another link in his chain of interconnected arguments against Milton's authorship of *De Doctrina Christiana*. Hunter claims: "I see no way to identify the chaos described in [*Paradise Lost*] with the inherent goodness of the original matter as the treatise defines it. As to whether it derives *ex nihilo* or *ex deo*, the poem is simply silent; and Milton never raises the question elsewhere." Hunter cites earlier criticism that has attempted to reconcile the contradictions between poem and treatise and claims that in *Paradise Lost*, chaos "exists in two distinct forms, all originally neutral, of which God transforms part to good, the limited material upon which he will found his creation." Hunter also explores the contradictory views of sexuality in the two works and concludes: "I do not see how the same man could classify sexuality as a 'secondary end' in *De Doctrina* and also create the sexual speeches and scenes that he included in *Paradise Lost* (for what would Paradise be without sex?)."

Like Hunter, Paul R. Sellin questions the provenance of *De Doctrina* in " 'If Not Milton, Who Did Write the *DDC?*': The Amyraldian Connection," in which he posits the involvement of Moyse Amyraut, a divine at the Huguenot academy of Saumur. Basing his thesis on his French translations of Amyraut's *Brief Traité de la Predestination et de ses principales dépendances* of 1634 and his own Latin translations of *De Doctrina*, Sellin argues for "an oddly conservative streak regarding predestination" in *DDC* that parallels Amyraut's eight components of predestination. Sellin thinks that this connection has been overlooked in Milton studies "partly because of its superficial resemblance to Arminianism, partly because of Amyraut's royalist political philosophy." Because *De Doctrina* is not the "coherent 'tractate' that Charles Sumner begot back in 1823," Sellin queries whether it might be "a composite rather along the lines of Jonson's *Discoveries* but arranged under borrowed orthodox headings, all strung together with sometimes organic but sometimes only superficially appropriate transitions" and counsels that "[u]ntil such questions are settled, it is perhaps vain and certainly premature to ask, 'if not Milton, who did write the *DDC?*' "

In an essay that counterpoints those of Hunter and Sellin, Kenneth Borris examines "Milton's Heterodoxy of the Incarnation and Subjectivity in *De Doctrina Christiana* and *Paradise Lost.*" Heterodoxy informs both works in their so-called theology of the Son, Borris argues: "Though the relation of *De Doctrina* to *Paradise Lost* is complex and indirect, their thematic and chronological interconnections are nevertheless both close and extensive. . . . [T]he fact that *Paradise Lost* could be published, unlike *De Doctrina*, shows that the poem approaches heterodoxy with much circumspection . . . by blurring its doctrinal positions" and "encoding controversial meanings. Through equivocation in his theological epic, Milton avoids hypocritically effacing the hard-won religious views explored in

De Doctrina." In particular, Borris sees *Paradise Lost* as "ground[ing] godly human relations, identity, and heroic potential in Milton's unique conception of its 'greater man': the Son unites with a specific and complete human person, not a generalized human nature as in orthodox accounts."

In the final essay, "Belial, Popery, and True Religion: Milton's *Of True Religion* and Antipapist Sentiment," Hong Won Suh offers a religio-political analysis of Milton's antipapism. Suh claims that *Of True Religion* is "a critique of the Test Act and more broadly of the use of civil power in ecclesiastical matters," especially Anglican policies regarding Nonconformists. Through the figure of Belial, Milton describes "the corrupting power of the pagan god" and "the vulnerability" of not only Roman Catholicism but also of Anglicanism and Presbyterianism to popish practices. For Milton, Suh argues, "the real danger is that, in the frenzy to eradicate popery, one faces the possibility of becoming that which one fears and hates," and in examining *Of True Religion,* Suh focuses "on Milton's definition of true religion and its opposite, popery," and views the pamphlet as a plea for toleration.

Individually, these essays represent the varied approaches that the range of Milton's "living texts" evokes. As a whole, the collection reveals the lively dialogue that his works, "imbalm'd and treasur'd up on purpose to a life beyond life," continue to stimulate more than three centuries after their "master spirit's" death.

NOTES

John Milton, *Areopagitica,* in *Complete Prose Works of John Milton,* 8 vols., ed. Don M. Wolfe et al. (New Haven: Yale University Press, 1953–82), 2:492–93.

1. John Milton, *Paradise Lost,* in *John Milton: Complete Poems and Major Prose,* ed. Merritt Y. Hughes (New York: Odyssey, 1957).

LIVING TEXTS

Adam's Story: Testimony and Transition in *Paradise Lost*

MICHAEL LIEB

1

At the completion of the dialogue on astronomy in book 8 of
Paradise Lost, Adam responds to the teachings of his angelic
guest by offering what he calls "My Storie" (205), a narrative at
least as fascinating as that related to the unfallen couple by Raphael during the course of his visit (7.41).[1] Beginning with
Adam's account of his first coming to consciousness after his
creation and culminating in his union with the newly created
Eve (8.250–520), the narrative that Adam shares with the "affable Arch-Angel" (7.41) is remarkable indeed. According to J.
Martin Evans, Adam's story is among "the finest and most imaginative things" in Milton's epic.[2] One would certainly be inclined to agree. For Adam's story not only brings to the fore some
of the most important themes that the poem as a whole raises
but also provides insight into the nature of Milton's artistry in
the transformation of biblical source into poetic text. As such,
Adam's story assumes paramount importance to the understanding of the thematic and artistic dimensions of *Paradise
Lost*.

As we all know, the immediate source of Adam's story is the
second chapter of Genesis.[3] There, Milton found a series of
events to be reconceived in the shaping of Adam's own narrative
in the epic. As delineated in the biblical text, these events include the forming of man from the dust of the ground, the plant-
ing of a garden eastward in Eden, the emergence of the Tree of
Life and the Tree of the Knowledge of Good and Evil in the midst
of the garden, the placement of man in the garden to dress and
keep it, the issuing of the prohibition, the decision to create a
"help meet" for the man, the naming of the creatures, the creation of woman from the man, and the recognition that man and

woman "shall be one flesh" (Gen. 2.7–24). If these events represent the biblical foundation of Adam's story in *Paradise Lost,*
Milton's reinscribing of them in the epic gives rise to an entirely
new way of understanding what in fact did happen "in the beginning."

To be sure, such a reinscription is already a feature of the biblical text itself. One need not subscribe to the "documentary hypothesis" of Julius Wellhausen and his school to be aware of
narrative differences between Gen. 1.1–2.3 (the so-called
"Priestly version") and Genesis 2.4–3.24 (the so-called "Jahwist
version").[4] Whereas the first version is distinguished by a divine,
indeed cosmic perspective supremely aloof yet festive in its celebration of God's creative acts, the second version is distinguished by an essentially human perspective immersed in the
drama of relationship and conflict. The differences that arise
among various versions of a biblical narrative are the very stuff
of "higher criticism." Applying this principle of exegesis to *Paradise Lost,* Evans distinguishes between Raphael's and Adam's
respective accounts of creation. If Raphael's account embodies
the Priestly perspective, Adam's embodies the Jahwist perspective. Raphael's narrative portrays the creation from above,
Adam's from below; Raphael's from the divine point of view,
Adam's from the human; Raphael's from the "outside," Adam's
from the "inside."[5] The differences are ones that Adam himself
invokes in introducing his story. Distinguishing his account
from Raphael's, Adam suggests that what he is about to share
with his angelic guest involves a descent from the "high pitch"
of celestial discourse to the "lower flight" of human discourse
(8.198–99). If Adam's distinction represents a polite gesture of
modesty and humility in the presence of so sublime a guest,
however, it nonetheless provides the means by which the host
may discreetly embark upon a narrative as elevated in its own
way as any related during the course of that wonderful interchange.

To engage Adam's account, his story, is to involve oneself in
the phenomenon of personal experience, the narrative of selfhood "writ large" ("On the Forcers of Conscience," 20). It is to
turn inward toward self and to experience with the teller the intimate details of his life. In fact, this is what Erich Kahler calls
"the inward turn of narrative," a phenomenon that he associates
principally with *Paradise Lost* as a crucial moment in the emergence of first-person narrative as a form of discourse for the revelation and exploration of the psyche. In works that subscribe to

this discourse, narrative undergoes an internalization through which "the springs of the inner life" find release.[6] Adam's story becomes such an act of self-disclosure, of testimony amounting to a revelation of his own experience. In the performance of that act, his story causes the events underlying his experience of coming to awareness of self, of God, and of union with the newly created Eve to become uniquely *his*. They are his because he experienced them and is in a position to retell them from his own point of view. Doing so bestows upon the events a new immediacy and a new authority sanctioned by the fact that what had been biblically conceived as third-person narrative is here reconceived through the eyes of Adam as his own story, as "autobiography," indeed, as "spiritual autobiography."

The phrase "spiritual autobiography" is to the point. In her study of the literary forms embedded in Milton's epic, Barbara Kiefer Lewalski appropriately defines Adam's story as "spiritual autobiography." Citing works ranging from Augustine's *Confessions* to Bunyan's *Grace Abounding* as "prototypes" of this genre, Lewalski views Adam's story as the consummate expression of it.[7] The phrase "spiritual autobiography" is a bit slippery, since neither an acknowledged literary genre known as "spiritual autobiography" nor even the word "autobiography" itself is attested until the beginning of the nineteenth century.[8] Nonetheless, spiritual autobiography is useful, for it does speak to Adam's determination as storyteller to organize the events of his life into a coherent "poetic" whole that maps the course of his spiritual awakening from the point of his coming to consciousness to his union with Eve, a journey that involves an ascent to ever higher realms of enlightenment. In this process, Adam experiences a remarkable "conversion" that transforms him into a being fully aware of the significance of God's providence.

Lewalski makes the telling point that within the compass of the larger epic narrative, it is actually Eve, rather than Adam, who "invents" the genre of autobiography. Complementing Eve's story, Adam's story must at the outset be viewed within the context of Eve's reflections on her own coming to awareness of self and "other" earlier in the epic (4.449–91). A self-contained narrative, her story is one of waking to life on a flowery bank, of responding to her own reflection in the pool, and of being led by God's voice to Adam, whom she accepts as her mate. According to Lewalski, Eve offers her tale not simply as autobiography but as exemplum, "a moralized life" designed to elaborate what she has learned from the first events of her existence. If Eve might be said to invent the genre of autobiography, Adam moves the genre beyond exemplum to a full-scale account of spiritual awakening in the initial stages of one's existence. Lewalski observes that Adam effectively "brings to higher perfection" the literary kind created by Eve.[9] Although the extent to which Adam's story is an "advance" on Eve's is open to question, the idea of interpreting his narrative as spiritual autobiography has much to recommend it as a means of gaining insight both into the nature of Adam's character and into his prelapsarian relationship with God.

As a source of such insight, Adam's story is framed by a prologue (8.204–49) and an epilogue (8.521–22). In both, Adam refers specifically to "My Storie" as kind of a narrative cue indicating that which is to unfold, on the one hand, and that which has transpired, on the other. "Now hear me relate / My Storie, which perhaps thou hast not heard" (8.204–5), Adam says to Raphael in the prologue; and "Thus I have told thee all my State, and brought / My Storie to the sum of earthly bliss" (8.521–22), he concludes in the epilogue. The artistry is deliberate and decisive here: the initial, spondaic placement of the phrase "My Storie" in both prologue and epilogue suggests a kind of self-conscious insistence on closure, coherence, and authority. This is "My Storie," my experience, Adam implies: it happened to me, and I am the one who best can tell it. The story Adam tells conforms to a tripartite structure of sleeping and awakening. Each part of that tripartite structure moves the speaker to a higher level of consciousness and awareness. Each part functions according to its own mode of discourse and its own set of narrative assumptions. Each part draws upon and reflects other aspects of the larger action that constitutes the epic as a whole. Whereas the first and third parts of the narrative are what might be called "event based," the second part (by far the longest of the three) is "dialogue based." If the second part as center of the threefold structure emphasizes the dialogic dimension of the individual's relationship with his Creator, the narrative from the very beginning moves inevitably toward the third and final part, which portrays the handiwork of God in the marvelous creation of one through whom Adam's desire for union is finally realized. Adam's story thereby becomes a self-contained performance, an act of self-disclosure with its own beginning, middle, and end. Taken as a whole, the three parts of the narrative represent a paean to God's ways, for Adam's story is a celebration of God in all his creative and providential power.

The first part (8.250–82) of the tripartite narrative encompasses three events: Adam's awakening to his new existence (250–66), his coming to awareness both of himself and of his native abilities (267–73a), and his desire to know and worship the source of his making (273b–82). Each of these three events involves a movement to a higher plane of experience. Progressively, each moves toward a knowledge of one's self, one's surroundings, and one's God. Adam's account of awakening to his new existence immediately places his narrative in the context of coming to awareness of oneself in relation to one's surroundings. As newly awakened from "soundest sleep," Adam says, "I found me laid / In Balmie Sweat," which the sun with its beams soon dried (253–56).[10] The reflexive construction ("I found me") underscores the mode of discovery. There is no disjunction between subject and object: they are one. Moreover, the immediacy and ease of finding one's self bathed in the aromatic, generative, and restorative fluids of one's birth is consistent with the sense of communion the newly formed creature enjoys with his surroundings. The discovery of self leads, in turn, to the discovery of other, an other centered in the sky with its bright sun:

> Strait toward Heav'n my wondring Eyes I turnd,
> And gaz'd a while the ample Skie, till rais'd
> By quick instinctive motion up I sprung,
> As thitherward endevoring, and upright
> Stood on my feet.
>
> (257–61)

As a narrative that comments implicitly upon the larger action of the epic, Adam's account recalls Eve's. In her narrative in book 4 (449–59), Eve too remembers awakening as if from sleep. In her newly awakened state, she likewise associates her birth with fluids, in her case issuing from a cave and spreading into a liquid plain. Rather than immediately springing up like Adam, however, Eve, Narcissus-like, lays herself down "On the green bank to look into the cleer / Smooth Lake" that to her "seemd another Skie" (458–59). There, she would have "pin'd with vain desire" (466) had not a voice led her to one with whom she experiences blissful union (467–91).

The experiences of Adam and Eve, in turn, find their demonic counterpart in that of Satan, through whose eyes we first behold Hell as the fallen angel lies "vanquisht, rowling in the fiery

Gulf" (1.52). "Prone on the Flood" (195), Satan awakens immersed in the horrible fluids of his own new "creation" (or "uncreation," as I long ago argued).[11] Only by the "will / And high
permission of all-ruling Heav'n" is he allowed to rise from the
burning pool (211–12). Raising himself "upright" (221), he sets
about to implement his "dark designs" (213), which ironically
serve only to undermine his cause further and to bring greater
glory to God (213–20). Satan's act of raising himself upright anticipates Adam's description of himself as one "rais'd / By quick
instinctive motion" (8.258–59) who springs upward and stands
on his feet. If humans are for Satan nothing but "A race of *up-
start* Creatures" (2.834; emphasis mine) who have usurped his
domain, his own attempt to raise himself upright is an affront to
the true motion of Adam's experience of springing upward and
standing on his feet as a reflection of his nobility and rectitude.

Adam's narrative—his spiritual autobiography—is one of undergoing a process of ascent. It is a process that works both physically and metaphorically. So his account of awakening and
arising to assume the posture of uprightness culminates in an
instinctive act of worshiping that divine source of creativity
through which he is able to realize his own aspirations as a
human being. Drawn upward by the source of light as a sign of
the enlightenment toward which he aspires, Adam observes the
natural world (hill, dale, woods, plains, streams, and the creatures of earth and air) of which he is a part but from which he
also stands apart. Surveying the prospect of his own body, "Limb
by Limb" (8.267), he comes to realize that, despite the animal
energy that empowers him to walk and run, his selfhood renders
him *sui generis*, for, through the operation of his innate mental
faculties, he has the power of speech and, with speech, the power
to name: "To speak I tri'd, and forthwith spake, / My Tongue
obey'd and readily could name / What e're I saw" (271–73). As
John Leonard has ably demonstrated, the power to name assumes an essential bearing in Milton's epic.[12] It is a power that
distinguishes God himself as a Being who brings the very world
into existence through the act of naming (see, for example, Gen.
1.5).

Such an act immediately renders Adam himself a "maker,"
that is, a poet in his own right. His first endeavor as a maker is
to produce a poem that seeks to know the source of this power
to make. Apostrophic in nature, the poem begins with an invocation to the sun as the source of light ("Thou Sun, said I, fair
Light") and then proceeds to celebrate the natural world "en-

light'n'd" by the sun (8.273–74). To the world of nature the poet turns with the invocatory request: "tell / Tell, if ye saw, how came I thus, how here?" (276–77). Accordingly, one of the first acts of the newly created being is to move to the point of conversion from an awareness of the natural world to an awareness of the divine world. Implicit in this awareness is a recognition that all creation is the result of a higher power, a recognition that Satan and his "Atheist crew" (6.370) attempt unsuccessfully to call into question in their claim to self-creation (5.853–63). Knowing instinctively that he was not self-produced, Adam seeks to discover how he might know and adore his "Maker" (8.278), that true Poet through whom Adam moves and lives and feels that he is happier than he knows (8.277–82). Recalling the kind of joyful exuberance that one finds as early as Milton's celebration of the "flaming Titan" [*Flammiger . . . Titan*, 5] in the "Elegiac Verses" (1624–25) accompanying the "Theme on Early Rising," Adam's paean to the sun is consistent with Milton's own Orphic hymn to the "rising god" [*surgenti Deo*] in the first Prolusion, a motif repeated throughout Milton's works.[13] As an Orphic hymn in its own right, the poem that Adam creates in response to his first awakening resonates with the "prompt eloquence" (5.149) that underscores the "orisons" of the Edenic couple "each Morning duly paid / In various style" to praise "thir Maker" (145–48). Unlike the newly created Adam who seeks to know through his paean "how came I thus, how here?" the Adam and Eve of the orisons are fully in possession of the answer to that question: their worship is not of the sun but of the true Maker, through whom the sun itself was fashioned (171–74). The paean of the newly created Adam represents the first gesture toward the realization of that profound truth.

The quest for answers that ultimately assumes a theological bearing underlies Milton's own paean that inaugurates the third book of his epic:

> Hail holy Light, ofspring of Heav'n first-born,
> Or of th'Eternal Coeternal beam
> May I express thee unblam'd? since God is light,
> And never but in unapproached light
> Dwelt from Eternitie, dwelt then in thee,
> Bright effluence of bright essence increate.
>
> (3.1–6)

In its own way, the paean of the newly created Adam looks forward to such an act of "hallowing" as it calls upon the world of

nature to lead him to a knowledge of the world of the divine. It
is this world that Satan not only refuses to acknowledge but also
insists upon cursing as he soliloquizes upon the Assyrian mount
before his entrance into Eden. Invoking "Heav'n and the full-
blazing Sun" (4.29) as reminders of his own lost divinity, he
cries:

> O thou that with surpassing Glory crownd,
> Look'st from thy sole dominion like the God
> Of this new World; at whose sight all the Starrs
> Hide thir diminisht heads; to thee I call . . .
>   and add thy name
> O Sun, to tell thee how I hate thy beams.
>
> (32–37)

If Adam's paean finds its demonic parody in Satan's maledic-
tion, that irony underscores the extent to which the act of coming to awareness of self in Milton's epic can be a source of joy on
the one hand and despair on the other. For the newly created
Adam who celebrates the sun, the emerging awareness of self results in joy. For the fallen Satan who curses the sun, the emerging awareness of self results in despair. As Adam relates the
story of his birth to Raphael, the apostrophe to the sun becomes
the means by which the storyteller delights in remembering his
first steps in coming to awareness of God. In his desecration of
the sun as a means of disavowing God, Satan despairs in the
memory of what he once was and can no longer be. For Adam,
the memory of his making is a source of life and renewal; for
Satan, the memory of his undoing is a source of death and despair. Recounting his paean, Adam delights in memory; engaging in his soliloquy, Satan seeks unsuccessfully to free himself
of it.[14]

2

Adam's paean represents the culminating event of the first
part of his tripartite narrative. As a narrative of ascent to succes-
sively higher levels of experience, his story moves to the transitional moment in which he realizes the object of his quest, that
of gaining access to the source of his creation. It is here that the
second part of the tripartite narrative unfolds.

Beginning with a detailed account of Adam's experience of

sleeping and awakening (8.283–316a), the second part (283–451) of the tripartite narrative encompasses a dialogue in two movements, the first establishing the prohibition against the fruit (316b–56), the second arguing successfully in behalf of the need for a companion (357–451). The account of Adam's experience of sleeping and awakening advances the story as a whole into the realm of visionary enactment. That enactment is delineated through Adam's description of his passing through sleep to what at first appears to be his "former state" (290), that is, his preconscious condition before awakening to an awareness of himself and his surroundings. It is at this point of potential dissolution that a dream suddenly appears in Adam's trancelike state of sleep (287). As Adam relates, this is a dream imbued with the aura of divinity:

> One came, methought, of shape Divine,
> And said, thy Mansion wants thee, Adam, rise,
> First Man, of Men innumerable ordain'd
> First Father, call'd by thee I come thy Guide
> To the Garden of bliss, thy seat prepar'd.
>
> (295–99)

Resorting to Gen. 2.8 ("And the Lord God planted a garden eastward in Eden; and there he put the man whom he had formed"), Milton transforms the biblical text into a moment of high visionary art. What in the Genesis account is described as the simple act of placing the newly formed creature into the garden becomes in Milton's epic the occasion for a visionary encounter of profoundest import. As Kristin Pruitt McColgan observes, the experience is one in which Adam first learns of God's presence in sleep.[15] The occasion for the emergence of that presence is Adam's desire to know and worship his Creator, who in turn manifests himself as a "shape Divine" to guide his newly formed creature to the higher realms. From the world of nature in the first part of the tripartite narrative, Adam is now prepared to move to the world of the divine. This is Adam's "Mansion," that which awaits him in his Father's house both in this world and in the next (John 14.2). In this world, its name is "Eden," literally, that *gan eden*, or garden of pleasure, that has been prepared for Adam as his "seat."

Describing the experience of being transported to that seat, Adam says that his "Guide" took him by his hand and raised him over fields and waters through the air to a woody mountain, the high top of which was enclosed with trees, walks, and bowers, a veritable *hortus conclusus* of delight. Within that garden, each tree was "Load'n with fairest Fruit" (8.307) that tempted him "to pluck and eat" (309). Having arrived at this blissful place, Adam awakened to find before his eyes "all real, as the dream / Had lively shadowd" (310–11). It is in this description that Milton makes clear how important the concept of ascent is to Adam's experience. The idea of rising from birth ("till rais'd / By quick instinctive motion up I sprung") is reiterated here with the ascent to the Edenic realm. In a parodic vein, we recall Satan's "ascent of that steep savage Hill" (4.172) that leads up to Eden. To violate the sanctity of that enclosure, Satan high overleaps all barriers with "one slight bound" and "sheer within / Lights on his feet" (181–83). By contrast, Adam's traversal of the enclosed world of the garden is not a violation at all: divinely sanctioned, it is realized as the result of God's own will. Significantly, its realization takes place in the world of dream, the world of vision. In a poem that is itself the product of visionary ascent to the celestial worlds, "the Heav'n of Heav'ns" (7.13), Adam's "flying dream" is one in which the dreamer wakes to find all real: appearance and reality are one. His is not the flying dream that Eve undergoes after she is guided in sleep by Satan to disobey the prohibition. Up to the clouds she flies with her false guide, who then disappears. She in turn awakens "To find this but a dream!" (5.93). Adam's dream, however, is of an entirely different order. It locates Adam's entrance into the Edenic world within an exalted context, one consistent with the ascent through vision to a realm in which all that dreams "lively [shadow]" (8.311) are the stuff of a higher reality, a dimension accessible only through the operation of faculties that extend their reach beyond the present. In this realm, the light of the sun that Adam beholds immediately after his creation finds its true source in that "Celestial light" that "shine[s] inward" and "Irradiate[s]" "the mind through all her powers" so that the seer "may see and Tell / Of things invisible to mortal sight" (3.51–55). This is as much an Eden of mind as an Eden of thing, as much a realm of the inside as a realm of the outside. It is indeed a realm where inside and outside are one, are real, where potential dislocations (between appearance and reality, inside and outside) are unknown.

It is this realm to which Adam has ascended in vision and which appears before his eyes in all its glory when he awakens from his visionary trance. Upon awakening, Adam beholds his

"Guide" appearing from among the trees. Falling in adoration before this "Guide," Adam is raised up by what he calls the "Presence Divine" (8.314), who identifies himself by declaring: "Whom thou [Adam] soughtst I am . . . Author of all this thou seest / Above, or round about thee or beneath" (316–18). If nothing else, the nomenclature itself suggests the milieu from which Adam's account at this point is drawn. "Presence Divine" corresponds to what is customarily known as the *Shekhinah,* or Dwelling Presence of God. Biblically, it finds its counterpart in the notion of deity enthroned between the cherubim on the Ark of the Covenant in the holy of holies. A phenomenon of crucial import to the rabbinical traditions extending from the early talmudic period to the later Middle Ages, the *Shekhinah* is a staple of Jewish mysticism and *kabbalah.* As I have discussed elsewhere, the concept is also a commonplace of Renaissance hermeneutics.[16] In various forms, the idea of the "Presence Divine" is invoked in *Paradise Lost* as an expression of God's self-manifestation.[17] Reinforcing this dimension is the self-referential statement by the "Presence Divine" that "Whom thou soughtst I am," an idea with its roots in the voice that emanates from the burning bush in Exodus. When asked for its name, the theophany responds to Moses, "I AM THAT I AM: . . . Thus shalt thou say unto the children of Israel, I AM hath sent me unto you" (Exod. 3.14). As Milton was well aware, God as "I AM" is a verbal play on the Tetragrammaton [*yod he vay he*].[18] Embodied in the Tetragrammaton is the profound mystery of all that the *Shekhinah* makes known as a manifestation of God's divinity. Between the *Shekhinah* and the Tetragrammaton, then, the milieu of Adam's visionary encounter is consistent with the idea of mystical ascents to the highest reaches, as a characteristic of the rabbinical traditions. Such a view is in keeping with William B. Hunter's study of the rabbinical contexts of the prophetic dreams and visions in *Paradise Lost.*[19] Adam's ascent to the Edenic realm has about it the aura of the "otherworldly," associated with such dreams and visions.

What becomes particularly important in this respect is the designation of the area into which Adam is placed as "Paradise": "This Paradise I give thee, count it thine / To Till and keep" (8.319–20), the "Presence Divine" says to Adam. On the face of it, the reference to "Paradise" hardly seems remarkable. So accustomed are we to associate Paradise with the Garden of Eden that we take the association for granted. After all, Milton himself refers to the garden as the "blissful Paradise / Of God,"

planted "in th' East / Of Eden" (4.208–10), a reference that identifies the "garden" [gan] of Gen. 2.8 with "Paradise." But we
need to remember that the term "Paradise," with its roots in the
Old Persian pairidâza (enclosure), makes its appearance canoni-
cally only three times and then only in the New Testament,
where it is invoked in celestial and apocalyptic terms.[20] In the
context of Adam's ascent in Paradise Lost, the one New Testament occasion that appears to be especially germane is Paul's account of his ascent to the celestial realms, a kind of spiritual
autobiography in miniature. "I will come," Paul says, "to visions and revelations of the Lord. I knew a man in Christ above
fourteen years ago, (whether in the body, I cannot tell; or
whether out of the body, I cannot tell: God knoweth;) such an
one caught up to the third heaven. . . . How that he was caught
up into paradise [paradeisos], and heard unspeakable words,
which it is not lawful for a man to utter" (2 Cor. 12.1–4). The
individual about whom Paul is speaking, albeit obliquely, is, of
course, himself. As I have suggested elsewhere, this text gave
rise to an entire literature of ascent in Jewish/Christian apocalyptic.[21] The point I wish to make here is not that the Pauline
text is a source for Adam's ascent in Paradise Lost, although it
comes about as close as any other text I can think of. Rather, the
Pauline text lurks in the background as a formative moment in
the experience of ascent that underscores Milton's own act of
casting Adam's movement into the garden in visionary terms.
Like Paul, Milton's Adam is in the position of one whose spiritual autobiography is about the experience of undergoing the
"visions and revelations of the Lord." If Adam's ascent is not
specifically to the third heaven, the shape of his experience is
distinctly tripartite. Moreover, his ascent, like Paul's, is con-
summated in an encounter with deity. Like Paul, Adam experiences a visio Dei.

It is in the dramatization of this event, however, that we discover a remarkable departure from the Pauline model. The final
sections of the second part of the tripartite narrative that Adam
relates transform vision into speech. Whereas Paul speaks of his
visio Dei as one in which the visionary hears "unspeakable
words, which it is not lawful for a man to utter," Adam engages
in a lively interchange with God that moves his story from the
realm of unspeakable mysteries to the realm of the dialogic, a
realm in which participants confront each other in a drama of
statement and counterstatement that, in this case, leads to a
wonderful resolution. The nature of the interchange is defined

by Adam himself as a "celestial Colloquie sublime" (8.455). As that which suggests the act of "speaking together," the dialogue between Adam and his Creator assumes, even in its sublimity, a kind of "conversational" bearing. It moves to that point, however, only after God has pronounced the stern prohibition against "the Tree whose operation brings / Knowledge of good and ill" (323–24), an interdiction the violation of which is fraught with "bitter consequence" (328) and the thought of which "resounds / Yet dreadful in [Adam's] ear" (334–35). The dread that surrounds this pronouncement is sufficient in itself to recall Paul's own reference to the "unspeakable words" uttered in his own vision. But the final movement of the action that constitutes the second part of Adam's story confirms his reference to the "celestial Colloquie sublime," for here the drama becomes ludic, indeed, even comic in its bearing. At the same time, the drama exhibits what Lewalski calls "a Socratic dimension," one that is the means through which Adam attains and manifests self-knowledge. As a result of this self-knowledge, "Adam is led to define for himself what it is to be human: that it is not to find company with beasts, or to be perfect in himself as God, but to seek completion, help, and solace in human companionship and human love."[22]

In keeping with Adam's earlier mention of his ability to name whatever he sees, God begins the colloquy by having Adam name the creatures. Approaching Adam as their master, the creatures "with low subjection" (8.345) acknowledge his superior power and authority. With the act of naming comes the ability to know and understand the nature of whatever is named (339–56). The act of naming moves Adam to the point of realization that, among the creatures he names, he "found not what [he] thought [he] wanted still" (355), that is, another individual who would be his companion. It is this desire that prompts him to engage in a dialogue with his Creator. Needless to say, Milton's bestowing upon Adam the desire for a companion and the courage to voice that desire represents a radical departure from the biblical text. There, it is God alone who takes the initiative to create a companion for his new creature: "And the Lord God said, It is not good that the man should be alone; I will make him an help meet for him" (Gen. 2.18). Only after arriving at this decision does the biblical God form the beasts of the fields and the fowl of the air for the man to name. Once that act is performed, God thereafter discovers that "for Adam there was not found an help meet for him" (Gen. 2.20). Milton changes all that.

In his version, it is not God but Adam who discovers the need for a "help meet." With that realization, Adam initiates a series of arguments to convince his Maker that this need has merit. At the conclusion of the dialogue, Milton's God acknowledges to Adam that he knew all along that it is "not good for Man to be alone" (8.445). God has been engaging in the colloquy with his new creation simply as a means of "trial" (447) to see how Adam "could'st judge of fit and meet" (448). Adam sustains the trial triumphantly and in the process does not hesitate to challenge the Creator and his ways. It is precisely this kind of challenge that God welcomes as a demonstration of Adam's ability to reason, to articulate, and to exercise his independence.

Having named the creatures about him, Adam accordingly petitions his Creator as one who far surpasses man's ability to name, a gesture that prepares the way for the challenge. As an all-providing deity, God has yet to provide a means to address the fact of Adam's solitude. The gesture pleases God, who argues in response that, as one surrounded by all the creatures he has provided, Adam certainly does not lack for companionship (369–75). God's counterargument is geared to advance his new creation to the point of recognizing his standing in relation to the standing of those he has named. By means of questioning Adam's desire for a proper companion, God moves his new creation to an awareness of hierarchy within the natural world as a reflection of hierarchy within the worlds beyond. "Hast thou not made me here thy substitute, / And these inferiour farr beneath me set?" (381–82) Adam asks his Creator.

> Among unequals what societie
> Can sort, what harmonie or true delight?
> Which must be mutual, in proportion due
> Giv'n and receiv'd.
>
> (383–86)

Adam's challenge is to the point. Its logic is drawn not from the second chapter of Genesis but from the first: "And God said, Let us make man in our image, after our likeness: and let them have dominion over the fish of the sea, and over the fowl of the air, and over the cattle, and over all the earth, and over every creeping thing that creepeth upon the earth" (Gen. 1.26). In his quest for a help meet, Adam argues in behalf of what the first chapter of Genesis takes for granted: the need for an "other" to fulfill all that is implied by the idea of God's image and likeness: "So God created man in his own image, in the image of God created he him: male and female created he them" (Gen. 1.27). It is the sense of mutuality and indeed equality that spurs Adam on to petition his Creator to provide what his new creation does not find among all the creatures that surround him in his paradisal abode.

This petition, in turn, moves Adam to the point of recognizing what is implied by the *imago Dei*. In response to God's final counterargument that he is "alone / From all Eternitie" and knows none "second to [him] or like, equal much less" (8.405–7), Adam distinguishes the state of his Maker's perfection, which is whole and complete within itself, from that of his own "single imperfection" (423). This fact justifies man's need for his "other" to "solace his defects" and to complement his imperfection, which in its propagation will "beget / Like of his like, his Image multipli'd, / In unitie defective" (423–25).[23] If mankind will never achieve ultimate perfection, he will strive toward it by means of concourse with the "other." Whereas God in his secrecy is best accompanied by his "self" as "other," Adam, then, requires a companion with whom to converse and to share "collateral love" (426). He requires, that is, another being with him at his side to fulfill the command issued in the first chapter of Genesis: "Be fruitful, and multiply" (1.28).[24] In the fulfillment of that command, mankind as the embodiment of the *imago Dei* will gloriously realize its calling. Adam's awareness of this calling is what renders him so noble. At this point in the "celestial Colloquie sublime," he becomes aware of the power of dialogue with his Creator to raise God's creature to the heights of concourse with deity, indeed, to the point of deification itself. At that point, Adam is imbued with a full sense of his own stature, his own abilities, and indeed of his own powers of discourse. He knows himself in a way that he had never thought to achieve when he first came to consciousness after his birth. So God praises him as knowing "not of Beasts alone" (8.438) but of himself, "expressing well the spirit within [him] free, / [God's] Image" (440–41). Having reached this point in his process of ascent, Adam is now ready to enjoy the fruits of his petition. So God declares to Adam:

> What next I bring shall please thee, be assur'd,
> Thy likeness, thy fit help, thy other self,
> Thy wish exactly to thy hearts desire.
>
> (449–51)

With that declaration, the second part of Adam's story is brought to a close.

3

Like the first two parts of the tripartite narrative, the third and final part (8.452–510) is divisible into three sections, the first encompassing the creation of Eve (452–90); the second, Adam's response to the creation (491–99); and the third, the union of the new couple (500–520). All three sections find their source directly in the Genesis account: "And the Lord God caused a deep sleep to fall upon Adam, and he slept: and he took one of his ribs, and closed up the flesh instead thereof; and the rib, which the Lord God had taken from man, made he a woman, and brought her unto the man. And Adam said, This is now bone of my bones, and flesh of my flesh: she shall be called Woman, because she was taken out of Man. Therefore shall a man leave his father and his mother, and shall cleave unto his wife: and they shall be one flesh" (2.21–24). Of particular note in the biblical account is the "deep sleep" that falls upon Adam in preparation for the creation of Eve. The presence of this sleep in the source text is no doubt what accounts for its use as a leitmotif to structure the three parts of Adam's story in *Paradise Lost*, each part of which commences with the idea of a profound sleep, followed by the awakening into a new consciousness. If such is the case, then an examination of the climactic moment of Adam's story might well begin with a consideration of precisely what is meant by this so-called "deep sleep" in the Genesis account.

The statement "And the Lord God caused a deep sleep to fall upon Adam, and he slept" uses two separate terms in the original as a designation for "sleep": the first is *tardemah*, the second *yashen*.[25] Appearing repeatedly throughout Hebrew Scriptures, *yashen* is used simply to denote the idea of falling into a state of sleep.[26] *Tardemah*, however, is a far different matter. Appearing seven times in Hebrew Scriptures, it is employed only on very special occasions and only in the context of divine agency. By means of his *tardemah*, God establishes a covenant with Abraham (Gen. 15.12), instructs Isaiah on the nature of prophecy (Isa. 29.9–11), and infuses Daniel with visions (Dan. 8.17, 10.9). Invoking the concept of *tardemah*, Job declares: "For God speaketh once, yea twice, yet man perceiveth it not. In a dream, in a vision of the night, when deep sleep [*tardemah*] falleth upon men, in slumberings upon the bed; Then he openeth the ears of men, and sealeth their instruction" (Job 33.14–16).

Clearly, the creation of a companion for Adam both in the biblical account and in the Miltonic account represents a momentous occasion, underscored by the visionary, prophetic, and indeed covenantal contexts to which the concept of *tardemah* gives rise in Hebrew Scriptures. In the course of the experience that Milton's Adam relates through his story of ascent to ever higher levels of consciousness, the pattern of sleeping and awakening from one stage to the next reinforces the significance of this ultimate moment of revelation when God creates for Adam "[his] likeness, [his] fit help, [his] other self, [his] wish, exactly to [his] heart's desire." Describing his own *tardemah*, Milton's Adam portrays the experience as an ecstasis or trance-like state through which his "internal sight" (8.461) becomes the vehicle for beholding the vision of the creation of his companion, as the glorious shape who has been his "Guide" now fashions from his rib a manlike creature, "but different sex, so lovely fair, / That what seemed fair in all the World, seemd now / Mean, or in her summ'd up, in her contain'd" (8.471–73).[27] As one who has ascended to the heights of Paradise, indeed, to the Heaven of Heavens within the sphere of the terrestrial world, Adam beholds what for him is the consummate fulfillment of all his hopes and desires. It is the high point in his visionary quest: that moment toward which all other moments have led, that joy in the presence of which all other joys are made to pale. On this supremest of supreme occasions, the narrative of ascent has realized its final destination.[28]

At that very point of consummation, the vision suddenly flees and leaves the seer in darkness: "Shee disappeerd," Adam says, "and left me dark, I wak'd / To find her, or for ever to deplore / Her loss, and other pleasures all abjure" (478–80). As has been noted before, Adam's experience recalls that of Milton in "Sonnet 23": "But O as to imbrace me she enclin'd, / I wak'd, she fled, and day brought back my night" (13–14). Whereas the blind seer of the sonnet is enveloped in darkness after he awakens, the newly created Adam of Milton's epic is able to enjoy the fruits of his vision, after all, as he beholds her,

> not far off,
> Such as [he] saw her in [his] dream, adornd
> With what all Earth or Heaven could bestow
> To make her amiable.
>
> (481–84)

"Led by her Heav'nly Maker, though unseen, / And guided by
his voice," she approaches Adam in her glory and as one already
informed

> Of nuptial Sanctitie, and marriage Rites:
> Grace was in all her steps, Heav'n in her Eye,
> In every gesture dignitie and love.
>
> (482–89)

From the simple statement of the Genesis account (the Lord
God "brought her unto the man"), Milton fashions an entire
drama of vision, potential loss, and ultimate fulfillment. The cel-
ebrative dimension of realization at the moment of awakening
portrayed here is complemented by Eve's own account, mentioned earlier. Upon hearing the voice of her own guide promising to "bring [her] where no shadow staies / [Her] coming"
(4.470–71) and to unite her with one "Whose image [she is]" (472)
and one to whom she "shall bear / Multitudes like [her] self"
(473–74), she exclaims: "What could I doe, / But follow strait, in-
visibly thus led?" (475–76). Although Eve's portrayal of her encounter with Adam contains additional details that supplement
the story that Adam tells, the individual perspectives through
which Adam and Eve's meeting is depicted reinforce the sense of
drama that infuses this most delightful of occasions. As a moment of utmost pleasure at this climactic point in Adam's story,
the encounter between first man and first woman brings the first
section of the third part of the tripartite narrative to a close.

The second section finds expression in the Miltonic rendering
of Adam's exclamation in the biblical text: "This is now bone of
my bones, and flesh of my flesh: she shall be called Woman, because she was taken out of Man. Therefore shall a man leave his
father and his mother, and shall cleave unto his wife: and they
shall be one flesh." In his own reinscription of that moment,
Milton provides a reading consistent with the action that underscores Adam's account of his visionary ascent. So the Miltonic
Adam declares:

> I now see
> Bone of my Bone, Flesh of my Flesh, my Self
> Before me; Woman is her Name, of Man
> Extracted; for this cause he shall forgoe
> Father and Mother, and to his Wife adhere;
> And they shall be one Flesh, one Heart, one Soul.
>
> (8.494–99)

The alterations are significant. "This is now bone of my bones, and flesh of my flesh" becomes "I now see / Bone of my Bone, Flesh of my Flesh, my Self / Before me." The Adam of Milton's epic imports into his exclamation the act of recognition so crucial to his story. Having beheld the "Presence Divine" in the form of the shape that guides him, Adam now beholds the new creation of that Presence in the form of the companion that has emerged from his own bones, his own flesh, indeed, his own being or "self" as it is positioned significantly "before him." It is this emphasis upon the "self before one's own self" that is so important to an understanding of the narrative at this juncture. For what Milton does is to render through a kind of play of language the true meaning of what we have come to know as "help meet." "And the Lord God said, It is not good that the man should be alone; I will make him an help meet for him." As I have argued elsewhere, Milton was quite aware that the phrase *"ezer keneghdo,"* rendered as "help meet" in the Authorized Version and elsewhere, implies much more than is suggested in the customary translations.[29] In the Hebrew, the phrase implies not simply that which is a "help" but that which is of a much higher order. In fact, the first part of the phrase [*ezer*] combines two ancient roots, one of which means "to deliver" and the other "to be strong." It is a term frequently applied to God as deliverer. As applied to the companion created for Adam, the word *ezer,* moreover, is in the masculine. Although a woman, the companion as *ezer* shares many of the properties of the being from which she is created. So Adam calls her "Manlike, but different sex" (471). The second part of the phrase [*keneghdo*] does not really mean "meet," as in "help meet." As a term of positioning, it implies (among other meanings) that which is *in front of* or *before* another, that which is *in sight of* another, that which is *opposite to* another, that which *corresponds to* another. Observing in *Tetrachordon* that the orginal Hebrew "is more expressive then other languages word for word can render it," Milton translates the phrase as *"another self, a second self, a very self it self"* (*YP,* 3:600). Clearly, at this juncture of profound recognition, one comes to realize the extent to which Adam's ascent to the terrestrial counterpart of the Heaven of Heavens situates the new "self" of the seer as the crowning achievement of God's handiwork.[30] One could not imagine a more triumphant moment than this.

The supreme elation that Adam experiences at this moment assumes its most festive bearing in the union of the two selves

celebrated in the final section of his narrative. What gives rise to
the action of this section is the fulfillment in the present of what
Adam declares will transpire in the future: that man shall "adhere" to his wife and that, as a result of this adherence, "they
shall be one Flesh, one Heart, one Soul." Reformulating the biblical text that "a man shall cleave unto his wife: and they shall
be one flesh," Milton intensifies the promised union by extending the "one Flesh" of the original to encompass "Heart" and
"Soul" as well.[31] In the portrayal of this adherence or cleaving
together of "Flesh," "Heart," and "Soul," the narrative recounts
what might be called Adam's act of "courting" Eve, followed by
the consummation of the courtship, an event commemorated
through an epithalamic hymn that celebrates the newly united
couple.

The final section begins with Adam's delightful account of his
courting. Responding to his call ("Bone of my Bone, Flesh of my
Flesh"), Eve turns away as one "That would be woo'd, and not
unsought be won, / Not obvious, not obtrusive, but retir'd"
(8.503–4). The play of language reinforces this sense of advance
and retreat, as the sense itself is suspended until the final moment when, upon seeing the one who has called, "she turned"
(507), only to be pursued by her suitor: "I follow'd her" (508),
says Adam; "she what was Honour knew, / And with obsequious
Majestie approv'd / My pleaded reason" (508–10). The idea of advance and retreat finds its counterpart in Eve's earlier description of hearing Adam's voice:

> Return fair Eve
> Whom fli'st thou? whom thou fli'st, of him thou art,
> His flesh, his bone . . .
>
> . . . .
>
> Part of my Soul I seek thee, and thee claim
> My other half: with that thy gentle hand
> Seis'd mine, I yeilded.
>
> (4.481–89)

Just as the two halves constitute the total being, the two perspectives constitute the total experience, one that culminates in
the act of cleaving together or adhering as "one Flesh, one Heart,
one Soul." Underlying this act of cleaving, of adhering, is the
very dynamic that underscores the notion of "cleaving" in Hebrew Scriptures. There, the term for cleaving is *"davak"* (Gen.
2.24), a word that denotes not only the union of two beings but,

in its usage in other contexts, the act of pursuing and finally overtaking as a result of pursuit.[32] If such an idea is absent from the narrative delineated in the Genesis account, it is very much present in the narrative of courtship that Milton provides for it in his epic. There, as we have seen, cleaving or adhering assumes a complex bearing as a result of the two perspectives that Adam and Eve accord it in their respective accounts.

With the consummation of Adam and Eve's courtship, the groom leads his bride, "blushing like the Morn" (8.511) to the "Nuptial Bowr" (509). To celebrate the occasion, "all Heav'n, / And happie Constellations . . . / Shed thir selectest influence" (511–13). Along with the heavens and the constellations, the entire paradisal world celebrates the union through a lovely epithalamium, one that Adam himself as the first of poets intones:

> the Earth
> Gave sign of gratulation, and each Hill;
> Joyous the Birds; fresh Gales and gentle Aires
> Whisper'd it to the Woods, and from thir wings
> Flung Rose, flung Odours from the spicie Shrub,
> Disporting, till the amorous Bird of Night
> Sung Spousal, and bid haste the Eevning Starr
> On his Hill top, to light the bridal Lamp.
>
> (513–20)

As Lewalski makes clear, this brief epithalamic hymn finds its counterpart in the extended epithalamic passage that graces book 4 (689–775). Celebrating the marital union of Adam and Eve, the extended epithalamium encompasses the description of the couple's "blissful Bower," the evening prayer at the entrance to the bower, and what Lewalski calls the bard's embedded lyric epithalamium hailing "wedded Love." As the bard focuses on the unfallen couple about to enter their bower for lovemaking and sleep (689–90), his epithalamium thereby accords with the definition indicated by the genre's name, *epi thalamou*, "a song sung at the bridal chamber door."[33]

It is in keeping with such an idea that Adam draws upon the entire paradisal world at the culminating moment of his tripartite narrative to celebrate his act of leading his bride to the "Nuptial Bowr."[34] Like the bard of book 4, Adam as an accomplished lyricist intones an epithalamium all his own. Doing so, he once again performs the function of the poet, one who no longer need apostrophize the world of nature in order to discover

the source of his making. Having discovered that source and fulfilled his longings for a companion with whom to achieve blissful union, he conceives of a poem in which heaven with its
constellations and earth with all the life that populates it are infused with the powers this union imparts. The joy that Adam
and Eve experience in their mutual love is the world's joy.
Blessed by the celestial spheres, the first couple receives the
"gratulations" of a totally animate nature. The melody of the
birds, the sound of the winds, the aroma of the flowers: all participate in the celebration of the poet who infuses new life into
the paradisal world with his Orphic song.[35] As a coda to that
song, "the amorous Bird of Night" sings spousal and bids "the
Eevning Starr" hasten "to light the bridal Lamp." All history is
obliterated here: this is a new beginning. The fate of the nightingale lies beyond the purview of the immediate occasion. The
bard is not blind, nor does "the wakeful Bird" that "sings darkling" (3.38–39) yet haunt his dreams or those of his spouse with
his "love-labor'd song" (5.41).[36] There is plenty of time for that.
For the time being, there is only bliss as the evening star is called
to perform her nuptial functions in commemoration of the light-
ing of the bridal lamp.

With that event, Adam concludes his story of selfhood, one
through which he has attained "the sum of earthly bliss" (8.522).
In the seamless web that Adam has woven during the course of
his narrative, the action has moved from his first awakening to
his last. Through successive stages of consciousness, he has
symbolically traversed the course of time from sunlight to the
appearance of the evening star, a traversal involving the act of
coming to awareness of self and of God and culminating in the
blissful union with his beloved. Such a traversal has involved a
process of ascent to higher levels of consciousness. If Adam's
story can be construed as spiritual autobiography, it is one that
assumes a distinctly visionary bearing, perhaps most immediately grounded in the Pauline ascent to the third heaven. However Adam's own ascent is construed, the experience he recounts
is structured with a consummate sense of artistry and skill.
Adam is a superb storyteller. More than that, he is both a poet
and an orator. The creator of superb lyrics, he is also capable of
engaging in a lively debate with his Creator. The story that
Adam shares with his angelic guest is a triumph of poetic art.
Witnessing that triumph, we are privileged to experience with
Raphael the first epic by the first man within the larger narrative
cosmos encompassed by *Paradise Lost*.

NOTES

1. John Milton, *Paradise Lost,* in *The Complete Poetry of John Milton,* ed. John T. Shawcross, rev. ed. (Garden City, New York: Doubleday, 1971). All references to Milton's poetry are to this edition and are cited parenthetically in the text.

2. J. Martin Evans, *"Paradise Lost" and the Genesis Tradition* (Oxford: Clarendon Press, 1968), 256. For an illuminating treatment of Adam's story, see Robert H. Bell, " 'Blushing like the morn': Milton's Human Comedy," *Milton Quarterly* 15 (1981): 47–54. According to Bell, "Book VIII exploits the comedy latent in the situation of a man telling the very happy story of how he met and wed his wife" (48). Although the comic element is certainly present and should not be underestimated, it is, I think, subsumed in a much greater whole. Other treatments of the topic are of corresponding interest. These include Claudia M. Champagne, "Adam and His 'Other Self' in Paradise Lost: A Lacanian Study in Psychic Development," *Milton Quarterly* 25 (1991): 48–59; Hugh MacCallum, *Milton and the Sons of God: The Divine Image in Milton's Epic Poetry* (Toronto: University of Toronto Press, 1986), 131–36; and Francis C. Blessington, *"Paradise Lost" and the Classical Epic* (Boston: Routledge & Kegan Paul, 1979), 25–34.

3. *The Bible: Authorized King James Version, with Apocrypha,* ed. Robert Carroll and Stephen Prickett (New York: Oxford University Press, 1997). All references to this edition are cited parenthetically in the text.

4. See Evans, *"Paradise Lost" and the Genesis Tradition,* 9–25, for a discussion of the backgrounds.

5. Ibid., 256–57. In fact, Raphael's account of the creation of first man and first woman is essentially a recapitulation of Gen. 1.26–30. Adopting the outlook of the Priestly version, Raphael relates God's speech and actions as follows:

> Let us make now Man in our image, Man
> In our similitude, and let them rule
> Over the Fish and Fowl of Sea and Air,
> Beast of the Field, and over all the Earth,
> And every creeping thing that creeps the ground.
> This said, he formd thee, Adam, thee O Man
> Dust of the ground, and in thy nostrils breath'd
> The breath of Life; in his own Image hee
> Created thee, in the Image of God
> Express, and thou becam'st a living Soul.
> Male he created thee, but thy consort
> Female for Race; then bless'd Mankind, and said,
> Be fruitful, multiplie, and fill the Earth,
> Subdue it, and throughout Dominion hold
> Over Fish of the Sea, and Fowl of the Air,
> And every living thing that moves on th' Earth.
>
> (7.519–34)

In his creation account, Raphael does not adhere strictly to the Priestly version. After describing the creation of first man and first woman, he reiterates the prohibition against the Tree of the Knowledge of Good and Evil as a warning not to disobey God: "but of the Tree / Which tasted works knowledge of Good and Evil, / Thou mai'st not; in the day thou eat'st, thou di'st" (542–44).

6. Erich Kahler, "Die Verinnerung des Erzählens," in *Untergang und Übergang* (Munich: Deutscher Taschenbuch Verlag, 1970). References are to *The Inward Turn of Narrative*, trans. Richard Winston and Clara Winston (Princeton: Princeton University Press, 1973), 9, 35, 107, 140, 143–44.

7. Barbara Kiefer Lewalski, *"Paradise Lost" and the Rhetoric of Literary Forms* (Princeton: Princeton University Press, 1985), 211. Kahler, *The Inward Turn*, 144, likewise cites Augustine's *Confessions* to Bunyan's *Grace Abounding* as prototypes of the internalization of narrative, here in confessional form.

8. See Paul Delany, *British Autobiography in the Seventeenth Century* (London: Routledge & Kegan Paul, 1969), 1. According to Delany, the word "autobiography" appears to have been coined by Robert Southey in 1809, an observation confirmed by the *Oxford English Dictionary*, s.v. See also Daniel B. Shea, *Spiritual Autobiography in Early America* (Princeton: Princeton University Press, 1968).

9. Lewalski, *"Paradise Lost" and the Rhetoric of Literary Forms*, 185–86, 211–12.

10. For a discussion of this aspect, see Geoffrey Hartman, "Adam on the Ground with Balsamum," *ELH* 36 (1969): 168–92.

11. Michael Lieb, *The Dialectics of Creation: Patterns of Birth and Regeneration in "Paradise Lost"* (Amherst: University of Massachusetts Press, 1970).

12. John Leonard, *Naming in Paradise: Milton and the Language of Adam and Eve* (Oxford: Clarendon Press, 1990). As an exploration of the divine perspective and its bearing on the idea of the "holy name," see Michael Lieb, *Poetics of the Holy: A Reading of "Paradise Lost"* (Chapel Hill: University of North Carolina Press, 1981), 171–84.

13. For the "Elegiac Verses" [*Carmina Elegiaca*], see Shawcross, ed., *The Complete Poems*, 7–8. For the "Theme on Early Rising," see *Complete Prose Works of John Milton*, 8 vols., ed. Don M. Wolfe et al. (New Haven: Yale University Press, 1953–82), 1:1,034–39, hereafter designated as *YP*, and *The Works of John Milton*, 18 vols., ed. Frank Allan Patterson et al. (New York: Columbia University Press, 1931–38), 12:286–91, hereafter designated *CM*. For *Prolusion 1* ("Whether Day or Night is the More Excellent"), see *YP*, 1:216–33; *CM*, 12:118–48.

14. For an illuminating treatment of the whole question of memory in Milton's epic, see Regina M. Schwartz, *Remembering and Repeating: Biblical Creation in "Paradise Lost"* (Cambridge: Cambridge University Press, 1988).

15. Kristin Pruitt McColgan, " 'God is Also in Sleep': Dreams Satanic and Divine in *Paradise Lost*," *Milton Studies* 30 (1993): 136–37.

16. For a full discussion, see Lieb, *Poetics of the Holy*, 212–45.

17. See especially Adam's lament:

> This most afflicts me, that departing hence,
> As from his face I shall be hid, depriv'd
> His blessed count'nance; here I could frequent,
> With worship, place by place where he voutsaf'd
> Presence Divine.

(11.315–19)

18. See discussion of the holy name in Lieb, *Poetics of the Holy*, 171–84.

19. William B. Hunter, "Prophetic Dreams and Visions in *Paradise Lost*," in *The Descent of Urania: Studies in Milton, 1946–1988* (Lewisburg, Pa.: Buck-

nell University Press, 1989), 21–30. For analogies in Dante, see also Manfred Weidhorn, *Dreams in Seventeenth-Century English Literature* (The Hague: Mouton, 1970), esp. 151–55.

20. Aside from 2 Cor. 12.1–4 (discussed in the text), see Luke 23.43: "And Jesus said unto him [the repentant malefactor], Verily I say unto thee, to day shalt thou be with me in paradise"; and Rev. 2.7: "He that hath an ear, let him hear what the Spirit saith unto the churches; To him that overcometh will I give to eat of the tree of life, which is in the midst of the paradise of God." For a discussion of the concept of Paradise in Milton, see Joseph E. Duncan, *Milton's Earthly Paradise: A Historical Study of Eden* (Minneapolis: University of Minnesota Press, 1972). For a discussion of the concept of Paradise in the ancient traditions, see John Armstrong, *The Paradise Myth* (New York: Oxford University Press, 1969). For the etymology and usage of "Paradise" [*paradeisos*] in the New Testament and the early literature, see *A Greek-English Lexicon of the New Testament and Other Early Christian Literature*, 4th ed., trans. and ed. W. F. Arndt and F. W. Gingrich (Chicago: University of Chicago Press, 1952), s.v.

21. See Michael Lieb, *The Visionary Mode: Biblical Prophecy, Hermeneutics, and Cultural Change* (Ithaca: Cornell University Press, 1991), esp. 180–81. References to the Greek text of the New Testament are to *The Precise Parallel New Testament*, ed. John R. Kohlenberger III (New York: Oxford University Press, 1987).

22. Lewalski, *"Paradise Lost" and the Rhetoric of Literary Forms*, 123–24, 214. Lewalski quite rightly compares the dialogue between God and Adam in book 8 with that between God and the Son in book 3 (123). For a detailed analysis of the dialogue between God and the Son in book 3, see Michael Lieb, *The Sinews of Ulysses: Form and Convention in Milton's Works* (Pittsburgh: Duquesne University Press, 1989), 76–97.

23. God's reference to himself as "alone / From all Eternitie" without "second to [him] or like, equal much less" has several classical antecedents. See the note to line 407 in *John Milton: Complete Poems and Major Prose*, ed. Merritt Y. Hughes (New York: Odyssey, 1957), 372, and the note to lines 406–7 in *The Poems of John Milton*, ed. John Carey and Alastair Fowler (London: Longman, 1968), 836–37. For a discussion of God's unity, see Milton's *De Doctrina Christiana*: "God is one ens, not two; one essence and one subsistence, which is nothing but a substantial essence, appertain to one ens" [Deus est unum ens, non duo; una essentia unius est entis, una etiam subsistentia, quae nihil aliud quam essentia substantialis est] (*CM*, 14:194, 195; for a corresponding translation, see *YP*, 6:212). Although the authorship of *De Doctrina* has been questioned, I shall (for the sake of argument) assume it is Milton's.

24. Underlying Adam's argument for an "other" to complete him is something of Aristophanes' argument in the *Symposium* concerning the need on the part of primeval man to find his "other half." With each half desiring the other, they come together and throw their arms around one another, "entwined in mutual embraces, longing to grow into one" (*The Dialogues of Plato*, 2 vols., trans. B. Jowett [New York: Random House, 1937], 1:317).

25. For detailed definitions of these terms, see *The New Brown—Driver—Briggs—Gesenius Hebrew and English Lexicon . . . Based on the Lexicon of William Gesenius*, ed. Francis Brown et al. (Peabody, Mass.: Hendrickson, 1979), s. v., hereafter designated *BDB*.

26. The term *yashen* is attested almost two dozen times in Hebrew Scrip-

tures. All references to the Hebrew Bible are to the *Biblia Hebraica Stuttgartensia*, ed. K. Elliger and W. Rudolph (Stuttgart: Deutsche Bibelstiftung, 1967–77).

27. Although the biblical account does not specify from which side of Adam God extracts the rib, Milton's Adam designates the "left side" (8.465) as the location closest to the heart, the place of "cordial spirits warm" and "Lifeblood streaming fresh" (466–67), an idea consistent with the traditions. (For explanation, see the note to lines 465–66 in the Carey and Fowler edition of *The Poems of John Milton*, 838.) Having earlier suggested the implications of Sin's own birth from the "left," or "sinister," side of Satan's head (2.755), Milton no doubt designates the left side of Adam as a proleptic gesture toward the coming disobedience and subsequent Fall.

28. That Milton viewed this sleep in distinctly visionary terms is discernible from Michael's own later statement concerning Adam's experience on the Hill of "Speculation" (12.589). Michael says to Adam:

> Ascend
> This Hill: let Eve (for I have drencht her eyes)
> Here sleep below while thou to foresight wak'st,
> As once thou slepst, while Shee to life was form'd.
>
> (11.366–69)

29. See Michael Lieb, "The Book of M: *Paradise Lost* as Revisionary Text," *Cithara* (1991): 28–35.

30. Few have explored the ironies implicit in the biblical Adam's declaration that "she shall be called Woman, because she was taken out of Man" in relation to the Miltonic rendering: "Woman is her Name, of Man / Extracted." As Umberto Cassuto (*A Commentary on the Book of Genesis*, 2 vols., trans. Israel Abraham [Jerusalem: Magnes Press, 1961], 1:136), among others, has made clear, the term for man [*ish*] and the term for woman [*ishsha*] in the Hebrew have different roots. Aside from a phonetic pun present in both the Hebrew and the English, the word "woman" is in no sense etymologically derived from the word "man." See also E. A. Speiser, trans., *Genesis, The Anchor Bible* (Garden City, New York: Doubleday, 1964). In the context of feminist discourse and sexual politics, such distinctions come to assume major significance in the establishment of "difference."

31. It is generally agreed (but by no means certain) that the narrator of the Genesis account (rather than Adam) declares: "Therefore shall a man leave his father and his mother, and shall cleave unto his wife: and they shall be one flesh." The Masoretic text contains no quotation marks. The act of placing the statement squarely in the mouth of his Adam is an important interpretive decision on Milton's part. For a discussion of the tradition underlying the concept of "one flesh" and Milton's use of it, see James Grantham Turner, *One Flesh: Paradisal Marriage and Sexual Relations in the Age of Milton* (Oxford: Oxford University Press, 1987).

32. See *BDB*, s.v. As a verb of pursuing and overtaking, *davak* in its various *binyanim* assumes a distinctly military bearing. See the texts indicated in *BDB*, Hiph., definitions 2 and 3. For the idea of pursuing, see Judg. 20.45, 1 Sam. 14.22, and 1 Chron. 10.2. For the idea of overtaking, see Gen. 31.23 and Judg. 18.22. As well as suggesting both faithfulness and loyalty (Ruth 1.14, 2 Sam. 20.2), *davak* may also assume a distinctly sexual (if indeed illicit) dimension. See the texts indicated under definition 2a in *BDB*, s.v. In the Jewish mys-

tical traditions, *davak* becomes *devekut*, the act of cleaving to God as the result of an ascent to the divine world. See Gershom Scholem, *Kabbalah* (New York: New American Library, 1974), 174–76. In *Tetrachordon*, Milton accords this cleaving a mystical status as well. Viewing the act of cleaving as a prefiguration of the *corpus mysticum*, as well as the Eucharist, Milton cites as his proof text Ephes. 5.30–32: "For we are members of his body, of his flesh, and of his bones. For this cause shall a man leave his father and his mother, and shall be joined unto his wife, and they two shall be one flesh. This is a great mystery: but I speak concerning Christ and the church" (*YP*, 2:606).

33. Lewalski, *"Paradise Lost" and the Rhetoric of Literary Forms*, 129.

34. Ibid., 213. Lewalski compares Adam's epithalamium here to that of Edmund Spenser in the *Epithalamion* and the bridegroom in the Song of Songs: both Spenser and the bridegroom celebrate their own wedding in an epithalamium.

35. This is a moment Milton envisioned as early as his plans for a drama on the Fall delineated in the Trinity manuscript. In the third draft (titled "Paradise Lost"), Milton refers to "the mariage song" sung by a chorus. "Evening starre" is likewise mentioned in the same context (*YP*, 8:554).

36. Still the best treatment of the significance of the nightingale to *Paradise Lost* is Anne Davidson Ferry, *Milton's Epic Voice: The Narrator in "Paradise Lost"* (Cambridge: Harvard University Press, 1967), 20–43.

Afterthoughts on Adam's Story

J. MARTIN EVANS

At the risk of committing what Yvor Winters identified as "the fallacy of imitative form,"[1] I would like to devote my afterthoughts on Adam's story to Adam's afterthoughts on the same subject. His description of Eve's creation and their consequent nuptial union appears at first to conclude at line 523 of book 8:

> Thus I have told thee all my State, and brought
> My story to the sum of earthly bliss
> Which I enjoy.
>
> (521–23)[2]

Although this may be the end of Adam's "relation" (247), it is not the end of his speech, not even the end of his sentence. For after only a comma, he launches into a prolonged exposition of the psychological and moral consequences of the events he has just described:

> Which I enjoy, and must confess to find
> In all things else delight indeed, but such
> As us'd or not, works in the mind no change
> Nor vehement desire . . .
> . . . .
> . . . but here
> Far otherwise, transported I behold,
> Transported touch; here passion first I felt,
> Commotion strange, in all enjoyments else
> Superior and unmov'd, here only weak
> Against the charm of Beauty's powerful glance.
>
> (523–33)

As the verb "confess" warns us at the outset, there is something seriously wrong with Adam's reaction to his wife's physical attractions. Unlike the other pleasures that God has provided, he tells the archangel, Eve's beauty carries him away into a state of

48

passionate excitement so strong that he literally loses his mind and becomes, in the original Latin sense of the word, "vehement."[3] In addition to the "trancelike state" in which he was led to his seat in Eden, and the *tardemah* (or, as the Greek Septuagint translated it, the *ecstasis*) in which he witnessed Eve's creation,[4] Adam now describes a third and very different form of "abstract" (462) experience, a kind of reverse *ecstasis* in which he is "transported" not out of his senses but into them, in which his mind is not freed from his body but his body is freed from his mind.

Despite his recognition of Eve's subordinate position in the divine scheme of things, Adam goes on to explain:

> yet when I approach
> Her loveliness, so absolute she seems
> And in her self complete, so well to know
> Her own, that what she wills to do or say,
> Seems wisest, virtuousest, discreetest, best;
> All higher knowledge in her presence falls
> Degraded, Wisdom in discourse with her
> Loses discount'nanc't, and like folly shows.
>
> (546–53)

As virtually every commentator on the poem has pointed out, and as the ominous verb "falls" already implies, here are the first symptoms of what "the Argument" to book 9 accurately diagnoses as "the vehemence of love" that will eventually lead Adam to eat the forbidden fruit, "fondly overcome with female charm" (9.999). The story that until line 523 seemed to be, in Michael Lieb's words, an account of "a process of ascent to ever higher levels of consciousness" culminating in "a celebration of God in all his creative and providential power"[5] is retroactively transformed by Adam's confession into something rather more sinister: an unsettling prologue to his temptation and fall.

In my opening sentence I described this act of self-analysis as an afterthought, and so it is if we look at it in purely chronological terms. Adam's subversive coda, that is to say, does not emerge from his consciousness until his "story" itself is over. For those of Milton's readers who were familiar with the exegetical traditions surrounding the text of Genesis, however, the feelings Adam confesses to Raphael would have been implicit in his narrative from the very beginning, for the notion that the first man's rational authority was undermined by his wife's sen-

sual attractions has its roots in one of the oldest surviving commentaries on Genesis in the history of the biblical narrative.
According to Philo of Alexandria, writing early in the first century of our era, the true significance of Eve's creation was essentially allegorical: when Adam, the representative of human
reason, fell asleep, that is to say when the mind relaxed its attention, Eve, the representative of the senses, was born. And
Adam's waking declaration that for this cause a man shall "leave
his father and his mother, and shall cleave unto his wife" (Gen.
2.24) signified that "for the sake of sense-perception, the Mind,
when it has become her slave, abandons both God the Father of
the universe, and God's excellence and wisdom, the Mother of
all things, and cleaves to and becomes one with sense-perception."[6] The creation of Eve while Adam was asleep thus constituted the beginning of the Fall, if not the Fall itself, as Philo
explained in purely literal terms in another of his works, *De
opificio mundi.* "Woman," he wrote, "becomes for [Adam] the
beginning of blameworthy life. For as long as he was by himself,
as accorded with such solitude, he went on growing like to the
world and like God." But when Adam first saw Eve, and desired
her, "this desire begat likewise bodily pleasure, that pleasure
which is the beginning of wrongs and violation of the law, the
pleasure for the sake of which men bring on themselves the life
of mortality and wretchedness in lieu of that of immortality and
bliss."[7] One could hardly want a better summary of the feelings
that Adam "confesses" to Raphael when his story is over.

During the centuries that followed Philo's observations, this
allegorical interpretation of the biblical text underwent a number of modifications at the hands of the church fathers, but as
late as the seventeenth century the original Philonic pattern was
still readily available to Milton and his contemporaries in a book
entitled *Conjectura Cabbalistica,* published in 1653 by the famous Cambridge Platonist Henry More. In this influential collection of Jewish lore relating to the book of Genesis, More, like
Philo, equated Adam with reason and Eve with the senses. When
Adam awoke from his divinely induced slumber and saw his
wife for the first time, More wrote:

> He straightway acknowledg'd that all the sense and knowledge of
> any thing he had hitherto, was more lifelesse and evanid, and
> seemed lesse congruous and grateful unto him, and more estranged
> from his nature: but this was so agreeable and consentaneous to his
> soul, that he looked upon it as a necessary part of himself, and called

it after his own name. And he thought thus within himself, For this cause will any one leave his over-tedious aspires to unite with the Eternal Intellect, and Universal Soul of the world . . . and will cleave to the joyous and chearful life of his [sensory] Vehicle.[8]

What Milton has done in *Paradise Lost*, I would submit, is to extract this allegorical reading of Eve's creation from its original narrative context in Gen. 2.24 and insert a literal version of it into the confession that Adam appends to the end of his story. Just as in Philo's original commentary, Adam's "mind" is enslaved by sensory pleasure and abandons the counsels of "Wisdom."

Something quite remarkably similar, we might note at this point, also happens to Satan when he sees Eve alone for the first time shortly afterward.[9] Just as she appeared to Adam to be "so lovely fair, / That what *seem'd fair* in all the World, seem'd now / Mean, or in her *summ'd up*, in her contain'd" (8.471–73), so, in Satan's eyes, "What *pleasing seem'd*, for her now pleases more, / She most, and in her look *sums* all Delight" (9.453–54). Just as Adam was "*transported*" by Eve's "*air*" (8.476) when she approached him with "*Grace* . . . in all her steps, *Heav'n* in her eye, / In every *gesture* dignity and love" (488–89), so Satan is "*transported*" (9.474) by his victim's "*Heav'nly* form / Angelic . . . Her *grace*ful Innocence, her every *Air* / Of *gesture*" (457–60). And just as Adam's "higher knowledge" was "Degraded" by the "*awe*" (8.558) of Eve's "loveliness," so Satan's "Malice" is "over*aw'd*" (9.460, 461) by her "beauty" (491). The devil's response duplicates Adam's in almost every detail.

Satan's moral transformation, of course, is only temporary, and he quickly recovers his true infernal nature:

> But the hot Hell that always in him burns,
> Though in mid Heav'n, soon ended his delight,
>
> . . . .
>   . . . then soon
> Fierce hate he recollects, and all his thoughts
> Of mischief, gratulating, thus excites.
>
>   (467–72)

The crucial question in book 8 is whether Adam, too, resists the "delight" that Eve inspires in him—whether he is simply revealing a psychological tendency that up to this point of the poem has not had an opportunity to manifest itself in a specific action or decision, and is therefore only *potentially* damaging, or whether he is describing an act of mental submission that he has already committed. At first sight it might well appear that Alastair Fowler is correct when he argues that the tendency Adam describes has so far been "held in check, so that it does not yet constitute a defect."[10] Michael Wilding, for instance, observes that "the Fall is presaged—but certainly has not occurred. . . . At this stage of the poem when Adam talks with Raphael, it is hard to say Adam's fully understandable passion for Eve is sinful. He may be failing to observe due order in things, but he is not corrupt."[11] And Stanley Fish, while recognizing Adam's susceptibility to "Commotion strange," concludes that "he keeps his balance (startled, not astounded) and retains his hold on the truth of things as he knows them to be. . . . Higher knowledge has *not* fallen degraded in Eve's presence."[12]

Adam himself, moreover, vigorously denies succumbing to his wife's physical attractions when Raphael subsequently accuses him of permitting his judgment to be swayed by his passion. Invoking the classic Augustinian distinction between *delectatio* and *consentio,* according to which the pleasurable contemplation of a sinful act may be guiltless provided that a conscious decision is not taken to commit it,[13] Adam insists that the delight he takes in Eve's company has never actually "foiled" (8.608) him.[14] He may "feel" (608) an inward commotion in the presence of "those graceful acts, / Those thousand decencies that daily flow / From all her words and actions, mixt with Love" (600–602), but he is still free to "Approve the best, and follow what I approve" (611). As Douglas Bush pointed out long ago, this ringing affirmation of moral integrity inverts Ovid's famous account of Medea's moral dilemma in the *Metamorphoses:* "I see the better, I approve it too: / The worse I follow" (7. 20–21).[15] In Bush's view, the echo is thoroughly ironic, providing the reader with a subversive counterstatement that directly challenges Adam's simple-minded assertion of his own innocence. But it seems equally possible that the whole point of Milton's allusion lies, rather, in the contrast between life before "Man's First Disobedience" (1.1) and life after it, that he invokes the Ovidian subtext to remind us that in the state of innocence it was possible to behave in a way no longer available to fallen human beings such as Jason's vengeful mistress.

Adam's interactions with Eve in books 4 and 5, at all events, betray not the slightest hint of mental weakness or sensory infatuation. The "superior Love" (4.499) with which he responds to Eve's account of her creation and marriage, the knowledgeable answer he provides to her question about the function of "glittering Star-light" (656), the reassuring explanation he offers for her "uncouth dream" (5.98), and the generous instructions he gives her when he first sees Raphael approaching all bespeak a mind that is fully in control of any carnal desires that Eve's beauty might stimulate in him. As Fish observes, Adam's "higher knowledge" has not been "Degraded" by her presence, and his "Wisdom" has nowhere taken on the appearance of "folly." In every respect, one is tempted to say, his behavior has been entirely exemplary.

The reason that critics such as Fowler, Wilding, and Fish are so concerned to defend Adam against the charge of "attributing overmuch to things / Less excellent" (8.565–66), of course, is their determination to maintain as clear a distinction as possible between prelapsarian and postlapsarian human nature and thus to refute E. M. W. Tillyard's argument, later amplified by Millicent Bell, that Milton ascribed to Adam and Eve "feelings which though nominally felt in the state of innocence are actually not compatible with it."[16] But as the church had been teaching for more than a thousand years, and as Adam explains to Eve after her dream, the difference between innocence and guilt has nothing to do with feelings, or even with thoughts, but with decisions. Even if Adam had permitted his judgment to be swayed by passion, even if his "higher knowledge" had "fallen" when he approached Eve's loveliness, his innocence would still be intact provided that his will had not consented to an evil deed. When Raphael leaves Adam at the end of book 8, he warns him to "take heed lest Passion sway / Thy Judgment to do aught, which else free Will / Would not admit" (635–37). The last ten words are crucial because they clearly specify that such a psychological disturbance would be sinful only if it eventuated in a decision to disobey the law of God.

It seems to me, therefore, quite unnecessary to deny that Adam has done what he says he has. Indeed, I would like to suggest that Adam *has* in fact allowed Eve's beauty to blur his mental faculties and that we have seen it happening at the precise narrative juncture from which Philo and More had extracted their allegorical descriptions of the mind's submission to the senses, the moment when Adam meets his wife for the first time—the "high point of his visionary quest," as Lieb describes it.[17] This is a particularly fascinating and complex moment, for it is the point at which Eve's story in book 4 intersects with Adam's here in book 8. As such, it is the only episode in the first

eight books that is narrated twice, and from two very different
points of view. According to Adam, when Eve originally approached him, "Led by her Heav'nly Maker" (8.485), her

> Innocence and Virgin Modesty,
> Her virtue and the conscience of her worth,
> That would be woo'd, and not unsought be won,
> Not obvious, not obtrusive, but retir'd,
> The more desirable, or to say all,
> Nature herself, though pure of sinful thought,
> Wrought in her so, that seeing me, she turn'd.
>
>   (501–7)

But this is not what really happened. In fact, it is a gross misrepresentation of what really happened, for as Eve had informed
Adam during the course of her autobiography in book 4, the reason that she turned away from him had nothing at all to do with
innocence and virgin modesty or anything vaguely resembling
them. After her Narcissus-like encounter with her own reflection immediately after her creation, she simply found her future
husband

>   less fair,
> Less winning soft, less amiably mild,
> Than that smooth wat'ry image; back I turn'd,
> Thou following cri'd'st aloud, Return fair Eve,
> Whom fli'st thou? whom thou fli'st, of him thou art,
> His flesh, his bone.
>
>   (478–83)

Adam has edited out of his story not only her "vain desire" (466)
for the figure she saw reflected in the pool but her self-confessed
preference for her own "wat'ry image" over that of her divinely
appointed mate.[18] What Eve "will[ed] to do or say" on that particular occasion does indeed now seem to Adam to have been
"wisest, virtuousest, discreetest, best." What in book 4 was a
frank admission that she found the "Shape" (461) she saw in the
"Smooth Lake" (459) more sexually attractive than her husband
has been transformed in book 8 into a natural impulse "pure of
sinful thought," an innocent example of "sweet reluctant amorous delay" (4.311). For a moment at least, "the charm of Beauty's powerful glance" seems to have deprived Adam of the
"knowledge" that Eve herself communicated to him earlier in
the poem. Either he did not really hear what she was saying to

him, or he has consciously or unconsciously suppressed the memory of it.

If we follow Lieb's advice and view Adam's story "within the context of Eve's reflections on her own coming to awareness of self and 'other,' " then we can hardly escape the conclusion that Eve's portrayal of her encounter with her husband not only "contains additional details that supplement the story that Adam tells" but contains additional details that totally subvert the story that Adam tells. Adam's romanticized misrepresentation of his wife's behavior is not merely "complemented by" Eve's account as Lieb generously suggests;[19] it is exposed by Eve's account as a pathetic exercise in self-deception, not in itself a sin, perhaps, since no violation of the divine law is involved, but an ominous foreshadowing of "the vehemence of love" that will lead him to eat the forbidden fruit in the next book.

NOTES

1. Yvor Winters, *The Function of Criticism* (Denver: Alan Swallow, 1967), 54.

2. John Milton, *Paradise Lost*, in *John Milton: Complete Poems and Major Prose*, ed. Merritt Y. Hughes (New York: Odyssey, 1957). All references to *Paradise Lost* are to this edition and are cited parenthetically in the text.

3. In Latin, Alastair Fowler points out in his note to 8.526, *vehe* means "lacking" and *mens* means "mind" (John Milton, *The Complete Poems of John Milton*, ed. John Carey and Alastair Fowler [London: Longman, 1968], 843).

4. See Michael Lieb, "Adam's Story: Testimony and Transition in *Paradise Lost*" on pages 21–47 in this collection.

5. Ibid., 42, 24.

6. Philo of Alexandria, *Legum allegoria*, in *Philo*, trans. F. H. Colson and G. H. Whitaker (Cambridge: Harvard University Press, 1962), 1:2.14.

7. *De opificio mundi*, in *Philo*, trans. Colson and Whitaker, 1:53.

8. Henry More, *Conjectura Cabbalistica* (London, 1653), 42–43.

9. I owe this insight to my daughter, Joanna R. Evans. All emphases in the following quotations are mine.

10. *The Complete Poems of John Milton*, ed. Carey and Fowler, note to 8.551–52.

11. Michael Wilding, *Milton's "Paradise Lost"* (Sydney: Sydney University Press, 1969), 90–91.

12. Stanley Fish, *Surprised by Sin* (London: Macmillan, 1967), 229.

13. Augustine, *De sermone Domini in monte*, 1.12. See also Peter Abelard, *Ethics*, trans. D. E. Luscombe (Oxford: Clarendon Press, 1971), 15: "[T]he will itself or the desire to do what is unlawful is by no means to be called sin, but rather, as we have stated, the consent itself."

14. According to Fowler, note to 8.608, "foiled" means "overcome, defiled,

or polluted," but the *Oxford English Dictionary*, s. v., records another meaning, drawn from the sport of hunting, which may also be operative here: "to run over or cross (scent or ground) so as to baffle hounds." In his pursuit of virtue, Adam paradoxically implies, his senses do not throw him off the scent. His reason still enables him to "follow what I approve" (8.611).

15. Douglas Bush, "Ironic and Ambiguous Allusion in *Paradise Lost*," *Journal of English and Germanic Philology* 60 (1961): 639. Like Bush, I quote from George Sandys's translation of the *Metamorphoses*, in *Ovid's Metamorphoses, English'd Mythologiz'd and Represented in Figures* (London, 1632).

16. See E. M. W. Tillyard, "The Crisis of *Paradise Lost*," in *Studies in Milton* (London: Chatto and Windus, 1951), and Millicent Bell, "The Fallacy of the Fall in *Paradise Lost*," *PMLA* 68 (1953): 863–83.

17. Lieb, "Adam's Story," 37.

18. Milton leaves us to imagine what Adam's motive might have been for misrepresenting his first encounter with Eve. Either he was deliberately deceiving the angel out of embarrassment, or he was unconsciously deceiving himself. In the final analysis, the latter explanation seems to me to be more likely.

19. Lieb, "Adam's Story," 23, 38.

John Milton, Object of the Erotic Gaze?

ANNA K. NARDO

In 1790, a coffin purported to be John Milton's was exhumed and rifled. Subsequently, a lock of hair assumed to be Milton's fell into the hands of poet and essayist Leigh Hunt, who showed it to his friend John Keats, who was so moved that he penned a poem on the spot. Hunt later gave the lock to Robert Browning, who kept it under glass near his writing desk.[1] Milton might have been amused at the irony: the remains of a revolutionary apologist for regicide, who once wrote a treatise entitled "Icon-Breaker," had now himself become a relic.

Despite the inconsistency, the Victorians venerated Milton—the sublime Puritan, the champion and martyr of English liberty, the author of their great national epic, *Paradise Lost*—as a kind of Protestant saint. The life story of such an exalted cultural hero was so well known that, in an 1855 review of Thomas Keightley's *An Account of the Life, Opinions, and Writings of John Milton*, George Eliot could claim "the principal phases and incidents of Milton's life are familiar to us all: . . . the journey to Italy where he 'found and visited the famous Galileo, grown old, a prisoner'; the prosaic transition to school-keeping in London City and inharmonious marriage with Mary Powell; his Latin secretaryship; his second and third ventures in matrimony, and small satisfaction in his daughters; the long days of blindness in which the *Paradise Lost* was poured forth by thirty lines at a time when a friendly pen happened to be near."[2] Every school-boy, Eliot says, knew these stories. But Victorian popular writers, not unlike twentieth-century journalists, were prone to sensationalize the life stories of their idols—especially the stories of their erotic life.

Briefly, I want to outline a cultural history of Victorian representations of Milton as a lover, with two goals in mind: first, to demonstrate how some of these fictions gratified the Milton idolaters by reversing Adam's love story told in *Paradise Lost* in

57

order to create a love story for the young Milton; and second, to show how Eliot's epic novel *Middlemarch* exposes the excesses of the cult of Milton by testing its folly against the truths of Milton's own epic vision.

1

To flesh out the scanty evidence of the young Milton's passions, several Victorian writers turn to hints in his poetry and even to legend. In an essay "Milton and Leonora Baroni" in *Memoirs of the Loves of the Poets* (1829), Anna Brownwell (Murphy) Jameson follows the lead of Milton's early biographer Jonathan Richardson (1734), who invented the supposed passions of Milton's youth from his early poetry, including three Latin epigrams addressed to Leonora Baroni, whom Milton heard sing at a soiree at the Barberini Palace in Rome. These poems, Jameson asserts, prove that Milton was "early touched by the softest passions, and during his whole life peculiarly sensible to the charm of female society." In youth, he possessed "an uncommonly fine person," and "like his own Adam, [a] fair large front and hyacinthine locks, serene and blooming as his own Eden." In her "disgust" at Samuel Johnson's attempt "to degrade the majestic, to disfigure the beautiful, and darken the glorious" and in her desire to vindicate England's "great and sacred" poet, Jameson recreates Milton in the image of the handsome young lover of romance fiction, who, in the tradition of Dante and Petrarch, wrote "a thousand most lovely and glorious passages scattered through his works, which women may quote with triumph, as proofs that we had no small influence over the imagination of our great epic poet."[3]

Whereas Jameson believed herself merely to be expanding on accurate biographical information in reconstructing Milton's erotic life, other writers consciously constructed fictions about Milton's passions—specifically, Edward Bulwer-Lytton in his poem "Milton" (1831), Major Vetch in his play *Milton at Rome* (1851), Max Ring in his novel *John Milton and His Times* (translated from German in 1868), and Anne Manning in her novel *The Maiden and Married Life of Mary Powell, afterwards Mistress Milton* (1855). Further embellishing the biographical speculations about Baroni, these writers resurrect a legend that circulated at Cambridge about its famous alumnus. One summer day, young Milton was supposedly dozing under a tree when a lovely foreign lady happened by. So captivated was she by his beauty that she left some Italian verses in the sleeping youth's hand.

> Occhi, Stelle mortali,
> Ministre de miei Mali,
> Se, chiusi, m'uccidete,
> Aperti, che farete?
> (Ye beautiful eyes! Stars of the earth!
> Though closed, my heart ye have wounded;
> What would life any longer be worth
> Should ye open with glory surrounded?)[4]

Upon waking, young Milton found the verses, but his secret admirer had disappeared. This legend had such currency that several artists painted the scene, including Henry Fuseli, whose painting of the foreign beauty gazing upon the sleeping Milton was exhibited with forty-seven scenes from Milton's poetry and life in the 1799 Milton Gallery.[5] Some versions of the legend even transform Milton's grand tour of Italy in 1638–39 into a quest for his secret admirer.

This romantic Cambridge interlude becomes the focus of Bulwer-Lytton's lush poem "Milton." When the traveling Italian lady sees the sleeping Milton, "O'er him she lean'd enamour'd, and her sigh / Breath'd near and nearer to his silent mouth."[6] Brushed by her dark curls, the poet awakes and for a moment they gaze into each other's eyes:

> The deep—deep love suppress'd
> For years, and treasur'd in each secret breast,
> Waken'd, and glow'd, and centred in their gaze.
>
> (259)

Impetuously Milton kneels adoringly to her, but the modest beauty flees "and left him mute and spellbound there" (260). Years later, however, Milton miraculously encounters this same beauty in Rome. He woos her, then asks her to marry him and return to England, where he must join the fight for liberty. Of course, the Italian beauty does not yield to Milton's call to "Come, be my guide, my partner, and my staff, / My hope in youth, my haven in my age!" (278). Remembering what domestic trials Milton will later face—the desertion of his first wife, Mary Powell; the death of his second wife in childbirth; and the rebellion of his teenaged daughters—any nineteenth-century reader would imagine the world of woes from which this first love might have saved Milton if she had consented to be the ideal helpmate he envisioned. Eventually, however, as an old woman, Bulwer-Lytton's Italian beauty returns to England, experiencing a reprise of her first vision of love. Herself unseen, she gazes on the blind, old man in defeat who once asked her to be "my solace, my reward" (278). Finally, she weeps over his tomb for three days, then dies of a broken heart.

It is very easy to laugh at Bulwer-Lytton's overwrought erotic language and high melodrama. But it will repay our attention to look at the source for his construction of the scene of budding passion. He describes the Italian lady gazing on the sleeping Cambridge student as a reprise of Milton's last sonnet and its revision in Adam's story of Eve's creation in book 8 of *Paradise Lost*. To entertain the angel Raphael, who has come to Eden to warn against Satan's wiles, Adam relates the story of Eve's creation:

> methought I saw,
> Though sleeping, where I lay . . .
> . . . .
>   a Creature . . .
> Manlike, but different sex, so lovely fair,
> That what seem'd fair in all the World, seem'd now
> Mean, or in her summ'd up, in her contain'd
> And in her looks, which from that time infus'd
> Sweetness into my heart, unfelt before,
> And into all things from her Air inspir'd
> The spirit of love and amorous delight.
> Shee disappear'd, and left me dark, I wak'd
> To find her, or for ever to deplore
> Her loss, and other pleasures all abjure.
>
> (8.462–80)[7]

In constructing this interpolated story, Milton had revised his own dream vision of his dead wife recorded in "Methought I saw my late espoused Saint" ("Sonnet 23"). In this poignant sonnet, the blind poet, although asleep, sees a vision of his beloved, deceased wife in whom shines "Love, sweetness, goodness . . . / So clear, as in no face with more delight" (11–12). "But O," he laments, "as to embrace me she inclin'd, / I wak'd, she fled, and day brought back my night" (13–14). In the subsequent passage from *Paradise Lost*, Adam, like the blind poet, sleeps, sees his beloved in a vision that infuses into his heart "Sweetness" and "love," then awakens to her absence. As in Petrarch's first glimpse of Laura or Dante's of Beatrice, this vision transforms Adam's life, refocusing his consciousness on the radiant object of his gaze. For Petrarch, Dante, and the blind poet of Milton's last sonnet, the object remains forever a lovely vision, never attainable on earth. In Adam's story, however, the lover comes to possess the object of his gaze, for God brings him Eve, the "fairest . . . Of all [God's] gifts" (8.493–94), to be his wife.

In Bulwer-Lytton's revision of this episode, the young Milton awakens to experience only a fleeting glimpse of the beauty who disappears, leaving him "mute and spellbound"—just as the blind husband awakens from his radiant vision to a day that is night, and as the vision of Eve disappears leaving Adam "dark." Fuseli, who painted all three of these scenes—the Cambridge legend, the dream vision of Milton's last sonnet, and Adam's account of the birth of Eve—seems to draw the same connection between biography and poetry as does Bulwer-Lytton.[8] But two of Fuseli's paintings—the foreign beauty finding the sleeping youth and the dead wife appearing before the sleeping husband—and Bulwer-Lytton's poem reverse the archetype of the male lover transfixed by gazing upon feminine beauty. In poem and paintings, the young man becomes himself the object of the feminine gaze. As in the myth of Diana and Endymion, the lady is captivated by gazing upon the beautiful youth. Bulwer-Lytton's Italian lady even returns one last time to gaze on the hero who lost his eyes, Milton claims in "Sonnet 22," "In liberty's defense" (11).

In different ways, all but one of the Victorian retellings of the Cambridge legend reverse Adam's story to make young Milton the object of the erotic gaze, while they recount his sacrifice of eros for a higher good. Major Vetch's justly obscure play *Milton at Rome* portrays Milton as freedom's outspoken champion, unwilling to curb his tongue even in Rome, and ready to die before leaving Rome without visiting Galileo's dungeon (never mind that Milton actually met Galileo when the old man was under house arrest in a villa outside Florence).[9] While reclining in a Roman garden imagining how he will describe the glorious Roman skies in his future poem of lost paradise, Milton falls asleep. Angelina, a young noblewoman who longs for the return of ancient Roman greatness, comes upon the sleeping poet, and is moved spontaneously to sing a variation on the verses left by the legendary beauty:

> Glory round that brow seems wreathing
>   All the hero's laurell'd fame;
> And those tuneful lips seem breathing
>   With the Muse's purest flame—
> Ah! I may not think what passion
>   In those shrouded eyes may be;
> Ere their lightning glance is flashing,
>   From the fatal bower I flee.

Here, the foreign beauty gazes less upon a lovely youth than on a prophetic image of a heroic poet. Again, Angelina disappears as Milton awakes, imagining he has had a vision of an angel.

Later that night at the Barberini soiree, when asked to demonstrate his poetic powers, Milton obscurely signals to Angelina that he recognizes the angel of his dream:

> As the Patriarch, in his dream,
>   Saw angelic forms descending,
> O'er the poet's sleep there came
>   Vision of an angel bending;
>   He, again to Britain wending,
> There to wake a song of Eden,
>   Memory of that vision blending
> Will pourtray an Eve unfading.

In this version of the legend, Vetch has not only removed the setting from Cambridge to Italy, but he has transformed the Roman singer Baroni into a prophetic heroine, who becomes Milton's inspiration for the episode of Adam's vision of Eve in book 8.

The young poet's aroused passions, however, must be sacrificed, although not without struggle, to his service to England: "O! this alone of earth-born trials unmans me," he laments, "Love and the patriot in my breast at strife / Contending for supremacy." Of course, Milton chooses England, and Angelina, who ironically would have become the supporting helpmate for whom he longed, applauds his choice: "There blazed the Roman soul!—his country's cause / Demands his heart entire." What Vetch has added to Milton's decision to deny eros for service to England is a revision of the conflict expressed by Adam after he tells Raphael the story of Eve's creation.

Having described his blissful union with the object of his gaze, Adam confides in Raphael his discomfort with the power of his erotic feelings:

here passion first I felt,
Commotion strange, in all enjoyments else
Superior and unmov'd, here only weak
Against the charm of Beauty's powerful glance.

(8.530–33)

In dialogue, Adam and Raphael agree that eros is one step on the scale of love that "Leads up to Heav'n, is both the way and guide" (613). In traditional poetry of the erotic gaze, the lover can never possess the beloved but instead transforms his frustrated passion into knightly service to his lady, or the preservation of the beloved's image as an eternal ideal, or a climb toward the beatific vision. Milton, however, allows the fulfillment of the erotic vision in Paradise, where eros is sanctified in the first marriage, because unfallen eros leads man up the scale of love to Heaven.

Both Bulwer-Lytton and Vetch revise Adam's dialogue with Raphael about passion and the scale of love as they imagine Milton's conflict between erotic attachment to an Italian beauty and service to England. Bulwer-Lytton has Milton pleading with his Italian love to become the ideal helpmate represented in the unfallen Eve of *Paradise Lost*. He would re-create the sanctified eros of Eden. Ultimately, however, the lady declines, and Milton chooses service to his country over erotic love. Like the older tradition of lovers, this Milton must translate his passion up the scale of love into higher service. In Vetch's play, Milton's love is again frustrated, but it is Milton who fails to recognize in Angelina the soul mate he would later seek in vain. Instead of having him seek a wife, Vetch has his version of Milton sublimate his passion into poetry, using his vision of Angelina to create Eve as the radiant object of Adam's gaze.

Ring's historical novel *John Milton and His Times* also recalls Adam's vision in book 8 and his dialogue with Raphael about his conflicted experience of passion. But Ring's transformation of this foreign beauty into Milton's Eve differs markedly from Vetch's and Bulwer-Lytton's idealizations. Early in Ring's novel, Henry Lawes, Milton's friend who composed the music for *A Masque Presented at Ludlow Castle*, recounts the legend of an Italian lady who found Milton sleeping in a garden and left him verses wrapped around a rose. The young Lady Alice Egerton (who actually played the heroine of *A Masque*, but who, in Ring's fantasy, becomes Milton's first love) hears the verses and exclaims, "That is charming, though it is much more suitable to address to a lady" (54). Lawes agrees, explaining that the episode resulted in Milton's nickname, "the Lady of Christ's College"—a sobriquet that allegedly originated in Milton's fair complexion and fastidious temperament. By linking the legend of the Italian beauty to Milton's Cambridge nickname, Ring pointedly emphasizes the reversal that places Milton in the feminine position as object of the erotic gaze. This early hint that Milton is being watched becomes a central theme in Ring's novel.

When Milton meets this same foreign beauty in Rome as Leonora singing at the Barberini soiree, he is overwhelmed by the seductive power of her voice. She seems "a true priestess of the goddess of art" (203), and he feels that "the ideal of his youth was not an unsubstantial image of the fancy; before him stood the magnificent embodiment of the reality" (205). At this stage of the novel, Ring has placed Milton, meeting the vision of his Cambridge dream again in Italy, in the position of Adam—dreaming of Eve, awakening to her disappearance, then being reunited with his vision as a reality. Now, however, the vision has become "my goddess! my Muse" (213).

Still, this realized vision turns out to be not the potential helpmate imagined by Bulwer-Lytton and Vetch, but Eve, the temptress. In Ring's revision of the dialogue with Raphael that follows Adam's account of the attainment of his dream, Milton is not smitten, as is Adam, by his beloved's "graceful acts . . . [and] thousand decencies that daily flow / From all her words and actions" but rather by "the charm of Beauty's powerful glance" (*Paradise Lost*, 8.600–602, 533). As a rare beauty with tendrils of hair that curl like serpents, as an artist whose song literally brings the impetuous young Milton to his knees, as an aristocrat living in a palazzo frescoed and decorated as a palace of art, Leonora embodies all the temptations of Rome. Milton, the poet, imagines yielding, for he realizes that in Rome "[i]nstead of heroism there is art; instead of battle cries there are the voices of singers, and strength has given way to beauty and grace" (207). Soon, however, Milton learns that he has been the object of observations far more sinister than the erotic gaze of a priestess of art. Since the days when he wrote the mask for Lord Egerton, he has been secretly watched by Catholic spies. When, at Ludlow Castle, Lawes first told the story of the foreign beauty, Sir Kenelm Digby was present. While playing the role of the evil sorcerer Comus, he was all the while plotting with Italian Jesuits to convert Lord Egerton to the Catholic cause. Now, Digby has reappeared in Rome and is using the beautiful Leonora as the siren to convert Milton, the potential champion of Protestant freedom, to Catholicism. Behind the lady's private, erotic gaze lies the public, political spying of the Roman Catholic Church. Discovering that he has been the dupe of spies, this Milton, like all the other fictional Miltons, rejects eros for the higher good of service to England's liberty.

2

Although often ludicrous in their sentimentality, ahistoricism, and melodrama, these three fictionalizations of Milton's life are not without interest as contributions to the cult of Milton. Public veneration of Milton was often represented through the fantasy of gazing on the blind, old poet. In an 1825 review of the recently discovered *De Doctrina Christiana*, the historian and statesman Thomas Babington Macaulay confesses his adoration and indulges his imagination: "We image to ourselves the breathless silence in which we should listen to his slightest word; the passionate veneration with which we should kneel to kiss his hand and weep upon it; the earnestness with which we should endeavour to console him, if indeed such a spirit could need consolation, for the neglect of an age unworthy of his talents and his virtues, the eagerness with which we should contest with his daughters; or with his Quaker friend Elwood, the privilege of reading Homer to him, or of taking down the immortal accents which flowed from his lips."[10]

The impulse behind such effusive tributes is visualized in the vogue (in England and on the continent, from the late eighteenth through the nineteenth centuries) for painting blind Milton dictating *Paradise Lost* to his daughters. George Romney, Fuseli, H. Decaisne, Eugène Delacroix, and Mihály Munkácsy, among others, painted this scene.[11] Of course, these paintings, engravings, and lithographs differ in their representations of Milton's daughters' attitudes toward their task. In Romney's version, for example, while one daughter bends diligently over her transcribing, the other glances furtively, fearfully, or perhaps rebelliously at her blind father. Nevertheless, in all these dramatizations of the scene of writing, the focus of the viewer's gaze is Milton. As his daughters look at him, they direct our eyes to his seated form, often illuminated by a shaft of light representing the spiritual enlightenment that Milton calls for in the invocation to book 3 of *Paradise Lost*—the "Celestial Light" (51) that must replace his physical blindness. In such representations, Milton becomes the object of the public's adoring gaze.

As the sightless bard of these paintings and the sleeping youth of fictions by Bulwer-Lytton, Vetch, and Ring—Milton is immobilized and passive, fixed as a beautiful or sublime icon to be venerated. A manifestation of the Milton cult, these Victorian fictionalizations of Milton's erotic life gratify the idolaters' desire to gaze by reversing Adam's story to retell Milton's. As the Italian beauties in these fictions gaze upon the youth destined to poetic greatness, so does the reader. Any danger potential in this eroticization of such a sublime hero is neutralized because these fictional Miltons always choose to deny eros for the higher love of country. What these projections of Adam's story onto Milton's life reveal is how some Victorians constructed the icon of Milton through a powerful erotic charge, aroused only to be denied.

But not all Victorians constructed Milton this way. Some nineteenth-century biographers and critics questioned whether such a sublime and ascetic figure was capable of experiencing passionate love. To the Reverend H. Stebbing, "The ordinary passions of our nature were, from the first dawn of manhood, subdued in [Milton's] bosom. . . . Love of woman never warmed him sufficiently to make him for a moment forget the severe assertion of authority, and in his character of child and father no melting tenderness, no irresistible flow of domestic joy, entered into his composition." To Peter Bayne, "Milton was never to any distracting extent in love. . . . [T]he piercing, wailing tenderness of Dante, the glorious transporting tenderness of Shakespeare, were beyond him."[12] Even the idolater Bulwer-Lytton confessed, in the preface to his poem, profound discomfort in attempting to eroticize Milton although using Milton's own poetry for warrant. He professes devotion to the Milton cult: "Aware how sacred and solemn is all connected with the Great Poet, I have endeavoured to touch upon so difficult a subject with all delicacy and all reverence. . . . But here—I confess with willingness my fear—that I may have erred by suffering the smallest mixture of fancy with truth" (255–56). The problem Bulwer-Lytton, as well as Vetch and Ring, failed to solve was this: how could a writer create a fictional Milton who was both the sublime, ascetic Puritan of the national mythology and a believable lover?

Anne Manning's novel *The Maiden and Married Life of Mary Powell, afterwards Mistress Milton* (1855) seems to have solved this aesthetic problem in a manner that pleased popular taste.

Manning's novel was so successful that it was reprinted in the Everyman's Library in 1859, together with its sequel about Milton's rebellious daughters entitled *Deborah's Diary*. Manning's strategy for representing Milton as a lover was to distance his experience of love from the reader's empathy. The novel takes the form of a diary kept by Milton's first wife, Mary Powell, who deserted him after barely one month of married life. The diary records her thoughts from the time of her girlhood in the pastoral world of her father's farm, through her marriage and desertion, until her penitent return to Milton three years later. Thus we see Milton's courtship and marriage wholly from Mary's perspective.[13] Only after she has left her husband does she hear the story of the unknown Italian beauty who found the young Milton asleep under a tree. Some old Cambridge friends, learning that Milton never told his wife the flattering story, relate it to illustrate Milton's modesty. Unlike these Cambridge friends (who seem to echo the Victorian idolaters), Mary does not take the position of an admirer gazing on the beauty of a young genius destined for greatness. Rather, she admits to her diary that her estranged husband is a genius, but she doubts that he was ever modest (116–19).

Although Mary eventually repents and learns to become a fit wife for a poetic genius, the young girl whom Milton comes to court gazes warily upon her suitor. To reconstruct a courtship that eventuated in desertion, Manning removes the motif of the lady gazing upon the young poet from the legend of the Italian beauty and translates it into a revealing moment of Miltonic wooing. One early diary entry records a pastoral ramble after Milton has just received Mary's father's consent to seek her favor:

> We sate a good Space under the Hawthorn Hedge on the Brow of the Hill, listening to the Mower's Scythe, and the Song of Birds, which seemed enough for him, without talking; and as he spake not, I helde my Peace, till, with the Sun in my Eyes, I was like to drop asleep; which, as his own Face was *from* me, and towards the Landskip, he noted not. I was just aiming, for Mirthe's Sake, to steale away, when he suddainlie turned about and fell to speaking of rurall Life, Happinesse, Heaven, and such like, in a Kind of Rapture; then, with his Elbow half raising him from the Grass, lay looking at me; then commenced humming or singing I know not what Strayn, but 'twas of *"begli Occhi"* [beautiful eyes] and *"Chioma aurata"* [golden hair] and he kept smiling the while he sang.
>
> (18)

Here the reader, but not the ill-educated, mischievous Mary, sees that Milton has fallen in love not with this country girl, but with an idealized vision, a composite image constructed from the reading that crystallized his poetic ideals of love: pastoral romances, Neoplatonic dialogues, and Petrarchan sonnets. With gentle humor, Manning constructs a complex scene that disrupts the traditional moment of the captivating gaze. As in the legend of the Italian beauty, Milton again becomes the object of a lady's gaze. But what the reader sees in Mary's report of what she sees is a poet gazing upon an ideal fantasy of his own creation. Through Mary's diary entry, the reader gazes not upon the poet but upon the poet's gazing. Thus we see Milton becoming a poet, not Milton falling in love, and we foresee the disastrous consequences of his marriage to an illusion.

Manning's fictionalization of Milton's erotic life differs markedly from the fictions by the male authors—Bulwer-Lytton, Vetch, and Ring. They gratify the reader's desire to gaze upon Milton, the cultural icon. But their fictions seem ludicrous and melodramatic to us, and they were not very popular in their own day. Manning, however, by writing from the point of view of a mischievous girl unimpressed by her wooer's sublimity, creates an ironic distance between the reader's gaze and Milton's gaze. This distance exposes Milton to the reader's laughter and pity, thereby creating a complex and believable character. Furthermore, Manning's irony exposes the poetic archetype of the erotic gaze to the withering realities of courtship, when the pretty girl being gazed upon just doesn't get the allusions to Italian sonnets.

3

In writing *Middlemarch*, that epic novel of life in nineteenth-century provincial England, George Eliot did not set out, like Bulwer-Lytton, Vetch, and Ring, to fictionalize Milton's life. Nevertheless, she does create a character whom her heroine venerates as a modern-day Milton and a young, handsome student who, while visiting Italy, is smitten by poetic love. Furthermore, like Manning, Eliot ironizes the plight of her Miltonic lovers to expose their blindness and illusions as they enact poetic fictions.[14]

As the novel opens, we meet the nineteen-year-old Dorothea Brooke, who (Eliot's distanced narrator warns us) possesses an engaging "eagerness to know the truths of life," but also "very childlike ideas about marriage." Dorothea imagines that "she would have accepted . . . John Milton when his blindness had come on; or any of the other great men whose odd habits it would have been glorious piety to endure," for "the really delightful marriage must be that where your husband was a sort of father, and could teach you even Hebrew, if you wished it."[15] Here, Eliot's heroine indulges a fantasy remarkably similar to that voiced by the learned statesman Macaulay, who imagined himself kneeling before Milton, listening to his wise words, reading to him, and consoling him in his blindness and loneliness. But Dorothea, not content with fantasy, acts out what the Milton idolaters only imagine. When she meets a neighboring scholar invited to dinner, she fancies him a modern-day Milton to whose work she could become "a lamp-holder" (18).

Unfortunately, Dodo (as her clear-eyed but prosaic sister Celia calls her) is near-sighted (30), and the scholar, as everyone except Dorothea sees, is not Milton, but "a dried bookworm towards fifty" (22), the Reverend Edward Casaubon, who has amassed copious notes toward a dry-as-dust Key to All Mythologies. Failing to notice his "white moles with hairs on them," his wagging head and blinking eyes, and the way he scrapes his spoon while eating soup, Dorothea sees only "the great soul in [his] face" (20), and she conceives an equally great plan. Since Casaubon claims to be " 'using up my eyesight on old characters' " (17), Dorothea offers, " 'Could I not learn to read Latin and Greek aloud to you, as Milton's daughters did to their father, without understanding what they read?' " (62–63). Whereas the Italian beauties in the previous fictionalizations of Milton's life gazed upon the sleeping Cambridge student and were moved by his beauty to compose poetry and song, Eliot's ardent young Protestant beauty gazes near-sightedly at a desiccated scholar and longs to save his eyes. While Bulwer-Lytton, Vetch, and Ring participate in the cult of Milton by making him the object of the erotic gaze, Eliot exposes the fantasy behind the cult by creating its embodiment in a young girl who yearns to devote her life to an idealized Milton of her own construction. Like Manning, Eliot employs irony, humor, and pathos to invent a love story for John Milton. But unlike Manning, Eliot creates a Milton figure with no poetry in his soul, while her heroine is the one deluded by poetic fantasies.

Dorothea, not her Miltonic husband, is blind. Casaubon, at least, recognizes his own emotional paralysis, concluding "that the poets had much exaggerated the force of masculine passion" (62). Dorothea, however, has failed to recognize the erotic component of her own ardent longings toward "the truths of life" (9), and the rest of the novel dramatizes the slow, painful purgation of her vision.

In order to represent her heroine's blindness and trace her gradual enlightenment, Eliot recounts Dorothea's courtship and marriage through strategic allusions to *Paradise Lost*, thereby testing her heroine's fantasy of marriage to Milton against Milton's own epic about marriage and its trials. On only the second day of their acquaintance, Dorothea has already imagined herself "a suitable wife" to Casaubon:

> Dorothea by this time had looked deep into the ungauged reservoir of Mr Casaubon's mind, seeing reflected there in vague labyrinthine extension every quality she herself brought; had opened much of her own experience to him, and had understood from him the scope of his great work, also of attractively labyrinthine extent. For he had been as instructive as Milton's "affable archangel"; and with something of the archangelic manner he told her how he had undertaken to show (what indeed had been attempted before, but not with that thoroughness, justice of comparison, and effectiveness of arrangement at which Mr Casaubon aimed) that all the mythical systems or erratic mythical fragments in the world were corruptions of a tradition originally revealed.
>
> (23)

In her epigraph to this chapter, Eliot had already prepared the reader for the following Miltonic allusion to Raphael's visit to Eden:

> Say Goddess, what ensu'd, when Raphael,
> The affable Arch-angel . . .
>   Eve
> The story heard attentive, and was fill'd
> With admiration, and deep muse to hear
> Of things so high and strange.
>   (7.40–41, 50–53)

Here, Eliot characterizes Dorothea as Eve, rapt at the wisdom of the visitor to her uncle's manor who discourses about high and serious subjects. But two less obvious allusions reframe our view of Dorothea's perception. Whereas this allusion represents Dorothea as Eve listening to an angel imparting Miltonic wisdom, Eliot's allusions to other episodes in *Paradise Lost* reveal what is beyond Dorothea's near-sighted vision.

While listening, Dorothea gazes upon "the ungauged reservoir

of Mr Casaubon's mind," and sees "reflected there in vague laby-
rinthine extension every quality she herself brought." In the
midst of the allusion to Eve's rapt attention to Raphael, Eliot interposes a second allusion likening Dorothea to a younger
Eve—as she remembers herself in the story she tells Adam about
her creation. Just coming to consciousness and hearing the mur-
mur of waters, Eve follows the sound, then "With unexperienc't
thought" lies down

> On the green bank, to look into the clear
> Smooth Lake, that to me seem'd another Sky.
> As I bent down to look, just opposite,
> A Shape within the wat'ry gleam appear'd
> Bending to look on me, I started back,
> It started back, but pleas'd I soon return'd,
> Pleas'd it return'd as soon with answering looks
> Of sympathy and love.
>
> (4.457–65)

Although at first reluctant to leave her own beautiful image, Eve
is led by God's voice beyond narcissism to union with her partner and guide, Adam. Likewise young and innocent, just awakening to life and longing "to see how it was possible to lead a
grand life here—now—in England" (28), Dorothea gazes into
what she imagines to be the profound reservoir of Casaubon's
mind. Failing to discern that it is only a labyrinth of scholarly
minutiae, she sees instead a reflection of her own yearning
toward truth as a guide for effective action. Ironically, Dorothea
longs to be called from "girlish subjection to her own ignorance," to be given "the freedom of voluntary submission to a
guide who would take her along the grandest path" (28)—in
short, to be the Eve who rejects narcissism and chooses to yield
to Adam, having learned that "beauty is excell'd by manly
grace / And wisdom, which alone is truly fair" (4.490–91). But
Eliot's allusion to Eve's gazing at herself in the lake makes it
clear that, in choosing Casaubon, Dorothea has chosen her own
fantasy not a wholly other self. Only later will she learn that Casaubon's mind does not reflect hers, that he has "an equivalent
center of self, whence the lights and shadows must always fall
with a certain difference" (205).

After their long morning conversation about Casaubon's
grand project, Dorothea hurries off for a solitary walk in order to
savor her realization that "Mr Casaubon might wish to make her

his wife, and the idea that he would do so touched her with a sort of reverential gratitude. How good of him—nay, it would be almost as if a winged messenger had suddenly stood beside her path and held out his hand towards her!" (27). What this angel offers, in Dorothea's fantasy, is "the completest knowledge" (28). Although Dorothea is "hardly more than a budding woman," she possesses "a great mental need, not to be satisfied by a girlish instruction comparable to the nibblings and judgments of a discursive mouse" (27). If she were to accept the hand offered by the winged messenger, she imagines, " 'I should learn everything then. . . . I should learn to see the truth by the same light as great men have seen it by' " (28). Following the epigraph that opens this chapter and the subsequent allusion to Raphael's visit to Eden, the reader at first assumes that, in imagining Casaubon as a winged messenger offering his hand, Dorothea returns to her fantasy of becoming an Eve who eagerly receives instruction from "Milton's 'affable archangel.' " But in *Paradise Lost*, Raphael does not suddenly appear, standing beside her path beckoning to Eve. He appears to Adam "through the spicy Forest onward come" (5.298) while Eve is inside their bower preparing lunch.

As Eliot and her readers knew, the only "winged messenger" who beckons Eve to higher knowledge appears in a dream inspired by Satan. As Satan sits "Squat like a Toad, close at the ear of Eve" (4.800), she dreams that a voice calls her "forth to walk" (5.36), and she follows "through ways / That brought me on a sudden to the Tree / Of interdicted Knowledge" (50–52). Beside the tree stands "One shap'd and wing'd like one of those from Heav'n" (55), who offers her the fruit of knowledge. Thus, while Dorothea sees Casaubon as a wise angel of light, Eliot's allusion to Satan in disguise reframes our view of Dorothea's perception, preparing us for her fall into a knowledge of married experience that brings only bitterness and sorrow.

In these two early allusions to *Paradise Lost*, Eliot tests Dorothea's fantasy of marrying Milton against Milton's own analysis of key moments in Eve's growing awareness of self. Through these allusions, Eliot exposes the blindness that leads Dorothea to marry a reflection of her own longings in order, she believes, to attain far-reaching knowledge. The rest of *Middlemarch* charts the clarification of Dorothea's vision of the fallen, middle world through which she must march with her less than perfect fellows. And again, Eliot represents the purgation of her sight in Miltonic terms.

4

Throughout the novel, the knowledge Dorothea so eagerly seeks is imaged as a vista from a high place. During Mr. Casaubon's thin-blooded courtship, Dorothea longs to begin studying Latin and Greek because "those provinces of masculine knowledge seemed to her a standing-ground from which all truth could be seen more truly" (63). Paradoxically, what brings Dorothea to that high "standing-ground" for seeing truly is her fall into the knowledge of suffering. As her illusions about marriage to Casaubon are stripped away, Dorothea repeatedly looks down on the world as she confronts her lonely, empty life. While on her honeymoon, as she begins to discover that her husband's knowledge of dusty trivia is devoid of feeling and life, she looks out on Rome, seeing "visible history, where the past of a whole hemisphere seems moving in funeral procession with strange ancestral images and trophies gathered from afar." But she is only oppressed by "this stupendous fragmentariness" and can gain no useful knowledge from this panorama of Rome's "glut of confused ideas" (187–88). Returning to England to the "stifling oppression of that gentlewoman's world," Dorothea often gazes from the windows of Casaubon's manor house as she struggles to discover some "sense of connexion with a manifold pregnant existence" (268, 318). But as the seasons pass, she sees only a winter landscape that mirrors the barrenness of her life (268) and the same landscape in a summer that brings no flowering to her marriage (362–63, 416).

In these scenes of Dorothea gazing down on her world from a high point of vantage, Eliot places her heroine in the position of Milton's Adam, who after the Fall is led by the angel Michael to "ascend / In the Visions of God" (11.376–77) up the highest hill in Paradise.[16] There

> Michael from Adam's eyes the Film remov'd
> Which that false Fruit that promis'd clearer sight
> Had bred; then purg'd with Euphrasy and Rue
> The visual Nerve, for he had much to see;
> And from the Well of Life three drops instill'd.
> So deep the power of these Ingredients pierc'd,
> Ev'n to the inmost seat of mental sight.
>
> (412–18)

Having purged Adam's eyes from the film of sin that, although promising knowledge, only obscures his vision, Michael shows

Adam a panorama of the results of his sin: all the murder, sickness, war, flood, wandering, and failure that make up postlapsarian history.

Whereas Adam's vision must be purged of the film of sin, Dorothea's innocent blindness is purged by bitter experience, as she comes to see the results of her folly, and these scenes of gazing down on her world mark the stages in the purgation of her vision. In the first stage of marital disillusionment, "the large vistas and wide fresh air which she had dreamed of finding in her husband's mind were replaced by anterooms and winding passages which seemed to lead nowhither" (190). Dorothea comes to see the Key to All Mythologies as futile scholarly quibbling that the fearful Casaubon will never finish. Second, she learns that her husband's proud suspicious reticence shuts her out from all married intimacy while shutting her up in his library away from his young, vibrant cousin Will Ladislaw. Refusing to share either his fears of death or his desires for scholarly immortality with a young wife who longs to comfort him, Casaubon demands that Dorothea complete his scholarly project, working "in a virtual tomb, where there was the apparatus of a ghastly labour producing what would never see the light" (466). Finally, after his death, Dorothea is shocked to learn what her naive trust and loyalty had occluded—that her withered husband was so jealous of his young cousin that he left a will disinheriting her if she remarries Ladislaw. What she does not yet see, however, as she gazes out of her manor house windows, is the power of her own passion.

Dorothea must descend to join her fellow middlemarchers in order to see the truth whole. Hoping to save her friend Lydgate's marriage, she goes to his wife Rosamond to vindicate him from a scandal that threatens his medical practice. There Dorothea has a searing vision that opens her eyes to the erotic life she has denied. Entering a supposedly empty room, she glimpses Will holding the hands of a tearful Rosamond, and in that tableau sees "in the terrible illumination of a certainty which filled up all the outlines" the reasons for Lydgate's distance from his wife, the reasons why her own husband might have had reason to suspect his young cousin, and the depth of her own passion for Will (764, 774).

After an agonized night of grieving for lost love, Dorothea resolves, despite her "terrible illumination," to return and try, at least, to save Rosamond and Lydgate's marriage because "All the active thought with which she had before been representing to herself the trials of Lydgate's lot, and this marriage union which, like her own, seemed to have its hidden as well as evident troubles—all this vivid sympathetic experience returned to her now as a power: it asserted itself as acquired knowledge asserts itself and will not let us see as we saw in the day of our ignorance" (776). At last, Dorothea has found, not in the "standing-ground" of Latin and Greek, but in her own experience of suffering, what she sought in marrying Casaubon: "the completest knowledge" that justifies right action. As she resolves to "clutch [her] own pain" and go again to her rival for Will's love, Dorothea "opened her curtains, and looked out towards the bit of road that lay in view, with fields beyond, outside the entrance-gates. On the road there was a man with a bundle on his back and a woman carrying her baby" (777). Gazing again from her manor window, what she sees is the fallen world into which Michael leads Adam and Eve in the final lines of *Paradise Lost*:

> In either hand the hast'ning Angel caught
> Our ling'ring Parents, and to th' Eastern Gate
> Led them direct, and down the Cliff as fast
> To the subjected Plain.
>
> (12.637–40)

Dorothea sees humankind beyond the gates of Eden, bearing Adam's burden of labor and Eve's of pain in childbearing, and she prepares to descend from her exalted position of vantage, "her luxurious shelter as a mere spectator," and join her fellows in "labour and endurance" (777).

Although Dorothea eventually learns that what she saw was not Will making love to Rosamond but his rejection of Rosamond's tearful advances, Dorothea never again retreats to her aloof vision. In marrying Will, Eliot says, she joins "Adam and Eve, who kept their honeymoon in Eden, but had their first little one among the thorns and thistles of the wilderness" (818). Like Adam and his modern counterpart bearing a bundle, Will must work in flinty soil that does not always repay one's sweat. As Eliot tells us in her epilogue, "Will became an ardent public man, working well in those times when reforms were begun with a young hopefulness of immediate good which has been much checked in our days" (822). And like Eve and her modern counterpart carrying a child, Dorothea, Eliot tells us, bears children and almost dies (823).

5

Eliot has constructed Dorothea's story as the rejection of the fantasy of devotion to a modern-day Milton and the painful process of coming to see the truth about her own passion and its consequences in the world of marriage, labor, and endurance. As we have seen, however, the nineteenth-century participants in the cult of Milton constructed their fictionalizations of Milton's life as stories about the rejection of passion for higher service to England. Although, in order to re-create Milton's erotic life, they retold episodes from *Paradise Lost*, their representations of love resemble the traditional love poetry of the erotic gaze more than Milton's portrait of married love in *Paradise Lost*. Their versions of Milton, like Petrarch and Dante, must reject erotic love, only retaining the image of the Italian beauty as a poetic vision.

In *Middlemarch*, Eliot, like Manning, spoofs this kind of ethereal love. While Dorothea tries to live out her fantasy of marrying Milton, Will tries to live out a literary fantasy of his own. In following Dorothea to England and taking up residence in Middlemarch, Will fantasizes himself sometimes as a chivalric knight rescuing Dorothea from Casaubon, whom he imagines as a monster "crunching bones in a cavern" (351). Sometimes, Will sees himself as a courtly lover, whose "remote worship of a woman throned out of . . . reach" (213) leads him to wish to "ever be of the slightest service" to her (219). And sometimes Will fancies himself a reincarnation of Petrarch or Dante, as he imagines that "[w]hat others might have called the futility of his passion, made an additional delight for his imagination: he was conscious of . . . verifying in his own experience that higher love-poetry which had charmed his fancy. Dorothea, he said to himself, was for ever enthroned in his soul" (460). As Will's fantasies expand, Eliot's irony encourages us to smile with Dorothea at the "passionate prodigality" of his exaggerations (352).

Acting on this fantasy, Will defies Casaubon's banishment from his home and sets out on a sunny Sunday morning in spring just to gaze on Dorothea in church—almost as if he were Petrarch, whose world was transformed by seeing Laura in church on Good Friday 1327. On his walk amid sunlight and "budding boughs," he sings of love sustained only by glimpses of the beloved:

> O me, O me, what frugal cheer
> My love doth feed upon!
> A touch, a ray, that is not here,
> A shadow that is gone.

When, however, his appearance only causes Dorothea pain at Casaubon's refusal to acknowledge his cousin's presence, Will feels mortified: "This was what a man got by worshipping the sight of a woman!" In acting out his literary fantasy, Will learns that he is neither a hero of romance who can rescue his love from "whatever fire-breathing dragons might hiss around her" nor a sonneteer who can live by a perverse code in which "the futility of his passion, made an additional delight for his imagination" (460–64). As Dorothea's vision must be purged of literary illusions, so must Will's.

Throughout the novel, Will discounts anything so prosaic as actually proposing marriage to Dorothea. Even in the final pages of the novel—after Casaubon's death and the restoration of Dorothea's faith in Will's fidelity—Will goes to her not to claim her as a partner to share his life. His goal is more poetic: "Until that wretched yesterday . . . all their vision, all their thought of each other, had been as in a world apart, where the sunshine fell on tall white lilies, where no evil lurked, and no other soul entered. But now—would Dorothea meet him in that world again?" (793). But Dorothea has no intention of living in a visionary paradise of lilies and sunshine. In proposing to Will, she asks him to descend with her into the world she saw from her manor window after her dark night of disillusionment, to walk beside that "man with a bundle on his back and . . . woman carrying her baby." In the end, Dorothea subsumes Will's aesthetic creed, "to love what is good and beautiful," into her own Miltonic vision of entering the fallen world of "thorns and thistles," taking up one's burden, and thereby "widening the skirts of light and making the struggle with darkness narrower" (382–83).

Ironically, Eliot, who exposes in *Middlemarch* the excesses of the Milton cult, is far more Miltonic than the cult members—Bulwer-Lytton, Vetch, and Ring. Whereas they reverse the tropes of traditional love poetry to make Milton the object of the erotic gaze, Eliot mocks any attempt to substitute the erotic gaze for lived life. Testing the folly of Milton idolatry by the light of Adam and Eve's experience in *Paradise Lost*, Eliot offers her characters, instead of poetic illusions, Milton's hard truths about marriage and labor in a fallen world.[17]

NOTES

1. James G. Nelson, *The Sublime Puritan: Milton and the Victorians* (Madison: University of Wisconsin Press, 1963), 4–5.

2. "Life and Opinions of Milton," in *Essays of George Eliot*, ed. Thomas Pinney (New York: Columbia University Press, 1963), 155.

3. Anna Brownwell (Murphy) Jameson, *Memoirs of the Loves of the Poets: Biographical Sketches of Women Celebrated in Ancient and Modern Poetry* (1829; Boston: Ticknor and Fields, 1863), 251–53. Jonathan Richardson, "Explanatory Notes and Remarks on Milton's *Paradise Lost*" (1734), in *The Early Lives of Milton*, ed. Helen Darbishire (London: Constable and Company, 1932), 204–5.

4. Jameson identifies the poem as a Guarini madrigal (254), which Anne Manning prints in *The Maiden and Married Life of Mary Powell, afterwards Mistress Milton*, in *Mary Powell, Deborah's Diary* (London: J. M. Dent and Company, n.d.), 118. The translation quoted here is from Max Ring, *John Milton and His Times: A Historical Novel in Three Parts*, trans. Rev. John Jefferson (London: John Heywood, 1889), 54. All references to these works are to these editions and are cited parenthetically in the text.

5. Marcia R. Pointon, *Milton and English Art* (Toronto: University of Toronto Press, 1970), 252.

6. Edward Bulwer-Lytton, "Milton," in *The Siamese Twins: A Satirical Tale of the Times, with Other Poems* (New York: J & J Harper, 1831), 259. All references to this work are to this edition and are cited parenthetically in the text.

7. John Milton, *Paradise Lost*, in *John Milton: Complete Poems and Major Prose*, ed. Merritt Y. Hughes (New York: Odyssey, 1957). All references to Milton's poetry are to this edition and are cited parenthetically in the text. Similarly, in "Elegy Seven," written when Milton was between nineteen and twenty-one, the young poet's eyes are captivated by a radiant young girl he sees walking on a spring day, but she disappears, never to return again to his sight ("*oculis non reditura meis*," 76).

8. For reproductions of Fuseli's paintings, see the catalog for the exhibit of all his extant work, held in Stuttgart, Germany (9 September 1997–1 November 1998): *Johan Heinrich Füssli: Das Verlorene Paradies*, Christoph Becker with Beiträgen von Claudia Hattendorff.

9. Major Vetch, *Milton at Rome* (Edinburgh: James Hogg, 1851).

10. Thomas Babington Macaulay, review of John Milton, *A Treatise of Christian Doctrine, Compiled from the Holy Scriptures Alone*, *Edinburgh Review* 42 (1825): 345–46.

11. Pointon, *Milton and English Art*, xxxiii–xxxv, 251–54. *The Romantics on Milton*, ed. Joseph Anthony Wittreich (Cleveland: Press of Case Western Reserve University, 1970), 563 n. 9. For Delacroix and Decaisne, see Lee Johnson, *The Paintings of Eugène Delacroix: A Critical Catalogue*, 6 vols. (Oxford: Clarendon Press, 1981–89), 1:123–26, 2:112. For Munkácsy, see Corvina Kaidó, *Mihály Munkácsy* (St. Paul, Minn.: Control Data Arts, 1981), plate 35.

12. Rev. H. Stebbing, "Memoir of Milton's Life and Writings," in *The Complete Poetical Works of John Milton* (New York: D. Appleton, 1844), xi. Peter Bayne, "Milton," *The Contemporary Review* 22 (1873): 431–32, 437.

13. However, in "Life of Milton," in *De Quincey's Works*, 16 vols. (Edinburgh: Adam and Charles Black, 1862), 10:83–84, Thomas De Quincey objected to Manning's giving Mary the chance to tell her version of the story: "We have seen in the hands of young ladies a romance bearing this title, which (whether meant or not to injure Milton) must do so if applied to the real facts of the case. . . . Every step which is made toward the white-washing of the

frivolous and unprincipled Mary Powell is a step towards the impeachment of Milton; and impeachment in a case which, if any within the records of human experience, drew forth and emblazoned Milton's benign spirit of forgiveness, and his magnanimous forbearance when a triumph was offered at once to his partisanship as a politician, and to his insulted rights as a husband."

14. Although in her exhaustive research for *Romola*, a historical novel set in fifteenth-century Florence, Eliot had read works by Jameson and Bulwer-Lytton, I can find no evidence in her diaries, journals, notebooks, and correspondence that she ever read Bulwer-Lytton's, Vetch's, Ring's, or Manning's fictionalizations of Milton's life. My goal, however, is not to chart a path of influence. It is to uncover a little-known cultural history of the eroticization of Milton in which *Middlemarch* participates and which Eliot transforms.

15. George Eliot, *Middlemarch*, ed. David Carroll (Oxford: Clarendon Press, 1986), 10. All references to this work are to this edition and are cited parenthetically in the text.

16. See Diana Postlethwaite, "When George Eliot Reads Milton: The Muse in a Different Voice," *ELH* 57 (1990): 201.

17. My reading of Milton's centrality to Eliot's vision in *Middlemarch* opposes the readings of Sandra M. Gilbert and Susan Gubar in *The Madwoman in the Attic: The Woman Writer and the Nineteenth-Century Literary Imagination* (New Haven: Yale University Press, 1979). They argue that Eliot was one of Milton's many spiritual daughters who internalized a misogynistic theology that imprisoned them in male texts. But in narrative violence that humbles, then kills off patriarchal males such as Casaubon, Eliot reveals her unconscious rage against female confinement and submission (451, 494–95). Although space does not permit a full exposition here, I would argue that not only does Eliot test her characters' experience against Miltonic paradigms, but she also tests Miltonic paradigms against the realities of Middlemarch life. What her tests uncover is the insufficiency of received assumptions as the basis for action—even assumptions transmitted through England's great epic.

"Wide Was the Wound": Cesarean Section and the Birth of Eve

SUSAN McDONALD

In recent years, literary, historical, and cultural scholars have begun the investigation into the interpretations, perceptions, and representations informing early modern midwifery and obstetrical practices. In 1993, and again in 1995, Louis Schwartz argued the relevance of such investigations to the study of Milton, reminding us that, as a man who was not only conversant in medical and scientific knowledge but one who had also lost two wives to the complications of childbirth, Milton could easily be understood as sensitive to the issues and tensions that surrounded childbirth in the seventeenth century. While Schwartz touches upon the relevance of cesarean section as practiced in the seventeenth century to Milton's vision of birth, he focuses primarily upon obstetrical matters other than cesarean section.[1] However, a consideration of the issues attending early modern childbirth and, in particular, cesarean section suggests Milton's invocation of the particular procedures and fears of that obstetrical method to indicate that which, ultimately, cannot be: childbirth without fear, pain, or death.

As numerous scholars have observed, *Paradise Lost* presents birth in various forms on various occasions. In *The Dialectics of Creation*, Michael Lieb maintains that the images of reproduction and generation represented within the work give expression to the struggles between good and evil, creation and degradation, as well as profane and pious poetics.[2] Most noticeably, fallen birth signals the degradation of those productive beings precisely because of its resemblance to postlapsarian human experience, although the womb itself frequently appears as a place of potential. Neither inherently good nor evil, the womb becomes a place of creation or, more ominously, uncreation. Thus, while Sin offers a recognizable image of postlapsarian childbirth, this contrasts with the "great mother" of the book 7 creation sequence and, throughout the work, the womb of Chaos, in which vectors of being and nonbeing intersect.[3] While Milton may present images of fallen childbirth as the consequence of transgression, and so foreshadow Eve's share in humanity's legacy, biblical narrative constrains him from representing unfallen human childbirth. Certainly, the descriptions of Sin's "Distorted . . . nether shape" (2.784)[4] and "sorrow infinite" (797) without "rest or intermission" (802) recall the physical changes and sufferings of pregnant and delivering women. Further, Scripture dictates that women undergo these changes and pains as part of their legacy, as coinheritors of Eve's part in humanity's downfall (Gen. 3.16). However, to suggest that Milton represents only fallen childbirth and, further, to argue that such limitations demonstrate either his or a culture-wide masculine indifference to or hostility for childbearing women fails to take into account not only other representations of birth within *Paradise Lost* but also Milton's personal experience with birth.

The repeated juxtapositions of life, degradation, and death within the domain of childbirth, as represented in *Paradise Lost*, take on special significance when we reflect on Milton's personal encounters with the risks of childbirth. Both Mary Powell, in 1652, and Katherine Woodcock, in 1658, died as a result of bearing Milton's children. Schwartz argues that Milton's grief for his wives and anguish for his role in their deaths bring him to a place occupied by many men: "Milton . . . finds himself not only helpless in the face of his wife's suffering but forced to recognize that this suffering is caused by his own desires to express love and to procreate . . . a man may love a woman just as God does, but the man's love causes painful death, not life." This conflict, Schwartz believes, finds expression in "Sonnet 23," which, in turn, functions as a framing text for Adam's dream of Eve's creation. In the epic, then, Milton translates his "own personal pain over confrontation with the grim physical facts of seventeenth-century childbirth" through the idealizing vision of Adam and Eve's brief time in Eden. Schwartz touches upon the relevance to Milton's depiction of Eve's creation of obstetrical procedures in use at that time, notably cesarean section as well as fetal dismemberment and extraction: "In suggesting obstetric surgery, Milton makes the instituting event an evocative reversal of one of the most troubling conditions of postlapsarian marriage; he could not have chosen a more loaded image." While he considers briefly cesarean section, he settles upon fetal extraction, a procedure in which a dead child was dismembered and removed from the womb of a living mother, as the source of Milton's description: "A dismembering extraction of a dead infant is even suggested and reversed in Eve's being formed out of a single, surgically removed piece of Adam's body." Further, he maintains that Milton resolves the tension underlying this representation by reversing the gender roles and placing Adam, the man, in the place of the childbearing woman.[5] This notion of Milton's achieving for men the experience of women also informs Schwartz's later essay, in which he examines the laboring body of Sin and concludes that the distortion of Sin's body and "expression" enables both men and women to assume, through affective identification, familiar roles within this allegorical representation of the laboring mother.[6] In his earlier essay, Schwartz identifies the particularly masculine experience of the witness to childbirth suffering endured by Milton and, moreover, identifies the other limited roles to which men were relegated in the business of childbirth; in his later article, he explores the ways in which Milton uses Sin's experience of birth to draw upon both sexes' experiences of and associations with painful labor and delivery. However, he leaves unexplored the depths of the male anxiety that motivates the account of Eve's birth.

In the cosmos of *Paradise Lost*, birth—both idealized and anomalous—appears frequently and in direct contradistinction. Fallen beings, such as Sin and Satan, experience birth as a painful and debilitating process that includes the unpleasant realities of monstrosity, miscarriage, and abortion.[7] Conversely, the unfallen give birth in a joyous burst of abundant creativity.[8] In Milton's epic cosmos, gender does not define one's ability to give birth; rather, the nature of the parent, and not his or her gender, determines the difference between fallen and unfallen experiences. Through the words of Sin in book 2, we first hear of birth as a fallen experience, as she reminds her father of her arrival:

> All on a sudden miserable pain
> Surprised thee, dim thine eyes, and dizzy swum
> In darkness, while thy head flames thick and fast
> Threw forth, till on the left side opening wide,
>
> . . . .
>
> Out of thy head I sprung.
>
> (752–58)

In its first appearance in *Paradise Lost*, birth seems an incapacitating experience for the birth giver for which even Lieb's

description of "pain and astonishment" seems an understate-
ment.[9] In laboring to deliver his "child," Satan experiences the
"sudden" onset of "miserable pain" that debilitates him to the
extent that he almost falls unconscious: "dizzy swum / In darkness." Sin inherits the pain of childbirth, as she recalls how

>   my womb
> Pregnant by thee, and now excessive grown
> Prodigious motion felt and rueful throes.
> At last this odious offspring whom thou seest
> Thine own begotten, breaking violent way
> Tore through my entrails, that with fear and pain
> Distorted, all my nether shape thus grew
> Transformed.
>
>   (2.778–85)[10]

Like her father before her, Sin experiences childbirth as a fearful
and painful event; worse, her ordeal continues through the rape
by her son, Death, and the ongoing tortures of the hellhounds.
In addition to the graphically depicted horrors of childbirth that,
Schwartz argues, incorporate "naturalistic" details, Sin's condition signals—a function she assumes at birth—"the general sin
of the postlapsarian existence *of which birth pain is a key manifestation.*"[11] However, Milton counters these painful images of
birth with a view of childbearing that bears no trace of anxiety,
pain, or dread.

In the unfallen realm, childbearing is eagerly anticipated,
fondly remembered, and afterward celebrated, in sharp contrast
to Sin's agonized memories and Satan's seeming amnesia. While
Schwartz argues that birth becomes "an occasion for celebration" in the closing passages of the epic, through the "Promis'd
Seed" that shall redeem humanity's transgression,[12] I propose
that such a perspective emerges earlier in prelapsarian Eden.
From their first mention as our "grand parents" (1.29), Adam and
Eve exist within *Paradise Lost* as progenerative beings. Eve's
earliest memories, recounted in book 4, reflect both the origins
of her identity in her progenerative destiny and, moreover, the
perception of that function as a cause for celebration. She recalls
being led from her reflection by a voice that tells her of another
to whom she shall "bear / Multitudes" like herself and, by so
doing, fulfill her name, "Mother of human race" (4.473–75).
Later, the narrator's voice joins with Raphael's greeting, enhancing the blessedness of prospective maternity:

On whom the angel Hail
Bestowed, the holy salutation used
Long after to blest Marie, second Eve.
  Hail mother of mankind, whose fruitful womb
Shall fill the world.

(5.385–89)

Unlike Sin, whose borne "multitudes" cause only "sorrow infinite," Eve's fecundity promises future joy.

While celebrating the joys of future motherhood may come easily to angelic beings who, unless they are fallen, do not experience even the pain of a sword blow, the prospective parents themselves show no signs of anxiety regarding their future childbearing. Between themselves, Adam and Eve talk of the "more" and "younger" hands that shall join them as a matter of course rather than as one of dread (9.207, 246). Their knowledge of birth, which seems more complete than their awareness of death, comes from the view of generation presented in Raphael's glorious and sexualized account of the creation in book 7. Their optimism derives from God's blessing to "Be fruitful, multiply, and fill the earth" (7.531).[13] Only after humanity's fall does birth become linked with "sorrow" (10.193).[14] Paradise Lost, then, offers visions of both unfallen and fallen birth. Although humans never experience birth without the threat of death, we may yet glimpse it through the metaphor of book 7 and, further, sense it through the anxiety-free celebrations of Raphael, Adam, and Eve. Perhaps to make the loss of unfallen childbirth more poignant, Milton juxtaposes suggestions of it with graphic depictions of that which fallen humanity must endure. Adam and Eve do not know of Sin's tale; we, the readers, do. Moreover, as dwellers in the fallen world, we bring our own postlapsarian associations of fear and anxiety to the birth experiences of these fallen and unfallen beings. Milton, twice widowed by childbirth, draws upon these associations and seems to echo his and other men's experiences as witnesses to fallen childbirth.

By presenting images of fallen birth before those of unfallen birth, Milton challenges the reader to lay aside his or her fallen experiences in order to perceive God's original design for human procreation.[15] However, such an exercise proves difficult. Fallen birth appears in vivid and graphic detail; unfallen birth must be assumed through promises and glimpsed through metaphors. Fallen birth resembles that with which Milton, as well as other readers, would be only too sadly familiar; unfallen birth remains a matter of wishful speculation for Adam, Eve, Milton, and the reader. That unfallen birth may only exist in the realm of the unreal or metaphorical does not imply, however, that Milton seeks to exclude the female body from the process, as some critics maintain.[16] Indeed, Milton invokes the very real anxiety of the specifically masculine witness to birth in order to provoke the responses and associations specifically linked to the principal roles accorded to men in early modern birth practices: the father and the surgeon.

In early modern culture, as now, childbirth provoked conflicting feelings of joy and fear for both women and men. The demands of propagation, the primitive methods for treating severely complicated deliveries, and the inability to cope effectively with infection (indeed, the contributory part played by medical procedures in these infections) resulted in an astounding level of risk for the fertile and childbearing woman through the medieval and early modern eras. While scholars debate the actual mortality rates for childbirth deaths, a married and childbearing middle- or upper-class woman residing in seventeenth-century London faced a "one-in-four chance of dying in childbirth," a sufficiently high incidence of mortality, Schwartz remarks, "for nearly everyone to have known someone who died in childbed."[17] This level of risk did not pass unnoticed; indeed, even surgeons who included obstetrical surgery in their practices appreciated the perils that women confronted. Sixteenth-century French surgeon Ambroise Paré comments that no woman would "desire the company of man, which one premeditates or forethinkes with her selfe on the labour that shee shall sustaine in bearing the burthen of her childe nine moneths, and of the almost deadly paines that she shall suffer in her delivery."[18] Paré's wonder, we must remember, arises from a consideration of a normal, uncomplicated delivery; the dread evinced by childbirth complications produces another set of reactions, driven by the anxiety with which one confronts this intersection of life and death. Further, for the man who contributes to his wife's "burthen," and thus to her "deadly paines," childbirth creates a moment of tension between his consciousness of God's imposition upon women and his sympathy for a suffering beloved. In this cultural, professional, and personal realm, the masculine presence signals the possibility of death.

The masculine witness to early modern childbirth occupied one of two positions: the surgeon, who delivered death, or the husband, who viewed the potentially fatal consequences of his expressed love and sexual desire. As Schwartz speculates, the man who watched his wife undergo the perils of pregnancy and delivery responded from the knowledge of his part in this suffering. These speculations seem borne out by the recorded responses of Ralph Josselin, a seventeenth-century minister, husband, and father. Josselin's diary, a chronicle of early modern family life, includes reports of illnesses, deaths, and births within his household and community. The pregnancies, miscarriages, and deliveries of his wife, Jane Josselin, appear in Josselin's accounts couched in gravest terms. He appears to wrestle with the seeming conflicts of sexual desire and God's commandment to procreate, on one occasion chiding himself: "I find a wantones in my heart, and private converse with my wife, the lord make mee more savoury in my spirit and towards her, and attend more attentively to the word and worke of god in my generacon."[19] Whether he became more attentive in his "generacon," or continued to indulge his "wantones" for "private converse," we cannot know; however, Jane Josselin's thirteen pregnancies feature prominently in his journal and, moreover, become occasions of increasing anxiety for both husband and wife. When she suffers a miscarriage, he expresses concerns for her health.[20] When her pregnancies progress to delivery, both become fearful of potential danger. Indeed, her fear of labor and childbirth informs his prayerful request that "the lord in mercy remember my deare wife, who lieth under many sad feares by reason of her approaching travaile."[21] The Josselins had reasonable cause to fear childbirth, as fatalities occurred within their circle of acquaintances. On 31 January 1645/46, Josselin records the death "in chilbed" of "Mrs Cooke, the Coll. wife"; a week later, he notes the sad denouement: "Mr Cookes child came to our towne at night and dyed next morning." On both occasions, Josselin gratefully acknowledges God's grace in "the preservacion of [his] whole family."[22] Yet, when he turns to God's word, he finds little comfort: "the lord was good to mee in the word preacht, and expounding, wherein, on the consideracion of Rachels calling her child Ben-oni. and on the contemplacion of this fact, such a passion surprized mee that I could not well speake, the Lord in mercy preserve my dearer then Rachel."[23] Apart from the husband's frank expression of concern, we may marvel at the wife's strength when we read the entry of 26 November 1663: "my deare wife after many sad pains, and sadder feares, in respect of the unkinlines of her labour. was yett through gods mercy, delivered of her 10th child."[24] In Josselin's diary, we see the verification of Schwartz's conjecture: not only could men suffer sympathetically with their childbearing wives, but they could also feel the unique anguish caused by the knowledge that they had contributed to that suffering. Further, that anxiety could be exacerbated, not quelled, by the acknowledgment of painful childbirth as divinely ordered. By impregnating a woman, a man contributed to the possible fatal consequences of childbirth; by assisting women in childbirth, men would also suffer the anxieties as deliverers of death.

While medical writings upon childbirth acknowledge the divine origins of painful delivery, they also advocate the alleviation of maternal suffering. In his 1637 *The Expert Midwife*, James Rueff locates both mother and midwife within divine intention as "the businesse wherunto God hath ordayned [midwives] of so great and dangerous consequence as concernes the very lives of all such as come into the world, and withall for preventing of great danger and manifold hazards, both unto the mother / and unto the infant." According to Rueff, laboring women endure the rightful legacy of their maternal ancestor; he suggests that God does not intend needless suffering but provides some measure of comfort through the efforts of the midwife, who "hath ever been useful for the relief & succour of all the daughter of Evah, whom God hath appointed to beare children into this world."[25] Normal births, those without serious complication, occurred within a ritualized female space. At labor's onset, the midwives and "gossips" would gather to assist the mother and to witness the birth and baptism, if necessary, of the child: the space, rituals, and attendance were reserved, normally, for women only.[26] Josselin's comments upon preparations for his wife's confinement capture this gender segregation: "after sermon having waited upon god in his house, my wife called her women and god was mercifull to me in my house giving her a safe deliverance, and a daughter which on Thursday April: (21st) was baptized by the name of Mary."[27] Only when complications exceeded the midwives' abilities would a man broach this feminine realm.[28] However, this compromising of the birthing space signaled the presence of death.[29] The surgeon's task included witnessing the death of either mother or child, if not both.

Early modern obstetrical procedures most commonly resulted from the declaration of maternal or fetal death: either mother or child, but seldom both, could survive severely complicated circumstances. While midwives could and did deal successfully

with a number of complications, including stalled labors and
breach births, male surgeons would intervene when either
mother or child appeared certain to die. If the baby died in utero,
and the mother was unable to deliver the body, her life could be
saved through the dismemberment and extraction of the unde-
livered child.[30] Conversely, if all agreed that the mother had
died, the child could be retrieved from the womb through cesarean section.[31] In short, as Adrian Wilson states, "The task of the
midwife was to deliver a *living* child, the task of the male prac-
titioner to deliver a *dead* one."[32] To expand upon Wilson's observation, cesarean section could only deliver a *living* child from a
dead mother and would be implemented only so that the child
could be baptized before it, too, perished.[33] Such dire considerations appear to generate the anxiety that informs so many professional discussions of cesarean section.

Medical writings upon cesarean section not only impress
upon the reader the desperate nature of the procedure, but they
also allow the anxiety created by the need for such measures to
surface through descriptions. Many surgeons write warily of cesarean section. Paré refers to it as a "desperate and dangerous"
act that should "not (in mine opinion) . . . be used."[34] Seventeenth-century surgeon Percival Willughby cites Solanus's description of the procedure, but he offers his own explicit
objections; the operation, Willughby argues via Solanus, may be
performed only "when finally the mother's chances of survival
are esteemed hopeless [so that] care must be taken only for [the
infant]."[35] James Guillimeau's reluctance takes bibliographic
form, as he introduces cesarean section last in his 1612 catalogue of midwifery and obstetrical techniques: "It now remaines
onely, that I speake of the last kind of deliuerie, which must be
practized, after the Mothers decease, that thereby the child may
be saued, and receiue Baptisme." For Guillimeau, the intersection of life and death that gives rise to the need for cesarean section creates a crisis of the conflicting needs for certainty and
speed;

> the Chirurgion . . . must obserue diligently, and be certainly assured,
> that the woman is dead, and that her kinsfolkes, friends, and others
> that are present, do all affirme and confess, that her Soule is de-
> parted: And then he must come presently to the handy-worke, *be-
> cause the deferring of it, might cause the childs death, and so make
> the worke vnprofitable.* . . . Now, to know certainly, and to be as-
> sured that the woman hath yeelded vp her last breath, you shall lay

vpon her lips, and about her nose, some light feathers; for if she breath neuer so little, they will flie away. And being thus assured that she is dead, the Chirurgion, presently *without any delay . . .* shall there make an incision.[36]

Guillimeau's instructions capture the tension between surgical necessity for speed and the social-cultural-religious process by which death emerges as a declaration of consensus. The surgeon must at once allow for and seek consultation with others, all the while remaining mindful of the necessity for precipitous action in order to save the child. Guillimeau's repeated cautions regarding the mother's death as prerequisite to cesarean section looks toward another matter of professional concern: the debated survivability of such a procedure.

While they acknowledge reports of women who survived cesarean section, these doctors discourage any notions that this procedure could be performed without maternal death. Guillimeau raises the question of survivable cesarean section and answers it from his own experience:

> Some hold, that this Caesarian section, may and ought to be practized (the woman being aliue) in a painfull and troublesome birth: Which for my owne part, I will not counsell any one to do. . . . [O]f fiue women, in whom this hath been practized, not one hath escaped [death]. I know that it may be alleaged, that there be some have been saued thereby: But though it should happen so, yet ought we rather to admire it, then practize or imitate it: For *one Swallow makes not a Spring,* neither vpon one experiement onely, can one build a Science.[37]

Paré also dismisses such reports as incredible: "I cannot sufficiently marvaile at the insolency of those that affirme that they have seene women whose bellies and wombe have bin more than once cut, and the infant taken out . . . which thing there is no man can perswade me can be done, without the death of the mother."[38] For doctors, then, cesarean section represents the final and desperate attempt to save one life through the declaration of another's death. The act itself arises amid the conflicting pressures to take scrupulous care in declaring maternal death and to act in a precipitous manner in order to save the infant's life. And, as if to reinforce the meticulous care necessary in a determination of death, these doctors dismiss reports of survivability as fantasy or, at least, bad science. The necessity of maternal death to cesarean section, so dire a prerequisite to medical writers, permeates folk culture iconographic representations of the procedure.

Traditional and folk representations of demonic or miraculous birth frequently proceed from such traditional, fatal associations with cesarean section. In medieval tracts, the Antichrist frequently appears as a cesarean birth, the offspring of either Satan's seed or, in an interesting parallel to Milton, as the child of an incestuous father-daughter coupling: such reported incidents include the detail of maternal death. Conversely, tales of miraculous cesarean sections depict maternal survival made possible by God's intervention, although the children perish in utero. Further, various tales tell of women who suffer because they cannot deliver babies who have died in the womb. In these accounts, an appeal to God results in either a spontaneous opening of the womb or, as in one case, an incision of the uterus by a divinely guided scalpel. Following "surgery" and the extraction of the fetus, the wounds heal, leaving scars that signify God's mercy and power.[39] The expectation of maternal death, then, figures in both demonic and miraculous treatments of cesarean section: the former preserves the feature familiar from real world medical practice; the latter invokes those expectations and overthrows them. Interestingly, in the miraculous tales the sign of God's power is the surviving, albeit scarred, mother, and not the living child.

Cesarean section, then, offered Milton a wealth of personal, medical, and cultural associations that intersected at a number of points. First, we may assume that Milton, as a man twice widowed by the complications of childbirth, felt at least some of the anxiety of the sort expressed by Ralph Josselin: cesarean section would make real the death that Josselin, and other men, feared. Second, as a man, Milton could identify with the foreboding that his masculinity would create within the usually feminine world of childbirth: the male presence at birth announced the introduction of death into the realm of birth. Third, Milton could look to medical writings and popular religious lore that drew upon the dire circumstances and consequences of cesarean section. Finally, specific to the creation of Eve, Milton could draw upon an artistic tradition that imitated the details of cesarean birth. As Renate Blumenfeld-Kosinski notes, cesarean birth served frequently as a model for medieval depictions of Eve's creation.[40] In *Milton's Imagery and the Visual Arts*, Roland Mushat Frye includes four representations of Eve's birth, all of which show Eve emerging fully fleshed from Adam's side.[41] Interestingly, two of the four images included in Frye's work show Eve arising from Adam's left side. Although Frye comments that the positioning of Adam, Eve, and the incision owes more to artistic composition, the presence of this particular motif suggests the incorporation of a detail, by artists and by Milton, repeatedly noted by those who describe the medical procedure.

In book 8 of *Paradise Lost*, Adam recalls Eve's birth in terms that at once allude to and expand upon Genesis. Scripture reports that God takes from Adam "one of his ribs" and "made he a woman" (Gen. 2.21–22).[42] Milton fleshes out this account by having Adam tell Raphael of his dreamlike memories of those events that he witnessed when God closed his eyes, "but open left the cell / Of fancy my internal sight" (8. 460–61). In this suspended state, Adam watches as God

> opened my left side, and took
> From thence a rib, with cordial spirits warm,
> And life-blood streaming fresh; wide was the wound,
> But suddenly with flesh filled up and healed:
> The rib he formed and fashioned with his hands;
> Under his forming hands a creature grew,
> Manlike, but different sex, so lovely fair.
>
> (465–71)

Milton's location of Eve's origin in Adam's left side has given rise to an interpretive tradition that reads this detail as a prolepsis of humanity's fall. Yet, in this seemingly trivial detail reside medical, artistic, and cultural traditions that originate in the obstetrical practice of cesarean section and that allow Milton to use the birth of Eve to address a range of concerns surrounding postlapsarian childbirth and, in the same moment, to dismiss them from Eden.

As Genesis does not specify from which side of Adam's body Eve is "born," some critics have interpreted Milton's identification of the left side as demonstrative of Eve's culpability in humanity's fall. The most detailed biblical account of Eve's creation reports only that God takes from Adam "one of his ribs" from which "made he a woman, and brought her unto the man" (Gen. 2.21–22). Milton expands upon this skeletal account, stating repeatedly that Eve originates as a rib drawn from Adam's *left* side (4.484, 8.465, 10.884–88).[43] For many critics, this detail marks Eve's connection with Sin, who also emerges from her parent's left side: "till on the *left side* opening wide . . . Out of

thy head I sprung" (emphasis mine). Invoking the Latin *"sinister,"* meaning "left," in a possible echo of Milton's fallen Adam,
some critics cast Eve and Sin as sister accomplices in humanity's fall.[44] Perhaps seeking to ameliorate the traditional damning
association of Sin and Eve, others suggest that Eve's place of origin locates her closer to Adam's heart.[45] While such readings en-
hance our perception of Milton's Eve, they neglect to appreciate
the influence of medical practice upon Milton's representation
of Eve's birth and therefore the invocation of all the anxieties
that attended complicated childbirth within this moment of creation.

Early modern European medical writings about the procedure
of cesarean section make repeated references to the incision site:
the left side of the woman's abdomen. In his fourteenth-century
Grande chirugie, Guy de Chauliac directs that the incision be
made on the left side of the body, so that the liver not obstruct
or inhibit the speedy extraction of the child. Bolognese surgeon
Piero d'Argellata, writing a few decades after de Chauliac, also
recommends incising the left side, again citing the liver as the
obstacle to be avoided. Eurcharius Rosselin, a sixteenth-century
German surgeon, cites de Chauliac's recommendation of left-
side incision. The practice of incising the mother's left side received enough acceptance to be acknowledged within the law. A
late fifteenth-century German statute governing midwives includes an intriguing change in the justification: "Many mothers
ask, when they feel that they are dying, to liberate the child by
an incision. In that case, the skillful midwife has to open up one
side, *but not the right one;* for in men the heart is located on the
left side, but in women on the right side."[46] Paré, Willughby, and
Guillimeau do not specify incision sites: we must recall, however, their explicit opposition to the irresponsible use of the
method. Their vagueness, therefore, need not necessarily indicate a change in either obstetrical method but rather may reflect
their hesitance either to perform or to encourage others to perform the procedure. Left-side incision, then, appears as an accepted standard in the performance of cesarean section: this
detail, moreover, emerges in artistic representations of Eve's
birth. Thus, Milton could adopt cesarean section as the trope of
woman's creation within an established tradition of representation and, further, incorporate details of its real-life practice.
Moreover, in so doing, Milton could also invoke the personal
and professional anxieties of those male witnesses to birth who
felt the burden of their contribution to maternal death in order

to suggest the distance between such horrific necessities of fallen childbirth and the unfallen childbirth possible in humanity's original condition.

Certainly, Milton's personal experience with childbed mortality and his interest in medical matters provided him with the motivation and the knowledge to introduce the image of cesarean section in *Paradise Lost*. Milton's knowledge of obstetrical procedures informs the many birth-related sequences of the poem: birth appears alongside darker images of miscarriage, abortion, and monstrosity.[47] Indeed, Schwartz speaks of the birth sequence recounted in book 8 in obstetrical-surgical terms: "[Adam] gives birth . . . successfully and painlessly, with God acting as male 'surgeon.' " Yet, Schwartz hesitates to type this birth a cesarean section: "It is possible, though at this point I have no concrete evidence, that Milton had knowledge of these traditions [of miraculous and demonic caesarean births]." Instead, he suggests that the birth of Eve resembles a "dismembering extraction of a dead infant," albeit one that is "reversed."[48] In part, I think, Schwartz's hesitance to type Eve's birth a cesarean derives from his perception of the significance of gender within this scenario. In both his essays, he suggests that Adam's and Sin's narratives perform, through language, a gender switch in the former and a gender reification, of sorts, in the latter. Sin's account forces us, men and women, to confront our respective roles in birth. More significant to my interests is Schwartz's suggestion that, in Adam's account, "Milton reverses gender roles: the man, not the woman, gives birth."[49] Adam does "give birth" to Eve, but does this action necessarily suggest a gender reversal? If we recall the significance of the male witness—the prospective father or the summoned surgeon—to childbirth in the fallen world and compound that with the anxiety expressed by Josselin and the reluctant doctors, we can find the grounds for Milton's use of cesarean section as witnessed by men at this point of *Paradise Lost*. Adam's experience becomes all the more miraculous precisely because he is a man viewing that which fallen men cannot. To respond to such suggestions as Elizabeth Harvey's that Milton presents a "metaphoric fantasy . . . of a birth that bypassed nature and the female body,"[50] I would argue that Milton, in fact, attempts the opposite: through the use of the male witness to birth and the clearly surgical nature of that birth, Milton invokes the very worst and most painful associations of fallen childbirth for men, suggesting the masculine experience through a speaking man. The fantastic quality of the episode derives not from misogynist notions regarding fallen birth but from the reality of the particularly self-conscious anxiety with which men witnessed birth.

By including cesarean section in the catalog of births, Milton invokes and dispels the anxieties that men brought to childbirth in order to demonstrate the joyous possibilities of birth before the Fall. As a voyeur to this unfallen realm, the reader may witness a method of death used as a means to greater, not lesser, life. At Eve's birth, Adam's masculine presence confounds fallen expectation: the male eye witnesses not death but only more life. Unlike Satan's painful and fallen experience of childbirth (which he appears to forget), Adam's recollection of birth includes not pain but a sense of detached wonder: "as in a trance methought I saw" (8.462). Unlike Ralph Josselin, for whom successive childbirths beget increasing anxiety, Adam's only and brief moment of anguish arises from the perceived loss of this new being: "I waked / To find her, or for ever to deplore / Her loss" (478–80). Thus, in overturning the traditional gender associations of childbirth, Milton overthrows the signification of man as deliverer of death to women: in describing the birth of Eve, moreoever, Milton presents the familiar—or, at least, the known—features of cesarean section but, as with the "miracle" tales, he does so in order to confound our expectations. The miraculous paradoxes of male birth, birth without fear, and cesarean section without death signal our entry into the realm of unfallen birth.

In describing Eve's birth, Milton draws upon both the practice and the perception of cesarean section: he retains details of the surgical procedure but, at a number of points, departs significantly from the fallen associations of that process in order to demonstrate the extent to which those associations originate with the Fall and not with creation. During Eve's birth, Adam's state resembles, with a significant difference, the death that both necessitates and initiates cesarean section. Through the "internal sight" of "fancy" (8.461), Adam watches as the shape "glorious" (464) sets to work: he "stooping opened my left side, and took / From thence a rib" (465–66). This waking sleep resembles death, the normal maternal condition in fallen practices, yet this unfallen "mother" does not die—nor even lose full consciousness. Rather, what Adam experiences more closely resembles the slumber that precedes unfallen birth.[51] The incision into Adam's left side echoes the specification of medical practice; in this realm, however, the wound becomes the sign of the miraculous nature of this birth, as fallen beings can understand it. Adam draws our attention to the size of the incision, "wide was the wound" (467), and invites us to wonder with him, although his astonishment derives not from any fallen associations but rather from the marvels being performed: "But suddenly [the wound was] with flesh filled up and healed" (468). The interjection of "But" signals another departure from fallen expectations, and the surprised note of "suddenly" confounds those expectations further. Through Adam's specifically male eyes, then, we can witness that which in the fallen world would be described as miraculous and, to many seventeenth-century (and earlier) men, that which would be ardently desired. Moreover, in invoking the miraculous iconographic association with cesarean section, Milton demonstrates the extent to which unfallen birth surpasses even miracles in the fallen world. Unlike those accounts, in which the children perish but the mother lives, in Eden both "mother" and "child" survive. Thus, God as "surgeon," as Schwartz types him, demonstrates the procedure that his fallen students can only imperfectly emulate: where surgeons in the fallen world can only ensure death, God creates life. Thus, Adam's experience of childbirth offers the reader a glimpse of what, according to biblical tradition, we can never hope to experience. His vision and Milton's expansion upon Genesis invoke the specifically masculine associations with fallen childbirth in order to illuminate more brightly the wonder of unfallen childbirth.

As Schwartz, Lieb, and others who discuss the implications of birth in *Paradise Lost* have noted, the depictions of procreation in Milton's work reveal much about the poet's equation of fallen and unfallen creativity. Schwartz argues rightly that Milton appears to include associations specific to a man who not only lost two wives to the complications of fallen childbirth but one who, moreover, was sufficiently conversant in medical procedures to allude to those practices in his representations of birth. Certainly, such seems to be the case in Milton's selection of cesarean section as the means by which to demonstrate the possibility of unfallen human childbirth. Moreoever, by incorporating that particular procedure, Milton invokes a variety of associations—medical, gender, iconographic—that expressed and engendered professional and personal anxieties. In so doing, however, Milton does not seek either to locate himself or Adam in the position of the childbearing woman or to attempt to displace woman from the process of procreation. Instead, Milton draws upon the specifically masculine experiences of childbirth, as father and surgeon, and the anxieties aroused by those experiences in order to suggest the possibility, and perhaps to intensify our understanding of the loss, of unfallen procreation.

NOTES

1. Louis Schwartz, " 'Spot of child-bed taint': Seventeenth-Century Obstetrics in Milton's Sonnet XXIII and *Paradise Lost* 8.462–78," *Milton Quarterly* 27 (1993): 98–109, and Louis Schwartz, " 'Conscious Terrors' and 'The Promised Seed': Seventeenth-Century Obstetrics and the Allegory of Sin and Death in *Paradise Lost*," *Milton Studies* 32 (1995): 63–89.

2. Michael Lieb, *The Dialectics of Creation: Patterns of Birth and Regeneration in "Paradise Lost"* (Amherst: University of Massachusetts Press, 1970), 7.

3. Ibid., 85–86, 16–17.

4. John Milton, *Paradise Lost*, ed. Alastair Fowler (London: Longman, 1971). All references to *Paradise Lost* are to this edition and are cited parenthetically in the text.

5. Schwartz, " 'Spot of child-bed taint,' " 101, 104, 104–5.

6. Schwartz, " 'Conscious Terrors,' " 80.

7. Kester Svendsen, *Milton and Science* (Cambridge: Harvard University Press, 1956), 183.

8. Lieb, *The Dialectics of Creation*, 75–78.

9. Ibid., 147.

10. In this passage, Schwartz, " 'Conscious Terrors,' " 67–69, detects Milton's incorporation of medical lore regarding the perineal damage incurred by many women in the process of childbirth.

11. Ibid., 79.

12. Ibid., 84.

13. Lieb, *The Dialectics of Creation*, 62. While the matter of Eve's presence during Raphael's visit continues to spur critical debate, her departure does not occur until after Raphael concludes the creation narrative. Thus, we may assume that she is as well schooled in the "facts of life" as is Adam.

14. Ibid., 165. Schwartz, " 'Conscious Terrors,' " 82–83, views Adam's minimizing of Eve's legacy of childbirth suffering as a demonstration of the distance that emerges between the promise of Christ's Second Coming, expressed in John 16.21–22, and Adam's obliviousness to the "cost" of childbirth "in terms of suffering and loss": Adam become the distant male witness to childbirth.

15. Of course, this point echoes Stanley Fish's observations in *Surprised by Sin: The Reader in "Paradise Lost"* (Berkeley and Los Angeles: University of California Press, 1967), 1. In Fish's view, however, we endeavor to prevent our "fallen" assumption from corrupting our readings of the "unfallen" text; in the case of birth, Milton forces us to confront the distance between fallen and unfallen beings by offering the most graphic images of fallen birth and only suggestions of unfallen procreation.

16. See, for example, Elizabeth D. Harvey, *Ventriloquized Voices: Feminist Theory and English Renaissance Texts* (London: Routledge Press, 1992), 150 n.

17. Schwartz, " 'Conscious Terrors,' " 72, 73.

18. Ambroise Paré, *The Workes of that famous Chirurgion Ambrose Parey Translated out of Latine and compared with the French by Tho. Johnson* (London, 1634), 887.

19. Ralph Josselin, *The Diary of Ralph Josselin, 1616–1683*, ed. Alan Macfarlane (London: Oxford University Press, 1976), 357. See also Alan Macfarlane, *The Family Life of Ralph Josselin* (Cambridge: Cambridge University Press, 1970), 83–84.

20. Lucinda McCray Beier, "In Sickness and in Health: A Seventeenth-Century Family's Experience," in *Patients and Practitioners: Lay Perceptions of Medicine in Pre-Industrial Society*, ed. Roy Porter (Cambridge: Cambridge University Press, 1985), 103–4.

21. Josselin, *The Diary*, 108.

22. Ibid., 54.

23. Ibid., 106.

24. Ibid., 502. See also Macfarlane, *The Family Life*, 84–85. Perhaps more marvelous is the fact that after enduring thirteen pregnancies (ten carried to full term), Jane Josselin survived her husband, albeit suffering from health problems possibly caused by her childbearing, as Beier, "In Sickness," 106, points out.

25. [J]ames Reuff, *The Expert Midwife, or An Excellent and most necessary Treatise of the genration and birth of man* (London, 1637), sig. A2v–3r.

26. Adrian Wilson, "Participant or Patient? Seventeenth-Century Childbirth From the Mother's Point of View," in *Patients and Practitioners*, ed. Porter, 134.

27. Josselin, *The Diary*, 12.

28. The rigidity of this segregation is demonstrated by the case of a fifteenth-century German surgeon who infiltrated the gender barrier by adopting female dress: being found out, he was executed and, in Donald A. M. Gebbie's wry observation, became "the first, and possibly the only, martyr in the service of obstetrics" (*Reproductive Anthropology: Descent Through Woman* [Chichester, England: John Wiley & Sons, 1981], 55).

29. Harvey, *Ventriloquized Voices*, 187.

30. Wilson, "Participant or Patient," 137.

31. Schwartz, " 'Spot of child-bed taint,' " 104.

32. Wilson, "Participant or Patient," 137.

33. Renate Blumenfeld-Kosinski, *Not of Woman Born: Representations of Caesarean Birth in Medieval and Renaissance Culture* (Ithaca: Cornell University Press, 1990), 2.

34. Paré, *The Workes*, 923.

35. Percival Willughby, *Observations in Midwifery* (1863; reprint, Wakefield, Yorkshire, England: S. R. Publishers, 1972), 101. Thanks to Richard F. Green for translation from Latin. Indeed, Willughby's use of Solanus could also reflect his inexperience with the procedure: "I never used this harsh and cruell way. Yet ignorant men have used it with happy successe. . . . *Vide* the schemes, and take that, which serveth best; for the Caesarean Section, I do not like it" (*Observations*, 101). According to Schwartz, Willughby never performed a cesarian section (personal correspondence).

36. James Guillimeau, *Childbirth or, The Happy Deliverie of Women . . .* (London, 1612), 185–86; emphasis mine.

37. Ibid., 187–88.

38. Paré, *The Workes*, 923.

39. Blumenfeld-Kosinski, *Not of Woman Born*, 131–37, 121, 122–24.

40. Ibid., 73.

41. Roland Mushat Frye, *Milton's Imagery and the Visual Arts* (Princeton: Princeton University Press, 1978), 259–61. See also figures 176, 179, 180, and 214.

42. All biblical references are to the King James Version and are cited parenthetically in the text.

43. Frye, *Milton's Imagery*, 260.

44. Lieb, 105 n. Schwartz, " 'Conscious Terrors,' " 81, suggests that Sin's childbirth pains also serve to connect her with Eve: the horrific and continuous labor foreshadows Eve's legacy of painful delivery.

45. Frye, *Milton's Imagery*, 260.

46. Blumenfeld-Kosinski, *Not of Woman Born*, 34–35, 37, 36; emphasis mine.

47. Svendsen, *Milton and Science*, 188, 193.

48. Schwartz, " 'Spot of child-bed taint,' "104–5.

49. Schwartz, " 'Conscious Terrors,' " 79–80; Schwartz, " 'Spot of child-bed taint,' " 104–5.

50. Harvey, *Ventriloquized Voices*, 150 n.

51. Lieb, *The Dialectics of Creation*, 64.

A Preliminary Study of Informed Consent and Free Will in the Garden of Eden: John Milton's Social Contract

LYNNE GREENBERG

Anthony Fletcher has described "[t]he master theme of seventeenth-century political theory" as "the great battle between patriarchalists and social contract theorists."[1] Patriarchal theory, the dominant ideology of this transitional period, supported several principles— the divine right of kings, monarchical absolutism, and female subordination—all of which derived support from biblical exegesis of the Fall. The alternative construct of the social contract, an emerging hegemony that would not gain full expression until later in the century, arose as a revolutionary response to patriarchal theory. The social contract model vindicated liberal constitutionalism, religious liberty, and freedom of choice. It, too, found its origins in the Genesis story.

John Milton's work, both his prose and poetry, resides in a liminal space in which the realm of patriarchal obedience and subordination vies with a simultaneous vision of a contract-based, egalitarian society. While critics have recognized the tension in Milton's work between two conflicting visions of society and have defined the former as patriarchal in nature, few have characterized the emerging world view as determined by contractarian principles.[2] This paper will provide a preliminary overview of the infusion in selected works by Milton, and crucial passages in them, of such a vision, one deeply indebted to contemporaneous legal, political, and religious theories of the contract.[3]

The contract emerged in seventeenth-century law as the predominant archetype for articulating the perimeters of individuals' associations with each other. The trope of the covenant also infused the rhetoric of political theory and religious discourse as a means of conceptualizing man's relationship with his government and God. Brief overviews of the legal, political, and religious conceptions of the contract foreground the extent to which Milton's own relational constructions depend upon the contractual paradigm. Milton's prose statements on marriage, divorce, and regicide, in particular, all find their precedent in contractarian ideals. It is in the Garden of Eden of *Paradise Lost* that Milton most compellingly actualizes a society legally constructed on such contractual principles. The poem presupposes a prelapsarian state dependent upon express agreements between the characters. Astonishingly, the poem does not simply register a vision of what has become our modern legal society but also exposes the submerged hypocrisies and iniquities of this system. The power dynamics emanating from the poem demonstrate how the contract functioned, and continues to function, as an official discourse of control and power. In particular, the poem illustrates the extent to which the social contract model embeds within itself patriarchal assumptions, undermining the two theories' supposed differences.

By the seventeenth century, the contractual model had established itself in the laws of marriage, annulment, and commercial agreements as the principal frame for delineating individuals' relationships with each other. Significantly, in all of its particular incarnations, both public and private, reciprocal consent emerged as the preeminent contract principle. In 1653, Oliver Cromwell established civil marriage by law, thus conceiving of marriage, not as a sacrament but "in no other light than as a civil contract. . . . And taking it in this civil light, the law treats it as it does all other contracts; allowing it to be good and valid in all cases, where the parties at the time of making it were, in the first place, *willing* to contract; secondly, *able* to contract; and, lastly, actually *did* contract."[4] Such requirements as solemnization in church were deemed merely "expedient."[5] Although the Restoration annulled this law, restoring church weddings by the Book of Common Prayer, the emphasis on voluntarism and reciprocity in forming marriage contracts remained intact. Throughout the seventeenth century, to create a legally binding marriage, "[a]ll that was needed . . . was a full, free and mutual consent"[6] of the individual parties to the contract. Nevertheless, the law did require some form of acceptance—either by words or deed: "[I]t is not sufficient if either of the Parties alone do promise . . . the silent Party in this Case [is not] presumed to consent."[7] The courts required not only an express but also the free consent of both parties to find a legally binding marriage. In a situation in which consent seemed coerced or forcibly obtained, the law declared the contract void: "It holdeth not when it is extorted by force, or by such a fear as may . . . [befall a constant man, because marriages ought to be free]."[8]

The original intention behind this legal formulation supports the contractual, rather than patriarchal, basis of marriage. Consent was regarded as a means of safeguarding individual freedom from the coercion of parental or family intrusions.[9] The patriarchal practice of arranging marriages may have continued during this period, particularly in aristocratic and landed families;[10] yet the legal system explicitly denounced this practice. The decision making of the church courts throughout the early seventeenth century likewise confirms that the legal system supported the concept of individual self-determination. Spousal litigation frequently turned on the validity of a contract. In those cases in which some doubt existed as to the intention of one of the parties or of the mutuality of the consent, the judges preferred to rule against a finding of an enforceable contract.[11] In summary, "[i]t is difficult to envisage a more subversively individualistic and contractual foundation for a marriage system."[12]

The law did not recognize divorce, per se, but only divorce *a mensa et thoro* (a legal separation entitling the parties to live apart, yet denying them the right to remarry) and divorce *a vinculo* (or annulment). One could annul a marriage only by establishing one of the delineated impediments to matrimony, including, importantly, the failure to establish true consent. Lack of consent could be adduced from proof of some form of coercion, duress, or constraint (even the fear of constraint) or of mistake.[13] The impediment of mistake turned on the failure of one of the parties to disclose certain critical information to the other party upon which such party had based consent. The law on this point proved gender-neutral, as both the male and female parties had the right to expect adequate freedom to choose and sufficient knowledge in order to make an informed consent.

While only in the nineteenth century did the true concept of a "meeting of the minds" become the standard definition of a valid commercial contract, by 1600 the modern sense of a contract dependent upon consent had already evolved. The common law defined a binding legal agreement as "a mutual agreement between the parties for something to be performed by the defendant in consideration of some benefit which must depart from the plaintiff, or of some labour or prejudice which must be sustained by the plaintiff."[14] The law of contract, then, like the law of marriage, required an arrangement between two parties freely consenting, without constraint, to be bound to each other. Each party prior to entering into the arrangement had the obligation to disclose all information necessary for the other party to make a reasoned and voluntary choice.

Nevertheless, a patriarchal framework still structured women's relationship to the law of contract. The law explicitly denied that married women had the legal capacity to enter into binding contracts (except in exceptional circumstances)[15] or even that they had any legal status at all. "By marriage, the husband and wife are one person in law: that is, the very being, or legal existence of the woman is suspended during the marriage, or at least is incorporated and consolidated into that of the husband."[16] Once a woman had consented to marriage, her power of consent was thereafter eviscerated. The consent, so central to the formation of the marriage contract, functioned as the only legally recognized consent of her life, a kind of catchall consent to have the law thereafter treat her as subsumed within her husband's person. To contract marriage, then, was to consent unalterably to her exclusion thereafter from the social contract.[17]

The exegesis of Genesis provided the most conspicuous rationale for a woman's legal status. Eve's responsibility for the Fall provided unassailable authority for a woman's present condition. As one seventeenth-century legal treatise explained: "Eve, because she had helped to seduce her husband, hath inflicted on her an especial bane. . . . [T]hy desires shall be subject to thy husband, and he shall rule over thee. . . . See here the reason . . . that women have no voice in parliament. They make no laws, consent to none, they abrogate none. All of them are understood either married or to be married, and their desires are subject to their husband: I know no remedy. . . . The common law here shaketh hand with divinity."[18] The story of Genesis here receives a traditional reading, used as a justification for patriarchal subordination of women.

So, too, the dominant political ideology of the period retained its patriarchal caste, even though contractarian principles did manage to imbue even its rhetoric. Interestingly, Robert Filmer's *Patriarcha* relied on the trope of an original contract as a vehicle to defend the divine right of kings and the hierarchical structuring of society. He conceived of an original contract as thereafter justifying absolute rule. The people had conveyed in an ancient compact all of their rights and power to an original monarch and had thereby divested themselves of it for all eternity. Filmer traced this original grant of government to the Fall when God declared Eve subordinate to the rule of her husband. Adam's rights over his wife established his, and his progeny's, political rights over the public sphere as well. Thus, the contractarian model did not initially present itself as a fundamental threat to the patriarchal order but rather proved a useful rhetorical tool for the entrenched political power.[19]

More radical theories of the contract, however, emerged during the Civil War period. Parliamentarian and republican writers began to argue for religious and individual liberty and limitations to a ruler's authority over his people, borrowing concepts of natural law, social and political contracts, popular consent, and trusteeship from the French Huguenots and New England Puritans, among others.[20] Social contract theorists found the genesis of political right not in an original and thereafter irrevocable contract but in ongoing and ever-alterable contracts made between men living in the postlapsarian state of nature. Such consent theories "rest[ed] upon the actions of the subject himself and not upon his duty to accept the political order agreed to by his ancestors."[21] After the execution of Charles I, the regicide was legitimized by arguing that Charles had failed to perform the terms and conditions of his Coronation Oath, thus breaching his covenant with the people of England. The Rump Parliament relied to such an extent on social contract theories to justify their establishment of a commonwealth that one historian has described the social contract as "the official theory of the Commonwealth party."[22] Interregnum and Restoration politics were also dominated by appeals to oath taking, or contract formations, meant to evidence and secure "voluntary" loyalty within Parliament, the army, the church, and the universities. The Solemn League and Covenant, the Negative Covenant, and the Engagement gave way in the Restoration period to the covenants of the Corporation Act, the Act of Uniformity, and the Test Act.[23]

Despite their differences, patriarchal and social contract theorists felt an equal compulsion to establish a historic foundation for their respective theories through the reliance on an originary contract embedded in Genesis and granted divine sanction. Such reliance testifies finally to "the preoccupation of seventeenth-century English political thought with origins . . . [which] dictated that political obligation could be found in, and had to be consistent with, the beginnings of government."[24]

The rhetoric of the contract is so wide reaching and pervasive in seventeenth-century Puritan theology, particularly on the

Continent, that simply the iteration of the broad principles of the covenant of grace, the covenant of works, and the covenant of redemption attests to the contract's centrality to Puritan thought. While the Old Testament covenant of works was conditioned upon the Hebrews' duty to obey ceremonial and moral law, the New Testament covenant of grace contemplated man's voluntary choice to believe, or have faith, as the condition upon which the contract depended. Again, the substance of covenant theology relied upon a contract legalistically construed: "By the word 'covenant' federal theologians understood just such a contract as was used among men of business, a bond or a mortgage, an agreement between two parties, signed and sworn to, and binding upon both."[25] Thus, foundational to the Puritan perception of the relationship between God and man is a "heavenly contract," with its connotations of revocability, reciprocity, and mutuality.[26] The federal Puritans' construction of the covenant of grace has particular relevance here, as they traced the covenant's origins once again to Genesis. In an effort to undo Augustine's teachings on original sin and the harsh consequences of predestination, Adam's sin was viewed as a violation of an external contract: "If the sin of Adam were regarded as the violation of a contract, it could . . . become externalized, forensic rather than internal, a punishable crime rather than an infinite sin. Seen in this light, the disobedience would amount to a bond broken, a lease violated."[27]

It is no surprise, given the preoccupation of seventeenth-century political theorists and theologians with establishing a genetic story for contractarian principles, that Milton himself should devote several of his prose arguments and an entire epic to the contract's origins. In fact, this essay's insistence on finding the rhetoric of the contract in Milton's writing derives from the social contractarians' and theologians' own insistence on treating the story of the Fall as a contractual issue. Milton's prose writing on marriage and divorce and the limits of a ruler's power, in particular, is determined by and derives from the contractual paradigm.

Milton supported Cromwell's parliamentary act of 1653 that removed marital affairs from the control of the church to that of the state. In his treatise *Considerations Touching the Likeliest Means to Remove Hirelings Out of the Church*, Milton emphasized that marriage was not a sacrament but a private and "civil ordinance, a household contract" (7:299).[28] He also subscribed to the legal formulation of marriage as contingent upon the free choice of the parties: "The first and most important point [in marriage] is the mutual consent of the parties concerned, for there can be no love or good will, and therefore no marriage, between those whom mutual consent has not united" (6:368).

The rhetoric of liberal contractualism likewise infuses Milton's prose statements on divorce, as he defended the right of *"mutuall[y] consent[ing]"* couples to divorce because of mental or emotional incompatibility (2:242). So, too, the failure of either party to the marriage contract to perform its conditions would lead to the contract's revocation: "Marriage beeing a Covnant, the very beeing wherof consists in the performance of unfained love and peace, if that were not tolerably perform'd, the Covnant became broke and revocable . . . for how can a thing subsist, when the true essence thereof is dissolv'd?" (2:747). And further: "If one of them perform nothing tolerably, but instead of love, abound in disaffection, disobedience, fraud, and hatred, what thing in the nature of a covnant shall bind the other to such a perdurable mischief?" (2:748). Yet, consistent with seventeenth-century law, the rhetoric of patriarchal subordination surfaces just as prevalently in Milton's writings on divorce. The mutual right to divorce is circumscribed later in *The Doctrine and Discipline of Divorce:* there can be no divorce "against the will and consent of both parties, or of the husband alone" (2:344).[29]

J. W. Gough credits Milton as one of the first English publicists to expound a "thorough-going" contract theory,[30] particularly in his arguments justifying regicide in *The Tenure of Kings and Magistrates.*[31] Consistent with later social contract theorists, Milton relied on an originary contract to explain the emergence of government. He envisioned a postlapsarian state of nature torn by anarchy and lawlessness. Upon realizing that humankind's behavior led to mutual destruction, individuals voluntarily agreed to exchange their freedom for legal protection and government restraints. Here again, one encounters the articulation of a genesis story that emphasizes the importance of the freedom to consent to a relationship. Significantly, Milton envisioned the contract between ruler and ruled not as irrevocable, but rather as conditional, subject to the ruler's continued and continual fulfillment of his obligation to his people. Otherwise, "if the king or magistrate prov'd unfaithfull to his trust, the people would be disingag'd" (2:200). Consistent with Puritan ideology, Milton even conceived of God's relations to man as contingent upon a mutually beneficial contract: God "appears to us as it were in human shape, enters into cov'nant with us, swears to keep [the Law], binds himself like a just lawgiver to his own prescriptions, gives himself to be understood by men, judges and is judg'd, measures and is commensurat to right reason" (2:292).

This brief look at Milton's prose work emphasizes the extent to which Milton subscribed to contractarian principles in his perceptions of several types of relations—that between man and wife, ruler and ruled, and God and man. These constructions conform to the legal, political, and religious definitions of a contract as willingly entered into by informed individuals for rational reasons. Ultimately, this contractarian ideal has significant bearing on Milton's vision of individual subjecthood. Milton's emphasis on man's autonomy and free will underpins the contractarian paradigm. Without a conception of the individual grounded in his capacity to make rational choices, it would be impossible to perceive of contractual transactions as enhancing autonomy or maximizing one's best interests, the classic arguments for privileging the contractual paradigm even today.[32]

So far this essay has focused on the "juridico-discursive" attributes of contract theory by stressing its legal, political, and religious constructions. These constructions emphasize how the social contract theory presents a genetic story of voluntarism and freedom—humankind has exchanged the risks of natural freedom for a civil freedom protected by the state, where all individuals have the authority to exercise their freedom of contract. It is now necessary to turn to the "power effects"[33] of contractarian ideology on individual relations in Milton's poetic writing. By exposing the level on which hegemonic values are actively lived and felt, it is possible to explore whether the ideal in fact conforms to reality. *Paradise Lost*'s articulation of the actual moments of contract formation has significant bearing on this question.

Milton's depiction of the relationship between God and his Son is extraordinary for its intermixing of controversial religious notions with those of modern contract doctrine. Milton does not permit the Son of God simply to inherit kingship over the universe and equal standing with God by birthright. Instead, Milton constructs the Son's elevation as part of an agreed-upon arrangement between God and his Son. The parties explicitly enter into a contract of reciprocal promises and duties with each other in book 3 of the poem, whereby the Son promises, in exchange for God anointing him universal king, to sacrifice himself for the redemption of humankind. As in *The Commonplace Book*, Milton reconceives hereditary rule, basing it on merit, rather than on blood (1:433–35).[34]

So, too, God's relationship with Adam originates in a legally construed contract, one premised upon an offer and acceptance of reciprocal promises and obligations, not simply a prohibitive command. At Adam's first moments of cognition, God appears before him and makes a formal offer of agreement. Adam is provided with the knowledge of the conditions of this contract (obedience to God in exchange for everlasting life and rule over life forms in Eden), his duties (not eating from the Tree of Knowledge[35] and tending of the garden), and a "liquidated damages" arrangement in the event of a breach of the contract (expulsion from the garden and death). Adam then freely accepts this arrangement. When he questions his relationship with God after the Fall, he uses the explicitly legalistic rhetoric of offer and acceptance, confirming the contractual nature of his relationship with God:

> inexplicable
> Thy Justice seems; yet to say truth, too late,
> I thus contest; then should have been refus'd
> Those terms whatever, when they were propos'd:
> Thou didst accept them; wilt thou enjoy the good,
> Then cavil the conditions?
>
> (10.754–59)[36]

The legal definition of a contract as a mutual, free, and informed arrangement thus operates as the principal frame for interpreting Adam's relationship to God.

The poem envisions a different relationship between Eve and God, however. While Adam's relationship with God is framed as a contract, the poem does not make definitively clear whether Eve even has a direct relationship with God. In a contested passage in the poem, Eve herself states to Adam: "God is thy Law, thou mine" (4.637). This statement, taken at face value, suggests that Eve's "acceptance" of her marriage to Adam functions as her only opportunity to consent meaningfully to an agreement in the poem, and that, in fact, she has not been granted the opportunity to covenant directly with God. This situation parallels a married woman's relationship to seventeenth-century law: she has no relationship. The "catchall" consent to marry functions here as the only consent Eve has the authority to make in the poem.

Nevertheless, one could choose to doubt Eve's statement, interpreting this passage as a misrepresentation of her relationship with God. Several passages in the poem imply that in fact Eve does have a direct and immediate relationship to God. Most forcefully, the text repeatedly makes clear that both Adam and Eve share in the contractual condition not to eat from the Tree of Knowledge (4.419–24; 514–15; 9.651–52). This negative duty derives from God alone—not from Adam—just as does the duty to tend the garden in exchange for everlasting life. So, too, only God, not Adam, has the authority to punish Eve for breach of the agreement. Thus, Eve's relationship to God has certain similarities with Adam's relationship to God in that it is based on a contractual relationship of reciprocal duties and promises and specifically delineated consequences in the event of a breach.

Yet, here the similarities end. For God does not approach Eve at the time of creation with an offer to contract or grant her the opportunity to accept formally such an offer. Only Adam enjoys this privilege. The voice that speaks to Eve simply directs her to Adam. Nor does God appear before Eve later in the text with a formal offer. Raphael does visit Adam and Eve in book 5, but he does not offer to contract with Eve. Raphael approaches only Adam. Acting as God's designated agent, Raphael provides Adam with more information concerning his duties and the specific negative performance or condition upon which the contract rests (i.e., the ban against eating from the Tree of Knowledge in the face of imminent satanic threat). God evidently deemed it necessary to impart this further information to Adam. Otherwise he would not have bothered sending Raphael. Thus, consistent with seventeenth-century commercial law, God provides Adam with the requisite knowledge necessary for him to make an informed choice as to his participation in and performance of the agreement.

The poem's treatment of Eve differs here again from its treatment of Adam, particularly in its formulation of the extent to which, and the manner in which, Eve actually acquires knowledge already deemed by God to be essential to performance of the agreement. God himself instructs Raphael to "Converse with Adam" (5.230). Unlike the designation "man," one cannot read "Adam" as generic enough to incorporate Eve within its meaning. God's instructions then are quite specific that Raphael need only provide Adam with the warning and information.

During the conversation itself between Raphael and Adam, Eve sits "retir'd in sight" (8.41). Such a posture already problematizes Eve's ability to obtain the necessary information from Raphael: Can she hear clearly? Does she lose out on important verbal and/or nonverbal communication? More disconcerting, Raphael does not treat Eve as if she is part of the discussion. He addresses Adam alone and refers to Eve in the third person. It is no surprise that, exasperated, she leaves the dinner. Of course, the text equivocates as to the reason for Eve's departure. Does she leave because she is disinterested in the discussion, because she is incapable of following the conversation, or because she already intuitively understands all that will be imparted to Adam? Yet, one must ask, why, if she is so disinterested in the discussion, does she later linger behind in a "shadie nook" (9.277), attempting to overhear what Adam and Raphael say to one another? Some of the information that Raphael imparts to Adam in response to his questions also corresponds to just that information Eve had sought from Adam earlier in book 4. Why then would she not be interested in finding out the answers? The text does provide a rationale for her departure: Eve would rather have information delivered to her secondhand through Adam, as she would find such information palatable only if interspersed by "conjugal Caresses, from his Lip" (8.56).

Because Eve does not play the role of a fully present and active subject in the conversation, as does Adam, she is not given the opportunity to learn through the process of discursive reasoning. Had the angel permitted Eve to participate, perhaps she would have had enough training in logic and the discursive process to withstand the serpent's syllogistic reasoning. The text's devaluing of Eve's ability to partake in discursive thinking merely acknowledges that she has not had the opportunity to learn as has Adam. Several critics, in their attempts to elevate Eve's character, have emphasized her intuitive knowledge and access to revelation. Yet Eve's relegation to the private sphere of dreams and internal illumination still underscores her unequal entry into the public sphere of logical discourse. Her gender construction here delimits her access to knowledge.

Eve's access not only to the discursive process, which leads to knowledge, but also to knowledge itself is incomplete. At the end of book 6, Raphael explains that he has told Adam of the War in Heaven in the hopes that Adam may "profit . . . t' have heard / By terrible Example" (6.909–10). Yet, he does not require Eve to so profit by example; otherwise he would have insisted on her active participation in the discussion. Or, alternatively, he would have insisted that Adam relate everything he has learned to Eve. Yet, Raphael only instructs Adam to "warn" her (6.908). This passage further implies that Eve has not been made privy to the entire conversation (if she had overheard everything, there would have been no need for Adam to warn her further).

In any event, Raphael does not provide a warning to Eve directly. Her knowledge of the satanic enemy comes only from what Adam remembers to pass on to her of his discussions with Raphael and from what she manages to overhear, initially sitting retired from view and subsequently hiding in the nook on her way back from gardening. While Eve acknowledges that Adam had informed her of Satan's presence in the garden (9.273–75), one cannot help but wonder whether Adam could indeed have communicated adequately the gravity of the information in a moment of erotic embrace. There lurks the added doubt of Adam's ability to translate accurately the information itself. Does he relay everything or only a small percentage of the information God wanted relayed? Does he objectively translate the information, word for word, or is the transmittal clouded by Adam's subjective interpretations of the information? It is at best questionable whether Eve obtains the sum total of what Adam learned and ultimately required in order to evaluate the risks of entering into the covenant with God. In summary, Eve's inability to have access directly to a divine source leaves her excluded both from receiving information necessary to the formation of the contract and from receiving training in the discursive process necessary to her performance of the contract.

This essay has devoted considerable attention to the issue of Eve's acquisition of knowledge because it must be emphasized again that one cannot legally form a valid and enforceable agreement without sufficient knowledge informing consent. God himself deemed the knowledge imparted by Raphael to Adam necessary to the formation and performance of Adam's agreement with God. Eve's likely failure to have obtained adequately this information invalidates any agreement she might independently have had with God.

Further, it puts into question Eve's, and women's, very relationship to the contractual model. Eve's experience, leading to her reinstatement in the private sphere without so much as a valid agreement tying her to the public sphere, has contemporary relevance. Feminist critics, including Catherine A. MacKinnon and Carole Pateman, have examined the extent to which the public sphere derives meaning from its opposition to the private sphere in terms of both influence and status and how this disparity coincides with inadequate legal protection in the private sphere.[37] *Paradise Lost* dramatizes both the social contract's effect of creating separate public and private spheres and the consequences of this separation. Milton's poem also sheds light on the power effects underlying contemporary gender construction and women's tenuous relationship to the contractual model. A woman's consent, if even requested in the first place, will either be invalidated, as based on inadequate information, or, as I will argue next, coerced.

The paradisal wedding functions as a critical scene for interpreting the actual role played by consent in the formation of marriage contracts. Milton specifically describes marriage as a "Law" (4.750), thus placing it firmly within the perimeters of the legal construction, which, as previously discussed, insists on mutual consent and abjures coercion. Yet, the voluntariness of Eve's consent is deeply problematical in the text.[38] In order to analyze the role of consent in Adam and Eve's marriage, one must begin nearly at the moment of their creation. A "voice" (467) draws Eve from her contemplation of herself in the water image. While critics have questioned whether this voice actually belongs to God, it is undeniable that this voice functions authoritatively: it pulls Eve from her independent musings and insists upon her compliance with its demands: "hee / Whose image thou art, him thou *shalt* enjoy / Inseparablie thine" (471–73; emphasis mine). Milton has thus constructed this marriage as an arranged one by a patriarchal figure who demands obedience—the very situation by which Milton was elsewhere so appalled. Note also that Eve, upon recounting this conversation, concludes, "what could I doe / But follow strait?" (475–76). This statement suggests the coercive element to her "choice"— or, more conclusively, that she really had no choice at all.

The sight of Adam still does not change Eve's reluctance, and she tries to return to the lake. Again, action is demanded, rather than asked, of her: "Return fair Eve" (481). Upon her return, Adam begins his "proposal" of marriage. The standard chain of circumstances needed to consent mutually to a legally recognized agreement, that is, an offer and acceptance, do not exist in this exchange. Adam simply states that he "claim[s]" her (487) and upon recognizing her lack of compliance, "Seiz[es]" her, albeit "gentl[y]" (488). Thus, Adam must rely on coercion for the formation of a contractual relationship between the parties, which under the seventeenth-century legal construction of a marriage, and even Milton's own construction of consent, would conceivably have rendered the contract null and void.

A further issue lurks in the formation of their marriage agreement, problematizing the legal status of their marriage. Eve does not affirmatively assent to their marriage, either by words or deed, as required by marriage law. She simply "yield[s]" to Adam (489), which he interprets as synonymous with consenting. Yet, silent submission, particularly in the face of coercion, would have invalidated the legality of this contract. So, too, in the description of the consummation of the marriage, Eve does not actively consent to conjugal sex. She is "led" (8.511) to the nuptial bower where

> Strait side by side were laid, nor turnd I ween
> Adam from his fair Spouse, nor Eve the Rites
> Mysterious of connubial Love refus'd.
>
> (4.741–43)

She neither initiates nor consents to sex but simply does not "refuse" it. MacKinnon, in a contemporaneous discussion of rape law, critiques this construction of a woman's consent: "[M]an initiates, woman chooses. Even the ideal is not mutual. Apart from the disparate consequences of refusal, or openness of original options, this model does not envision a situation the woman controls being placed in, or choice she frames, yet the consequences are attributed to her as if the sexes began at arm's length, on equal terrain, as in the contract fiction."[39]

One final depiction of the marriage is remarkable for its neat encapsulation of gender construction and the actual meaningfulness of a woman's consent, regardless of the legal construction. Adam interprets Eve's reluctance to consent to their marriage not as an indication of her real feelings but rather as her participation in a mating ritual:

> Yet Innocence and Virgin Modestie,
> Her vertue and the conscience of her worth,
> That would be woo'd, and not unsought be won,
> Not obvious, not obtrusive, but retir'd,
> The more desirable, or to say all,
> Nature her self, though pure of sinful thought,
> Wrought in her so, that seeing me, she turn'd.
>
> (8.501–7)

Adam here reinterprets Eve's "no" as a "yes," and, again, Eve's "yielding" becomes synonymous with Eve's "consenting." Most disturbing—and of critical importance to the future of Milton studies—is the continued persistence of reading the marriage between Adam and Eve as one of mutual free will and consent in an effort to accommodate the subordinate position of Milton's Eve. Problems in this construction arguably derive from the paradoxes inherent in the contractual model itself, which Milton unwittingly reproduced in his poem.

This essay has traced the centrality of contractual theories to the legal doctrines and political and theological discourse of the first half of the seventeenth century in order to provide an alternative screen for interpreting *Paradise Lost*. This screen, because of its endurance as dominant ideology, has ongoing relevance. The power effects emanating from the poem are surprisingly contemporary in their exposure of a submerged critique of the social contract model.[40] Eve's relationship—or lack of one—to God evidences her difficulties in achieving full access to public discourse. As such knowledge informs consent, sometimes quite critically, Eve's experience emphasizes women's precarious relationship to the contractual model: lack of information can quickly nullify her consent or free exercise of choice and so leave her out of the public network of contractual relations altogether. Once more finding herself relegated to the private sphere, Eve's relationship to Adam illustrates how a woman's experience there will be constructed. Because the marriage contract may well be contingent upon forced acceptance, a system of dominance and obedience, patriarchal in nature, prevails.

As Milton's writing so poignantly illustrates, the contractual arrangement, despite its rhetoric of voluntarism, does not provide the paradigm of a free agreement but rather one of coerced participation. The genesis of the social contract resides not in mutual and voluntary agreement but rather in the forced submission of women. This scenario has continuing ramifications, as the initial story of origins creates residing social relations constructed on a hierarchical system of sexual difference. The contract thus functions as a means of normalizing the perimeters of human relationships and delineating the acceptable roles of the contractees. Social contract theory has not replaced patriarchal theory, but rather it has subversively reappropriated and subsumed it within its own ideology. For a system founded upon and glorifying the principles of rational and informed consent and free will, this final insight proves devastating.

Notes

1. Anthony Fletcher, *Gender, Sex and Subordination in England 1500–1800* (New Haven: Yale University Press, 1995), 292.

2. Prior discussions of the contractual elements in Milton's work appear in Victoria Kahn, "The Metaphorical Contract in Milton's *Tenure of Kings and Magistrates*," in *Milton and Republicanism*, ed. David Armitage, Armand Himy, and Quentin Skinner (Cambridge: Cambridge University Press, 1995), 82–105; Jason P. Rosenblatt, *Torah and Law in "Paradise Lost"* (Princeton: Princeton University Press, 1994); John T. Shawcross, "Milton and Covenant: The Christian View of Old Testament Theology," in *Milton and Scriptural Tradition*, ed. James H. Sims and Leland Ryken (Columbia: University of Missouri Press, 1984); Michael Lieb, "*Paradise Lost* and the Myth of Prohibition," in *Milton Studies* 7 (1975): 233–65; and Joseph Duncan, *Milton's Earthly Paradise: A Historical Study of Eden* (Minneapolis: University of Minnesota Press, 1972), 132–47. On the eve of publication, I also became aware of Laura Lunger Knoppers's unpublished dissertation, " 'League With You I Seek': Milton's Concept of Covenant" (Ph.D. diss., Harvard University, 1986), which investigates Milton's prose and major poetry in light of Puritan covenant theology. Her thorough examination of Puritan conceptions of theological, marriage, and political covenants provides an invaluable resource. She also presents a compelling analysis of the contractarian values underlying God's relationships with Satan and the Son of God in *Paradise Lost*. Nevertheless, Knoppers and I come to radically different conclusions as to Milton's depiction of the relationships between God, Adam, and Eve in the poem.

3. Part of my intent in this essay is to promote more comprehensive examinations of Milton's contractarian vision and the issues of consent and free will necessarily implicated by such a vision, the results of which may well modify, counteract, or reinforce this preliminary study.

4. William Blackstone, *Commentaries on the Laws of England: A Facsimile of the First Edition of 1765–1769*, vol. 1 (Chicago: University of Chicago Press, 1979), 421. For marriage legislation and regulation during the seventeenth century, see Chris Durston, " 'Unhallowed Wedlocks': The Regulation of Marriage During the English Revolution," in *The Historical Journal* 31 (1988): 45–59; Martin Ingram, *Church Courts, Sex and Marriage in England, 1570–1640* (Cambridge: Cambridge University Press, 1987); Alan Macfarlane, *Marriage and Love in England: Modes of Reproduction 1300–1840* (New York: Basil Blackwell, 1986); Chilton Latham Powell, *English Domestic Relations: 1487–1653. A Study of Matrimony and Family Life in Theory and Practice As Revealed by the Literature, Law, and History of the Period* (New York: Russell & Russell, 1972), 28–100.

5. Powell, *English Domestic Relations*, 56.

6. *A Treatise of Feme Coverts: or, the Lady's Law* (London, 1732), 25.

7. Henry Swinburne, *A Treatise of Spousals, or Matrimonial Contracts: Wherein All the Questions Relating to that Subject Are Ingeniously Debated and Resolved* (London, 1686), 70.

8. [T. E.?], *The lawes resolutions of womens rights: or, The lawes provision for woemen* (London, 1632), 59. The bracketed section of the quotation is a translation of the original phrase in Latin by Joan Larsen Klein, *Daughters, Wives, and Widows: Writings by Men about Women and Marriage in England: 1500–1640* (Urbana: University of Illinois Press, 1992), 36.

9. Ingram, *Church Courts*, 132–35. See also Martin Ingram, "Spousal Litigation in the English Ecclesiastical Courts," in *Marriage and Society: Studies in the Social History of Marriage*, ed. R. B. Outhwaite (New York: St. Martin's Press, 1982), 47, 35–57.

10. Ingram, *Church Courts*, 137–40. See also Margaret J. M. Ezell, *The Patriarch's Wife: Literary Evidence and the History of the Family* (Chapel Hill: University of North Carolina Press, 1987), 20–35.

11. Ingram, *Church Courts*, 199, 210.

12. Macfarlane, *Marriage and Love in England*, 129.

13. J. H. Baker, *An Introduction to English Legal History*, 3d ed. (London: Butterworths, 1990), 560.

14. *Slade v Morley* (1598 hearing), in J. H. Baker and S. F. C. Milsom, *Sources of English Legal History: Private Law to 1750* (London: Butterworths, 1986), 485.

15. See *Baron and Feme: A Treatise of the Common Law Concerning Husbands and Wives* (London, 1700), 4. For background on women's legal status in the period, see Baker, *An Introduction to English Legal History*, 550–57, and Leonore Marie Glanz, "The Legal Position of English Women Under the Early Stuart Kings and the Interregnum, 1603–1660" (Ph.D. diss., Loyola University of Chicago, 1973).

16. Blackstone, *Commentaries on the Laws*, 430.

17. Peter Goodrich, "Gender and Contracts," in *Feminist Perspectives on the Foundational Subjects of Law*, ed. Anne Bottomley (London: Cavendish Publishing, 1996), 17–46.

18. [T. E.?], *The lawes resolutions*, 6.

19. On patriarchal uses of contractarian rhetoric, see Gordon J. Schochet, *Patriarchalism in Political Thought: The Authoritarian Family and Political Speculation and Attitudes Especially in Seventeenth-Century England* (Oxford: Basil Blackwell, 1975).

20. The literature on many of the more radical groups, for example the Levellers and the Diggers, and their employment of the social contract is vast. For a helpful introduction to the history of the social contract, see J. W. Gough, *The Social Contract: A Critical Study of Its Development* (Westport, Conn.: Greenwood Press, 1978). For a discussion of the analogy between marriage contracts and political contracts and the conflicting uses of this analogy during the Civil War period, see Mary Lyndon Shanley, "Marriage Contract and Social Contract in Seventeenth-Century English Political Thought," *Western Political Quarterly* 32 (1975): 79–91.

21. Schochet, *Patriarchalism*, 8–9.

22. Gough, *The Social Contract*, 99.

23. Susan Staves, *Players' Scepters: Fictions of Authority in the Restoration* (Lincoln: University of Nebraska Press, 1979), 24–29, 191–252.

24. Gough, *The Social Contract*, 143–44. For discussions of the importance of originary stories and ancient custom to political theory of the period, see Gordon J. Schochet, "Sir Robert Filmer: (2) Patriarchalism and the Descent of Adam's Power," in *Patriarchalism*, 136–76, and J. G. A. Pocock, *The Ancient Constitution and the Feudal Law: A Study of English Historical Thought in the Seventeenth Century* (Cambridge: Cambridge University Press, 1957).

25. Perry Miller, *The New England Mind: The Seventeenth Century* (Cambridge: Harvard University Press, Belknap Press, 1939), 375. On Puritan covenant theology and its uses of contractarian rhetoric, see also Kahn, "The

Metaphorical Contract," 85–88; Knoppers, "Milton's Concept of Covenant"; David Zaret, *The Heavenly Contract: Ideology and Organization in Pre-Revolutionary Puritanism* (Chicago: University of Chicago Press, 1985); Gough, "Puritanism and the Contract," in *The Social Contract*, 84–103; Perry Miller, "The Marrow of Puritan Divinity," in *Errand into the Wilderness* (Cambridge: Harvard University Press, Belknap Press, 1956), 48–98; William Haller, *Liberty and Reformation in the Puritan Revolution* (New York: Columbia University Press, 1955), 65–78; John von Rohr, "Covenant and Assurance in Early English Puritanism," *Church History* 54 (1961): 195–203.

26. Zaret, *The Heavenly Contract*, 4.

27. Miller, *The New England Mind*, 400.

28. John Milton, *Considerations Touching the Likeliest Means to Remove Hirelings Out of the Church*, in *Complete Prose Works of John Milton*, 8 vols., ed. Don M. Wolfe et al. (New Haven: Yale University Press, 1953–82). All references to Milton's prose are to this edition and are cited parenthetically in the text.

29. For an analysis of Milton's formulation of divorce as deriving from a subordinationist vision of woman's autonomy, see Janet E. Halley, "Female Autonomy in Milton's Sexual Politics," in *Milton and the Idea of Woman*, ed. Julia M. Walker (Urbana: University of Illinois Press, 1988), 230–53.

30. Gough, *The Social Contract*, 100.

31. For a discussion of *The Tenure of Kings and Magistrates* and the implications of its "metaphorical contract" with the reader, as well as a further overview of seventeenth-century political and theological uses of the contract, see Kahn, "The Metaphorical Contract."

32. See, for example, Richard Posner, *The Economics of Justice* (Cambridge: Harvard University Press, 1981).

33. The distinction between a "juridico-discursive" theory of power and an analysis that explores the effects of power derives from Foucault, particularly in Michel Foucault, "Two Lectures," in *Power/Knowledge: Selected Interviews and Other Writings* (New York: Pantheon Books, 1977), 78–108, and Michel Foucault, *The History of Sexuality: An Introduction*, vol. 1, trans. Robert Hurley (New York: Vintage Books, 1980), 81–91. For a parallel discussion using a Foucauldian analytic, see David Weisberg, "Rule, Self, Subject: The Problem of Power in *Paradise Lost*," in *Milton Studies* 30 (1993): 85–107.

34. Stevie Davies, *Images of Kingship in "Paradise Lost": Milton's Politics and Christian Liberty* (Columbia: University of Missouri Press, 1983), 129–32. See Knoppers, "Milton's Concept of Covenant," for a similar conclusion.

35. Regardless of Milton's statement in the *Christian Doctrine* that God's prohibition not to eat from the tree was not a "covenant of works" (6:352), this essay must insist that Milton depicts this prohibition as part of a voluntaristic and mutual arrangement between God and Adam.

36. John Milton, *Paradise Lost*, in *The Complete Poetry of John Milton*, ed. John T. Shawcross (New York: Anchor Books, 1963). All references to *Paradise Lost* are to this edition and are cited parenthetically in the text.

37. Carole Pateman, *The Sexual Contract* (Stanford, Calif.: Stanford University Press, 1988), and Catherine A. MacKinnon, "Feminism, Marxism, Method, and the State: Toward Feminist Jurisprudence," in *Signs* 8 (1983): 635–58.

38. I am indebted to the following works for their similar interpretations of this scene and of its problematic portrayal of Eve's consent: Lee A. Jacobus,

Sudden Apprehension: Aspects of Knowledge in "Paradise Lost" (Paris: Mouton, 1976), 35, and Halley, "Female Autonomy," 248.

39. MacKinnon, "Feminism, Marxism, Method," 655.

40. These observations are based on the conclusions in Pateman's *The Sexual Contract*, which furnishes the most radical feminist critique of social contract theory to date. In this work, Pateman provides her own retelling of the genesis story, arguing that a marriage precedes the social contract. This marriage, as *Paradise Lost* so beautifully illustrates, is not structured on a contract but rather on the conjugal or sex right of the husband over the wife. Women do not perform the role of subjects to the agreement but rather of objects, or gifts of exchange. For other discussions of the way in which marriage contracts served to obliterate women's ongoing relationship to the social contract, see Goodrich, "Gender and Contracts," and Shanley, "Marriage Contract and Social Contract." For a discussion of the extent to which Eve is figured as just such a divinely bestowed gift of exchange between God and Adam, see Mary Nyquist, "The Genesis of Gendered Subjectivity in the Divorce Tracts and in *Paradise Lost*," in *Critical Essays on John Milton*, ed. Christopher Kendrick (New York: G. K. Hall, 1995), 165–93.

"Aside the Devil Turned / For Envy": The Evil Eye in *Paradise Lost*, Book 4

CHERYL H. FRESCH

Over the past twenty-five years, both genre theory and postmodernist theory have enriched readings of the intertwined roles of Satan and the bard in book 4 of *Paradise Lost*. In *"Paradise Lost" and the Rhetoric of Literary Forms*, for example, Barbara Kiefer Lewalski, pointing out that Milton concentrates many epithalamic topoi in the fourth book of his epic, explains that within this sequence Milton casts himself as "choragus or master of ceremonies," much as does Catullus in his epithalamic lyric 61.[1] Gary M. McCown, in "Milton and the Epic Epithalamium," anticipated Lewalski in this reading, recalling that the traditional choragus "uses language magically to make things happen," as when the Miltonic bard "addresses the deity presiding over these nuptials 'Hail wedded Love' " (4.750) or when he "addresses Adam and Eve directly" with "Sleep on / Blest pair" (773–74).[2] McCown also argues that Milton's epithalamium presents both Satan and the bard as choragus, thereby establishing them as "rival choragi who vie to control the outcome of [Adam and Eve's] wedding": "It is Satan's presence within the garden, of course, which makes the poet anxious for the future. And it is through Satan's eyes, moreover, serving as a kind of sin-tinted glass that we observe the couple's danger throughout the epithalamium."[3] Reexamining this application of genre theory, Sara Thorne-Thomsen departs from both Lewalski's and McCown's readings by identifying Satan and the bard as rival choruses, like those in Catullus's lyric 64, rather than rival choragi, but (in agreement with McCown) she also proposes that Satan and the bard have a "shared perspective." Thorne-Thomsen notes, however, as McCown does not, that Satan's departure well before the bard's encomium to marriage, "Hail wedded love," precipitates a change in the bard that she believes leaves him "chastened."[4]

118

Because Adam and Eve have been married for some time when Eve's "matron lip" (501) meets Adam's, however, the genre theorists' emphasis on epithalamium seems somewhat inappropriate. In addition, if a choragus "uses language magically to make things happen," the utter pointlessness of the bard's telling Adam and Eve to sleep when they have already managed to do that on their own highlights the bard's feebleness as choragus. Furthermore, of course, neither rival choragus actually causes anything at all to happen in this scene. McCown himself also concedes another point against his own thesis when he explains that although the bard as choragus should "prophesy a happy future for the marriage," he really "prophesies the opposite" by invoking an apocalyptic warning voice when he opens book 4.[5] Regardless of how firmly or loosely epithalamic conventions can therefore be said to shape the contours of book 4, what certainly remains to be delineated more clearly is the role in terms of which Milton is here presenting the bard, as well as Satan, with whose presence in Eden the bard's presence is clearly intertwined.

While not sharing the emphasis on epithalamium common to these earlier studies, Regina M. Schwartz has also focused attention on Satan's and the bard's ways of seeing and speaking in book 4 of *Paradise Lost*. Fundamental to Schwartz's reading is the feature downplayed or neglected by the genre theorists—the secrecy of that seeing. Satan spies, Schwartz stresses in 1988, "in order to gain mastery over the object of his sight," and "[h]is sightings are not so much a prelude to attacking his prey, as they are the first phase of the attack: his eye is his weapon."[6] According to Schwartz, Satan's eye is the eye of a voyeur: "The impulse to seize control is . . . apparent in the voyeuristic gaze of Satan who watches Paradise from a position of concealment, seeing, but unseen."[7] What both of Schwartz's analyses overlook, however, is Satan's sudden and painful departure as Adam and Eve kiss: "aside the devil turned / For envy" (502–3). More than fifty years ago, C. S. Lewis also overlooked Satan's turning aside and, perhaps most memorably, first charged the devil with voyeurism, describing him as "a mere peeping Tom leering and writhing in prurience as he overlooks the privacy of [Milton's] two lovers."[8] William Empson subsequently rejected Lewis's characterization of Satan as a voyeur, of course, by pointing to the jealousy that compels the tormented devil to flee the sight he secretly observes.[9]

Schwartz's assertion that "the eye of Satan is lethal"[10] nevertheless firmly urges us toward identifying Satan's role in this sequence, as it also urges us toward recognizing that while the role may fulfill, it also most certainly extends far beyond, epithalamic conventions. It is my view that Satan is not so much an epithalamic choragus, an epithalamic chorus, or a voyeur in book 4 as he is what the classical writers of marriage songs—among a significant body of other authorities—identified as the *fascinum*, "the evil eye," and furthermore, that Milton's blind bard, insofar as he shares Satan's perspective, also participates in that role within the fourth book of *Paradise Lost*.

Those who understood vision to result from the seeing extromissive eye sending forth rays, rather than the seeing intromissive eye receiving rays that had been sent forth by the object thereby seen, conceived of the evil eye as the envious eye, the invidious eye that, emitting destructive rays, looks askance on the happiness of others. "So extensive was this belief in earlier periods," Frederick Thomas Elworthy explains in *The Evil Eye*, "that every malady, all adversity, and almost anything undesirable in life was regarded as the inevitable result of the fatal glance of some person or animal. Belief in the evil eye is probably the oldest and most widespread of superstitions. It was strongly adhered to in ancient Egypt and Babylonia; and its existence was attested to in the Bible and in Greek and Roman writings of classical antiquity. An early Northern European reference to it may be found in one of the Eddas."[11]

The various literatures to which Elworthy refers reveal that triumphant generals, adorable children, successful farmers, and prosperous merchants—in addition to eager bridegrooms and beautiful brides—had to be protected against the power of the evil eye. Protection basically meant diverting the evil eye from the object it envied. In *Catullus: A Commentary*, C. J. Fordyce notes that "the singing of ribald extempore lines was a regular accompaniment of the Roman marriage ceremony" and that this device, designated the *fescennina iocatio*, was employed as an "attempt, at moments of human happiness, to cheat the power of the evil eye, of *invidia* . . . by 'taking down' the fortunate person."[12] In Catullus's lyric 61, the foremost model of the classical epithalamium, the *fescennina iocatio* involves teasing references to the groom's earlier love of boys, servant girls, and all "former smooth cheeks." All these, the choragus-poet jokingly cautions the groom, "were the licensed joys, / but the licence / expires / with your marriage."[13] Such references to sexual license have been noted as a traditional element in the genre by most scholars of the epithalamic nature of Milton's fourth book, but none has associated the *fescennina iocatio* with the other traditional epithalamic element, the *fascinum*.[14]

Spying in the garden in book 4 of *Paradise Lost*, Satan manifests that Milton has adapted the traditional concept of the evil eye. Like the *fascinum* threatening Roman marriage celebrations, Satan intends to destroy the happiness of the young couple, as he announces while he secretly peers at their naked embrace:

> Live while ye may,
> Yet happy pair; enjoy, till I return,
> Short pleasures, for long woes are to succeed.
>
> (533–35)

Embracing this tradition of the *fascinum*, the dramatic situation in which Milton develops his response becomes strikingly ironic, however. Milton's secretly peering thing *vows* to destroy happiness; that is, he does not actually destructively eye the happy couple he envies, as does the traditional *fascinum*. Further enfeebling the power traditionally assigned the *fascinum* is the fact that Milton's *fascinum* does not make his vow until he is in the process of departing the presence of the married couple.

Yet another element in Milton's ironic development of Satan as *fascinum* in book 4 is that although he thinks he sees secretly, Satan is himself actually being seen. The eye of Uriel, whose "perfect sight, / Amid the sun's bright circle . . . / See[s] far and wide" (577–79), followed the flight of the zealous spirit who had asked directions of him, and Uriel's eye "soon discerned his looks / Alien from heaven" (570–71). Rather than creating evil by malevolently eyeing the happiness others enjoy, Satan's looks in book 4 of *Paradise Lost* are therefore seen to expose his own evil to the eye of one with perfect sight. Schwartz concludes that being seen by Uriel is "the dreaded event" for a voyeuristic Satan:

In "Instincts and Their Vicissitudes" (1915), Freud outlines a mechanism of reversal in which the aggression toward an object is turned back upon the self, and the once active subject (sadist, voyeur) assumes the role of passive object (masochist, exhibitionist). Because in "normal" seeing, the roles of object and subject are continually substituted, either of the extremes—only seeing or only showing—represent a hysterical fixation. That response is driven by the fear of loss. In order to shift positions, the scopophiliac must move his gaze away from the object and endure temporary loss until he can become the object of another's sight. Similarly, the exhibitionist will not vacate his object position for fear that it will be left empty. When Satan is apprehended by Uriel, the dreaded event occurs: the viewer is viewed.[15]

Here, too, however, Schwartz's analysis requires that she overlook Satan's earlier departure from Adam and Eve. The torment that Satan experiences as he secretly watches the naked Adam and Eve kissing undermines, if it does not indeed invalidate, claims that identify the devil as a voyeur. While Satan's being seen by Uriel does perhaps bring into question the success of his spying mission, his being seen by Uriel even more clearly subverts his power as *fascinum*, but that which most strikingly compromises Satan's power as *fascinum* is the care with which Milton compels his reader to see Satan, indeed to see Satan most precisely, at the moment when he utters his third soliloquy:

> aside the devil turned
> For envy, yet with jealous leer malign
> Eyed them askance, and to himself thus plained.
> Sight hateful, sight tormenting!
>
> (502–5)

Even as he looks askance (that is, out of the corner of his eye) and simultaneously looks askance (that is, enviously and malignantly) on the happiness of Adam and Eve, Satan is being driven from this scene. What cheats the power of the evil eye in *Paradise Lost*, though, is neither the ribald singing, *fescinnina iocatio*, of the classical epithalamium, nor the "perfect sight" (577) of the Christian archangel. However powerful Satan is as secret watcher, that which Milton's peering thing sees is obviously even more immediately powerful. In the fourth book of *Paradise Lost*, Satan as the evil eye is actually overpowered by the object he views, the sight, that is, of Adam pressing Eve's "matron lip / With kisses pure" (501–2).

That Satan should be driven away by the sight of Adam and Eve's naked kiss remains very much in keeping with the traditional understanding of the evil eye. At a more lighthearted level, wedding songs lewd and obscene, directed toward making the groom look more laughable or pitiful than enviable, were intended to defeat the *fascinum* by trickery; and finger gestures such as the *mano fica* or *mano cornuto* continue to be understood as serving the same purpose. Symbols of the "generative powers," however, as Richard Payne Knight first nominated them in his pioneering and extremely controversial study *A Discourse on the Worship of Priapus* (1786), have long been seen as most profoundly and most universally to defeat the evil eye by symbolizing "the first principles of . . . religion, the knowledge of the God of Nature, the First, the Supreme . . . the creator of all things."[16]

Furthermore, as Thomas Wright continued to explain in *The Worship of the Generative Powers During the Middle Ages of Western Europe* (1866), which extended Knight's work as to geography, chronology, and religion, "[t]he figure of the female organ, as well as the male, appears to have been employed during the middle ages of Western Europe far more generally than we might suppose, placed upon buildings as a talisman against evil influences, and especially against witchcraft and the evil eye, and it was used for this purpose in many other parts of the world."[17] Like Knight and Wright, Elworthy has studied the amulets carrying these protective symbols, both those amulets presented in public art and those personal amulets carried on the body. Explaining that "[t]he intent often was to depict on the protective device a representation of the thing against which it was desired that a protective influence should be exercised,"[18] he established that while the commonest Egyptian amulet against the evil eye was the Eye of Osiris, amulets with sexual symbols appear to have been most widely employed against the evil eye.[19] That *fascinum* was the name that the Romans gave to both the phallic amulet and the erect male member simply reinforces Elworthy's note about the Eye of Osiris; the *fascinum* that was the evil eye, that is, was to be warded off by the phallic *fascinum*. This same point is also furthered by the associations between the eye and the female genitalia not only salaciously asserted long ago by Chaucer's Miller, who concludes his tale "And Absolon hath kist hir [Alison's] nether ye,"[20] but also sustainedly and clearly being investigated and elaborated in current research by archeologists, anthropologists, and feminist scholars.[21] The female eye shared with the phallic eye the power to ward off the evil eye.

Quite common therefore are amulets combining symbols of both male and female sexuality. For example, today's researchers point to "numerous Roman *tintinnabula* representing a winged phallos having a phallos of its own and a phallic tail. This assemblage, [sic] often surmounts several vulvae, or is hung with bells, which are symbols of the vulva, as are the wings."[22]

As Pierre Bettez Gravel has most recently and most succinctly reminded us, however, "The most obvious symbol of fertility is the act of procreation."[23] What torments the devil's evil eye as Adam and Eve nakedly kiss in book 4 of *Paradise Lost* is just such a symbol of fertility, as Milton's text itself establishes (immediately before Satan breaks out in his painful third soliloquy), by describing Adam and Eve so as to associate their kiss with the generative powers of Jupiter and Juno. Adam smiles on Eve,

> as Jupiter
> On Juno smiles, when he impregns the clouds
> That shed May flowers; and pressed her matron lip
> With kisses pure: aside the devil turned
> For envy, yet with jealous leer malign
> Eyed them askance, and to himself thus plained
> Sight hateful, sight tormenting!
>
> (499–505)

While Jupiter and Juno are here called upon to illumine a profound truth about the generative powers of human love, a power threatening enough to drive away the eye of evil itself, Jupiter and Juno remain in *Paradise Lost* among those devils who only in the fallen world come to be adored for deities. So, too, within the Christian world of *Paradise Lost* where free will makes evil a matter of reasoned choice, not chance sighting, the concept of the evil eye must be seen as a superstition and a falseness but a superstition and a falseness that, like Jupiter and Juno, can be used to illumine the truth. Disposing his arguments, Francis Bacon framed his essay "On Envy" (1625) within biblical references, noting in his first paragraph that "Scripture calleth envy an *evil eye*" and in his final paragraph that envy "is the proper attribute of the devil, who is called *the envious man*," but the body of Bacon's essay studies the social and political rather than the theological significance of envy and the evil eye.[24] Unlike Bacon, the essayist, Milton, the Christian prophet-poet, was obliged more forthrightly, more imaginatively, to contend with the evil eye superstition that he chose to bring into such prominence. Perhaps recalling the dramatic device of Comus's hasty exit from the Ludlow masque, which leaves the audience wondering about the potential of the tempter's persuasive powers, Milton structures this scene in book 4 of *Paradise Lost* so that the "generative powers" expressed by Adam and Eve's kiss drive off Satan, thereby sustaining, if not heightening, the remarkable sense of dramatic tension within the scene while also avoiding—at this point—the doctrinal need to untangle the metaphysical snare created when superstition encounters Christian theology. With the bard who remains after the devil flees, however, Milton most remarkably adapts the superstitious concept of the evil eye to serve the purposes of Christian truth.

Satan's forced departure from the presence of Adam and Eve is followed by Uriel's entrance into Eden on a sunbeam, as "the setting sun / Slowly descended, and with right aspect / Against the eastern gate of Paradise" (540–42). Uriel, the archangel of the sun, comes to warn Gabriel of the "evil thing" (563) whose looks have disclosed his nature, and Gabriel and Uriel thereby come to share the same perspective on Eden. This episode of shared angelic perspective then becomes the transitional and thematic device by which Milton returns to the scene from which Satan has already fled, thereby displacing the earlier perspective on that scene, which the bard had shared with Satan, and preparing the reader for the complex, eventual triumph of the bard's vision.

While the bard no longer shares Satan's perspective, the change in him is much more meaningful than is suggested by Thorne-Thomsen's description, "chastened."[25] The bard, for example, continues to inhabit darkness, even when released from the physical presence of Satan. While Satan disappears from sight into darkness, as Uriel reports to Gabriel, "Mine eye pursued him still, but under shade / Lost sight of him" (572–73), the bard now becomes uniquely and fully visible as he sings from within darkness: "as the wakeful bird / Sings darkling, and in shadiest covert hid / Tunes her nocturnal note" (3. 38–40). The bard's singing "darkling" must nevertheless be seen to sustain, albeit in a new way, his association with the concept of the evil eye. The bard's physical blindness, established most poignantly as he invoked "holy Light" (1) in book 3, hides him in the "shadiest covert" whence he "Sings darkling." Furthermore, as one of the evil consequences of Adam and Eve's Fall, the Fall that, within the action of the poem, has not yet occurred, his blindness symbolizes evil. Freed though it may be from a perspective shared with Satan's evil eye, the bard's blind eye is therefore seen to bring evil into Eden, not, of course, inflicting evil according to the popular superstition of the evil eye, but both suffering evil and revealing evil according to the Christian understanding of original sin.

Consequently, although Satan's eyes may have provided a

"sin-tinted glass" through which Adam and Eve's danger was earlier observed, the bard's blind eyes function similarly after Satan's departure. Indeed, speaking out of future human darkness, the bard's blind eyes more memorably taint and contaminate the reader's view of Eden than did Satan's, since the bard experientially knows, as the reader also experientially knows—and as the departed Satan did not—the detailed miseries of fallen human love. While Satan had only vowed to bring "long woes" to ruin the happiness of Edenic marriage, the blind bard enters Eden dragging the knowledge of long centuries of future human hypocrisy, lust, and greedy selfishness behind him:

> the bought smile
> Of harlots, loveless, joyless, unendeared,
> Casual fruition . . . court amours
> Mixed dance, or wanton mask, or midnight ball,
> Or serenade, which the starved lover sings
> To his proud fair, best quitted with disdain.
>
> (4.765–70)

Most ironically, however, the focus on this new detailed vision of the future corruption of marital happiness is sharpened while the blind bard struggles rather to show and to celebrate unfallen Edenic love. The voice of the blind bard proleptically and—insofar as he is fallen—necessarily taints human love; in spite of that, however, as he observes Adam and Eve proceed "into their inmost bower / Handed" (738–39), the bard simultaneously experiences the dawning awareness of the divine significance of marriage within this Christian epic. The bard comes to glimpse the most profound meaning of wedded love, to perceive, that is, that wedded love is a "mysterious law," while it is also the "true source / Of human offspring" (750–51), and by so tightly juxtapositioning the eschatological meaning and the almost bluntly biological consequence of wedded love, the bard points toward the basis of the divine significance of Christian marriage.

In *Paradise Lost*, Adam and Eve not only symbolize what Knight calls the "generative powers," but, as they share "the rites / Mysterious of connubial love" (742–43), Adam and Eve also activate those powers. Expressing "the first principles of religion, the knowledge of the God of Nature, the First, the Supreme . . . the creator of all things," as they did when placed on Egyptian or Roman amulets, those generative powers as symbolized and realized by Milton's presentation of Adam and Eve have been adapted within book 4 to express the first principles of Christianity and to express the bard's growing knowledge of the Christian God. While the generative powers symbolized by the protective symbols on the Egyptian or Roman amulets were thought capable of driving off the *fascinum* that was the evil eye, evil within the Christian epic is not to be magically deflected but rather to be mysteriously defeated through the ultimate Christian realization of those generative powers, through, that is, the seed of the woman.

What "Hail wedded love" proceeds most remarkably to establish, then, is the bard's divided perspective on the love shared by Adam and Eve. Milton's reader here comes to see Adam and Eve not through Satan's demonically evil eye, with which the bard's eye had also earlier viewed Eden, but through both the bard's humanly evil eye—an eye that unremittingly symbolizes and expresses evil within this Christian epic—and the bard's prophetic eye—an eye that, illuminated by the knowledge of God, also expresses and illuminates that knowledge so that others may see. Focusing on the bard's invocations as she concludes her essay on voyeurism, Schwartz writes that the bard's "sight depends upon the light looking inward."[26] The sight that Satan's evil eye could not endure, the sight of human love as Adam and Eve nakedly kissed, is the sight that comes to look inward and to enlighten the bard's blindness as Adam and Eve enter the nuptial bower and lie "Straight side by side" (4.741). Some modern readers of *Paradise Lost* seem annoyed by what they understand as Milton's failure to envision and show prelapsarian sexual intercourse. To such readers, McCown explains that "Milton's reticence in depicting the sexual act . . . affirms the Christian humanists' conception of it as a private and natural rather than a public or ceremonial occasion."[27] But it is assuredly not priggishness, even priggishness concealing itself as Christian humanism, that turns aside the bard's eye from the Edenic lovemaking. What does in fact come to be seen here is rather that which sees, what comes to be seen here is the very eye of the emerging prophet: "nor turned I ween / Adam from his fair spouse, nor Eve the rites / Mysterious of connubial love refused" (741–43).

Crucial to our proper reading of this sequence is the key term *ween*. With this very line from *Paradise Lost* as its example, the *Oxford English Dictionary* (1.h) explains that "I ween" does not govern the sentence in which it occurs but is parenthetical. "I

ween" does not, as has often been assumed, serve to cast doubt
on the event of Edenic sexual intercourse. Instead, "I ween"
serves to establish—and to mark as extraordinary—the fact that
the blind bard succeeds in envisioning the "rites / Mysterious."
For *to ween* is also "to imagine" or "to fancy." What the phrase
intimates is that the bard's fallen eye has been illuminated by
the light of the sight of love and is thereby manifesting itself as
the eye of visionary prophecy.

When the bard does look back to envision the lovers within
the nuptial bower, they are asleep:

> These lulled by nightingales embracing slept,
> And on their naked limbs the flowery roof
> Showered roses, which the morn repaired.
>
> (4.771–73)

Before he turns aside from this sight of love, however, the bard
speaks, recalling but poignantly inverting Satan's earlier words
when a powerfully similar sight compelled him to turn aside:
"Sleep on / Blest pair; and O yet happiest if ye seek / No happier
state, and know to know no more" (773–75). What Milton may
be evoking as he concludes this sequence is the concept that the
rabbis called the Good Eye, as opposed to the Evil Eye. Brigitte
Kern-Ulmer has explained that "the possessor of a Good Eye is
invariably a good person. One who has the Good eye [sic] is involved in the performance of *mizvot*. In a midrash, Moses is said
to have had a Good Eye because he shared the Torah with Israel.
Consequently, the Torah should be taught with a Good Eye."[28]
The prophetic eye of Moses as he shared the Torah, and the prophetic eye of Milton's bard as he here shares the "mysterious
Law" of marriage, may therefore be seen to share the same visionary perspective as they did in book 1 when the bard first un-
dertook to "assert eternal providence, / And justify the ways of
God to men" (25–26) after having evoked the memory of "That
shepherd, who first taught the chosen seed" (8). Associated with
the one who has the midrashic Good Eye, who "In addition to
blessing others . . . is given the honor of reciting benedictions,"[29]
Milton's bard finally then proceeds to deliver his benediction
over the sleeping lovers: "Sleep on / Blest pair." And although
other nightingales have already lulled Adam and Eve to sleep,
the reader of *Paradise Lost* who hears the bard sing darkling is
immediately blessed by the song, as the reader, the blind bard,

and the sleeping lovers will eventually all be blessed by the mysterious marriage celebrated within that song.

NOTES

I wish to thank Professor William B. Hunter Jr. for his most insightful comments and his even more valuable reservations about my argument when I presented the reading version of this paper at the Conference on John Milton in October 1997.

1. Barbara Kiefer Lewalski, *"Paradise Lost" and the Rhetoric of Literary Forms* (Princeton: Princeton University Press, 1985), 190.

2. Gary M. McCown, "Milton and the Epic Epithalamium," *Milton Studies* 5 (1973): 43. John Milton, *Paradise Lost,* ed. Alastair Fowler (London: Longman, 1971). All references to *Paradise Lost* are to this edition and are cited parenthetically in the text.

3. McCown, "Milton and the Epic Epithalamium," 60, 59.

4. Sara Thorne-Thomsen, "Milton's 'advent'rous song': Lyric Genres in Paradise Lost" (Ph.D. diss., Brown University, 1985), 30.

5. McCown, "Milton and the Epic Epithalamium," 59.

6. Regina M. Schwartz, *Remembering and Repeating: Biblical Creation in "Paradise Lost"* (Cambridge: Cambridge University Press, 1988), 54, 55. See also Regina M. Schwartz, "Rethinking Voyeurism and Patriarchy: The Case of *Paradise Lost,"* *Representations* 34 (1991): 85–103. In "Rethinking Voyeurism," 100, Schwartz questions the polarization of seeing that makes the secret watcher or voyeur the aggressor and the object of that visual aggression its victim. She notes, for example, that if the invocations in *Paradise Lost* "become occasions for the narrator to enact the polarization of aggressive voyeur and passive exhibit, of sadism and masochism, it is only to reject these formulas."

7. Schwartz, *Remembering and Repeating,* 55.

8. C. S. Lewis, *A Preface to "Paradise Lost"* (London: Oxford University Press, 1942), 97.

9. William Empson, *Milton's God* (London: Chatto and Windus, 1961), 68.

10. Schwartz, *Remembering and Repeating,* 55.

11. Frederick Thomas Elworthy, *The Evil Eye: The Origins and Practices of Superstition* (New York: Julian Press, 1958), v.

12. C. J. Fordyce, *Catullus: A Commentary* (Oxford: Clarendon Press, 1961), 247, 248.

13. Catullus, *The Poems of Catullus,* trans. Peter Whigham (Baltimore: Penguin, 1966), 126–27.

14. See Lewalski, *Rhetoric of Literary Forms,* 190; McCown, "Milton and the Epic Epithalamium," 44; Thorne-Thomsen, "Milton's 'advent'rous song,'" 23.

15. Schwartz, *Remembering and Repeating,* 55. A more sustained and wider investigation of the mechanism of voyeur-exhibitionist reversal in *Paradise Lost* is central to Schwartz's later essay, "Rethinking Voyeurism."

16. Richard Payne Knight, *A Discourse on the Worship of Priapus,* in *Sexual Symbolism: A History of Phallic Worship* (1786; reprint, New York: Julian Press, 1957), 28.

17. Thomas Wright, *The Worship of the Generative Powers During the Middle Ages of Western Europe* (1866), in *Sexual Symbolism*, 48.

18. Elworthy, *The Evil Eye*, vii.

19. Ibid., 126.

20. Geoffrey Chaucer, *The Canterbury Tales*, in *The Norton Anthology of English Literature*, 6th ed., 2 vols., ed. M. H. Abrams et al. (New York: W. W. Norton, 1993), 1:117. While Chaucer apparently never elsewhere uses the expression "nether ye" and while the scholarship on "The Miller's Tale" seems to assume that Absolon kissed the same anatomical feature on both Nicholas and Alison, my research on the evil eye strongly suggests that Chaucer meant by Alison's "nether ye" her uniquely female lower eye.

21. See, for example, O. G. S. Crawford, *The Eye Goddess* (London: Phoenix House, 1957); Michael Dames, *The Silbury Treasure: The Great Goddess Rediscovered* (London: Thames and Hudson, 1976); Marija Gimbutas, *The Language of the Goddess* (San Francisco: Harper and Row, 1989); Marija Gimbutas, *The Civilization of the Goddess* (New York: HarperCollins, 1991); Pierre Bettez Gravel, *The Malevolent Eye: An Essay on the Evil Eye, Fertility, and the Concept of Mana* (New York: Peter Lang, 1995).

22. Gravel, *The Malevolent Eye*, 55.

23. Ibid.

24. Francis Bacon, *The Essays*, ed. John Pitcher (New York: Penguin, 1985), 83, 87.

25. Thorne-Thomsen, "Milton's 'advent'rous song,' " 30.

26. Schwartz, "Rethinking Voyeurism," 100.

27. McCown, "Milton and the Epic Epithalamium," 53.

28. Brigitte Kern-Ulmer, "The Power of the Evil Eye and the Good Eye in Midrashic Literature," *Judaism* 40 (1991): 346–47.

29. Ibid., 347.

Satan and Servius: Milton's Use of the Helen Episode (*Aeneid*, 2.567–88)

RAPHAEL FALCO

This brief essay has two aims. The first is to establish a plausible new classical—or pseudoclassical—source for Milton's Satan. And the second, less definitive aim is to explore the possibility that in his poetry Milton responds to Renaissance commentaries of standard authors (in this case Vergil). Although I do not foresee a new *Quellenforschung* coming into fashion in Milton studies, it seems likely nonetheless that as we begin to explore the resources of the various commentary traditions, new influences on Milton and his contemporaries are bound to surface. Early modern Neo-Latin poetic and biblical commentaries, as well as their vernacular counterparts, form a great mass of unmined practical criticism, containing all manner of intellectual debate from poetics to history to moral philosophy.[1] Of course, the commentaries can be tough going, repetitive and pedantic, written sometimes in obscure shorthand. But their value as compendiums of culture has yet to be realized in English literary criticism of the early modern period. Craig Kallendorf once remarked to me that he thought the poetic commentaries might well supply the missing link in Renaissance studies. I am inclined to agree with him, at least provisionally, until more work has been done to disprove such a conjecture. It seems counterintuitive, as my essay indicates, that learned English authors would have failed to acknowledge and to respond to the aggregation of critical opinion in the margins of editions of their favorite authors.

Milton in particular, considering his vociferous engagement in intellectual matters, is unlikely to have ignored learned commentary. Commentary and response constitute the sine qua non of humanist literary production, the Roman forum of the *res publica litterarum*. Born long after the height of the movement, Milton might nonetheless be seen as an ideal product of Renaissance humanism, an advocate and admirer of the classical past whose efforts in ancient genres are exemplary. Thanks in large measure to his own prodding, we tend to think of him in direct engagement with Homer, Vergil, Ovid, Horace, and many others. The thought that there might be some fillip of mediation between Milton and his great models almost seems a heresy. Yet I am convinced that such mediation had a considerable effect on Milton's writing: specifically, I think that Milton—like every other learned author—read Vergil, Ovid, and Horace, maybe even Homer, against the background of a lively and voluminous tradition of commentary. Thus what we often regard as a direct response to a passage in, say, Vergil, is very possibly a response to a commentator's exegesis of Vergil and moreover to the marginal debate surrounding a particular canonical passage in Renaissance editions of the classical works.

This essay explores one such response to a controversial passage in Vergil. Milton would not have read the *Aeneid* without also having read commentaries on the poem—indeed, the controversies raised by commentators were ubiquitous in intellectual culture. It follows, therefore, that Milton would have been unable to avoid the extensive Renaissance debate over the legitimacy of what we now refer to as the Helen Episode in the second book of the *Aeneid*. The scholia of virtually all commentators reflect the debate, from Servius to humanist writers such as Landino, Parrhasius, Scaliger, and Pontanus. I would like to suggest that, far from avoiding the debate, Milton deliberately engages the Helen Episode—that in some degree he bases Satan, the fraud and counterfeit, on the possibly spurious Aeneas of this episode. His aim would have been to exploit a situation in which the Fraudulent Tempter himself, like his specious reasoning, rests for his very existence in the poem on a doubtful source. The result would be a kind of baroque textual joke, a model of imitation that keeps disappearing into the margins.

In any case, using the spurious passage and its marginal controversy as a source could not be construed as classical imitation in the conventional sense, regardless of whether one takes Aristotle or Seneca as one's guide. Nor is it conventional humanism, for which commentary by and large remains subordinate to, or at least separate from, poetry. Rather, there is something palpably transitional about depending on the commentary tradition and acknowledging that dependence in one's verse, something in my view characteristically Miltonic. But it would be difficult in the brief space of this essay to do much more than conjecture about Milton's enigmatic place between humanism and neoclassicism. So let me try simply to establish that he might have used the Helen Episode in conjuring up Satan.

One word of caveat: as many critics have shown, Satan has numerous textual origins, from Elizabethan tragedy to Midrash. I do not mean to displace these other sources. The Helen Episode merely complements them, adding a component of textual doubt to all the other dubiety surrounding Satan's character in the poem. I would also venture to say that in identifying the Helen Episode as a possible source we might have stumbled on a witty exculpation of the poet who plans "to justify the ways of God to men" (1.26):[2] if the text Milton imitated is itself spurious, then how can he be blamed that his character turned out to be such a liar? Like Eve, Milton has been deceived—he by the clever pseudo-Vergilian disguise of the Helen Episode.

THE HELEN EPISODE

The Helen Episode occurs in book 2 of the *Aeneid* (567–88), during Aeneas's narration of the fall of Troy. At this point in the narrative, as will be recalled, Aeneas finds himself on the roof of the palace, looking out over the burning city after having just witnessed the murder of Priam. Surveying the chaotic street, he suddenly sees Helen in the doorway of a temple:

> Iamque adeo super unus eram, cum limina Vestae
> servantem et tacitam secreta in sede latentem
> Tyndarida aspicio: dant clara incendia lucem
> erranti passimque oculos per cuncta ferenti.
> illa sibi infestos eversa ob Pergama Teucros
> et Danaum poenam et deserti coniugis iras
> praemetuens, Troiae et patriae communis Erinys,
> abdiderat sese atque aris invisa sedebat.
> exarsere ignes animo; subit ira cadentem
> ulcisci patriam et sceleratas sumere poenas.
> "scilicet haec Spartam incolumis patriasque Mycenas
> aspiciet, partoque ibit regina triumpho?
> coniugiumque domumque patris natosque videbit
> Iliadum turba et Phrygiis comitata ministris?
> occiderit ferro Priamus? Troia arserit igni?
> Dardanium totiens sudarit sanguine litus?
> non ita. namque etsi nullum memorabile nomen
> feminea in poena est nec habet victoria laudem,

exstinxisse nefas tamen et sumpsisse merentis
laudabor poenas, animumque explesse iuvabit
ultricis flammae et cineres satiasse meorum."
talia iactabam et furiata mente ferebar.

(1:2.567–88)[3]

[And so now I remained alone, when I saw Helen watchful on the threshhold to the temple of Vesta, silently lurking in that secret place. The fires gave clear light to my wandering steps, my eyes glancing everywhere. Dreading the anger of her abandoned husband, the hostile Trojans in their ruined citadel, and the punishment of the Danaans, she, the hated sight, hid herself and squatted at the altars, a Fury both to Troy and to her native country. The flames blazed up in my mind: rage rose in me to avenge my falling country and to inflict punishment on such wickedness. "Shall she, unharmed, behold Sparta and Mycenae in triumph? Shall she see her native land and her husband's home, all the while attended by enslaved Trojan handmaids? Shall Priam be slain by the sword for this? And Troy burned? And the Dardanian shore so many times bathed in blood? It shall not be! Even if one gains neither renown in punishing a woman nor glory for victory over one, nevertheless I will be praised for destroying that abominable creature and for exacting deserved punishment. It will please me to glut my soul with the flames of vengeance and to appease the ashes of my ancestors." I pondered these words and bore mad thoughts in mind.]

This passage, which does not appear in any of the ancient manuscripts of the *Aeneid* that we have, was preserved for the Renaissance by the fourth-century Vergilian scholar Servius. But, as G. P. Goold has pointed out, the so-called Servius of the Servian commentary is really "an amalgamation of Servius's commentary . . . with a large mass of non-Servian scholia."[4] So far as learned opinion can guess (and there is dispute on every aspect of the reconstruction) the non-Servian scholia were combined with the Servius commentary by a seventh-century compiler, thought (for pretty thin reasons) to have been Irish. The expanded Servian commentary, which includes Servius himself as well as the non-Servian scholia, was first edited in 1600 by a Frenchman called Pierre Daniel, so that we now refer to this complete text as the Servius Danielis. What is important for our analysis is that until the nineteenth century, Servius Danielis was considered the authentic and finally complete text of Servius alone, when in fact it was considerably longer than Servius's actual manuscript because it included commentators from before the fourth century as well as commentators on Servius himself.

Thus, Renaissance editions of the *Aeneid* respond to "Servius" when in reality they are sometimes responding to commentators who disagree with Servius. This leads to a good deal of confusion, which, however, is not in itself relevant at this stage. More to the point is the Servian treatment of the Helen Episode. Servius prints the Helen Episode in his preface, along with the famous *"ille ego"* opening to the *Aeneid;* he does not comment on the twenty-two lines at 2.567 of his text except to note that "sumpost hunc ver hi versus fuerunt, qui a Tucca et Vario obliti sunt" [after this verse (566) there were verses that were removed by Tucca and Varius (Vergil's friends and literary executors)].[5] Servius gives no reason for the executors' removal of the passage but at line 592 points out "hinc versus constat esse sublatos, nec immerito" [these verses continue to be canceled, but undeservedly].[6] He—or, actually, the amalgamated commentary (known as Servius *auctus*)—reports the reasons that the verses continue to be kept out of the poem:

> nam et turpe est vir forti contra feminam irasci, et contrarium est Helenam in domo Priami fuisse illi rei, quae in sexto (495) dicitur, quia in domo est inventa Deiphobi, postquam ex summa arce vocaverat Graecos, hinc autem versus fuisse sublatos Veneris verba declarant dicentis (601) *non tibi Tyndaridis facies invisa Lacaenae.*[7]

> [because it is a disgrace for a powerful man to be wrathful toward a woman, and (because the verses) contradict that Helen was in the palace of the great King Priam: it is said in book 6 (line 495) that she revealed Deiphobus in the palace after she had summoned the Greeks from the highest stronghold. But the words of Venus's speech (line 601) declare, "Not for you (to avenge) the hated face of Laconian Helen" (referring to the canceled verses).]

Servius and those who followed him restored the Helen Episode, based essentially on his assertion that Venus makes reference to lines included in the expurgated Episode, which supposedly would be impossible unless Vergil had written both passages. This so-called rehabilitation prepared the way for the editorial debate, which focused not on the external evidence (that is, the manuscript's veracity) but rather on the internal evidence.

Commentators argued chiefly about aesthetic consistency, ethics, and decorum. They objected that, as Servius himself noted, the Helen of the Episode is inconsistent with the Helen

of book 6, in which she appeases Menelaus by summoning the
Greeks and showing them where her new husband Deiphobus is
hiding. This objection was countered by the observation that
just because Helen tried to appease Menelaus does not mean she
succeeded in doing so. But the objectors added that anyway
Helen was long gone from Troy by the time it fell, according to
Herodotus, who says the Trojans sent her to Egypt before the
Greeks overran the city. This objection was easily rejected, however, by the suggestion that Vergil apparently did not know that
fact; and in any case he had poetical tradition on his side in the
auspicious persons of Homer and Euripides, who place Helen at
the scene of the fall. So much for Helen.

Much more important to the commentators—and to Milton, I
suspect—is Aeneas's character. The chief objection to the Episode from this perspective, as Servius records, is that it is shame-
ful for a heroic figure to want to kill a woman, let alone kill her
in a temple. The corollary of this objection is that the passage
must be spurious because Vergil never would have broken decorum in such a way and allowed his hero to have such unsavory
and pointless desires.[8] Aeneas's rage for vengeance, especially
against a woman, is seen to be utterly out of character with the
pius Aeneas whose mission is to found Rome.

The responses to this objection during the sixteenth and
seventeenth centuries are numerous and contradictory, ranging
from peremptory cancellation of the verses in some editions to
the bracketing of the Episode in others to lengthy justifications
in the marginal scholia of still other editions.[9] I will confine myself to Jacobus Pontanus, whose comprehensive commentary on
Vergil's works was published in Augsburg in 1599. Clearly in
possession of numerous prior commentaries including those of
Servius, Pontanus has three folio pages of marginal remarks on
the Helen Episode. After a brief review of the Servian tradition,
citing Julius Caesar Scaliger's defense earlier in the century,[10] he
launches into his support of the Episode:

> Non est obstrependum Aeneae adversus Helenam irascenti. Nam et
> ipse ibi disputat, et ita movetur, ut vincat melior sententia: quam
> divinus poeta meritò adscribit deae. . . . Disputationem ecce qualem.
> *namque etsi nullum memorabile nomen Fominea in poena est, nec*
> *habet victoria laudem.* Non quaerit igitur aut nomen, aut laudem,
> sed iustitiam, ut suorum deleat ignominiam. Quis enim patiatur af-
> fines suos, foeminas primarias premi servitio impudicae mulieris?
> Igitur rectè interpretatur factum suum sic: *Extinxisse nefas.* Nullius

enim non interest nefas tollere. Vir enim iustus nullum malum superesse pati debet. Quare Grammaticuli, qui hosce luculentissimos, operosissimosque versus sublatos volvere, vulgaribus moti affectibus, ignoratis rationibus, iustitiam de sapiente abstulere.[11]

[It is not disturbing for Aeneas to be enraged with Helen. That point is itself disputed and set in motion there (in the text), and better judgment prevails, which the divine poet ascribes to the goddess. . . . There is also dispute over the lines: "Even if one gains neither renown in punishing a woman nor glory for victory over one, nevertheless I shall be praised for destroying that abominable creature and for exacting deserved punishment." Thus Aeneas does not seek either renown or praise, but justice, so that he might blot out the dishonor of his people. Who indeed would suffer his loved ones, women of the first rank, to be forced into servitude to a shameless female? It is correct to interpret his deed so: "to destroy the abominable creature." Yet it is of no importance to anyone to kill a wicked woman. Indeed the just man must allow no evil to overcome him. For which reason, according to the most distinguished and painstaking grammarians, to consider the verses canceled—moved by common feelings, ignorant arguments—is to remove justice from sapience.]

Pontanus's analysis is very subtle. In agreeing with Servius that the lines deserve to be printed, he faults neither Aeneas nor Vergil. Rather, he sees Aeneas's vengeful wrath as a thirst for justice. But he recognizes that to fulfill that wrath would both divert Aeneas from his course and redound poorly on his honor as a just man. So he praises Vergil for structuring the scene so that the goddess, bringing a holy beam of light to the dark moment, enlightens Aeneas and sets the tale back on course.

The phrase *"iustitiam de sapiente abstulere"* is especially provocative if we can translate it "to remove justice from sapience," as I have done. Sapience, as is well known, has profound significance for Milton in *Paradise Lost*. Misunderstood, disastrously incomplete sapience has a crucial place in the poem. Moments after plucking and eating the fruit in book 9, Eve, "jocund and boon" (793), addresses the Forbidden Tree:

> O Sovran, virtuous, precious of all Trees
> In Paradise, of operation blest
> To Sapience, hitherto obscur'd, infam'd,
> And thy fair Fruit let hang, as to no end
> Created.
>
> (795–99)

Eve's mistake echoes the mistake of misguided commentators who, to quote Pontanus, "remove justice from sapience." That it is justice she will receive for her sin (albeit assuaged by mercy through the Son's sacrifice) only reinforces Pontanus's association of the two virtues. In fact, to my mind, the prominence of the word sapience in Pontanus's defense of the Helen Episode alongside its moral and philosophical prominence in *Paradise Lost* plausibly suggests a Miltonic response to the marginal commentary. Apart from the usefulness of the Episode as a source, the commentary on that source—indeed the existence of controversy itself—seems to furnish Milton with poetic material.

SATAN

In contrast to Pontanus's Aeneas, Milton's Satan never gets set back on course. He retains the very traits that the vengeful Aeneas must lay aside. My suggestion, then, is that Milton, while probably aware of such rationalizations as Pontanus's, recognized the tenuous nature of the Helen Episode and simply put the marginal justifications into Satan's mouth. The several parallels between the character flaws of the spurious Aeneas and the flawed character of Satan would consequently owe their existence to the commentary tradition. Milton could have seen these flaws himself, but, again, the marginal exegeses would reinforce his impressions.

The parallels in fact begin with the setting. The Helen Episode and books 1 and 2 of *Paradise Lost* both occur against a background of flames and destruction. In terms of classical antecedents, Milton's Hell does not resemble the Homeric or Vergilian underworld so much as it resembles the smoking shambles of Vergil's Troy. And Satan, while not staring at his "*cadentem patriam*" precisely as Aeneas does, nevertheless stares out over the burning marl at fallen comrades in arms. This is not really Dante's Hell, either, nor any of the numerous medieval versions; this is a Hell populated by defeated soldiers. And in their defeat by Milton's God and Son, the fallen angels are prototypes of the fallen Trojans: Troy falls, after all, because the gods cause it to fall, as Venus emphasizes in counseling her son against taking revenge on Helen and Paris. (That the fallen angels will themselves become the pagan gods, and be responsible for the destruction of Troy, in this context reinforces the familiar Miltonic irony.)

In the first line of the Helen Episode, Aeneas finds himself alone [Iamque adeo super unus eram]. The fires of the ruined city give clear light to his "wandering steps," and the word for wandering in the passage is *erranti*, in my view too close to Milton's "err" and "erring" to be ignored. Rory B. Egan has noted, in regard to Aeneas, that he is a "distraught and delusion-prone hero" and that he is "making mental mistakes at this time— wandering with his mind at least as much as with his feet."[12] The same might be said for Satan in book 1 (and increasingly as the poem progresses). When we first see Satan, he, like Aeneas, finds himself alone, awaking amid the flames and "utter darkness" (72) of the burning lake. Aeneas, alone on the palace roof *"oculos per cuncta ferenti"* [cast his eyes everywhere about]; similarly, Satan "round . . . throws his baleful eyes / That witness'd huge affliction and dismay / Mixt with obdurate pride and steadfast hate" (56–58). There certainly seems to be a parallel in these lines, and in fact Milton immediately associates Satan with Aeneas. Satan's famous first words to Beelzebub, "If thou beest hee; But O how fall'n! how chang'd" (84), are an allusion to Aeneas's remark to Hector's ghost: "quantum mutatus ab illo / Hectore qui redit exuvias indutus Achilli" (*Aeneid*, 2.274–75) [how changed from that Hector who returned clothed in the arms of Achilles].[13] This places Satan squarely in book 2 of the *Aeneid*. The meeting with Hector's ghost occurs not in the underworld of book 6, as one would expect, but in Aeneas's dream on the night of the fall of Troy, only moments before the Helen Episode in Aeneas's narrative.

We suspect that Satan is the spurious Aeneas of the Episode rather than the legitimate Aeneas of the dream, however, when we recognize his motives. Simply put, he wants vengeance and he plans to kill a woman to get it. Just as Helen crouches near the altar of the temple of Vesta, Eve is in her Edenic temple when Satan approaches her, "This Flow'ry Plat, the sweet recess of Eve" (9.456). By his actions Satan may, as Pontanus says of Aeneas, hope to "blot out the dishonor of his people." But, regardless, in Milton's terms he is the prototype of the figure overcome by wrath and hatred; and in textual terms he might well have derived his rationalizations from those of the Aeneas of the Helen Episode. "The flames blazed up in my mind," recounts Aeneas; "rage rose in me to avenge my falling country and to inflict punishment on such wickedness." If we substitute "innocence" for "wickedness," Satan might well utter the same sentence, with particular emphasis on "falling" [*cadentem*] in Milton's mind. As Satan stands observing Eve in book 9, he suddenly (and briefly) becomes "abstracted . . . From his own evil" (463–64). But soon his abstraction ends, and as is the case with Aeneas, flames blaze up in his mind: "the hot hell that always in him burns," says Milton,

> soon ended his delight,
> And tortures him now more, the more he sees
> . . . then soon
> Fierce hate he recollects.
>
> (467–71)

In a comparable mood, Aeneas, staring at the unaware Helen, says in perfect Satan-speak, "It will please me to glut my soul with the flames of vengeance."

Let me conclude, therefore, by saying simply that I think Milton echoes the Helen Episode in books 1 and 2, and perhaps in book 9 as well. In many of Satan's scenes, Milton's consciousness of the Episode seems all but certain. And while it is difficult to claim a similar certainty regarding his response to the commentators, at times the two influences seem interlocked, as in Pontanus's word "sapiente" and Milton's "sapience."[14] It would be possible, I think, to multiply the echoes and parallels, referencing both the Episode and the scholia. But in the final analysis, I doubt that Satan should be identified narrowly with any character, not even a spurious one, nor with any one literary controversy. Although Milton might have used the Helen Episode to furnish the nuances of Satan's character, Satan has a more complex relation to the classical past and to the humanist incursions into classical tradition. He comes to represent—and of course to predict, in the time scheme of the poem—the defeat of Troy itself when he rises up among his vast army of fallen angels "proudly eminent" (1.590) and "like a Tow'r" (591). It would not be amiss, amid Milton's repeated descriptions of that ever-burning lake, to recall Vergil's description of the final Trojan conflagration, the collapse of what Marlowe calls "the topless towers of Ilium" (*Doctor Faustus*, 5.1.98).[15] But there are other towers and other defeats to consider as well. Satan, no matter which way we take him, is certainly a spurious figure. Consequently, it is reasonable (and provocative) to suggest that some aspect of his literary original might well be spurious, too.

If so, then Milton has balanced his most classically heroic figure on a fine line drawn between classical authority and humanist revision, between Vergil and myriad Vergilian authorities—between, finally, the text and the margin. I think he does this largely to discredit his antihero. But, in terms of literary history, Milton's balancing act also captures a moment in the transition from humanist classicism to the considerably altered neoclassicism of the eighteenth century.

NOTES

1. Debora Shuger examines Neo-Latin biblical commentary, chiefly from the seventeenth century, in *The Renaissance Bible: Scholarship, Sacrifice, and Subjectivity* (Berkeley and Los Angeles: University of California Press, 1994), esp. 1–53. On poetic commentaries, see Anthony Grafton, "Quattrocentro Humanism and Classical Scholarship," in *Renaissance Humanism*, 3 vols., ed. Albert Rabil Jr. (Philadelphia: University of Pennsylvania Press, 1988), 3:23–66.

2. John Milton, *Paradise Lost*, in *John Milton: Complete Poems and Major Prose*, ed. Merritt Y. Hughes (New York: Odyssey, 1957). All references to *Paradise Lost* are to this edition and are cited parenthetically in the text.

3. *The Aeneid of Virgil*, 2 vols., ed. R. D. Williams (New York: St. Martin's Press, 1972). The Helen Episode ends here with Vergil's "cum mihi se non ante oculis tam clara, videndam . . . alma parens" [when I saw my mother before my eyes more clearly than ever]. Venus then persuades Aeneas to return home to save his family and to leave vengeance to the gods. All references to the *Aeneid* are to this edition and are cited parenthetically in the text. Translations are mine unless otherwise indicated.

4. G. P. Goold, "Servius and the Helen Episode," *Harvard Studies in Classical Philology* 74 (1970): 103.

5. *Servianorum in Vergilii Carmina Commentariorum*, 2 vols., ed. E. K. Rand (Lancaster, Pa: American Philological Association, 1946), 2:462. See 2:2–3 for the *"ille ego"* opening and the text of the Helen Episode. This edition is known as the Harvard Servius.

6. Ibid., 2:463.

7. Ibid., 2:463–64.

8. In 1902, Richard Heinze echoed this sentiment in his influential *Vergils epische Technik*, setting the tone for the twentieth-century's rejection of the passage. See the recent edition of his book, *Virgil's Epic Technique*, trans. Hazel Harvey, David Harvey, and Fred Robertson (Berkeley and Los Angeles: University of California Press, 1993), esp. 26–30. Other important discussions of the Helen Episode in the twentieth century include Goold, "Servius and the Helen Episode"; T. Berres, *Vergil und die Helanaszene mit einem Exkurs zu den Halbversen* (Heidelberg, 1992); R. G. Austin, ed., *P. Vergili Maronis "Aeneidos" Liber Secundus* (Oxford: Clarendon Press, 1964), 19, 217–28 (Austin does not think the lines are by Vergil); R. G. Austin, "Virgil, Aeneid 2.567–88," *Classical Quarterly*, n.s. 11 (1961): 185–98; and most recently Rory B. Egan, "A Reading of the Helen-Venus Episode in *Aeneid 2*," *Echos du Monde Classique/*

Classical Views 40, n.s. 15 (1996): 379–95. Egan provides numerous bibliographic references and calls attention to Berres's study as a "major watershed
in the history of scholarship on the subject" (379). For his part, Egan puts forth
a new thesis, arguing for Vergil's authorship: Egan claims that Aeneas, in his
deluded state, thinks he sees Helen ("a simulacrum of Helen," 391) when in
fact he is really looking at Venus, his mother. When Venus speaks to him, he
realizes his mistake and comes to his senses. This is an ingenious, if not
wholly convincing, argument; Egan marshals both linguistic and literary-his-
torical evidence. In terms of the present essay, it should be noted, however,
that I have never come across a similar argument in Renaissance commentaries.

9. See, e.g., such editions as J. P. Valerianus, *P. Virgilii Maronis Opera* (Venice, 1544), 2 vols., facsimile edition (New York: Garland Publishing, 1976),
which includes the older commentators Servius, Donatus, Probus, Mancinel-
lus, Ascensius, Augustinus Dathus, Jacobus Constantius Phanensis, Domitius
Calderinus, and (representing the moderns) Filippo Beroaldo and Angelo Polizi-
ano (see also Valerianus's 1533 edition); Andrea Naugerius, *P. Virgilii Maronis
Opera* (Venice, 1552), with notes by Pietro Bembo in addition to Servius, Donatus, and Pierius; (Lambertus) *Lamberti Hortensii Montfortii Enarrationes in
sex priores libros Aeneidos Vergilianae* (Basel, 1559); (Guellius) *P. Virgilius
Maro, et in eum commentationes, et paralipomena Germani Valentis Guellii*
(Antwerp, 1575), which includes commentary by Joseph Scaliger; Jacobus Pontanus, *Symbolarum Libri XVII Virgilii* (Augsburg, 1599), 3 vols., facsimile edition (New York: Garland Publishing, 1976), with commentators similar to
Valerianus's editions. This is merely a sample list, by no means exhaustive. It
should be noted, moreover, that a complete bibliography of Renaissance editions of Vergil does not yet exist. Giuliano Mambelli's *Gli Annali delle Edizi-
oni Virgiliane* (Florence: Leo S. Olschki, 1954) has significant gaps; scholars
have begun to catalog editions for particular cities and publishers, but no comprehensive work has emerged. More significantly, we have only spotty evidence regarding which editions might have been available and in use in
England during the sixteenth and seventeenth centuries. This is unfortunate
because to assess the direct influence of the commentaries it is imperative that
we try to establish the editions of standard authors that English authors used.

10. Julius Caesar Scaliger, *Poetices Libri Septem* (1561), facsimile edition
(Stuttgart-Bad Cannstatt: Frommann-Holzboog Verlag, 1987), 90 (book 3, section 11).

11. Pontanus, *Symbolarum Libri*, 2:936.

12. Egan, "A Reading," 388.

13. Cf. Williams, *Aeneid*, 1:234 n. 274–75, who cites Milton's passage. He
translates *exuvias* as "trophies."

14. Another somewhat less striking example might be Pontanus's use of the
verb *"superare"* [to overcome] as in "the just man must allow no evil to overcome him." He uses the verb several times in different forms throughout his
comments. We might compare Milton's use of the verb "overcome," especially
where revenge is concerned, as when Satan declares,

> All is not lost, the unconquerable Will,
> And study of revenge, immortal hate,
> And courage never to submit or yield:
> And what is else not to be overcome?

(1.106–9)

Already overcome by the need for revenge in exactly the way Pontanus says the just man never could be, Satan ironically thinks of his revenge plot as a form of resistance to being overcome by God's will.

15. Christopher Marlowe, *The Complete Plays*, ed. J. B. Steane (London: Penguin, 1986).

Theosis and *Paideia* in the Writings of Gregory of Nyssa and the Prelapsarian Books of Milton's *Paradise Lost*

CLAUDE N. STULTING JR.

One of the central ideas in the writings of the Fathers of the early Greek church is that of *theosis*, or the deification of humankind. This idea—that humankind is to find communion with God through assimilation to him, that humankind is to be glorified and become divine itself—finds its *locus classicus* in Athanasius's statement that God became human so that we might become God. "For he [the Word of God] was made man," Athanasius declares, "that we might be made God."[1] Gregory of Nyssa concurs. He holds that the very purpose of the Incarnation, Death, and Resurrection of Jesus is to deify humankind and render it immortal through its union with and participation in the divine nature. "In the suffering of His human nature," Gregory writes, "the Godhead fulfilled the dispensation for our benefit, that all the corruptible may put on incorruption, and all the mortal may put on immortality, our first-fruits having been transformed to the Divine nature by its union with God."[2] Following the Fall, humankind is to be restored to the original divine image in which it was made through being elevated and made partakers of the divine nature. This idea is reiterated throughout Gregory's writings.[3]

But *theosis* is not merely humankind's postlapsarian destiny; it is also humankind's *pre*lapsarian possibility. And as it is with humankind after the Fall, so it is here, too: *theosis* is inherently a dynamic process whose means is a divine *paideia*. Gregory's ideas on this matter can, I think, illuminate our understanding of Milton's prelapsarian Adam and Eve in *Paradise Lost*.

144

THEOSIS IN THE GREEK FATHERS

In *On the Making of Man*, Gregory makes a useful comparison to the natural world to describe humankind's prelapsarian condition:

> [W]e say that in wheat, or in any other grain, the whole form of the plant is potentially included—the leaves, the stalk, the joints, the grain, the beard—and do not say in our account of its nature that any of these things has pre-existence, or comes into being before the others, but that the power abiding in the seed is manifested in a certain natural order, not by any means that another nature is infused into it—in the same way we suppose the human germ to possess the potentiality of its nature, sown with it at the first start of its existence, and that it is unfolded and manifested by a natural sequence as it proceeds to its perfect state, not employing anything external to itself as a stepping-stone to perfection, but itself advancing its own self in due course to the perfect state.[4]

This passage suggests what Gregory believes about the status of prelapsarian humankind, i.e., that at creation humankind was not made perfect and complete, but only *potentially* perfect, not "originally perfect, except in possibility."[5] Gregory says that "in us is the idea or seminal possibility of all good, of all virtue and wisdom."[6] Humankind was created as a participant in the good that is God, but, like the seed of wheat, it possesses full participation only as a prospect.

What Gregory says about the seed of wheat also illustrates the dynamic character of deification. The realization of humankind's *potentia* lies in the exercise of its freedom to bring to completion the fullness of the divine image in which it is made, but given the nature of humankind, this freedom is inherently dynamic. According to Gregory, humankind was created mutable, because, as he explains it, we were brought into being from nonbeing, so we who derive existence from this change of state cannot be free from the movement of change. Change is also that quality that distinguishes humankind from God. The archetype—God—is *being* and thus not subject to change, but the image or the icon of the archetype—humankind—is *becoming* and mutable.[7] Whereas God is immutable and unchangeable, humankind, by virtue of its having been brought into being from nonbeing, is ever subject to change.[8] This dynamic and vital nature of humankind Gregory also considers in *On the Soul and the Resurrection*, in which he compares the nature of the body to a burning flame. Just as a flame ceaselessly changes, ever new and fresh, and never remains the same, so, too, does the human body, which during its life is always increasing or decreasing, moving from one state to another. It is, as Gregory says, "his nature to be always in movement."[9]

The significance of this is that the free realization of human perfection not only has the character of a dynamic process; attaining union with God, for other Greek Fathers as well as for Gregory, is also a *never-ending* process. In a key passage in *On the Making of Man*, Gregory writes that humankind, if it chooses to move toward the good, will "never cease moving onwards to what lies before it," because the "course" of that journey is infinite. The good, the telos, has no boundaries that might be fully grasped; because the good is God, it is infinite and uncircumscribed, and so can never be fully apprehended in a way that would bring an end to one's movement toward it: "Now that which is always in motion, if its progress be to good, will never cease moving onwards to what lies before it, by reason of the infinity of the course to be traversed:—for it will not find any limit of its object such that when it has apprehended it, it will at last cease its motion."[10] Gregory, in describing this dynamism as "a perpetual movement toward a different state," says that "its progress is continual, since there is no conceivable limit to the distance it can go. . . . By reason . . . of its impulse toward change and movement, our nature cannot remain essentially unchanged. Rather does the will drive it toward some end, desire for the good naturally setting it in motion."[11] Gregory speaks here, in *On the Making of Man*, of prelapsarian humankind, which as originally conceived possesses a vocation—to exercise its free will in order to realize in an ever-dynamic process the fullness of the good in which it was made. So, humankind's prelapsarian life is partly gift and partly task: on the one hand, it is constituted by God's creation of humankind in his own image; on the other hand, it is constituted by humankind's dynamic capacity to realize that image in the exercise of its own free will, to more fully share and participate in God's goodness.

But this movement requires what Gregory calls *paideia* [education], a Greek philosophical ideal to which his understanding of *theosis* is closely related. Transforming the classical Greek understanding of *paideia* and making it a distinctly Christian education, Gregory maintains that if the goal of humankind is *theosis*, then the way to this is by means of *paideia*. This is not merely a matter of doctrinal teaching or right belief but of *mor-*

phosis (the gradual development and formation of the entire person and his or her spiritual potentia)l. It is a perpetual and dynamic effort, a lifelong process of achieving perfection. In this way, more is required than the formulation and acknowledgment of correct dogma ("orthodoxy" in the Western Christian sense); it requires right worship ("orthodoxy" in the Eastern Christian sense) and the attainment of a "perfect life based on *theoria* or contemplation of God and on ever more perfect union with him."[12]

Gregory's *On the Inscription of the Psalms* epitomizes his concern for this cultivation of what the Greeks called *arete*. In this work, Gregory arranges the Psalms in five sections that reflect the ascent of the soul to higher and higher levels of participation in God. Such an arrangement, Gregory is convinced, represents the mystical progression of *theognosia* [knowledge of God], but it also coincides with the "steps in the gradual formation *(morphosis)* of the perfect Christian."[13] This is the *metamorphosis* that Paul urges upon his audience: "And be not conformed to this world: but be ye transformed by the renewing of your mind, that ye may prove what is that good, and acceptable, and perfect, will of God" (Rom. 12.2).[14] The various virtues that the soul cultivates during its ascent Gregory compares to the links of a chain and the steps of a ladder.[15]

Just as humankind, the sovereign of creation, brings nature to perfection by means of conferring form upon it, so through a divine *paideia* does God, in cooperation with human freedom, lead humankind to full communion, *theosis*, by means of creating in the individual a new *morphe*, a transfigured form. In Gregory's understanding, the deification of humanity through a divine *paideia* is the fulfillment of its nature and destiny. But this fulfillment is not restricted to humankind; it extends throughout all of creation. In its own deification, humankind sanctifies the whole creation, so that "no part fails to share in the divine fellowship." Deification completes what creation began. "In that way the earthly [is] raised to union with the divine, and a single grace equally extends through all creation."[16]

THE DEIFICATION OF ADAM AND EVE

In Milton's *Paradise Lost*, we find a similar kind of spiritual aspiration for communion with God, which George Santayana describes as "something perfectly Greek."[17] This process is, I want to propose, that of *theosis*. It is Raphael, who in his "onto-logical" speech to Adam, initially spells this out. Raphael says:

> O Adam, one almighty is, from whom
> All things proceed, and *up to him return,*
> If not depraved from good, created all
> Such to *perfection,* one first matter all,
> Indued with various forms, various degrees
> Of substance, and in things that live, of life;
> *But more refined, more spiritous, and pure,*
> *As nearer to him placed or nearer tending*
> *Each in their several active spheres assigned,*
> *Till body up to spirit work,* in bounds
> Proportioned to each kind. So from the root
> Springs lighter the green stalk, from thence the leaves
> More airy, last the bright consummate flower
> Spirits odorous breathes: flowers and their fruit
> Man's nourishment, by gradual scale sublimed
> To vital spirits aspire, to animal,
> To intellectual.
>
> (5.469–85; emphasis mine)[18]

Raphael's discourse clearly articulates Adam's and Eve's prelaps-arian spirituality, and it is one that bears remarkable similarity to how Gregory of Nyssa conceives of it. Milton proclaims, as does Gregory of Nyssa, that Adam and Eve are created primarily for participation in and communion with God; that their telos, in brief, is deification. All things come from God, and they are created to return to him in full participation. God is he "from whom / All things proceed, and up to him return"; God "created all / Such to perfection." Because matter issues from God, it is holy and can return to God; it can be, as Harry F. Robins puts it, "purified until it arrives at that incorporeal state in which it is suited for assimilation into the Heaven of Heavens, and eventu-ally into God."[19] The image of the plant conveys this. From the root of the plant (the heaviest part) comes the green stalk ("lighter"), from which springs the leaves ("more airy"), then, finally, the flower ("bright consummate").

There are at least two dimensions to this image. At one level, it is simply that, i.e., a trope for the progressive development of humankind. The plant "represents" or "stands for" the organic and spiritual growth of the human being, who recapitulates the growth of the plant. At a deeper level, however, the plant's own "transubstantiation" from lower to higher forms becomes the material means for humankind's deification. That is, the plant's own transfiguration, its metamorphosis, as John C. Ulreich Jr. says, "participates in the transformation of the human being, so that the relation of the image to idea is also a relation of part to whole."[20] The flowers and fruit of the plant quite literally become the food and nourishment for the development of humankind's bodily and spiritual potential. So in eating the fruit of the plant, humankind, by "gradual scale" ascends from "vital spirits" to "animal" and then, finally to "intellectual," the source of understanding and reason. From there, as Raphael suggests, humankind, working its way up from body to spirit, may eventually attain the end for which it was created—*theosis:*

> Wonder not then, what God for you saw good
> If I refuse not, but convert, as you,
> To proper substance; time may come when men
> With angels may participate, and find
> No inconvenient diet, nor too light fare:
> And from these corporal nutriments perhaps
> Your bodies may at last turn all to spirit,
> Improved by tract of time, and winged ascend
> Ethereal, as we, or may at choice
> Here or in heavenly paradise dwell.
>
> (5.491–500)

Raphael's speech serves to place the act of eating in the context of Adam and Eve's cosmic destiny: for them deification is to be achieved through eating. They are created for "perfection," and eating is largely (if not exclusively) the sacramental means of realizing that potential.

To be sure, a number of commentators have noted the significance of eating. William Empson remarks that "God expects them to manage to get to heaven, and that what they eat has something to do with it."[21] Mary Irma Corcoran comments, somewhat more hesitantly, that Adam and Eve's "[e]arthly nourishment might be to them the means of bodily immortality and ultimate spiritualization."[22] And more recently, John Rumrich has analyzed the significant role that nutrition plays in the realization of God's will. He contends that if God's will is the formal cause of humankind's destiny, then eating is the "material path through which God's will is accomplished." The consumption of food, he goes on to say, is the means of divine communion, the "motion of creation toward God and apocalyptic glory."[23] All of these comments reflect the thrust of my own argument, but what is lacking in them is a broader historical perspective that would identify the Miltonic dynamic of eating and growth as *theosis*, an idea that, as we have seen, was developed during the fourth century C.E. by Fathers of the Eastern Church such as Gregory of Nyssa.

Alexander Schmemann, a modern Orthodox theologian, draws out the significance of the Greek Fathers on this matter and indirectly sheds light on the dynamic of eating and *theosis* in Milton. According to Schmemann, we find, unwittingly, the primary biblical sense of humankind in Ludwig Feuerbach's materialistic dictum that "Man is what he eats."[24] In the Bible, human beings are created hungry creatures who must eat, creatures for whom the whole world is given food: "Behold, I have given you every herb bearing seed . . . and every tree, in the which is the fruit of a tree yielding seed; to you it shall be for meat" (Gen. 1.29).[25] Humankind eats in order to have life, but eating, as is the case in *Paradise Lost*, is more than a matter of sustaining bodily functions. It is a matter of appropriating the world, literally taking it into one's body, and transforming it into flesh and blood so that all of creation may participate in the divine goodness. The whole world is a banquet table, Schmemann says, and this is the central biblical image for humankind at the beginning, creation, and at the end, the fulfillment of time, "that you may eat and drink at my table in my Kingdom."[26] Of this cosmic banquet, humankind is the priest, the one who eucharistically returns to God the world with which he has been blessed. Humankind, Schmemann writes, "stands in the center of the world and unifies it in his act of blessing God, of both receiving the world from God and offering it to God—and by filling the world with this eucharist, he transforms his life, the one that he receives from the world, into life in God, *into communion with Him*. The world was created as the 'matter,' the material of one all-embracing eucharist, and man was created as the priest of this cosmic sacrament."[27] As priest of the world's banquet, as *homo adorans*, humankind consumes the very material—food—that leads to participation in and communion with the glory of God; in short, it is the means of humankind's deification.

The related themes of eating and *theosis* are perhaps summed up best when Raphael, in narrating to Adam the story of the War in Heaven, speaks of the angels' own repast:

> Forthwith from dance to sweet repast they turn
> Desirous; all in circles as they stood,

> Tables are set, and on a sudden piled
> With angels' food, and rubied nectar flows
> In pearl, in diamond, and massy gold,
> Fruit of delicious vines, the growth of heaven.
> On flowers reposed, and with fresh flowerets crowned,
> They eat, they drink, and in communion sweet
> Quaff immortality and joy.
>
> (5.630–38)

We are reminded here of Raphael's meal with Adam, but nowhere is it more clear that eating, even for angels, is charged with spiritual value. It is that activity that, for Milton's prelapsarian pair, leads to communion with God and the continuation of immortality, just as in the Orthodox Eucharist eating leads to communion with God. Raphael's discourse on eating also creates powerful images of the way in which *all* of nature is transfigured and redeemed by humankind's sacramental relation to the created order. The transfiguration of nature at the physiological level in the realization of *theosis* reiterates in an inward way what Adam and Eve effect outwardly in the exercise of their royal and priestly vocations.

Other passages in *Paradise Lost* indicate that *theosis* is humankind's telos and that Milton's theological vision approximates the patristic doctrine of *theosis*. Adam's response to Raphael's discourse, for example, suggests that deification is the proper end of humankind:

> Well hast thou taught the way that might direct
> Our knowledge, and the scale of nature set
> From centre to circumference, whereon
> In contemplation of created things
> By steps we may ascend to God.
>
> (5.508–12)

The ascent to God by "steps" through the "contemplation" of creation recalls the way in which Gregory of Nyssa articulates the dynamics of *deificatio*. And immediately after the defeat of the rebel angels in Heaven and before the Creation, God muses that he can repair the depopulation of Heaven; in eloquent sacramental tones, he declares that he

> in a moment will create
> Another world, out of one man a race
> Of men innumerable, there to dwell,

> Not here, till by degrees of merit raised
> They open to themselves at length the way
> Up hither, under long obedience tried,
> And earth be changed to heaven, and heaven to earth,
> One kingdom, joy and *union* without end.
>
> (7.154–61; emphasis mine)

Even more explicit is Adam, who relates to Raphael his conversation with God before the creation of Eve. Adam, complaining to God because he has no companion, articulates the reason God needs no partner:

> Thou in thy secrecy although alone,
> Best with thy self accompanied, seek'st not
> Social communication, yet so pleased,
> Canst raise thy creature to what highth thou wilt
> Of *union* or *communion, deified.*
>
> (8.427–31; emphasis mine)

In these passages, the distinctive diction that echoes Greek patristic thought—"union," "communion," "deified"—certainly suggests Milton's theological kinship with Gregory of Nyssa and his conception of deification.

For all of its importance in attaining *theosis*, however, eating is not the *sole* requisite. Milton also makes it abundantly clear that deification is attained by virtue of obedience, especially obedient eating.

> Death is the penalty imposed, beware,
> And govern well thy appetite, lest Sin
> Surprise thee, and her black attendant Death.
>
> (7.545–7)

The fruit of creation is, to be sure, Adam and Eve's "nourishment" that will enable them to transubstantiate body into spirit and ascend to participation in a life of bliss, but this remains a possibility only, as Raphael tells Adam, "If ye be found obedient, and retain / Unalterably firm his love entire / Whose progeny you are" (5.501–3). This, too, is the import of Raphael's statement to Adam that all things are intended to return to God "If not depraved from good." Such obedience, of course, presupposes that humankind possesses the freedom to be obedient. On this Milton is insistent. He repeatedly asserts the freedom of Adam and Eve, and this is an emphasis that runs throughout the poem. "I made him just and right," God pronounces to the Son, "Sufficient to have stood, though free to fall" (3.98–99). Later, God instructs Raphael to inform Adam and Eve of their "happy state, / Happiness in his power left free to will, / Left to his own free will, his will though free, / Yet mutable" (5.234–37). So Raphael warns Adam that "good he made thee, but to persevere / He left it in thy power, ordained thy will / By nature free" (525–27). Significantly, the last matter that Raphael mentions before he departs concerns freedom: "I in thy persevering shall rejoice," he tells Adam, "And all the blest: stand fast; to stand or fall / Free in thine own arbitrament it lies" (8.639–41). Above all else, Adam and Eve's *imago Dei* consists of their free will. This echoes unmistakably the Greek tradition, especially Gregory of Nyssa, who also identifies freedom as that which more than anything else constitutes the image of God.[28]

Not unrelated to the freedom to obey is love. To love, as Raphael says, is tantamount to obedience. "Be strong, live happy, and love, but first of all / Him whom to love is to obey" (8.633–34). So it is that Raphael tells Adam that love is "the scale / By which to heavenly love thou mayest ascend" (591–92). By love, Adam and Eve hold the prospect of attaining participation in divine love itself, that is, of attaining *theosis*. Love, obedience, and eating thus converge as a constellation of themes that define humankind's ultimate end as *theosis*.

The necessity of obedience on the part of Adam and Eve brings us to another Miltonic theme that recalls Gregory of Nyssa. Adam is clearly puzzled by Raphael's statement that he may become deified only "If ye be found obedient." So he inquires about this: "But say, / What meant that caution joined, *If ye be found / Obedient?* (5.512–14; emphasis in the text). And when Raphael responds, "God made thee perfect, not immutable" (524), it becomes clear that obedience is a dynamic process. Inasmuch as free obedience and love are requisite for *theosis*, that, too, is an ongoing project. A fortiori when Raphael describes the gradual ascent from body to spirit—the attainment of union with God—by virtue of eating, it is clear that Adam and Eve's station has an indelibly progressive character.[29] Their perfection is thus not to be construed as a static condition, something fully and inexhaustibly given. Quite the contrary, their prelapsarian perfection is, as it is for Gregory of Nyssa, something they possess only *in potentia*.

This, to be sure, has been extensively noted by many commentators: Merritt Y. Hughes,[30] Arapura Ghevarghese George,[31]

A. Bartlett Giamatti,[32] J. B. Broadbent,[33] Joseph H. Summers,[34] Walter Clyde Curry,[35] J. Martin Evans,[36] Mary Irma Corcoran,[37] Northrop Frye,[38] and Barbara Kiefer Lewalski.[39] Rumrich, in particular, has observed and analyzed more thoroughly than others this dynamic nature of Adam and Eve's ascent to communion with God. Milton, in Rumrich's view, does not stress the Platonic distinction between appearance and reality but rather the Aristotelian distinction between potency and act, the progressive development of matter from chaos into more perfect forms. Substance, which underlies all creatures, does not subsist in a static condition; it is subject to perpetual movement, to a process that can lead either to its disintegration in evil or to the glorification of God. He asserts that Adam and Eve, indeed all creatures, "*must* change in order to participate in the ultimate apotheosis of creatures with God." This change, he maintains, occurs primarily through eating.[40] Rumrich continues:

> Milton's Aristotelian dichotomy between potency and act . . . presumes that change and motion are necessary to a creature's substantial development toward the final perfection of its being. . . . Milton's unorthodox vision of the material community of creation and creator allows [Adam and Eve's] moral and epistemological progress to be accompanied and symbolized by a natural process of aspiration, a nutritional, alchemical process accompanied through the ingestion and assimilation of God's bounty. The perfect communion of the apocalypse represents the final stage of this metamorphic process, in which recognition and desire are finally fulfilled as fully realized creatures unite with the source and object of glory.[41]

Rumrich could well be describing the perspective of a fourth-century Greek Father or of a contemporary Orthodox theologian. His analysis of the dynamic metamorphosis of Milton's creation is extraordinarily insightful. However, neither Rumrich nor the other commentators cited above recognize that Milton's thinking on this matter has rich antecedents in the theological tradition of the Greek Fathers, especially that of Gregory of Nyssa.[42]

This dynamic character of Adam and Eve's obedient eating as the way to their deification constitutes a divine *paideia*. Evans remarks of Adam that he "is serving a kind of spiritual apprenticeship; he is a novice learning to take his place in the order of perfection, not a member of it already. He has first to undergo the preliminary discipline of 'long obedience' " (7.159).[43] That Adam and Eve's deification requires a dynamic growth in obedience indeed defines their experience as a divine *paideia* in the way that Gregory of Nyssa understands it. Just as Adam and Eve provide creation with form, in the same way that they are responsible for the metamorphosis of nature, they themselves undergo a change of form whose goal is *theosis*. If this is for Milton, as for Gregory, humankind's telos, then the way is, again as for Gregory, *paideia*. Such a *paideia* occurs throughout *Paradise Lost*.

Adam and Eve grow in knowledge and perfection through their actively seeking out new experiences and new knowledge; they are the ones who assume the initiative in interpreting their condition. From the moment of their creation, they undertake an educational venture, and in that way they become more complete and perfect. The ways in which this *paideia* is evident are manifold. Following his creation, Adam discovers through reason and discourse with God who he is, his nature and purpose, and he convinces God that he needs a companion (book 8); Eve, following her creation, begins to question who she is, comes to know her proper relationship to Adam, and asks about astronomical matters (book 4); Eve's dream serves to develop both her and Adam's understanding of the nature of evil (book 5); Raphael's visit, of course, explains many matters: the diet of angels (book 5), the ontological structure of the universe (book 5), which in turn explains how they are to grow toward perfection, the War in Heaven (books 5–6), the creation of the world (book 7), astronomical issues (book 8), and the experience of sex (book 8).[44] In all these ways, Adam and Eve learn about the nature of the world so that they may employ their free will appropriately and ascend to communion with God. Milton's emphasis clearly falls upon the formation of Adam and Eve, upon what Gregory calls *morphosis*, the growth of the human personality and its spiritual potential. Lewalski says aptly that for Adam and Eve, life is a "process whereby [they] grow in knowledge and acquire experience within the State of Innocence, and thereby become more steadily complex, more conscious of manifold challenges and difficulties, more aware of larger responsibilities, and by this very process, more complete and more perfect."[45] What Lewalski describes unawares here is the Nyssan ideal of Christian *paideia*. What Milton does is pick up on Gregory's understanding of Christian *paideia*, which concerns the development and formation of the human personality, and apply it to the prelapsarian life of Adam and Eve.[46]

Adam and Eve's destiny is constituted by a dynamic ascent to a progressively fuller communion with and participation in the life of God by a process that for both Milton and Gregory is continual and reaches its fulfillment only in God's cosmic restoration of all of creation, *apocatastasis*. Adam and Eve are to become godlike in a process that summons them to live as the sovereigns and priests of creation, simultaneously transfiguring creation with form, consuming it in obedience, and offering it to God as Eucharist. In this ascent, humankind's "nobler end" (11.605) is, as Milton puts it, with a diction worthy of Gregory of Nyssa or any of the fourth-century Greek Fathers, "conformity divine" (606). Creatures who achieve this end attain "perfection" and are "accomplished" (5.29, 4.660). Creation itself supports this end as the sacrament of God's presence. Even before creation is completed, Milton remarks

> That earth now
> Seemed like to heaven, a seat where gods might dwell,
> Or wander with delight, and love to haunt
> Her sacred shades.
>
> (7.328–31)

The "gods" here referred to need not be understood as angels or some other deities from the heavenly court; they can rightfully be understood as anticipating the presence of Adam and Eve as potentially divine creatures. After creation's completion, Milton writes: "Witness this new-made world, another heaven / From heaven gate not far" (7.617–18). There Adam and Eve are to dwell, worship God, and fulfill their destiny as partakers of the divine nature, along with all of creation.

The resemblance between Gregory of Nyssa's ideas of *paideia* and *theosis* and Milton's description of Adam's and Eve's prelapsarian possibilities has, I think, significant historical ramifications. Werner Jaeger has pointed out that the impact of Gregory of Nyssa's Christianization of Greek *paideia* upon the Latin world is an issue that remains largely "unexplored." And he maintains that the Greeks who emigrated to Italy in 1453 exerted an influence upon the Renaissance in Italy and the rest of Europe that remains an "unsolved problem."[47] In general, Jaeger claims that the lines of influence can be traced from the Renaissance through the Middle Ages back to the "Christian humanism of the fathers of the fourth century and to their idea of man's dignity and of his reformation and rebirth through the Spirit."[48] It is an intriguing possibility that Milton's poetics of deification represent a partial solution to this "unexplored" and "unsolved" Latin transformation of the ideal of divine *paideia* first articulated by Gregory of Nyssa.

NOTES

1. Athanasius, *On the Incarnation*, sec. 54, in *Christology of the Later Fathers*, ed. Edward R. Hardy (Philadelphia: Westminster Press, 1954), 107. Literally, Athanasius's statement reads, "He was humanized that we might be deified."

2. Gregory of Nyssa, *Contra Eunomium*, bk. 2, sec. 13, in *A Select Library of Nicene and Post-Nicene Fathers*, 2d ser., vol. 5, ed. Philip Schaff and Henry Wace (New York: Charles Scribner's Sons, 1890–1900), 127; see also 101, 179.

3. In *On Virginity*, for example, Gregory defines virginity as the cardinal virtue by which humankind attains perfection and becomes assimilated by God. Uniting God and humankind by virtue of the image that they share, virginity is the power that brings God down to humankind and elevates humankind to divinity. Virginity, Gregory writes, "brings God down to a sharing in human life and lifts man up to a desire of heavenly things, becoming a kind of binding force in man's affinity to God" (*Fathers of the Church: A New Translation* [Washington, D.C.: Catholic University of America Press, 1947–], 58:11).

Gregory's *On the Soul and the Resurrection* also speaks of humankind's "union" with the divine and its being "joined to God." When the soul imitates the divine nature, "there is complete assimilation to the divine." And at the time of the Resurrection, the dead will be "transformed into an immortal nature." Through this, God will restore humankind to its original state and achieve his overarching purpose, which is the perfection of all of creation. "For Him," Gregory writes, "the one goal is this, the perfection of the universe through each man individually, the fulfillment of our nature" (*Fathers of the Church*, 58:224, 238, 260, 267).

4. Gregory of Nyssa, *On the Making of Man*, chap. 24, sec. 3, in *A Select Library*, bk. 2, 5:421.

5. William Moore and Henry A. Wilson, "The Life and Writings of Gregory of Nyssa," in *A Select Library*, bk. 2, 5:23.

6. Gregory of Nyssa, *On the Making of Man*, chap. 16, sec. 11, trans. Paulos Gregorios, in *The Human Presence: Ecological Spirituality and the Age of the Spirit* (Warwick, N.Y.: Amity House, 1987), 69. See also *A Select Library*, bk. 2, 5:405.

7. Gregory of Nyssa, *An Address on Religious Instruction*, sec. 21, *Christology*, 297.

8. Gregory of Nyssa, *On the Making of Man*, chap. 16, sec. 12, in *A Select Library*, bk. 2, 5:405.

9. Gregory of Nyssa, *On the Soul and the Resurrection*, in *Fathers of the Church*, 58:263.

10. Gregory of Nyssa, *On the Making of Man*, chap. 21, sec. 2, in *A Select Library*, bk. 2, 5:410–11.

11. Gregory of Nyssa, *An Address on Religious Instruction*, in *Christology*, 298.

12. Werner Jaeger, *Early Christianity and Greek Paideia* (New York: Oxford University Press, 1961), 90.

13. Ibid., 97.

14. All biblical references are to the King James Version and are cited parenthetically in the text. See also 2 Cor. 3.18: "But we all, with open face beholding as in a glass the glory of the Lord, are changed into the same image from glory to glory, even as by the Spirit of the Lord."

15. Jaeger, *Early Christianity*, 86–99. The comparison of humankind's ascent on the links of a chain or the steps of a ladder is especially interesting in light of the rich Renaissance tradition concerning Jacob's ladder. The Renaissance made extensive use of Homer's "golden chain" to articulate the sense of order that pervades the universe and the providence of God over creation. Jacob's ladder came to signify this as well as other things among Protestants. Many endorsed John Chrysostom's interpretation of Jacob's ladder as signifying "the gradual ascent by means of virtue, by which it is possible for us to ascend from earth to heaven, not using material steps, but improvement and correction of manners" (*In Joannem Homilia*, 83:5, in *A Select Library*, bk. 1, 14:312; quoted in C. A. Patrides, *Premises and Motifs in Renaissance Thought and Literature* [Princeton: Princeton University Press, 1982], 31–51, esp. 43–45]. Milton, of course, had recourse to this tradition.

16. Gregory of Nyssa, *An Address on Religious Instruction*, sec. 6, in *Christology*, 279.

17. George Santayana, "The Christian Epic," in *The Life of Reason on the Phases of Human Progress* (New York: Charles Scribner's Sons, 1954), 219. See also George W. Whiting, *Milton and This Pendant World* (Austin: University of Texas Press, 1958), 192–93.

18. John Milton, *Paradise Lost*, ed. Alastair Fowler (London: Longman, 1971). All references to *Paradise Lost* are to this edition and are cited parenthetically in the text.

19. Harry F. Robins, *If This Be Heresy: A Study of Milton and Origen* (Urbana: University of Illinois Press, 1963), 83, 79. Robins compares Milton and Origen and the latter's understanding of "man's ascension to God" and his "intellectual journey toward perfection" through mental discipline (107–8). But Robins is here referring to *Paradise Lost*, 12.575–87, not the "ontological" passage, and so has in mind humankind's postlapsarian spiritual prospects.

20. John C. Ulreich Jr., "Milton on the Eucharist: Some Second Thoughts about Sacramentalism," in *Milton and the Middle Ages*, ed. John Mulryan (Lewisburg, Pa.: Bucknell University Press, 1982) remarks on the symbolic character of the plant imagery: "The growing plant is a symbol, in Coleridge's terms, rather than a mere similitude: it 'partakes of the reality which it renders intelligible' " (42). This is similar to the Eastern Orthodox Christian understanding of symbol. See Alexander Schmemann, *For the Life of the World: Sacraments and Orthodoxy* (Crestwood, N.Y.: St. Vladimir's Seminary Press, 1973), 135–51. I discuss Schmemann in a different context below.

21. William Empson, *Milton's God* (London: Chatto and Windus, 1961), 150.

22. Mary Irma Corcoran, *Milton's Paradise with Reference to the Hexaemeral Background* (Washington, D.C.: Catholic University Press, 1967), 128.

23. John Rumrich, *Matter of Glory: A New Preface to "Paradise Lost"* (Pittsburgh: University of Pittsburgh Press, 1987), 68, 118.

24. Schmemann, *For the Life of the World*, 11.

25. The epic puts it thus:

> He brought thee into this delicious grove,
> This garden, planted with the trees of God,
> Delectable both to behold and taste;
> And freely all their pleasant fruit for food
> Gave thee.

> (7.537–41)

26. Schmemann, *For the Life of the World*, 11.

27. Ibid., 15 (emphasis mine). This recalls the title of Rumrich's book on Milton, *Matter of Glory*, a study that resonates, I think, with the Eastern Orthodox sacramental sense of the world.

28. Another seminal theologian in the Orthodox tradition, John of Damascus, reiterates Nyssa's emphasis on human freedom. See, for example, his *On the Orthodox Faith*. On the importance of freedom in Milton's epic, see also Robins's *If This Be Heresy*, 59, 84–85, 129, 141.

29. Dennis Burden, *The Logical Epic* (London: Routledge and Kegan Paul, 1967), 36.

30. The image of the tree is "an emblem of man's *potential* divinity in obedience to God" (Merritt Y. Hughes, ed., *John Milton: Complete Poems and Major Prose* [New York: Odyssey, 1957], 194; emphasis mine).

31. "Adam's characterization in *Paradise Lost* shows his potentialities of perfection" (Arapura Ghevarghese George, *Milton and the Nature of Man: A Descriptive Study of "Paradise Lost" in Terms of the Concept of Man as the Image of God* [New York: Asia House, 1974], 61).

32. Giamatti suggests that neither the garden nor Adam and Eve is statically perfect; they possess the potential for change, for good or evil (A. Bartlett Giamatti, *The Earthly Paradise and the Renaissance Epic* [Princeton: Princeton University Press, 1966], 299–330).

33. Adam and Eve's "innocence is a moment of potential: it must change: either develop into something richer, or be lost" (J. B. Broadbent, *Some Graver Subject: An Essay on "Paradise Lost"* [London: Chatto and Windus, 1960], 180, 184–85).

34. "And in contrast to our world, fulfillment in Paradise never implies a cessation of motion and action, but continuous and fruitful motion. Each joy of man here perfectly follows the preceding joy and perfectly prepares the ensuing" (Joseph H. Summers, *The Muse's Method: An Introduction to "Paradise Lost"* [Cambridge: Harvard University Press, 1962], 73).

35. Walter Clyde Curry points to the ontological passage as giving Milton's scheme a dynamic character. According to Curry, however, this is a new idea, unlike that found in Duns Scotus and Origen (*Milton's Ontology, Cosmogony, and Physics* [Lexington: University Press of Kentucky, 1957], 170). He suggests that the source of this dynamism lies in Neoplatonic thought (171–73) and observes that in Milton's own time, the Cambridge Platonists, e.g., Henry More and Ralph Cudworth, recognize the idea of a dynamic soul (173–74).

36. "Throughout the poem Milton insists that on this earth perfection cannot be a condition of stability. The perfection of Adam and Eve no less than the perfection of the garden they inhabit is nothing if not conditional, for it requires their constant vigilance to preserve the balance of forces on which it depends. These forces, being natural, are always trying to grow, so they must

be controlled" (J. Martin Evans, *"Paradise Lost" and the Genesis Tradition* [Oxford: Clarendon Press, 1968], 269).

37. "It is an axiom of *Paradise Lost* that man was created for God. To this end, then, all of his physical, mental, and moral powers must tend. However, the movement toward God was to be a matter of growth, of perfection according to each stage of this progress rather than of mystical contemplation enjoyed from the outset." We find not static being but a "growing apprehension of God" (Corcoran, *Milton's Paradise*, 128; see also 89).

38. "[T]he creature moves upward toward its creator by obeying the inner law of its own being, its telos or chief end which is always and on all levels the glorifying of God" (Northrop Frye, *Return of Eden: Five Essays on Milton's Epics* [London: Routledge and Kegan Paul, 1966], 53).

39. "In *Paradise Lost* the Edenic life is radical growth and process, a mode of life steadily increasing in complexity and challenge and difficulty but at the same time and by that very fact, in perfection." In Adam and Eve's prelapsarian experience, life is not static, stable, and uncomplicated. Lewalski, however, like Curry, believes that Milton's conception of the state of innocence is unlike that of traditional theology (Barbara Kiefer Lewalski, "Innocence and Experience in Milton's Eden," in *New Essays on Paradise Lost*, ed. Thomas Kranidas [Berkeley and Los Angeles: University of California Press, 1969], 88, 99–100).

40. Rumrich, *Matter of Glory*, 170; see also 70.

41. Ibid., 83, 53–69. Rumrich is right to stress the dynamic character of humankind's relation to God as a progressive growth in perfection and participation in divine glory. But Rumrich puts too much stock in defining "glory" [*doxa*] as right opinion or knowledge. This constitutes, in his view, true glory for humankind (45, 49, 108–9, 123, 168, 170). *Doxa*, it seems to me, can be understood more fruitfully, especially in light of Rumrich's own analysis, not as "right opinion" but in the way the Eastern Church construes it, as "praise" or "worship." Hence, *orthodoxa* is not "right opinion" but "right praise" or "right worship." The content of humankind's growth in perfection is, therefore, found not in right opinion *about* God but in its right worship *of* God.

Doxa, the subjective aspect of glory as Rumrich describes it, amounts to obedience. For him, that comes first and is essential (139, 144). It seems, however, that it is, as Regina M. Schwartz argues, gratitude that comes first and that establishes the motive for obedience (*Remembering and Repeating: Biblical Creation in "Paradise Lost"* [Cambridge: Cambridge University Press, 1988], 69–74). So the problem in *Paradise Lost* is not, as Rumrich defines it, that obedience and submissiveness come first but that the eucharistic sensibility and the sacramentality of the world are lost for postlapsarian humankind and are not offered by Milton as possibilities for restoration. In any event, even on Rumrich's terms, the obedience required of Adam and Eve by virtue of God's interdiction is not a matter of an arbitrary gauntlet thrown at the feet of the creature to challenge him but a matter of providing *form*—an identity—for him. This identifies the gift aspect of humankind's life.

42. Corcoran, *Milton's Paradise*, 103 n. 21, in reference to *Paradise Lost*, 8.429–31, is the only one I know of who suggests that Milton was familiar with and employed the idea of deification. She describes this as "the elevation of the human soul to a supernatural state," though not as a participation in the essence of God. Remarkably, however, Corcoran cites only Aquinas and Lombard as sources for the idea of deification; she makes no mention at all of the Greek Fathers on this matter.

43. Evans, *"Paradise Lost" and the Genesis Tradition,* 245–46.

44. Lewalski, "Innocence and Experience," 99–116. Lewalski also points to the ways in which Adam and Eve frequently begin with faulty assumptions and false starts and then grow in understanding.

45. Ibid., 116.

46. Robins, *If This Be Heresy,* 152, notes, in citing *Paradise Lost,* 12.561–71, that for postlapsarian Adam and Eve, "the world is a training school in virtue."

It is worthy to note, I think, that my reading of Adam and Eve as engaged in the process of a divine *paideia* is paralleled by Stanley Fish's interpretation of *Paradise Lost* in *Surprised by Sin: The Reader in "Paradise Lost"* (Berkeley and Los Angeles: University of California Press, 1967), i.e., that it is the *reader* who undergoes a similar kind of divine education. It would appear on the surface, at least, that Fish has taken the idea of Greek *paideia* as transformed by Gregory of Nyssa and employed it in a reader-response interpretation of Milton's epic.

47. Jaeger, *Early Christianity,* 99–101.

48. Ibid.

Riding the Hebrew Word Web

PEGGY SAMUELS

As a result of the explosion of Hebrew learning in the sixteenth century, seventeenth-century readers of Hebrew were able to draw readily on the use of lexicons, concordances, and polyglots as they negotiated the Hebrew Bible.[1] These aids to reading record particular ways of thinking about and handling the language. In looking both at the prefatory material that describes the Hebrew language and at the treatment of individual words, we can gather a sense of how readers were working with the language. Written while modern philology was in its formative years, early modern dictionaries of Hebrew sometimes reveal a motivated shaping of the knowledge that was being gathered and transmitted via the dictionaries. Edward Leigh's dictionary, *Critica Sacra. Observations on all the Radices, or Primitive Hebrew words of the Old Testament,* and the more scholarly *Lexicon Hebraicum* of Johannes Buxtorf, demonstrate the labile nature of the meanings of individual Hebrew words and illuminate the ways in which Milton and other seventeenth-century readers widened the meanings of Hebrew words.[2]

According to David Katz, "For most seventeenth-century English language theorists, the very words of Hebrew were divinely significant."[3] Don Cameron Allen writes that "there is no doubt that like most of his contemporaries Milton believed that Hebrew was the original mother tongue."[4] We can glimpse the emotional force behind these beliefs in Brian Walton's preface to the polyglot of 1656.[5] Walton states that God's goodness, so manifest in the world, was demonstrated vividly in his having "poured out on the first men" (145) this divine language. Walton thinks of divine wisdom as having been scattered in other languages because "certain remnants of [Hebrew] are found in all languages" (147). He claims that those long centuries "when the whole earth ha[d] been buried in deep shadows of error" (148) can only be reversed by trying to grasp at these scattered, tiny shards of light located in Hebrew. Walton studied Hebrew lexicons, biblical translations and Targums, hoping to be able to gain access to those "divine mysteries concerning the eternal well-being of humanity, which were established and first passed on in this language" (148). When Walton imagines the reader gaining entrance to the Hebrew language, he says that it is as if one who had always had to view sacred things from a distance was now "admitted into the sanctuary with priests[;] he himself [the one who knows Hebrew] is a witness and a judge of all those things which are going on in the inner rooms" (150). *Areopagitica*'s imagery of gathering the scattered body of truth, like the fragmented pieces of Osiris, is also the image that occurs in the preface to Walton's polyglot, between the covers of which the fragments of Hebrew and of other languages that revealed its meanings were collected.

The collectors of these shards, the lexicographers and translators, were primarily attempting to "clarify" scriptural meaning. With the knowledge of Hebrew, Leigh claims, "how easily . . . might divers knotty places . . . be opened and interpreted. The literall sence of the place is usually to be followed, there cannot be a better helpe for the finding out of that, then skilfullnesse in that tongue wherein the Scripture was first written" (*Critica Sacra*, A7–8). However, beyond clarity, or more accurately, on the way to clarity, scholars found other prominent characteristics of the divine language. If we try to compile the features of this language according to the seventeenth-century commentators, we find that in addition to the "exact meaning of words," the "perfection" of Hebrew involves "purity, elegance, and energy" (Walton, 145). It is mostly the great compression of Hebrew that these men notice; compactness makes the language seem purer, more divine than other tongues. Leigh writes, "The Holy Ghost translateth one Hebrew word by many Greek, to shew what ample wisdome is comprised in the mother tongue" (*Critica Sacra in two parts*, A3). Commentators agree on the impossibility of translating a single Hebrew root by a single Latin equivalent. However, when scholars describe in more detail this compression, they begin to remark not on clarity and exactness of meaning but rather on the multiplicity of meanings. Robert Boyle writes: "Hebrew is the very opposite of a copious language, and the words which compose it being very limited in number, abound in consequence with acceptations [that is, significations] widely different from each other."[6] Describing the way in which Hebrew is built upon the triconsonantal root, Wal-

ton says, "many or most of its words . . . regularly stand upon
three letters . . . and [this triliteral root] has a simple and primary
importance *from which nevertheless, other things are derived
with great elegance"* (149; emphasis mine). That is, Walton
thinks of the Hebrew roots as expressing meaning with brevity
and strength, but when he comes to discuss that meaning, he
ends by admiring the additional meanings that can be derived
from the first. Thus compression and brevity arise because many
meanings are concisely contained in one root. Leigh says that
"one Hebrew root hath sometimes contrary and usually various
significations (*Critica Sacra*, A4). Leigh believes that these "contrary" or "various" significations will give access to truth.[7]
Leigh calls the multiple meanings of the roots the "force" and
"fullness" of the sacred language (*Critica Sacra*, A5). Likewise,
Walton watches "the modulation of words through various conjugations," a process that allows him to see the multiple meanings, or ambiguities, locked inside of a single Hebrew root. This
is the feature of Hebrew that, he says, is lost in translation and
that can best be shown in a lexicon. "Ambiguity cannot always
be shown through translation: hence, a meaning passed on [in
the translations now available] is not complete, but defective,
while perhaps each of the two meanings is saved in Hebrew"
(151).

I will return to Walton's phrase "modulation through various
conjugations," but first let us look at a simple example of several
meanings inhering in one root. The word *nachash* is recorded by
both Buxtorf and Leigh to have two meanings: the noun "serpent" and the verb "to search diligently, to search over curi-
ously." The word can refer to practicing divination or augury,
reading omens, learning secret things, and the gathering of
knowledge by unauthorized means. In *Paradise Lost*, we find
Milton emphasizing the theme "search" when he is describing
Satan. After his first view of the human pair, Satan announces,
"I must walk round / This Garden, and no corner leave unspi'd"
(4.528–29).[8] He is described by Gabriel as "A Spirit, zealous, as
he seemd, to know" (565). And, later, in book 9, "the Orb [Satan]
roam'd / With narrow search; and with inspection deep / Consider'd every Creature" (82–84). Having chosen the serpent, in
order to locate him, Satan continues to "prie / in every Bush and
Brake" (159–60). And, "Like a black mist low creeping, he held
on / His midnight search" (180–81). In addition, Milton's Satan
is associated with searching by chance and by signs. For example, he announces to Sin that he will "search with wandring

quest a place foretold / Should be, and, by concurring signs, ere now / Created" (2.830–32).

Milton is interested in thematizing legitimate and illegitimate means of acquiring knowledge, so we needn't be surprised to find Satan associated with searching for knowledge illegitimately or for illegitimate purposes. Yet, these characterizations of Satan as intensively searching and relying on chance or signs are in addition to the expected thematic association, in the conversation with Eve, of offering immediate access to wisdom of the gods by eating the fruit. The working out of, or dilation of, the theme of overly curious searching may be thought of as Milton's bringing into the view of his English-reading public—that is, "translating" as fully as possible—the multiple meanings contained in a single Hebrew word. The lexicographers use the phrase "to open a word" when they are elucidating its meanings. To "open" a word is to gain entrance to its meanings, as if each word is a door, leading to a new conceptual stream. This view of the Hebrew language can contribute to Milton's sense that he is "opening" rather than adding to Scripture. A full, complete reading or rendering of Scripture would have to include these links between "serpent," "overly curious searching," and "searching by augury."

Some of these multiple meanings, particularly the ones that are based on etymological (often false etymological) connections, are familiar to us because the Bible mentions them when speaking about the name of a child or a place. For example, Renaissance dictionaries follow the biblical text in making an etymological connection between Moses (in Hebrew, *Mosheh*) and the verb "to draw out" [*mashah*]. Of the many ways that Milton conceptualized himself as a kind of Moses, one of the most powerful nodes of identification may have been through this false etymology of the one who "draws out"—not just the one who was drawn out of the water but the one who draws out water from the rock. Milton describes the poet's work as making "the sense variously drawn out from one Verse into another" (250) in his note on "The Verse" of *Paradise Lost* preceding the lines at the opening of the epic when he equates himself with Moses. For a Renaissance reader of Hebrew, within the word *Moses* resides the additional resonance of one who draws out.

Often, the occurrence of two meanings within a single Hebrew root arises from the feature that Walton calls "the modulation through various conjugations." He uses the phrase to describe what he is watching as he is studying the meaning of

Hebrew words. He is referring to the way that the verbal system
in Hebrew depends on varying the form of a verb in order to convey sometimes intensified, sometimes additional meanings. To
give a simple example, the word *naga'* [to touch] has also the
intensified meaning of "to strike" when it moves through what
Walton calls another "conjugation."[9] And, in the passive, *naga'*
denotes "to be stricken," as in defeated in battle, or struck (by
the plague), or (of fate) to befall. "Touch," "harm," "strike," "to
be defeated," "to be stricken (with the plague or fate)": the language feels like a series of palimpsests in which one word has
other words above and below it. Or, as an alternative image, one
can think of it as overtones on a flute in which one can hear the
meanings hovering over (or under) the meaning that is invoked.

To turn to an example that also occurs as a thematic strand
in *Paradise Lost*, the verbs "to place" and "to rest" are actually
different forms of the same root (*noach*). In *Paradise Lost*, Satan
cannot have found a true place for himself because he is unable
to rest. Adam and Eve lose their place as they lose their ability
to find repose. Certainly these thematic links have a long history in Christian tradition and literature. They also have an ele-
mental relationship to one another in the verbal system of the
Hebrew language. It would be difficult for someone learning Hebrew (not necessarily a native speaker of Hebrew) to forget
"rest" [*noach*] as he/she reads "and he placed him" [*yanichahu*].
So as God "places" man in the Garden of Eden to work it [*avdah*]
and watch over it [*shamarah*], the idea of "rest" is inside, or resonates within, the verb "to place," intensifying the sense that one
can be at work (placed there to serve and to watch over) while
simultaneously being at rest. Milton's construction of an Eden
in which human labor never seems to counteract the feeling of
repose surely has cultural causes, yet the Hebrew language provides a grounding from which such a cultural construction can
both find confirmation and unfold.

In many cases the "modulation of conjugations" gives an opposite signification to the verb ("touch"/"strike," for example).
So, rather than seeming as though there are multiple meanings
residing within one word, each use of the word exists as an alternative to absent but hovering potential uses. Such a feature im-
pels a continuous comparative move in the reader.[10] Each use of
a word recalls its former use, in another verse, and sets up a comparison between the two contexts. For example, the word
"send" [*shalach*] is used for "to send a messenger" or, with an
increased sense of honor, "to send on a mission" or "to send off"

as in escorting part way; in the next conjugation, however, the meaning alters, becoming "send away," "dismiss," "cast out." In *Paradise Lost*, Milton uses the full range of meanings for the verb. He deploys its forms when describing the satanic crew "sent" (cast out) from Heaven (1.750), angels "sent" (as messengers) to the garden (7.72), Christ "sent" as Judge and Savior (10.209), and Adam and Eve "sent" out of the garden (11.261). Milton needs to have one English word bear this range of oppositional meanings (even if he sometimes also uses the words "cast out") in order to create a correlative to the way the Hebrew word holds within itself a comparison of different kinds of "sending." By repeating the word in different contexts, Milton can lead his reader simultaneously to hold onto the different contexts for the word's use. To hold in one's mind the extremes of this range ("to cast out," "to send on a divine mission") has an impact on the resonance of Milton's final use of the word as Adam and Eve are sent out of the garden. That moment of leave-taking, then, hovers between the sense of "expelled" and "sent out as if destined" (as messenger or angel or Christ is sent out to perform a mission). Adam and Eve's experience of being sent out of the garden is held in tension between all of the meanings "sent" has acquired during the poem.

This weblike effect, in which any one meaning of a word stands in tension with other uses of the same word, is accentuated by the experience of reading the Bible in Hebrew. A Renaissance reader of the Hebrew Bible was able to establish the meaning of a word primarily by encountering it in scriptural context after scriptural context. The Hebrew lexicons provided a shortened, intensified, and selective experience of that kind of sequence of contexts. Reading the entry for a word in a Renaissance Hebrew lexicon was like moving, as in a concordance, from one scriptural context to another. The words are used in such a variety of contexts that it becomes clear that the meaning of the word can only be understood by studying, much as Quentin Skinner argues, "the circumstances in which the word can properly be used to designate particular actions or states of affairs."[11] The whole method of *Paradise Lost*, in which Milton plays a word or a concept over and over in varying contexts, allowing the word to be used with such wildly varying intents and meanings, and frequently causing the word to turn into its opposite, is a use of language that closely resembles the reading of the Bible in Hebrew, especially as it was facilitated by lexicons and concordances. In *Paradise Lost*, Milton creates a range of meanings for a single word (trying it out, as it were, in a range of circumstances) and so clarifying (and implicitly evaluating) its uses.[12]

Thus, if we are to conceive of Milton's relationship to the Bible as a "gathering of places,"[13] we will need to attend to the repetition of Hebrew words, sometimes widely scattered in the text, as a possible tool for Milton's determining which verses were to be "gathered" together. The lexicographers provide a picture of such "gathering" because they cite scriptural verses as they seek to trace the various uses of a word. Through this process, single words sometimes widen in meaning to take on the connotations of the scriptural verses in which they appear.

For example, the verb "to turn" [panah] and the noun "face" [panim] share the same root. So, as in the example of "serpent"/ "overly curious searching," we have an association between a verb and a noun—"turn" and "face." While the more scholarly Buxtorf defines panah first as "he turned," Leigh quickly establishes the association between the noun and the verb by defining panah as "he turned his face." He defines the word using scriptural citations as reference points: "He turned his face, he turned himself, he has been turned from one thing to another, he reversed, he has been turned towards something, by turning himself towards something he saw, he turned towards it, he looked at it again, he inspected it, he inclined, he declined, he returned, Jer. 6.4. [In the next conjugation, the meaning becomes] by clearing obstacles, by cleaning filth and by evacuating from sight, he removed, he purged, he evacuated, drove out, prepared, Gen. 24.31. Ps. 80.10" (190). In his entry for panah, Buxtorf includes another construction, "when the evening approached" (literally at the "turn" of evening) and "when it approached early in the morning" (literally, at the "turn" of morning). For this construction, Buxtorf cites Gen. 24.63, when Isaac, at the "turn" of evening, walks into the fields and, lifting up his eyes, sees camels coming; his wife-to-be, Rebekkah, is arriving. She, for her part, slips off her camel and asks the servant, "What man is this that walketh in the field to meet us?" (Gen. 24.64–65).[14] There is a sense of an implicit (but not actually spoken in the text) face-to-face encounter (as both lift up their eyes to see one another but Rebekkah veils herself as soon as she learns who the man is). In the next conjugation, when the word denotes "purge," Leigh cites Gen. 24.31 (Laban clearing the house in order to receive the servant of Isaac and the camels that came with him). Buxtorf instead emphasizes the sense of "prepared" and cites Mal. 3.1 ("he has prepared the way before me").

From the list of denotations, one can see first that a thematic cluster can potentially form (turn, return, face, purge, prepare). The full resonance of the thematic cluster, however, comes from the biblical contexts in which the terms appear: for example, not just turning one's face, but an emotional moment of encountering a human face (Isaac meeting—almost—Rebekkah) or not simply a purging but a purging that prepares the way for the entrance of a divine being (Malachi's messenger preparing the way for the Lord's coming). A marginal note in Leigh's dictionary shows his formation of a thematic cluster that draws on scriptural verses. He draws on his citation of Ps. 80.10 (in which God *clears* a place for the vine of Israel to grow) and Jer. 6.4 (in which *at the decline of day,* the destruction of Israel is imminent; emphasis mine). These two scriptural contexts of imminent destruction and God's assistance establish the ground for Leigh's marginal comment linking *panah* to "paean," which he defines as "a song or hymn praying for the ceasing of a plague or war, nay for the preventing of apparent hurt." To clinch his case, he then links the frequent psalm genre, praying for God to turn his face upon Israel, to "paean," using the similarity between *panah* and "paean" to forge this synthesis of bliblical and classical literary forms.

Milton also creates a thematic cluster drawn from these definitions and citations. In the proem to book 3, the poet returns to the Muse, who does not return to or turn toward ("revisit") the poet's seemingly upturned face (21). The moment of the "turn" of the day is fully imagined as a time of glimpsing a human face, a moment that has reverberations of meeting the divine: "Seasons return, but not to me returns / Day, or the sweet approach of Ev'n or Morn, / Or sight of vernal bloom . . . or human face divine" (41–44). Finally, the poet links these themes to purging and preparation: he prays that the "Celestial light . . . all mist from thence / Purge and disperse" (51–53). The purging serves as preparation for the poet to "see and tell" (54). As he writes his paean, Milton appears to be calling on these contexts, associating the "turn" of evening and morning, the highly charged nonglimpse of a human face as a divinelike experience, and the purging or preparing for another return of the divine.

I have not reported all the scriptural citations that occur in the definitions of these words but have focused only on those citations that might have contributed to Milton's thematic cluster

in the proem. *Panah* and *panim* are far too common in Hebrew
Scripture for any two readers to "gather" the same verses when
working with the root. Yet, the process of working on that root,
or reading the dictionary, sets up many potential verses to be
gathered. Any one reader will focus on different associations between meanings and gather different verses. The lexicons provide a selection of verses that have been gathered and sometimes
reveal the lexicographer creating thematic associations among
the range of meanings inside the root.

In some cases the Latin terms chosen to translate the Hebrew
set up associations between two verses of the Bible. For example, the term *rafak* occurs only once in the Bible, in the Song of
Solomon: "Who is this cometh up from the wilderness, leaning
[*rafak*] upon her beloved?" (8.5). It is likely that any reader
would have to use the dictionary (or turn to a Latin or vernacular
Bible) to figure out this word. Buxtorf and Leigh use the Latin
term *adhaerere* in their definitions, and Leigh uses the English
"cleave" in the margin. Both choices would bring the reader to
Gen. 2.24 ("Therefore shall a man leave his father and his
mother, and shall cleave unto his wife"), where the Vulgate uses
adhaerebit and the King James "cleave" to describe the relation
between man and woman after the woman's creation. Thus the
term "leaning," with its eroticized connotative context taken
from the moment of "leaning" in Song of Sol. 8.5, would provide
a gloss for the "cleaving" in Gen. 2.24. Milton uses the term
"leand" in such an eroticized context to describe Adam and Eve
after Eve tells of her coming up from the lake shortly after her
creation: Eve "with eyes / Of conjugal attraction unreprov'd, /
And meek surrender, half imbracing leand / On our first Father"
(4.492–95).

Certainly, the seventeenth-century religious concerns of Milton or Leigh would partly direct which associations would be
made or emphasized when working on Hebrew words.[15] For example, while listing the various definitions of "send" [*shalach*],
Leigh is clearly most struck by the word's use in God's sending
Christ to man. He notes that the word harbors "a rich, weighty,
precious importance, To design or destine, to install or conse-
crate, to give commission for some great office" (253). And, he
sees the word *noach* as apt in combining the meanings of "comfort" or "rest" and "repentance" because "the only true comfort
comes from true repentance." This is not a connection that
twentieth-century philologists would accept, but it is important
to Leigh. As the two huge webs of language came into contact,

as Hebrew was translated into Latin, and a possible dispersal of meaning threatened to occur (since any one Hebrew word could and did lead to many Latin words), the Christian theological concerns acted as a stabilizing grid. Of the many possible meanings that could ensue when the dictionary maker began to define a Hebrew word, the attentiveness to the potential effect on interpreting difficult scriptural passages, or the potential for "proving" that some already-known Christian truth was herein expressed with utmost brevity and strength, would act as a brake.

Nevertheless, the Hebraic material is not merely being Christianized. In fact, Leigh makes one more association between "purge" and "face" without applying a Christian concept to the Hebrew words but rather by drawing out of the words a seemingly new concept. Leigh links "purge" and "face" by claiming, "The Hebrew word signifies to effect, as the natural face of something with obstacles removed, comes into sight." That is, in linking the two meanings of the root, Leigh generates the idea of clearing away obstacles so that the natural face of a thing can be seen. So, too, any individual reader of the Renaissance Hebrew lexicons would not only have closed down the dispersal of meaning by applying an already-composed Christian grid but also would have looked for Christian concepts to be enriched or transformed by the new thematic connections revealed in studying Hebrew. As Matthew Poole demonstrates in his preface to the reader, new derivations will give rise to new concepts. Adam, he tells us, is not to be derived from 'adamah [ground] as it has traditionally been thought but rather from a root that signifies "beauty" or "to be beautiful."[16] Here, two concepts, "Adam" and "beautiful," are set in relationship to one another, which previous to the work of the lexicographers would not have been considered to be intimate acquaintances. So, too, "leaned" and "cleaved" bring together Adam and Eve with the lovers in Song of Solomon.

In working on a particularly difficult Hebrew word, commentators, translators, and lexicographers would employ all of the aforementioned methods: the links between nouns and verbs via a common root (serpent/overly curious searching), the modulation of conjugations (send/cast), and thematic clusters derived from scriptural citations that share the same root (face/return/turn of evening/purge/prepare). One of the notoriously difficult terms on which commentators deployed their skills was *ezer cnegdo*, which the King James translated by "help meet for him" (Gen. 2.18). In *Tetrachordon*, Milton says that God "contents not himself to say, I will make him a wife, but resolving to give us first the meaning before the name of a wife, saith graciously, *"I will make him a help meet [ezer cnegdo] for him"* (2:599).[17] That is, Milton declares that the "meaning" of "wife" resides in this term. He suggests that it demonstrates the "fullness" of Hebrew when he writes, "the originall heer is more expressive then other languages word for word can render it" (2:600).[18] We can get some sense of the fullness of the term by looking at the compilation of comments about it in Poole's *Synopsis Criticorum*.[19]

The word *cnegdo* can be taken as qualifying the noun "helper," so the commentators are primarily working to determine what kind of helper is denoted in *cnegdo*, which grammatically falls into three parts:

1. *c* = a preposition usually denoting like or according to.[20]
2. *neged* = in front of (facing, opposite), against, contrary.
3. *o* = him (third person masculine pronominal suffix).

Putting the parts together, one can imagine a meaning that has the woman as likeness facing (or standing opposite to) Adam. Such a sense of the word occurs in some of the many, variegated interpretations that Poole collects and which I list below:

(a) *cnegdo* conveys likeness (" 'c' is a note of likeness").
(b) *cnegdo* conveys equality of stature in a conflictual relationship ("from his opposite, he responds"). Poole cites 1 Sam. 17.4 and gives a quotation from another source ("Princes do not fight except with princes").
(c) *cnegdo* conveys closeness ("near to his face, next to him"). This idea of "closeness" is then qualified in various ways: in his possession; always close so that she may listen; close so that she may act as a substitute or help, acting like a fulcrum so that a burden is halved.
(d) *cnegdo* conveys presence. The Latin term used in the translation, *"coram,"* takes on the Roman significance of a client present at the patron's house, standing before him and ready to minister to the patron. Poole cites Dan. 1.5, Ezek. 44.11, 1 Sam. 29.8, and 1 Kings 10.8.
(e) *cnegdo* conveys throwing oneself before him, in a pleading posture. Poole cites 2 Kings 1.13.

(f) *cnegdo* conveys sexual intercourse ("a woman who will re-
cline in front of him"). This interpretation comes from
false etymological connections to an Arabic word.

(g) *cnegdo* conveys a true help. Poole cites Fagius ("I will act
as aid to the man, not empty, but true, certain and solid, as
it is done truly face to face").

(h) *cnegdo* conveys the joining of two like selves ("another
self, a similar nature, conjoined in love; of the same nature,
and soul and will, customs and habits"). Poole cites the
Septuagint's Greek translation here.

(i) *cnegdo* conveys a mirror relation or a relation of image or
formal likeness of the self ("face to face, or against, or from
in front of him, or in answer to him . . . close to what corresponds to him. Himself, although [really] another self, con-
cordant in shape and form"). At this point, Poole quotes
another Hebrew construction that means "one like him,
standing in front of him" and pronounces that *cnegdo* conveys that meaning more "elegantly."

The sheer variety of interpretations and emphases reveal both
the difficulty of defining the term and the way that interpreters,
while translating, cite scriptural verses and thereby transport additional concepts inside the word. In (b), the citation of 1 Sam.
17.4 (Israel lined up opposite the Philistines, ready for war) casts
an aura of equals battling, which is then reinforced by the quotation "Princes do not fight except with princes." In (d), the citations of Daniel, Ezekiel, Samuel, and Kings all suggest that the
woman's standing in front of the man conveys a readiness to
serve. In (e), the citation of 2 Kings 1.13 releases a theme of
pleading (as well as an offer to serve). In (f), the reference to etymological connections to an Arabic word recasts the denotations as primarily referring to coitus.

Milton's depiction of Adam and Eve includes many of the aspects of the man/woman relationship that commentators found
in the "fullness" of *ezer cnegdo*. The poem plays out the implications of being in the other's presence (and leaving that presence), reclining, ministering, listening, and responding to/
battling one of equal (comparative to other creatures) status. The
idea of the couple standing in a mirroring relationship to one another, in which the woman is both the image of the man and
uses him as a substitute mirror, engaged Milton's interest in *Paradise Lost*. The Hebrew literally suggests a likeness standing in
front of him, whereas the Vulgate [*adjutorium simile sibi*] con-

tains the idea of likeness without necessarily implying a standing before or in front of or against. Thus the Hebrew suggests
standing in front of a mirror-image of the self, and this theme is
accentuated at the end of the list [item (i)]. Although Poole cites
Rivetus for this view, Buxtorf, too, included it in almost exactly
the same words as part of his definition of the word *neged*. This
is not to say that Milton's, or the seventeenth century's, concept
of husband and wife serving as mirrors for one another derives
from the study of this Hebrew word. The sources for such a
theme are multiple, just as the uses of the theme are multiple.
Yet, for those translators or commentators who either generated
or chose to find convincing the definition of *cnegdo* as the self
facing a likeness, the Hebrew word could function as validating
the cultural concept. It could also prompt certain avenues of thematic development in *Paradise Lost*. The characterization of
Eve as image of Adam ("hee / Whose image thou art" [4.471–72])
does not have a biblical source outside of the word *cnegdo*.
Adam concurs in this characterization: "Best Image of my self
and dearer half, / The trouble of thy thoughts this night in sleep /
Affects me equally" (5.95–97). The Narcissus myth certainly
serves as substratum of the scene in which Eve reflects on her
mirror image in the water, but so does that single, tantalizing,
obscure word *cnegdo* that readers found mysteriously, darkly
shadowing the word "helper" in Genesis.

Poole's collection of commentaries can serve only as a hint of
the kinds of fullness Milton and his contemporaries found in a
Hebrew word that was both a significant term (promising to contain God's intentions for the relation between man and woman)
and one that was notoriously difficult to translate. *Doctrine and
Discipline of Divorce* provides evidence that Milton used the
"modulation of conjugations" to unpack the compact word
cnegdo. In his entry on *neged*, Leigh related the root to the verb
higid (to speak). It is this connection that Milton appears to have
grasped when he declares that the wife should be a "speaking
help" (2:251). Milton is translating *ezer cnegdo* as "a speaking
help" because of the root, *ngd*, (in hiphil construction, "speak"),
which is, as it were, hidden inside the term *cnegdo*. Milton's attribution of the adjective "speaking" to the noun "helper" aptly
demonstrates that links between words, links established by the
Hebrew roots, enabled an associational fluidity for concepts in
English. While a term that was as difficult to discern as *ezer
cnegdo* became a site upon which commentators and translators
could project their own cultural concerns and beliefs, the He-

brew triconsonantal root system served as a pathway by which those concerns could both formulate themselves and *re*formulate themselves *differently*. The Hebrew word, with its web of meanings gathered from etymology, conjugations, and scriptural contexts, shakes up or reconfigures the relations between words and concepts in English. Milton certainly believed that all doctrinal points were easily enough understood through vernacular translations of the Bible ("Therefore are the Scriptures translated into every vulgar tongue, as being held in main matters of belief and salvation, plane and easie to the poorest" [7:302]). But to render the fullness of the Hebrew into English required a means of opening and presenting the rich web of associations locked inside the Hebrew roots.

NOTES

1. See Moshe Goshen-Gottstein, "Foundations of Biblical Philology," in *Jewish Thought in the Seventeenth Century*, ed. Isadore Twersky and Bernard Septimus (Cambridge: Harvard University Center for Jewish Studies, 1987). For Hebrew learning in sixteenth-century England, see G. Lloyd Jones, *The Discovery of Hebrew in Tudor England: A Third Language* (Manchester: Manchester University Press, 1983).

2. Edward Leigh, *Critica Sacra. Observations on all the Radices, or Primitive Hebrew words of the Old Testament in order Alphabetical . . .* (London, 1642), hereafter designated *Critica Sacra; Critica Sacra in two parts: the first containing Observations on all the radices, or primitive Hebrew words of the Old Testament . . .*, 3rd ed. (London, 1662), hereafter designated *Critica Sacra in two parts;* Johannes Buxtorf, *Lexicon Hebraicum* (London, 1646). All references to these works are to these editions and are cited parenthetically in the text. All references to words in Leigh's dictionary are to the 1662 edition, *Critica Sacra in two parts*. Definitions in these dictionaries are s. v. On Buxtorf's dictionary, see Stephen G. Burnett, *From Christian Hebraism to Jewish Studies: Johannes Buxtorf, 1564–1629, and Hebrew Learning in the Seventeenth Century*, Studies in the History of Christian Thought, vol. 68 (Leiden, Netherlands: E. J. Brill, 1996), 120–33.

3. David Katz, *Philo-semitism and the Readmission of the Jews to England, 1603–1655* (Oxford: Clarendon Press, 1982), 71.

4. Don Cameron Allen, "Some Theories of the Growth and Origin of Language in Milton's Age," *Philological Quarterly* 28 (1949): 5.

5. Brian Walton, *In Biblia Polyglotta Prolegomena*, ed. Frances Wrangham (Cambridge: J. Smith, 1828); all references to this work are to this edition and are cited parenthetically in the text.

6. Robert Boyle, *Some Considerations on the Style of the Holy Scriptures*, trans. Rev. P. Panter (London: C. and J. Rivington, 1825), 19.

7. Attention to multiple meanings of the roots provides one means of access to the "compound sense" of Scripture; see Hugh MacCallum, "Milton and Figurative Interpretation of the Bible," *University of Toronto Quarterly* 31

(1962): 397–415, for the argument that Protestant interpreters, including Milton, retained an idea of "compound sense" even while asserting their belief in the literal, plain sense of Scripture.

8. John Milton, *Paradise Lost*, in *The Complete Poetry of John Milton*, ed. John T. Shawcross, rev. ed. (New York: Doubleday, 1971). All references to Milton's poetry are to this edition and are cited parenthetically in the text.

9. Renaissance grammarians often used grammatical terms based on Latin to describe the structure of Hebrew. I will be following their usage of the term "conjugation" rather than the terms used by twentieth-century grammarians. The definitions for *naga'* are taken from Francis Brown, S. R. Driver, and Charles A. Briggs, *A Hebrew and English Lexicon of the Old Testament* (1907; reprint, Oxford: Clarendon Press, 1951).

10. Rabbinic commentary often discusses these plays on words. More recently, Martin Buber and Franz Rosenzweig, *Scripture and Translation*, trans. Lawrence Rosenwald with Everett Fox (Bloomington: Indiana University Press, 1994), as well as Everett Fox, "Translator's Preface," *The Five Books of Moses* (New York: Schocken Books, 1995), have conceived of the Bible as structured by such word relationships. Other recent literary critics of the Bible have used these word relationships when working on biblical texts; see for example, J. P. Fokkelman, "Genesis 37 and 38 at the Interface of Structural Analysis and Hermeneutics," in *Literary Structure and Rhetorical Strategies in the Hebrew Bible*, ed. L. J. de Regt, J. de Waard and J. P. Fokkelman (Assen, Netherlands: Eisenbrauns, 1996), 152–87.

11. Quentin Skinner, "Language and Social Change," in *Meaning and Context: Quentin Skinner and his Critics*, ed. James Tully (Princeton: Princeton University Press, 1988), 122.

12. My explanation is not meant to replace others that are equally true. Sharon Achinstein, *Milton and the Revolutionary Reader* (Princeton: Princeton University Press, 1994), 117–223, has discussed the strategies for problematizing representation and reference in *Paradise Lost*, attributing them to Milton's desire to educate the audience to make sound judgments in the emerging public sphere.

13. Dayton Haskin, *Milton's Burden of Interpretation* (Philadelphia: University of Pennsylvania Press, 1994), has taught us to see Milton's primary mode of biblical hermeneutics as the laborious comparing or "gathering" of scriptural fragments.

14. All biblical references are to the King James Version and are cited parenthetically in the text.

15. Jerome Friedman, *The Most Ancient Testimony: Sixteenth-Century Christian Hebraica in the Age of Renaissance Nostalgia* (Athens, Ohio: Ohio University Press, 1983), covers the range of Christian approaches to the study of Hebrew (see especially, 125–35).

16. Matthew Poole, preface to *Synopsis Criticorum, aliorumque sacrae scripturae interpretum ac commentatorum adornata* (Frankfurt am Main: B. C. Wustii, 1694), n.p.

17. John Milton, *Tetrachordon*, in *Complete Prose Works of John Milton*, 8 vols., ed. Don M. Wolfe et al. (New Haven: Yale University Press, 1953–82). All references to Milton's prose are to this edition and are cited parenthetically in the text.

18. See Michael Lieb, "Adam's Story: Testimony and Transition in *Paradise Lost*," in the present collection, 21–47.

19. Poole, *Synopsis Criticorum*, 25. Translations of quotations from this work are cited parenthetically in the text. For their able assistance in translating from the Latin of Poole, Buxtorf, and Walton, I would like to thank Gloria Rojas and Dennis McManus.

20. The parts of the word have more complex definitions than my brief summary here can accommodate.

When Worlds Collide: The Central Naturalistic Narrative and the Allegorical Dimension to *Paradise Lost*

SARAH R. MORRISON

Addison and Johnson very early faulted Milton for his handling of "such airy beings" as Sin and Death in his epic,[1] and generations of readers have followed them in expressing distaste for the clashing of two seemingly incompatible narrative planes in those scenes that have the profound psychological portrait that is Satan conversing with—and, in one instance, almost coming to blows with—personified abstractions. As Kenneth Borris observes, the "allegorical aspect of *Paradise Lost* has embarrassed many subsequent Miltonists who have ignored or sought to restrict or deny it."[2] There is considerable disagreement about the precise nature and extent of the allegory Milton employs in his grand epic. Critics continue to haggle over issues of decorum, genre, intentionality, and narrative authority raised by Milton's use of allegory in *Paradise Lost*.[3]

Why are the allegorical elements in Milton's epic so disturbing to so many readers? Many modern readers, of course, simply dislike allegory and react negatively to blatantly allegorical representations. Some critics, aware that in the seventeenth century allegory was increasingly viewed, in Gordon Teskey's words, "as an empty and tedious game,"[4] have difficulty reconciling the dualistic philosophical implications of its use with other elements in the poem. The central, naturalistic narrative of *Paradise Lost* would seem to validate experiential reality and, in keeping with Milton's Christian materialism, attempts to join almost seamlessly the physical realm and the spiritual. Allegory by its very nature posits a higher reality and reduces physical representation to the symbolic. And it seems reasonable to assume that Milton—even if he did not actually share his contemporaries' disenchantment with allegory—was aware of the

178

problematic philosophical implications of its use. But Milton's use of allegory in *Paradise Lost* is troubling to even unsophisticated or casual readers for yet another reason. Because the purely allegorical figures of Sin, Death, and Chaos intrude boldly into the naturalistic plane of *Paradise Lost*, are ascribed physical agency, and interact directly with Satan, who is regularly viewed as the most vital and dynamic character in the naturalistic narrative, the literal truth of the narrative is, if only indirectly and by implication, called into question. The range of critical opinion is great, but the general assumption seems to be that Milton could not have desired this.

Teskey, taking an extreme stance, argues, "[t]o avoid the subordination of a literal narrative to its figurative meaning, Milton refuses allegory."[5] Although Stephen M. Fallon agrees with Teskey that Milton views allegory as suspect, Fallon sees allegory as operating importantly in *Paradise Lost*. But for him, allegory in *Paradise Lost* is always carefully contained and purely parodic, meant to further diminish Satan and thus to underscore the Augustinian conception of evil as negation and vacuity. "Milton's genius," he claims, "is to have reserved allegory, the reality of whose characters was more than suspect, for [the] non-beings" Sin and Death.[6] More recently, critics have argued that Milton's use of allegory in *Paradise Lost* is both extensive and highly original. Borris insists, "[a]voiding simple allegory does not necessarily imply any aversion to more complex kinds."[7] Catherine Gimelli Martin, who challenges the view that the allegorical elements in *Paradise Lost* must be "hostile to naturalistic narrative,"[8] displays an unusual degree of comfort with Milton's commingling of the mimetic and figurative in *Paradise Lost*. Martin sees in seventeenth-century allegory and in *Paradise Lost* in particular a new kind of deliberately ambiguous "meta-allegory" that "creates the linguistic equivalent of perpetual dialectic, a self-reflexive vehicle everywhere dissolving the borders of the literal and the figurative dimensions that (re)-organize it."[9] I, too, see allegory as infusing the poem, but I regard the various threads of narration as more cleanly maintained and the poem as carefully structured to bring the allegorical and naturalistic into direct conflict.

I believe that Milton allows the allegorical elements of *Paradise Lost* to undercut the central naturalistic narrative because to do otherwise would be to appear to endorse parascriptural elements of doubtful authority that go well beyond the bare and self-contradictory scriptural account of creation and the Fall: his

highly fictionalized interpretation of sacred history must necessarily contain within itself subtle indications of its nature as an
accommodated version *of* accommodated scriptural truth. The
occasional and startling intersection of the naturalistic plane
and the allegorical is, in fact, a controlled tactic by which Milton
deals with problems inherent in his sacred subject and materials. Paradoxically, this subtle undercutting of the naturalistic
narrative stemming from Milton's concern not to endow speculative embellishments with the authority of Scripture purchases
Milton the freedom of invention he employs throughout *Paradise Lost*. Milton may treat the story of Adam and Eve's creation
and the Fall so loosely precisely because he provides the means
for readers to ascertain that *Paradise Lost* is ultimately more allegory than history.

Teskey understandably insists that we not "read [the 'allegorical tropes in *Paradise Lost*'] in any sense but the literal."[10] The
problem, of course, is that admitting the "non-being" of Sin and
Death encourages an allegorical rendering not only of the gates
they guard but also of the physical locales of Hell and Chaos and
forces an acknowledgment that the larger narrative may be con-
taminated as well. In fact, the very stage on which the cosmic
action unfolds privileges the symbolic and figurative over the
literal or factual. Absolutely no one thinks that Milton attempts
anything but a symbolic rendering of the relation between God
and his creation and of man's place in the universe when he
maps out his cosmography. Everyone understands it to be the
moral condition of man that is the real concern of the poet when
he suspends the sphere containing the planets and stars from the
base of Heaven over the dual threats of Chaos and Hell. As Walter Clyde Curry notes, "the meeting of three ways at the World's
zenith is of tremendous importance in the poet's epic design;
here are made 'visible' the roadways to three universes hence-
forth involved in the struggle for the soul of Man."[11] Yet within
this fanciful framework, Milton jarringly introduces the serious
scientific question of whether man occupies a geocentric or he-
liocentric system and pointedly refuses to provide an answer—
even though for the educated portion of his seventeenth-century
audience at least the Copernican model would already have sup-
planted the Ptolemaic.[12] Critics typically read in Raphael's refusal to satisfy Adam's curiosity on this point a humbling
caution not to misdirect intellectual energy. But Milton's reticence may as well be read as a signal to his audience not to ex-

pect or seek literal truth in his epic but rather to delve beneath the surface for accommodated essential truth.

After acknowledging that "[n]o evidence could be found in this world to establish numerous features of Milton's reality in *Paradise Lost*," Earl Miner insists that "such concessions offer but another way of saying that narrative may establish the terms of its own reality and so carry conviction."[13] *Paradise Lost* does so impressively in the opening scenes in Hell of the first two books. But Milton goes on repeatedly to violate the "terms" or premises of his own narrative; and we can here see how Milton's very free treatment of scriptural history can be reconciled with his scrupulous concern (most fully expressed in the *Christian Doctrine*)[14] to separate sound "scriptural doctrine" from "parascriptural tradition."[15] *Paradise Lost*, while on one level exploiting the parascriptural tradition of the Fall (and freely adding to it), contains within itself elements that undercut the most doubtful components of the legend that built up around the sparse scriptural account.

Milton was undoubtedly well aware that the version of the Fall he employs evolved, winning out over several competing accounts in the first centuries after Jesus.[16] Indeed, the scantiness of the Genesis account and the fullness of the parascriptural theological, literary, and folk traditions surrounding Satan especially may partly explain Milton's selection of the Fall over other biblical subjects and his heavy dependence upon the character Satan to fuel narrative interest and define the plot.[17] Significantly, as Dennis Danielson observes, "the rest of the Old Testament makes no clear mention of the story of Adam and Eve, and its only biblical interpretation is given in the New Testament by St. Paul [in 1 Corinthians 15.21–22, 45], who reads it typologically."[18] Satan, as John Carey notes, although mentioned more frequently in Scripture, is nonetheless grounded in far less certain biblical authority:

> There is very little in the Bible about Satan. In *Christian Doctrine* Milton collects all the available biblical evidence in a few sentences. It amounts to little more than that Satan is the author of all evil and has various titles (YP 6:349–50). As Kastor has shown, it was not until about AD 200 that official Judaism began to absorb popular concepts of Satan. From then on appearances of Satan in literature, subliterature, and theology multiplied.[19]

And as Kastor also points out, "[r]eferences to Satan are far more numerous in the New Testament" than in the Old Testament, "but they are also scattered. As a whole they present not only a paucity of details, but also contradictory and inconsistent bits of description."[20] In particular, the linking of the serpent in Genesis with Satan became firmly established in Christian tradition only with Augustine around A.D. 400.[21] If Satan is suspect, certainly other of Milton's fallen angels, however fully conceived and dramatically rendered, are assuredly not historical personages: "Two of Milton's devils, Belial and Mammon, he knew were—a matter of historical fact—only popular personifications of the abstractions that were originally meant by the two names" (i.e., "lust" and "avarice").[22] I wish to argue that Satan and other less suspect characters in *Paradise Lost* are highly allegorized and that the level of narration I prefer to term "historical" is much more limited than has been supposed and is tightly interwoven with allegory throughout the epic. Milton's tactics have their source, I believe, in his views on the limitations of language and the human mind, and in particular in the example of authorial accommodation to be found in Scripture.

Milton stresses the ineffability of God and, while he clearly views Scripture as divinely authored, he basically regards it as "dummied down" for the limited capacities of human beings. An oft-quoted passage from the *Christian Doctrine* cautions:

> When we talk about knowing God, it must be understood in terms of man's limited powers of comprehension. God, as he really is, is far beyond man's imagination, let alone his understanding. . . .
> It is safest for us to form an image of God in our minds which *corresponds* to his representation and description of himself in the sacred writings. Admittedly, God is always described or outlined *not as he really is* but in such a way as will make him conceivable to us. Nevertheless, we ought to form just such a mental image of him as he, in bringing himself within the limits of our understanding, wishes us to form.
>
> (6:133; emphasis mine)

This statement accords with Milton's consistent practice of reading many Old Testament passages figuratively to reconcile their meaning with portions of the New Testament. In *Reason of Church-Government*, for example, we find the following explicit caution concerning the interpretation of the description of "the stately fabrick & constitution of [the] Church" in Ezekiel: "[I]ndeed the description is as sorted best to the apprehension of those times, typicall and shadowie, but in such manner as never yet came to passe, nor never must literally, unlesse we mean to annihilat the Gospel" (1:757). Despite discussion of Milton's claim to a prophetic voice in his writings, he assuredly does not aspire to accomplish more than Scripture itself and thus can only offer a similarly accommodated version of the truths to be found in the Bible. Milton's strongly qualified acceptance of the "representation and description" of God in the Bible as a portrait accommodated to limited human understanding allows him to take considerable liberties in his depiction of God in *Paradise Lost* so long as his characterization of the Almighty "corresponds" to what appears in Scripture.

Critics, whether sympathetic to Christianity or not, and whether inclined to accept Milton's reasoned defense of the Almighty or not, have found fault with Milton's depiction of God. Some have found him too shadowy a figure; others have complained that Milton's God, described by the hymning angels as "invisible" and "inaccessible" (*Paradise Lost*, 3.375, 377), while too scantily characterized in some respects is yet crudely anthropomorphized at times—as when the Father jests with the Son at the possibility God will be dethroned (5.729–32). Milton's God and the Son, of course, pose the greatest challenge in terms of characterization, for poetic license here could easily shade into blasphemy. In particular, Milton avoids the kind of "anthropopathy, or the ascription of human feelings" to the Deity that he felt resulted in "the nonsense poets write about Jove" (*Christian Doctrine*, 6:134). Milton does not overstep the bounds in his portrayal of the Father and the Son, for he presents little more than what he regarded as sound doctrinal argument through their dialogue and ascribes only essential attributes to them, carefully refraining from "fleshing out" their characters as he does Satan's. When faced with the task of depicting God so as to "justify the ways of God to men" (*Paradise Lost*, 1.26), Milton feels free to present an anthropomorphic God only to the extent the Scriptures do. It is in narrative strategies that complement and amplify the naturalistic plane of narration, allegory among them, that Milton finds a way to "figure forth" that larger conception of God otherwise quite beyond the reach of human beings.[23]

Offering a general observation about the way allegory works, Fallon states that "allegorical agents represent parts of a divided whole. . . . [A]n aspect is separated from the whole and embodied."[24] Milton's scantily characterized, anthropomorphized God encompasses but part of his conception of the Deity. The rest is parceled out and conveyed indirectly, partly through the allegorical figure of Chaos and the personified abstraction divine Justice. Milton employs the allegorical representation of Chaos and the personification of Justice, I believe, to deflect adverse reactions to the most troubling aspects of God—the Deity's denial of responsibility for the existence of evil in a universe under his control and his insistence upon the necessity of judgment upon humankind.

As John Rumrich notes, "Milton scholarship has characteristically defined relations between the disorder of chaos and the order of God exclusively as adversarial."[25] By implication, Milton might at first appear in his depiction of Chaos to be endorsing the concept of pre-existent matter, which conveniently allows for the possibility that evil is inherent in the matter itself and thus absolves God of responsibility for evil. But Milton, in fact, believed in creation *de deo*, of God himself, and rejected the view that matter existed independently of God from all eternity. Why, then, does Milton in *Paradise Lost* establish what would appear to be an antagonism between God the Creator—or at least, his creation—and the matter out of which he creates?

Creation *de deo* absolutely insists upon the inherent goodness and unity of all creation, but for this very reason the philosophical and theological problem of accounting for evil without calling into question God's goodness looms all the larger.[26] It is largely through his allegorical representation of Chaos in *Paradise Lost* that Milton succeeds in distancing the raw material of creation—and the imputation of responsibility—from God;[27] and yet by subtle means Milton also identifies Chaos with God. Rumrich, who admits that there exists "strong narrative evidence of the malignancy of chaos," points out that this is "a narrative impression left early in the epic" countered by later developments that posit the " 'authoritarian' " Satan as the true enemy of Chaos and by God's description of Chaos as—like the Deity himself—"infinite and boundless."[28] Rumrich is comfortable with the idea that "Milton's materialist understanding of the deity is implicitly paradoxical" and argues persuasively that "chaos is God's womb" and that Chaos allegorically "represents the infinite material dimension of God."[29] Similarly, Justice may be viewed as a gloss on the paradoxical nature of God's omnipotence.

Fallon cites as "the best implicit evidence for Milton's increasing dissatisfaction with the allegorical mode, or at least with the mixing of allegorical and mimetic characters," his systematic elimination of "allegorical personifications in the successive drafts for a drama on the fall in the Trinity manu-script."[30] I am more struck by the particular personifications that Milton chooses to retain, namely Justice and Mercy, charac-ters that (along with Wisdom) in the third draft of the drama "will debate 'what should become of man if he fall' "[31] and can thus be more easily recognized as aspects of God. Justice, like Chaos, is by Milton carefully distanced from God, for God is not to be understood as willfully requiring a payment for a debt that he possesses the power to cancel:

> Die hee [Man] or Justice must; unless for him
> Some other able, and as willing, pay
> The rigid satisfaction, death for death.
> *(Paradise Lost,* 3.210–12)

God may temper justice with mercy, but he is bound by Justice to exact a penalty for man's transgression. Milton, to justify God, must avoid several pitfalls: one is the dark possibility that God is in no way limited and can choose to do good or evil, that is, to *be* good or evil. The problem here of course is that such a god is at least potentially evil. Milton must also sidestep volun-tarism, the notion that God's will is *by definition* good whether it answers to human notions of justice or not. Milton adopts the alternative theological position: his God does not arbitrarily de-cree what is good and what is evil. Rather, God is bound by natu-ral necessity: his nature is such that he can participate only in the good. Thus, somewhat paradoxically, we have an omnipo-tent God who *cannot* abrogate justice.[32] By representing divine Justice as outside of or apart from the character God, Milton sub-tly renders this element of compulsion that comes from within God's own nature. Allegory and personification thus allow Mil-ton both to distance troubling aspects of God's nature from his anthropomorphized figure of God and at the same time to sub-sume these under a larger conception of the Deity.

The problematic characterization of God reveals Milton's blending of personification and allegorical representation with naturalistic narrative and realistic characterization. The full cast of characters in *Paradise Lost* may be ranged in a variety of ways along some sort of continuum, from the fullest to the flat-test, from the most "perfect" to the least, from degrees of evil or corruptness to the good, for example. Critics, however, regularly treat the mimetic or historical and the allegorical as discrete cat-egories. But if—without assuming anything about a character's "legitimacy"—one looks at the extent to which Milton assigns characters believably human motivation and personality and precise physical characteristics and ascribes physical agency to them, then Sin, at least, of all the allegorical figures, moves to the other end of the scale. Clearly, dividing characters and incidents into two groups and assigning them to either the allegorical plane or a level of narrative termed mimetic or naturalistic obscures significant differences among the full range of characters in *Paradise Lost*. The unmistakably allegorical figures with tidy identifying labels range from the vague personification Justice to flat characters such as Death and Chaos that merely define and illustrate the abstractions they embody to the elaborately characterized Sin, who demonstrates human personality and emotion to a remarkable degree. The diffuseness of God's characterization and the seeming completeness of Sin's should alert us to the unwisdom of assigning a character to either plane purely on the basis of the fullness or depth of characterization. This consideration should make it easier to reconsider Satan's allegorical dimension for all his convincing psychology.

A number of critics have explored the allegory that surrounds Satan, but they typically balk at even momentarily contemplating Satan himself as an allegorical figure. Cherrell Guilfoyle observes that in the transformation of Satan from Promethean tragic hero to serpent, "Milton has achieved a superb allegorical summation of the two-faced Adversary," but Guilfoyle clearly regards the allegory as unquestionably subordinate to Satan's realistic characterization.[33] Borris, who finds in "Satan's cosmic journey . . . a hitherto unnoticed yet expansive allegory that shows how thoroughly *Paradise Lost* appropriates and redevelops heroico-romantic allegory for its own purposes," similarly sees the allegory as safely contained: "Rather than somehow becoming simpler or flatter for being allegorical, then, Satan's characterization assumes added dimensions and complexity."[34] Borris does, however, call for the "serious consideration" of "the allegorical potential of other parts of the poem, including even those with some scriptural basis."[35] Carey acknowledges the troubling implications of the "episode with Sin and Death at the gate between Hell and Chaos (2.648–870)" but backs away from any direct speculation about Satan's "reality": "The status of the sequence in terms of the poem's '*reality*,' and *the level on which we are to read it*, are not matters about which we can obtain any firm directives. This means that, in this strange episode as in much else, Satan slips from our knowledge. We can see that he is implicated in depths, but the nature of them eludes our understanding" (emphasis mine).[36] Joseph H. Summers, who argues that Milton "used and then 'broke' allegory" to accomplish his ends, perhaps goes further than anyone else when he cautiously states that "the brilliance of Milton's portrait of Satan should not lead us to assume that he is of an entirely different order of reality from his offspring," but he does not pursue this line of inquiry.[37] What is evident in the critical discussion is readers' discomfort at the prospect of viewing Satan primarily as an allegorical figure and their reluctance to regard his realistic characterization as at any time subordinate to his allegorical function.

It is certainly possible that Milton questioned the existence of Satan. Milton we know believed that a number of views labeled heretical by the church establishment were more in accord with Scripture than orthodox opinion. Again, the *Christian Doctrine* offers this passage, which sums up Milton's independent-minded and critical stance: "For my own part, I devote my attention to the Holy Scriptures alone. I follow no other heresy or sect. I had not even studied any of the so-called heretical writers, when the blunders of those who are styled orthodox, and their unthinking distortions of the sense of scripture, first taught me to agree with their opponents whenever these agreed with the Bible" (6:123–24). Noting some striking points of similarity between Milton's views and Socinian or Anabaptist doctrine as expressed in "ten points of doctrine" drawn up by "a most important Anabaptist council held in Venice in 1550," Leonora Leet Brodwin observes in passing that this group "denied" the "existence" of Satan "along with that of the angels."[38] The *Christian Doctrine* does of course refer explicitly to the "Bad angels" who "are kept for punishment" (6:348) and declares that "[t]he devils have their prince," Beelzebub or Satan (6:349): "Their chief is the author of all wickedness and hinders all good. . . . As a result he has been given a number of titles, which suit his actions. He is frequently called *Satan*, that is, enemy or adversary" (6:349–50). The *Christian Doctrine* also lists the fallen angels' ultimate defeat and "everlasting punishment" (6:625) as among the events to accompany Christ's Second Coming. It does not, however, expound upon Satan's nature or influence. Nor does the discussion of sin, reprobation, and regeneration in the *Christian Doctrine* stress the role of Satan or the other devils in tempting human beings. These devils seem tame and shadowy compared to the devils in *Paradise Lost*: "[S]ometimes they are able to wander all over the earth, the air, and even heaven, to carry out God's judgments. . . . But their proper place is hell, which they cannot leave without permission" (6:348–49). Rather, the *Christian Doctrine* insists upon man's full responsibility for original sin, emphasizing—in complementary fashion—man's (relative) perfectibility and the individual's responsibility for specific sinful acts. Any heightened portrayal of Satan and his minions would seem to run counter to the whole tenor of the *Christian Doctrine*. What is interesting, of course, is that in *Paradise Lost* Milton goes well beyond such cautious conclusions about Satan (or Beelzebub) and the lesser fallen angels as we find in the *Christian Doctrine* to embrace the dubious parascriptural traditions that make Satan a formidable and fascinating figure. Milton does not exhibit the concern evident in his portrayal of God and the Son to make the portrait "correspond" to sound scriptural doctrine—precisely because, I would suggest, the scriptural evidence that Satan is anything more than evil personified is slight.

If we consider that Milton may not have been entirely convinced that Satan was an actual historical personage and that Christian tradition notwithstanding there is scant biblical authority to connect Lucifer, Satan, and the serpent, the possibility that the Satan of *Paradise Lost* is an allegorical representation of evil in the mind of man seems likelier. Looked at in this light, Satan's encounters with Sin and Death seem less startling. It seems more and more appropriate for Satan to be the single character so aligned with personified abstractions. Sin and Death—emanating from Satan, and thus traceable to humankind—become a further demonstration of man's ultimate responsibility for his own suffering and loss. Fallon notes, "[w]ith surprising frequency in the seventeenth century, poets mix allegorical and mimetic characterization and narration."[39] I see this fusion of modes within *Paradise Lost* as occurring most strikingly within the character of Satan himself. In what may be termed the "historical" plane of the poem, I would tentatively locate God, the Son, and, less surely, the angels and Adam and Eve—all biblical "characters." In the patently allegorical plane, we can confidently place Sin, Death, Chaos, Night, and lesser personifications without speaking roles. Satan stands apart as a figure with a dual function who simultaneously invests the naturalistic level of narrative with power and betrays the essentially allegorical nature of the myth of the Fall.

Understandably, Satan has been regularly viewed as the major actor in the naturalistic narrative plane of *Paradise Lost*. Milton accomplishes any number of things by making Satan so convincing and compelling—indeed, so *human*—a character. Yet, it is not merely in the "embarrassing" scenes with Sin and Death and with Chaos that Milton undercuts this impression. Although the fallen Satan converses with angels, he is kept at one remove from God and the Son. Satan interacts directly with the allegorical figures Sin, Death, and Chaos—and is the *only* character from the seemingly mimetic plane to do so. Satan never confronts Adam and Eve in his "true" form. And, while Milton inherited the notion that Satan adopted the guise of a serpent to tempt Eve, the earlier "temptation" scene in which Satan is found "Squat like a Toad, close at the ear of Eve" (4.800) is pure invention on his part. The earlier scene suggests subconscious promptings, or "Fancy" (5.102); the second—which marks the actual Fall—conscious reasoning acted upon. Satan's shape changing and insinuation into Eve's psyche can be seen as indicative of his allegorical function, his role as the "Evil [that] into the mind of God or Man / May come and go" (117–18).

The more one explores the allegorical dimension of key players in *Paradise Lost*, the more one is led to question the degree to which the "truth" of the epic resides in the naturalistic level of narrative. The allegorical thread that exists throughout *Paradise Lost* and periodically forces itself to the fore underscores Milton's grasp of revelation as essentially metaphorical and exposes the compromises dictated both by his audience's and his own human limitations. We might here recall Raphael's justification for "relat[ing] / To human sense th' invisible exploits / Of warring Spirits" (564–66) in what many have seen as ludicrously physical terms:

> what surmounts the reach
> Of human sense, I shall delineate so,
> By lik'ning spiritual to corporal forms,
> As may express them best.
>
> (571–73)

How Adam and Eve, innocent of the experience of a fallen world, are to understand the martial imagery employed throughout Raphael's account is not explained, but of course this device exists for our benefit as readers. Raphael—and the epic poet—are here copying the tactic of the Deity, couching what is beyond human comprehension in "easy-read" terms. And yet, the lengthy account of the battle is not entirely self-contained: Satan and his fallen compatriots speak of the great conflict in similar corroborating terms, and the same figurative tactic extends throughout the whole of *Paradise Lost*. Book 1 offers descriptions of the fallen army, their "Banners," "Spears," "Helms," and "Shields" (545–48) and the "Martial sounds" resounding through Hell (540). In book 2, in her efforts to prevent a fight between Satan and Death, Sin speaks of Satan's "bright Arms, / . . . temper'd heav'nly" (812–13) and of Death's "fatal Dart" (786) and "deadly arrow" (811).

The authorial disclaimer comes late and is placed in the mouth of Raphael, not the epic narrator, but it is hardly possible to see the technique as confined to Raphael's account of the War in Heaven. This narrative accommodation is clearly Milton's and operates throughout the poem. In books 1 and 2, Milton is in fact at great pains to establish the *impression* of a naturalistic or mimetic narrative without giving us that at all. For, as Raphael tells Adam, the warring angels are "invisible" (5.565), lacking in "corporal forms" (573), and beyond "the reach / Of human sense" (571). What is interesting is that Milton waits until book 5 to expose—indeed, flaunt—this inescapable tactic of narrative accommodation.

Johnson's complaint, echoed by critics down to this day, is that Milton confounds the "real" and the "figurative" dimensions of the poem when he allows the "non-entit[ies]" Sin and Death to "stop the journey of Satan, a journey *described as* real" (emphasis mine).[40] Critics still often speak as if the naturalistic or mimetic narrative plane and the allegorical plane in *Paradise Lost* are neatly discrete *except* at such embarrassing moments as when Satan encounters Sin and Death. There are many reasons to see these narrative planes as tightly interwoven throughout the poem. I would like to suggest that we might do well to distinguish not merely between the "real" (or mimetic) and the "figurative" (or allegorical) levels of *Paradise Lost* but to consider that events or actions "presented as real" within a portion of the narrative may in fact better be described as a kind of latent allegory, for later developments call their "reality" into question.

If Satan is allowed to be an allegorical figure, then what are we to conclude about Milton's characterization of Adam and Eve? The existence of a long tradition that reads the Fall allegorically, seeing Adam as Reason or Mind and Eve as Passion or the Senses, by itself provides some justification for considering Milton's Adam and Eve as allegorical figures. If one judges by the *Christian Doctrine*, Milton appears to recognize Adam and Eve as historical personages who in one "atrocious offence . . . broke every part of the law" (6:383). Yet Milton everywhere displays a remarkable degree of comfort with *accommodated* literal readings of obscure or inconsistent Old Testament passages when nothing in the New Testament provides a key to unlocking possible figurative meanings; and I have already noted the spareness of biblical reference after Genesis to Adam and Eve. Milton clearly regarded much of Scripture as a historical record. However, his conviction that the New Testament must take precedence over the Old Testament and, indeed, is altogether clearer, the theory of divine accommodation he embraced, and his reticence on certain subjects in the *Christian Doctrine*, taken together, suggest that he may not have been so convinced of the literal truth of certain portions of the Old Testament: "Surely the obscurity of the law and the prophets should not be used to refute the light of the gospel. On the contrary, the light of the gospel should be used to illuminate the obscurity and the figurative language of the prophets" (*Christian Doctrine*, 6:255). Indeed, what one finds in the *Christian Doctrine* is the abiding conviction that the *truth* of any scriptural passage is in its doctrinal import and not its historical accuracy.

If some doubt is admitted as to Adam and Eve's historical status, Milton's Adam and Eve can be considered more readily as generic types of Man and Woman whose fall dramatizes humankind's (collective and individual) alienation from God. The prelapsarian and postlapsarian Adam and Eve—like Satan, who is the complete type of the reprobate—figure forth spiritual states. But suggestions in Milton's text that Adam and Eve share "one Flesh, one Heart, one Soul" (*Paradise Lost*, 8.499) invite us to go further to consider *Paradise Lost* as a psychomachia. That Eve is *more* allied with the physical or sensual and Adam with the intellectual or spiritual (however Milton may qualify this scheme) provides even more justification to push an allegorical interpretation of the Fall in *Paradise Lost* further and link Milton's rendering of the Fall to the allegorical tradition that stretches from the first-century Alexandrian theologian Philo Judaeus to Milton's contemporary the Cambridge Platonist Henry More.

Citing the long tradition that reads the Genesis account of the Fall allegorically, Diane Kelsey McColley emphasizes that "Adam and Eve are each whole personages, both reasonable and imaginative, both sensuous, passionate and pure" and insists that "[o]ne of the habits of mind that Milton revises in *Paradise Lost* is the allegorizing of Scripture that makes Adam reason, mind, or soul, Eve passion, sense, or flesh, and the Garden abstract moral virtue."[41] If there is an occasional staginess or flatness to their characterization before the Fall, there is also a naturalness even then—and certainly after the Fall—that makes them believably human figures. Their individuation, however, comes largely from Milton's efforts to present *essential* human nature, masculine and feminine, in a state of perfection. Neither *can* be strongly marked by such "humors" or traits as distinguish one man or one woman from another and make for variety in a fallen world. And, as we have seen, full or realistic characterization does not preclude allegory.

But as the tradition that reads the Fall allegorically is, as McColley notes, blatantly "dualistic," positing "nature and spirit, body and soul, [and] passion and reason" as "inherently antithetical,"[42] such a reading would seem at first to be incompatible with Milton's monism and his Christian materialism. Furthermore, allegory would seem to depend upon the clear, if not exclusive, association of Adam with Reason and Eve with the Senses, and Milton's Adam and Eve, in their likeness to one another, do, as McColley and others have pointed out, challenge the tradition that regards woman as man's antithesis. The tradition, however, posits two Adams, or two sides to Man, discoverable in the two creation myths in Genesis: a higher that desires a more spiritualized state and a lower dominated by physical appetite.[43] Woman, by contrast, is one-dimensional and lacks the potential even to envision and desire a higher state: she is both woman as seductive object and the personification of the pull of the senses within Adam. The Adam of tradition, like Milton's Adam, experiences a conflict and exhibits passions not well regulated; and it is by having *Eve* exhibit intellectual and spiritual depth that Milton departs from this tradition. But if Milton's allegorization of Adam and Eve is seen as deliberately evocative of the tradition without endorsing it fully, then his resistance to a discrete, oppositional characterization becomes a statement upon the indivisibility of spirit and body and a different kind of challenge to the tradition's dualist assumptions. One *can* see Milton's Adam as Reason or Mind and Eve as Passion or Body, but ultimately the statement in *Paradise Lost* is that flesh and spirit are one. Milton is revising, certainly, but not necessarily rejecting the traditional allegorical reading of the Fall.

Allegorical readings of Scripture, of course, may accompany a view of biblical figures as historical or may make them purely figurative representatives of human propensities and potential. Philo, despite his commitment to "allegorical readings" that "turn specific characters who speak and act according to ordinary narrative realism into the impulses and faculties of the inner world of the human soul" and allow man "to retrieve Moses' deliberately hidden message," exhibits as well a concern to preserve the literal level of meaning: his "dual allegiance requires him to convince his audience that both literal and nonliteral readings are plausible interpretations of the same text that do not cancel one another."[44] By sharp contrast, as Joseph Levine notes, Henry More's "elaborate" interpretation of "the allegory of Adam and Eve" was prompted by his fear that in the intellectual climate of seventeenth-century England "the story of Creation taken by itself [i.e., in its literal meaning] might actually foster atheism by helping the unregenerate to think that the whole business of religion was no more than a fable."[45] Milton, whose life spans roughly the same years as More's, may have recognized as well that a substantial portion of his contemporary audience would not have regarded the myth of the Fall as literally true.

An allegorical reading of the Fall does not preclude a belief in Adam, Eve, and Satan as historical personages, but an allegorical reading has the advantage of not insisting upon their historical existence as the basis of a belief in the spiritual truth contained in the myth of the Fall. And while allegorical readings may be imposed on any text, certainly some texts are more amenable to such treatment than others. Milton opens the door to a full-blown allegorical reading of *Paradise Lost* when he introduces unmistakably allegorical figures, creates clear points of intersection between the undeniably allegorical plane and the seemingly naturalistic or mimetic narrative plane, and echoes the tradition that views Adam and Eve as aspects of the human psyche or soul. Milton's design preserves at its core the bare literal account found in Genesis, yet *Paradise Lost* builds upon Scripture in a way that both affirms the myth's essential truth and resists confirming its literal truth.

A major investment in allegorical representation does not necessarily imply philosophical or theological dualism. Milton's fusion of the allegorical and naturalistic in *Paradise Lost* seems entirely in keeping with his compulsion to synthesize and incorporate disparate elements, which in turn is symptomatic of his monism and his Christian materialism. Moreover, if allegory must be seen as disrupting or undercutting the naturalistic narrative, calling into question the very premises upon which it appears to rest and exposing Milton's tactics of narrative accommodation, we might do better to ask why Milton might wish to unsettle his narrative in this fashion. Such a "flaw" seems the necessary implicit recognition of the gap between truth and human apprehension of truth.

NOTES

1. Samuel Johnson, "Milton," in *Lives of the English Poets*, ed. George Birkbeck Hill (Oxford: Clarendon Press, 1905), 185. Joseph Addison, *Critical Essays from "The Spectator,"* ed. Donald F. Bond (New York: Oxford University Press, 1970). Of the eighteen Spectator papers devoted to *Paradise Lost*, five (nos. 273, 297, 309, 315, and 357) make particular mention of the allegorical figures Sin and Death. Addison praises Milton's "beautiful extended allegor[y]" but considers it "not agreeable to the nature of an heroic poem" (155); for his general comments upon "such shadowy and imaginary persons as may be introduced into heroic poems," see Spectator 357, 155–57.

2. Kenneth Borris, "Allegory in *Paradise Lost*: Satan's Cosmic Journey," *Milton Studies* 26 (1990): 101.

3. John Milton, *Paradise Lost*, in *John Milton: Complete Poems and Major Prose*, ed. Merritt Y. Hughes (New York: Odyssey, 1957). All references to Milton's poetry are to this edition and are cited parenthetically in the text.

4. Gordon Teskey, "From Allegory to Dialectic: Imagining Error in Spenser and Milton," *PMLA* 101 (1986): 16.

5. Ibid.

6. Stephen M. Fallon, "Milton's Sin and Death: The Ontology of Allegory in *Paradise Lost*," *English Literary Renaissance* 17 (1987): 342.

7. Borris, "Allegory in *Paradise Lost*," 126.

8. Catherine Gimelli Martin, "Ithuriel's Spear: Purity, Danger, and Allegory at the Gates of Eden," *SEL* 33 (1993): 175.

9. Catherine Gimelli Martin, *The Ruins of Allegory: "Paradise Lost" and the Metamorphosis of Epic Convention* (Durham, N.C.: Duke University Press, 1998), 4, 42. Martin's full-length study of allegory in *Paradise Lost* appeared as I was preparing this manuscript for publication. She follows others in reading *Paradise Lost* in the context of seventeenth-century thought but departs from earlier approaches that emphasize Milton's antecedents and regard his grand epic as "the culmination of the privileged Renaissance mode" (2). Crediting Milton with the almost prophetic ability "to foresee the demise of post-Cartesian culture," Martin approaches *Paradise Lost* as "a vision of the demise of the mode that would succeed it" (2). Such a view does not, however, sufficiently credit the role of the scriptural exegetical tradition in shaping Milton's heightened awareness of the limits of language. Martin also links the theory of accommodation and Milton's poetic practice but places, from my perspective, too great an emphasis upon Milton's distrust of language and humankind's fallen nature and too little upon his faith in the power "of learning

... to repair the ruins of our first parents by regaining to know God aright" (John Milton, *Of Education*, in *Complete Prose Works of John Milton*, 8 vols., ed. Don M. Wolfe et al. [New Haven: Yale University Press, 1953–82], 2:366–67). All references to Milton's prose are to this edition and are cited parenthetically in the text.

10. Teskey, "From Allegory to Dialectic," 19.

11. Walter Clyde Curry, *Milton's Ontology, Cosmogony, and Physics* (Lexington: University Press of Kentucky, 1957), 157.

12. By deliberately embracing in *Paradise Lost* an outmoded plan of the cosmos and by introducing dialogue (between Adam and Eve in 4.657–88 and between Adam and Raphael in 8.15–197) that exposes the inadequacy of human reason to unlock the secrets of the universe, Milton is refusing to view *any* model of the universe as authoritative. As Martin points out, contemporaries of Milton including "scientists like Robert Boyle . . . typically called in question *both* Ptolemaic and Copernican models of the universe in an attempt to conserve some *un*mechanistic role for its First Mover" (" 'Boundless the Deep': Milton, Pascal, and the Theology of Relative Space," *ELH* 63 [1997]: 58).

13. Earl Miner, "The Reign of Narrative in *Paradise Lost*," *Milton Studies* 17 (1983): 12.

14. Milton's authorship of the *Christian Doctrine* has recently been questioned. It seems equally impossible to ignore this work or to base much of my argument upon it. I attempt to make cautious use of the treatise, regarding it as a compilation of views accepted by Milton if not entirely authored by him.

15. James H. Sims, "The Miltonic Narrator and Scriptural Tradition: An Afterword," in *Milton and Scriptural Tradition: The Bible into Poetry*, ed. James H. Sims and Leland Ryken (Columbia: University Press of Missouri, 1983), 194–95.

16. Frank S. Kastor (*Milton and the Literary Satan* [Amsterdam: Rodopi N. V., 1974], 8–9) sums up the history of "Satan's genesis": "Satan appears first in Hebrew Scripture written after the Babylonian Exile (586–538 B.C.)— although not for some years afterwards, which accounts for some of the uncertainty of his genesis. (He is first mentioned in I Chronicles, xxi, dating from about 400 B.C.) The Old Testament as a whole offers little information concerning him. Satan's great and marked development begins only after the Jewish canon of the Old Testament had been completed and in the period of approximately 200 B.C.–200 A.D."

17. David Masson ("A Brief Life of Milton," in *Paradise Lost: A Norton Critical Edition*, ed. Scott Elledge [New York: Norton, 1993], 324) lists the range of possible subjects considered by Milton: "How he wavered between Biblical subjects and heroic subjects from British history, and how many of each kind suggested themselves to him, one learns from a list in his own handwriting among the Milton MSS. at Cambridge. It contains jottings of no fewer than fifty-three subjects from the Old Testament, eight from the Gospels, thirty-three from British and English history before the Conquest, and five from Scottish history." For the full list of subjects considered by Milton, see David Masson, *The Life of John Milton*, 7 vols. (1859–94; reprint, New York: Peter Smith, 1946), 2:104–16.

18. Dennis Danielson, "The Fall of Man and Milton's Theodicy," in *The Cambridge Companion to Milton*, ed. Dennis Danielson (Cambridge: Cambridge University Press, 1989), 116.

19. John Carey, "Milton's Satan," in *The Cambridge Companion to Milton*, ed. Danielson, 131.

20. Kastor, *Milton and the Literary Satan*, 9.

21. Denis Saurat, *Milton, Man and Thinker* (New York: Haskell House, 1970), 273.

22. Merritt Y. Hughes, ed., in *John Milton: Complete Poems*, 183.

23. Barbara Kiefer Lewalski examines God and the Son as "literary portraits" and argues that Milton "employed a special strategy of generic multiplicity" in his characterization of the Deity, a characterization that she terms a "radically metaphoric but yet insistently biblical imagination of God" ("Generic Multiplicity and Milton's Literary God," in *A Fine Tuning: Studies of the Religious Poetry of Herbert and Milton*, ed. Mary A. Maleski [Binghamton, N.Y.: Medieval and Renaissance Texts and Studies, 1989], 163, 164, 165).

24. Fallon, "Milton's Sin and Death," 333.

25. John Rumrich, "Milton's God and the Matter of Chaos," *PMLA* 110 (1995): 1039.

26. James P. Driscoll (*The Unfolding God of Jung and Milton* [Lexington: University Press of Kentucky, 1993], 14–15) states that Milton "rejected" creation *ex nihilo*, or creation out of nothingness, because it is "illogical," but Driscoll observes that creation *ex nihilo* is more easily reconciled with the "Augustinian doctrine that evil is *privatio boni*" (i.e., has no positive existence but is merely the privation of good) than is creation *de deo* (i.e., "creation out of [God] himself"): "Although Milton doesn't acknowledge it, creation *de deo* discredits *privatio boni* and thereby lays the problem of evil in God's lap."

27. Dennis Danielson (*Milton's Good God: A Study in Literary Theodicy* [Cambridge: Cambridge University Press, 1982], 47–48) explains that "Milton in *Paradise Lost* expands the creation from two stages to three, so going beyond both tradition and his own prose treatise": "The traditional two-stage theory has the limitation that all of Chaos gets used up in the second stage. But just as Milton needed the doctrine of *creatio ex deo* in order to establish that the 'original matter . . . was good, and . . . contained the seeds of all subsequent good' (*CD*, p. 308), so, in order that he might do justice also to the fact of *evil*, he needed to retain an infinite Chaos even after the world was created."

28. Rumrich, "Milton's God and the Matter of Chaos," 1041, 1036, 1040, 1043.

29. Ibid., 1043. Rumrich carefully distinguishes between chaos the place and Chaos its ruler.

30. Fallon, "Milton's Sin and Death," 340.

31. Ibid., 341.

32. See Danielson (*Milton's Good God*, 151) for an explanation of this aspect of Milton's Arminianism.

33. Cherrell Guilfoyle, "Adamantine and Serpentine: Milton's Use of Two Conventions of Satan in *Paradise Lost*," *Milton Quarterly* 13 (1979): 133.

34. Borris, "Allegory in *Paradise Lost*," 103–4.

35. Ibid., 125.

36. Carey, "Milton's Satan," 142–43.

37. Joseph H. Summers, *The Muse's Method: An Introduction to "Paradise Lost"* (1962; reprint, New York: Norton, 1968), 40, 39.

38. Leonora Leet Brodwin, "The Dissolution of Satan in *Paradise Lost*: A Study of Milton's Heretical Eschatology," *Milton Studies* 8 (1975): 193. Brodwin also regards Milton's Chaos as "signify[ing] not a geographic dislocation of the earth but a figurative statement of the process of dissolution" and Milton's Hell as "not a physical but a psychological state" (174).

39. Fallon, "Milton's Sin and Death," 338.

40. Johnson, *Lives*, 185–86.

41. Diane Kelsey McColley, *A Gust for Paradise: Milton's Eden and the Visual Arts* (Urbana: University of Illinois Press, 1993), 126.

42. Diane Kelsey McColley, *Milton's Eve* (Urbana: University of Illinois Press, 1983), 3.

43. Philo's two Adams correspond rather neatly to the two sides of Milton's conflicted Adam, whose superior (to Eve's) reasoning powers are short-circuited by his "uxorious[ness]" (*Christian Doctrine*, 6:383):

> Recognizing the same two stories of creation in Genesis 1–3 that modern biblical scholars have identified as the work of the Priestly Writer (P) and the Yahwist (J), Philo understands "Adam" to be a composite figure whose identity shifts between an ideal, nonmaterial Adam of Genesis 1 and a material Adam of Genesis 2–3. The first, ideal Adam of Genesis 1, copied after the image of God, desires to be like his divine archetype. . . . [C]reated Adam (as both ideal Adam and material Adam) desired to overcome his difference from his creator. But succumbing to the serpent's temptation, material Adam exchanges a desire for the Same (that is, for the God who has established the world of archetype and copy correlation) for a desire for the Other [i.e., Eve] . . . —for the woman, despite enormous similarity to Adam, is different from him (and different from God) (David Dawson, *Allegorical Readers and Cultural Revision in Ancient Alexandria* [Berkeley and Los Angeles: University of California Press, 1992], 88–89).

44. Ibid., 100, 76, 100–101.

45. Joseph Levine, "Latitudinarians, Neoplatonists, and the Ancient Wisdom," in *Philosophy, Science, and Religion in England 1640–1700*, ed. Richard W. F. Kroll, Richard Ashcraft, and Perez Zagorin (Cambridge: Cambridge University Press, 1992), 99.

Milton, Lucretius, and "the Void Profound of Unessential Night"

JOHN LEONARD

A. B. Chambers, writing in 1963, declared that Milton's Chaos in *Paradise Lost* was in one key feature wholly original: "Milton's chaos, unlike others, continues to exist, in part, even after the creation."[1] The Chaos of Hesiod, Plato, Ovid, Claudian, Du Bartas, and others was all used up. Chambers does acknowledge that "the atomists . . . supposed that worlds other than ours might come to be from those atoms yet remaining in space," but he concludes: "no writer known to me maintained that chaos as such continued to exist."[2] Even if we set the atomists aside for a moment, Milton is not quite as original as Chambers supposes. Spenser's Chaos also "continues to exist":

> in the wide wombe of the world there lyes,
> In hatefull darkeness and in deepe horrore,
> An huge eternall Chaos, which supplyes
> The substances of natures fruitfull progenyes.
>
> (3.6.36)[3]

Spenser's Chaos nevertheless differs from Milton's. Spenser's Chaos lies "in the wide wombe of the world"; Milton's lies outside our universe "In the wide womb of uncreated Night" (2.150).[4] Spenser's Chaos is an integral part of nature, which it continually "supplyes" with "substances." Milton's Chaos, having made one contribution at creation, is forever after shut out.

This exclusion has implications for the much-debated question of whether Milton's Chaos is "good," "neutral," or "evil." Chambers had no doubt that Chaos and Night are "malevolent."[5] Although I have more sympathy with this view than with the current orthodoxy that Chaos is good, I should say at the outset that I am unhappy with the words "good" and "evil" as they are used in this debate. They frame the argument in narrow

198

moral terms. To some extent this is unavoidable, given Milton's allegorical personification of Chaos. Critics on my side usually cite Chaos's line "Havoc and spoil and ruin are my gain" (2.1009) as if it settled the question of his moral allegiance. Perhaps it does, but I have always found Chaos the person to be a pale shadow of Chaos the place, and I shall say little about him in this essay. Even Chaos the person harbors no special malice against mankind. He resents the universe, but he never so much as mentions its occupants. He might not even know of their existence. To my mind, this ignorance or indifference is more alarming than Hell's hatred. Satan's malevolence at least reassures us that we matter. Chaos might annihilate us and not notice.

In what follows, I shall argue that Milton's conception of Chaos and Night is deeply indebted to Lucretius.[6] Chambers claims that the atomists were unconcerned "with Chaos as such," and it is true that Lucretius never uses the Latin word "Chaos."[7] But in *De Rerum Natura* (5.436) he does relate how our world arose from a "strange storm" [*nova tempestas*] or "shapeless mass" [*moles*] of warring elements.[8] More importantly, he anticipates Milton's model of a finite, spherical universe surrounded by an infinite void in which atoms randomly collide for all eternity. Lucretius argues that innumerable universes must have been formed and destroyed by chance atomic collisions in infinite space (2.1086). Milton (in a line borrowed from Lucretius) calls his abyss "The womb of Nature and perhaps her grave" (*Paradise Lost*, 2.911) and boldly conjectures that God might draw on the "dark materials" of Chaos "to create more worlds" (916). Lucretius's influence on Milton has received little comment from editors and critics,[9] presumably because of the doctrinal gulf that separates the two poets. Milton's contemporaries often reviled Lucretius as an atheist.[10] Even Lucy Hutchinson hedges her translation with marginal comments deploring the Roman poet's "[h]orribly impious" beliefs.[11] Lucretius's belief that chance had produced our universe is irreconcilable with Christianity. Milton's God explicitly declares that "Necessity and Chance / Approach not me" (*Paradise Lost*, 7.172–73). Clearly, it would be absurd to argue that Milton shared Lucretius's atomist beliefs, but it would also be rash to suppose that these left no trace in *Paradise Lost* when its universe owes so much to that of Lucretius. At the very least we have a right to ask why Milton should have drawn upon atoms and the void when constructing his universe and infinite space.

A part of the answer is no doubt that Milton, like Giordano Bruno, Pierre Gassendi, and Henry More, wanted to appropriate infinite space for God, who deserves no less ("Boundless the deep, because I am who fill / Infinitude" [7.168–69]). Anxiety nevertheless attends the appropriation, for atoms and infinite space threaten to dislodge God from his privileged position as Creator. It is hard to believe that beings like ourselves could have come about by chance in a finite universe. But the odds are not so long in an infinite universe, where what can happen, will happen.

Johannes Kepler, partly for reasons of piety, had denied the possibility of an infinite universe.[12] Walter Clyde Curry argues in like vein that such Miltonic phrases as "vast infinitude" (3.711) and "infinite abyss" (2.405) "must not be taken literally." These are "epic phrases" appropriate to "epic grandeur," but they express "merely an hyperbolical infinitude" since "only God is infinite."[13] The problem with this line of argument is that it diminishes Milton's imagination in precisely those places where it is most sublime. The equation of "epic grandeur" with the "merely . . . hyperbolical" rings especially hollow. Yet, as we shall see, many critics have followed Curry's lead and tried to cut Chaos down to size. We can reverse this trend by approaching Chaos through Lucretius. Lucretius, more than any other poet before Milton, was imaginatively alive to the wonder and terror of infinite space, and his wonder and terror both find expression in *Paradise Lost*. The debate as to whether Chaos is "good" or "evil" too often deprives Chaos of this wonder and terror. Lucretius can help us to respond to Milton's abyss with due awe.

Milton's created universe is surrounded by a "firm opacous globe" (3.418) which acts as a "partition firm and sure" (7.267) between us and "vast infinitude." Critics have been hard-pressed to find precedents for this protective outer shell. The universe of Aristotle and Ptolemy was spherical and finite, but nothing (not even space or time) could exist outside it. The Stoics imagined that the universe was surrounded by an infinite void, but they did not posit the existence of a dividing shell. Nicholas Cusanus, Thomas Digges, Bruno, and René Descartes saw the stellar universe itself as infinite. Critics have found vague hints of a shell like Milton's in rabbinical sources, as well as in St. Augustine and St. Thomas.[14] Harinder Singh Marjara has recently found an analogue in Henry More, who believed that a "hollow Expansion, firm and transparent" protected us from inundation by the waters above the firmament.[15] Milton's shell does share some features with More's, but (as Marjara notes) it serves a different function. More's shell protects us from the waters of Gen. 1.6; Milton's protects us from "the destructive nature of extramundane space."[16] I think that the real source of Milton's shell is in *De Rerum Natura*. Lucretius surrounds our universe with something he calls "*moenia mundi*," [the walls of the world]. Lucretius uses this phrase at least ten times. It first appears in *De Rerum Natura* 1.73, where Lucretius refers to "the flaming walls of the world." This does not sound like a firm globe, but in book 5, where Lucretius describes the genesis of our world, he gives an account of the *moenia mundi* that clearly looks forward to Milton. The *moenia mundi* are formed of small, round atoms, squeezed out from the earth when the universe first divided into separate regions. Ascending in the form of "fiery ether" (5.458–59), some of these atoms became the sun, moon, and stars, but others rose still higher, spreading out in all directions to form a solid globe:

> Sic igitur tum se levis ac diffusilis aether
> Corpore concreto circumdatus undique flexit
> Et late diffusus in omnis undique partis
> Omnia sic avido complexu cetera saepsit.
>
> (5.467–70)

Hutchinson translates:

> So heavens light bodies did in vapors rise
> Till all was hemd in with concreted sides,
> Which spred themselves to such a vast extent
> As made the all-embracing firmament.
>
> (5.484–87)

Lucretius's "*concreto*" (faithfully translated by Hutchinson's "concreted") means "solidified." Milton draws directly on Lucretius's account, and even borrows the image of "walls," when Uriel recalls how he saw ether spring from earth at the Creation:

> this ethereal quíntessence of heav'n
> Flew upward, spirited with various forms,
> That rolled orbicular, and turned to stars
> Numberless, as thou seest, and how they move;
> Each had his place appointed, each his course,
> The rest in circuit walls this universe.
>
> (3.716–21)

By "the rest" Uriel means the ether that was not "turned to stars." This remaining ether formed a wall around the universe, a "partition firm and sure" between us and Chaos. Alastair Fowler rightly cites Lucretius as Milton's source but does not explore the implications.[17]

Lucretius's image of walls has military implications that Milton develops. Lucretius predicts that the walls of the world will at last collapse, having been stormed from all sides: "Sic igitur magni quoque circum moenia mundi / Expugnata dabunt labem putreisque ruinas" (2.1144–45). Milton never concedes so much power to Chaos, but its hostility is unmistakable when it falls back from Nature's "outmost works a broken foe" (2.1039). "Works" there means "fortifications" (Oxford English Dictionary 12) as well as "creation, handiwork" (OED 9). Milton's universe, like that of Lucretius, is besieged. I am aware that it is unfashionable, at the present time, to associate Chaos with warfare. John Rumrich, in particular, has urged us to see Chaos as a womb rather than a war.[18] Even if Chaos's womblike qualities have been neglected (and I shall return to this point), that is not an argument for discounting the war imagery. Milton's Chaos is not less but more violent than that of other poets. Many poets have depicted Chaos as a fray of warring elements; Milton, following Lucretius, adds the much more disturbing image of belligerent atoms rising from the void to assault our fragile universe.

Critics sometimes protest that the violence exists only in Satan's imagination ("the scene is . . . Satan's view in more ways than one"),[19] but Chaos appears just as hostile when Satan is not present. When the good angels look down from Heaven's gates, they see

> the vast immeasurable abyss
> Outrageous as a sea, dark, wasteful, wild,
> Up from the bottom turned by furious winds
> And surging waves, as mountains to assault
> Heav'n's heighth, and with the centre mix the pole.
>
> (7.211–15)

That is very close to Lucretius's account of the final collapse of the moenia mundi. John Evelyn translates:

> The Worlds bright wals would vanish suddenly
> Through the vast Voyd dissolv'd, the rest would be
> After the same sort hurried, that from high

Would drop the thundring Turrets of the Skie:
And under foot the sinking earth to bend,
Whilst the same ruin Earth with Heaven would blend.[20]

That last line translates the Latin words "Inter permistas terrae, caelique ruinas" (1.1107). This is very close to "with the centre mix the pole."[21] Evelyn's "the vast Voyd" translates *"inane profundum"* (1.1108), a phrase that Milton borrows and translates literally as "the void profound" (2.438). The *OED* credits Milton with the earliest English instance of "the void," meaning "the empty expanse of space" (*OED* 4). The *OED* also cites Milton's "Space may produce new worlds" (1.650) as the earliest instance of "space" in its fully developed astronomical sense (*OED* 8). But Evelyn and Hutchinson refer to "space" and "the void" in their translations of Lucretius. The Latin terms are *"spatium"* and *"inane."* It looks very much as if Lucretius inspired both of Milton's supposed neologisms.

Lucretius and Milton both liken Chaos to a storm. Lucretius tells how atoms will gather out of the infinite *[Ex infinito]* and "overwhelm this sum of things in a violent hurricane" [corruere hanc rerum violento turbine summam] (5.367–68).[22] Milton speaks in like vein of "ever-threat'ning storms / Of Chaos blust'ring round" (3.425–26). Milton's most violent depiction of Chaos, however, is this double simile describing the noises that assault Satan's ear:

> Nor was his ear less pealed
> With noises loud and ruinous (to compare
> Great things with small) than when Bellona storms,
> With all her battering engines bent to raze
> Some capital city; or less than if this frame
> Of heav'n were falling, and these elements
> In mutiny had from her axle torn
> The steadfast earth.
>
> (2.920–27)

Together, the two similes imply that our universe is a city that Chaos might take by (military) storm. But even the end of a universe would be a small event in Chaos. Milton invokes cosmic destruction while comparing "Great things with small." Earl Miner has recently demonstrated that this phrase is a classical topos used by Herodotus, Thucydides, Virgil, Cicero, Ovid, Statius, and others.[23] Yet Milton uses it quite differently from these authors. Their "small things" (a beehive, a lover's distress, a private bath) really are small. Milton's "small things"—the sack of a city, the crunching of the cosmos—would be great in any other poem.

I have so far been emphasizing the similarities between Milton and Lucretius. But there are also important differences. Lucretius, for all his storms and sieges, welcomes stray atoms into the universe. The *moenia mundi* are not impassable. The universe even needs to be fed and sustained by atoms wandering in from outside. Lucretius goes so far as to conjecture that it will be a dearth of such atomic intruders that will at last cause the walls of the world to weaken and collapse (2.1105–45). Lucretius's universe could not survive without a continued supply of matter from the void. Milton's universe, having once been created, is "enclosed / From Chaos and th' inroad of Darkness old" (3.420–21), and no new atoms may enter it.

Milton also differs from Lucretius on the relationship between Chaos and free will. Although Lucretius has not received his due in Milton criticism, many critics have imposed an atomist notion of freedom onto Milton's Chaos. Dennis Danielson argues that "God 'retires' himself" from Chaos in the same way that he withdraws from "creaturely freedom."[24] Rumrich identifies Chaos as God's "capacity for otherness" and avers that "the psychological correlative of this substantial, divine capacity is freedom of the will, the foundation of Milton's ethical beliefs at least since the composition of *Areopagitica*."[25] If Chaos looks like "Satan's accomplice," Rumrich argues, that is because temptation presupposes freedom. Chaos, like free will, is good in itself. Although I am unpersuaded, I do find this argument useful. It gets hold of the right thing by the wrong end. Lucretius, following Epicurus, had argued that an unpredictable "swerve" [clinamen] in atomic motion accounted for free will, and the idea was developed in Milton's time by Pierre Gassendi and Walter Charleton.[26] Milton would have been aware of the theory, but it may be doubted whether he warmed to it. We should not conclude that Chaos and freedom are alike just because they both preclude determinism. We should look at Milton's own description of atomic motion before we leap to any conclusions. He writes:

> Hot, Cold, Moist, and Dry, four champions fierce
> Strive here for mast'ry, and to battle bring
> Their embryon atoms; they around the flag
> Of each his faction, in their several clans,

Light-armed or heavy, sharp, smooth, swift or slow,
Swarm populous, unnumbered as the sands
Of Barca or Cyrene's torrid soil,
Levied to side with warring winds, and poise
Their lighter wings. To whom these most adhere,
He rules a moment; Chaos umpire sits,
And by decision more embroils the fray
By which he reigns: next him high arbiter
Chance governs all.

(2.898–910)

Milton's atoms move randomly, not spontaneously. They are "Levied" (both "raised" and "enlisted") by the four contraries, which dash them hither and thither like grains in a sandstorm. Lucretius's atoms move *"ipsa / sponte sua"* (2.1058–59), of their own free will. Both poets are speaking metaphorically, but it matters that Chance, not free will, "governs all" in Milton's Chaos. Those critics who argue for the goodness of Milton's Chaos too often elide freedom with chance. Catherine Gimelli Martin, in a recent defense of Chaos, refers to "the 'randomness' of free will." Those quotation marks around "randomness" acknowledge that there is a problem but conspicuously fail to address it.[27] The difficulty for all such critics is that Milton identifies freedom with responsibility, not randomness. He even parodies atomist notions of freedom when he calls Chance a "high arbiter." The latter word evokes freedom *[arbitrium]* in order to exclude it. When Lucretius writes of swerving atoms, he uses *"arbitrium"* without irony to equate the atoms' freedom with our own (2.281). Milton's "arbiter" means "one who has power to decide or ordain according to his own absolute pleasure" (*OED* 3). The word smacks of tyranny, not freedom. Chance's arbitrary edicts are no doubt "capricious, uncertain, varying" as well as "despotic" (*OED* s. v. "arbitrary," 3, 4)—but so were those of Charles I. Caprice is something quite different from the freedom that was "the foundation of Milton's ethical beliefs." When Raphael says "to stand or fall / Free in thine own arbitrament it lies" (8.640–41), he is warning Adam to exercise moral choice. He is not inviting him to take a chance and let Chaos govern all.

Rumrich is deeply committed to Chaos, and he argues with passion, intelligence, and wit. Like others before him, he cites Milton's approval of primal matter in *De Doctrina Christiana*: "[T]his original matter was not an evil thing, nor to be thought

of as worthless: it was good, and it contained the seeds of all subsequent good. It was a substance, and could only have been derived from the source of all substance. It was in a confused and
disordered state at first, but afterwards God made it ordered and
beautiful" (6:308).[28] This passage is a favorite with those who see
Chaos as good, but there is a difference between it and *Paradise
Lost*. In *De Doctrina Christiana*, Milton insists that matter was
always "good." In *Paradise Lost*, God specifically identifies
"goodness" as the quality that Chaos lacks:

> Boundless the deep, because I am who fill
> Infinitude, nor vacuous the space.
> Though I uncircumscribed myself retire,
> And put not forth my goodness, which is free
> To act or not.
>
> (7.168–72)

Critics cite these lines as if they clinched the case for "goodness
in action,"[29] but God's goodness is out of action so far as Chaos
is concerned. Rumrich, quoting the lines, falls back on para-
phrase. Where God speaks of "goodness," Rumrich substitutes
"governing" and "control." God, he writes, "does not exercise
control . . . he is absent as an active, governing agent."[30] Rumrich
puts even more rhetorical pressure on "governing" and "control" in an earlier version of his argument, published in *PMLA*.
In the space of one paragraph we hear: "[T]he father does not exercise control," "the father is absent as an active, governing
agent," and "God refrains from being there as a governing
agent."[31] Rumrich's change of "goodness" to "governing" is
more significant than might at first appear. The change effectively turns God's words on their head, for Rumrich sees governing as bad. He repeatedly associates the word with Satan. Where
Milton's God withholds "goodness" from Chaos, Rumrich's
God withholds something satanic, and so makes Chaos better
than ever.

It is now time to turn to "ancient Night." Critics often con-
flate Chaos with Night, but I shall argue that they are distinct,
and that Night is in some ways the more sinister of the two. But
what *is* Night? Chambers conjectures that she is primal, "imper-
ceptible matter."[32] He distinguishes Night from Chaos, which is
visible and so must have form.[33] The problem with this learned
distinction is that Milton describes Chaos as "formless" (3.708)
and "unformed" (7.233). He nowhere implies that Night is mat-

ter. He speaks instead of "the void profound / Of unessential Night" (2.438–39), "the womb / Of unoriginal Night" (10.476–77), and "th' unreal, vast, unbounded deep" (10.471). From this I infer that Night is dark, infinite, uncreated space, identical with the deep, the abyss, the void. True, Milton does call Night "eldest of things" (2. 962), but Night is a "thing" in accordance with the atomists' theory that the void, though unreal, exists.[34]

A failure to distinguish Night from Chaos (void from matter) vitiates even the best Milton criticism. Rumrich rightly emphasizes the importance of womb imagery in Milton's abyss, but he distorts Milton's picture by attributing the womb to Chaos. He confidently declares: "[N]o one disputes that in *Paradise Lost* chaos is the 'Womb of Nature.' "[35] But I do dispute this. It is Night—"the abyss"—that is "The womb of Nature and perhaps her grave" (2.911). Belial speaks of "the wide womb of uncreated Night" (2.150), and Satan tells how he was "plunged in the womb / Of unoriginal Night and Chaos wild" (10.476–77). I admit that there is a syntactical ambiguity in that last phrase, but Milton elsewhere speaks of Chaos as "embryon atoms" (2.900) within Night's womb. Night is an "abortive gulf" (441) that conceives, but cannot deliver, embryonic matter. Rumrich is altogether too celebratory when he associates Chaos with Eve's "fruitful womb" (5.388). He performs rhetorical wonders in arguing that "chaos is to God as Eve is to Adam,"[36] but even his lyrical prose cannot disguise the horror of ancient Night:

> Before their eyes in sudden view appear
> The secrets of the hoary deep, a dark
> Illimitable Ocean without bound,
> Without dimension, where length, breadth, and heighth,
> And time and place are lost.
>
> (2.890–94)

Rumrich takes "Milton scholars" to task for ignoring "the link between chaos and sexual fruition,"[37] but many critics have remarked on the sexuality of ancient Night. Twenty years ago, Edward Le Comte noted how "secrets" in the above lines contains a pun on "secret parts, genitals" (*OED* 1j). Le Comte also hears a pun on "whore" in "hoary."[38] Some might think this far-fetched, but it accords with George Chapman's "Hymnus in Noctem," in which primal Night "(Most harlot-like) her naked secrets shows" (74).[39] "Hoary" might also play on "hory" meaning "foul, dirty, filthy" (*OED*). Rumrich chides Regina Schwartz for seeing Chaos "entirely in military terms,"[40] but Schwartz explicitly writes that the "epithets most frequently attached to chaos" are those of "an aborted birth, a womb that miscarries."[41] No one denies that Ancient Night is presented in sexual terms. The point at issue is whether Night's womb is so horrific as to preclude eroticism. Rumrich repeatedly uses the word "excess" to link Chaos with Eve, but Night, for all its immensity, is characterized by privation rather than abundance. As Le Comte notes, Night is "darkness, nothingness, the void, the bottomless pit."[42] Schwartz agrees that "it is as Nothing" that Chaos is "most threatening."[43] We should recall, in this context, that "nothing" was slang for female pudenda. Rumrich wants Chaos to be a material womb, teeming with life, but it is as a vast vacuity that Night's "secrets" appall the beholder. Nothing could be further from Eve's naked majesty than this "sudden view" of total privation.

Eve's fruitful womb is the source of human life. Milton never allows us to forget that we are all her children. Ancient Night is an "abortive gulf" that threatens "utter loss of being" (2.441, 440). It is the sheer sight of the void, rather than any physical contact with it or in it, that oppresses the would-be space-traveler. Night robs one of all sense of bearings, both spatial and moral. Satan on Hell's brink looks *up* into an "abyss" (910, 917). This is disorienting because the literal meaning of "abyss" (Greek ἄβνσσοϛ, Latin *abyssus*) is "bottomless pit" and Milton has until now encouraged us to think of Hell as an absolute bottom. As Robert Adams notes, Satan, by falling for nine days from Heaven to Hell, "creates a range of physical and moral possibility for man; he structures the cosmos. A universe consisting of just two parts, Heaven and Chaos, is essentially undirected and incomprehensible. . . . Satan, by falling, gives the cosmos a bottom and a sense of moral and physical distance."[44] That is well said, but Adams underestimates Night's power to circumvent this moral structure. Satan, too, had thought that he was at rock bottom and could only go up. But as he looks up into bottomlessness, he is from deep to deeper plunged. Milton forces this point home when Satan encounters a "vast vacuity" (932) and plummets downward. Had chance not intervened, he would be falling "to this hour" (934). Critics have shrunk from the implications of that phrase, but Milton really does open the possibility of a fall lasting thousands of years. Compared to this, Satan's nine-day fall is a cosmic jaunt and Hell a suburb of Heaven in the purlieus of light. Lucretius, describing the void, says that bright lightning [*"clara fulmina"*] would take eternity to traverse it (1.1003).[45] Lucretius and Milton would have had no difficulty in grasping the notion of "light-years." Milton's abyss, refusing to be tamed by Satan's nine-day fall, mocks God's notions of "moral and physical distance."

Night's most disturbing feature, however, is darkness. Milton repeatedly stresses it. To cite just a few instances, Night is "The dark unbottomed infinite abyss" (2.405), "a dark / Illimitable Ocean" (891–92), "the hollow dark" (953), "the dark abyss" (1027, 10.371) stretching "dark, waste, and wild" (3.424) "Through all the coasts of dark destruction" (2.464). For us, the darkness of outer space is so obvious that Milton's repeated epithet might seem redundant. As C. S. Lewis remarks in *The Discarded Image*, "nothing is more deeply impressed on the cosmic imaginings of a modern than the idea that the heavenly bodies move in a pitch-black and dead-cold vacuity."[46] Milton's stellar universe is not like this. In *Paradise Lost*, as in *A Masque Presented at Ludlow Castle*, Milton adopts the old model of a bright universe "Where day never shuts his eye" (978). We must make an imaginative effort to visualize this model. Here Lewis is invaluable:

> [N]owhere in medieval literature have I found any suggestion that, if we could enter the translunary world, we should find ourselves in an abyss of darkness. . . . And as they had, I think, no conception of the part which the air plays in turning physical light into the circumambient colour-realm that we call Day, we must picture all the countless cubic miles within the vast concavity as illuminated. Night is merely the conical shadow cast by our Earth. It extends, according to Dante (*Paradiso*, IX, 118) as far as to the sphere of Venus. . . . When we look up at the night sky we are looking through darkness but not at darkness.[47]

It is hard to say just when our ancestors realized that the darkness really was out there between the stars. Edward Harrison in *Darkness at Night* tells us that "the invention of the telescope at the dawn of the scientific age destroyed the old belief in celestial light and plunged the heavens in darkness."[48] By the late seventeenth century, natural philosophers were accustomed to the idea that outer space is dark. In 1672, Otto von Guericke pointed to interstellar darkness as proof that the stars must be finite in number. If the stars continued indefinitely, von Guericke argued, every line of vision would end on a star and the night sky would be bright. Harrison traces the origins of this riddle (now known as "Olber's paradox") to Thomas Digges's "A Perfit Description of the Caelestiall Orbes" (1576).[49] Milton's bright universe seems to have been out of date by 1667—at least among astronomers—though it no doubt still struck a familiar chord in the consciousness of his first readers.

Milton's universe certainly is bright. Satan, standing on its brink, looks down through the celestial day and sees terrestrial night as a remote shadow:

> Satan from hence now on the lower stair
> That scaled by steps of gold to Heaven Gate
> Looks down with wonder at the sudden view
> Of all this world at once . . .
> . . . .
> Round he surveys, and well might, where he stood
> So high above the circling canopy
> Of night's extended shade.
>
> (3.540–57)

The "circling canopy" is the earth's shadow "revolving like the hand of a clock."[50] From his high vantage point, Satan sees the universe in its true glory. A few lines later he glides down through "the pure marble air" (564). "Marble" (from Greek μαρμάρεοζ) means "sparkling." Satan passes through skies that are bright, warm, and (probably) thronged with life. Whatever his anxieties about outer space, Milton had no difficulty accepting the existence of life on other worlds. It is the thought of dark emptiness that chills him. He even hints at a solution to a problem that had tormented others. As Satan passes other planets, they resemble "those Hesperian gardens famed of old" (568). The allusion to the apples of the Hesperides hints that other worlds have their own forbidden fruit and so might not have fallen with Adam and Eve. Directly contradicting his own later statement that "Hesperian fables true" are found "only" in Adam and Eve's Paradise, Milton now boldly hints that other (perhaps unspoiled) Paradises might be strewn throughout the cosmos. Bruno had been burned alive for daring to suggest as much.

After this wonderful description of a bright universe it comes (or it *should* come) as a surprise to find ourselves in a dark one just 150 lines later. Directing Satan to the earth, Uriel says:

> Look downward on that globe whose hither side
> With light from hence, though but reflected, shines;

That place is earth the seat of man, that light
His day, which else as th' other hemisphere
Night would invade, but there the neighbouring moon
(So call that opposite fair star) her aid
Timely interposes.

(722–28)

This is odd. Terrestrial night had been a merely local privation. Now darkness is everywhere except for a few places ("that light," "His day") where heavenly bodies hold it in check. Uriel underestimates Night's powers when he says she *would* invade." In the space of 150 lines, Night *has* invaded our universe and conquered almost all of it. This contradiction is never resolved in *Paradise Lost*. When Raphael descends to earth, he sails between worlds and worlds like an Aegean "pilot" sailing through the "Cyclades" (5.264) to "Delos or Samos" (265). This lovely simile implies that the "vast ethereal sky" (267) is as blue as the Mediterranean, with planets inviting the island-hopping space traveler to rest. But when Eve asks Adam why the stars shine, Adam's answer assumes a dark universe. Stars shine, he says, "Lest total darkness should by night regain / Her old possession, and extinguish life / In nature and all things" (4.665–67). Here, as in Uriel's lines, primal darkness pervades our universe. How can we explain the contradiction? The simple answer is that Milton has it both ways because he does not know which is right. But we should not assume that he therefore does not care or that nothing is at stake.

What is at stake is the relation of our universe to ancient Night. A bright universe would be wholly distinct from outer darkness. A dark one would be uncomfortably like it. Describing the shell around our universe, Milton says that "bounds were set / To darkness" (3.538–39). Satan crossing this boundary is likened to "a scout" (543) who, having traveled "All night" (543) "Through dark and desert ways" (544) at last climbs a hill and sees a glorious city "by break of cheerful dawn" (545). Passing from Chaos to Creation, Satan passes from night to day. It is disconcerting, then, to find ourselves back in darkness just 150 lines later. To my mind, Milton's ambivalence about the brightness of our universe betrays a real anxiety that cannot be explained away. Milton wanted very much to believe that we inhabit a bright universe, bathed in light and love, but he could not shake the fear that our earth is "An atom" (8.18) in the void profound of unessential Night. Adam's metaphor of an atom implies more than just small size. Lurking in the background is the Epicurean notion that there is nothing but atoms and void.

The darkness of space never seems more oppressive than when Milton likens our whole universe to one of its own faint stars. Approaching from the depths of Night, Satan sees Heaven in the distance and "fast by hanging in a golden chain / This pendent world, in bigness as a star / Of smallest magnitude close by the moon" (2.1051–53). By likening the universe with all its stars to one of its own faint stars, Milton briefly evokes the image of an encompassing night that is utterly black. Standing on the outer shell of the universe, Satan surveys "a boundless continent / Dark, waste, and wild, under the frown of Night / Starless exposed" (3.423–25). A little earlier, Milton had described the shell of the universe as "Firm land imbosomed without firmament" (75). "Without" there means both "outside" and "not possessing" (OED 1, 2). Satan is on the outside of our firmament, and he has no firmament above him. The oxymoron "imbosomed without" perfectly captures the isolation and fragility of a universe that is embosomed in nothing but itself. What all these images have in common is a sense of exposure. It is as if the sky had been rolled away to reveal a boundless abyss. I have been arguing that something like this did happen in the seventeenth century, and that *Paradise Lost* is, among other things, an attempt to come to terms with the new "darkness visible."

We have seen that Milton calls Night "eldest of things." He also places "God and his Son" in the category of "Created thing" (2.678–79). The blasphemy shocked Richard Bentley, and the shock is only half-allayed by the pious discovery that Milton did think of the Son as a creature. Can it be that Night is as old as God the Father? Danielson dismisses the possibility of an eternal Chaos. In his view, "Satan alone in *Paradise Lost* speaks in dualistic terms, referring to his voyage through '*unoriginal* Night and Chaos wild' (10.477) and implying thereby the pagan view of some primordial state that is uncreated and without origin."[51] But it is in his own voice as poet that Milton refers to "eternal Night" (3.18) and the "Eternal anarchy" (2.896) of "eldest Night / And Chaos, ancestors of Nature" (894–95). Rumrich intriguingly points out that "the terms 'anarchy' and 'anarch,' the latter which seems to have been Milton's own coinage, can themselves be taken to mean that the eternal night of chaos lacks a beginning as well as governance (etymologically, both are possible translations of 'an-arch').'"[52] Rumrich is untroubled by the eternity of Chaos because he sees Chaos as an aspect of God. But Milton is troubled by the antiquity of darkness. He wants light to be primal:

> Hail holy Light, offspring of Heav'n first-born,
> Or of th' Eternal co-eternal beam
> May I express thee unblamed? Since God is light,
> And never but in unapproachèd light
> Dwelt from eternity.

(3.1–5)

If light was created, darkness must antedate it. This thought troubles Milton, who wants to think of darkness as a shadow cast by light. In *De Doctrina Christiana*, he goes out of his way to refute the idea that God sat in darkness for countless eons. Heaven must be bright and eternal: "It is not likely that God built a dwelling-place of this kind for his majesty only the day before yesterday, only, that is, from the beginning of the world. If God really has a dwelling-place where he pours forth his glory and the brightness of his majesty in a particular and extraordinary way, why should I believe that it was made at the same time as the fabric of this world, and not ages before?" (6:311). God's Heaven is certainly older than our universe in *Paradise Lost*. Chaos resents the encroachment of Hell and the new Creation, but even he cannot recall a time when Heaven was not. The natural inference is that Heaven and Night are coeternal. One might rescue this scheme for orthodoxy by arguing, along Rumrich's lines, that the darkness is somehow within God. Something must be conceded to this argument. God clouds himself with "the majesty of darkness" (2.266), and even the Son is "Gloomy as Night" when driving out the rebel angels (6.832). But Night's darkness differs from God's. God is "Dark with excessive bright" (3.380); Night's darkness is unremitted and unremitting.

To sum up: ancient Night in *Paradise Lost* combines Lucretius's void with the black interstellar space that we have learned to live with but whose existence was not finally admitted until the seventeenth century. This black void is a thing of darkness that Milton is reluctant to acknowledge. He tries to expel it from our universe, but it creeps back in his despite. The void is threatening because it raises uncomfortable questions about our importance and about the Creator's power and even his existence. Critics have either brushed these questions aside or tried to tame them. Rumrich liberates both Milton and Chaos when he bravely admits that Chaos is eternal, but he promptly binds Chaos again when he insists it is just an aspect of God. Danielson cannot admit that Chaos is eternal, but he does recognize that it is Godless. "What a fine picture of any world without God!" he cogently remarks of 2.898–916, but then he, too, reaches for the shackles: "The scene is certainly Satan's view in more ways than one."[53] But we cannot, and should not, shrink from the abyss with murmured complaints about "Satan's view." The telescope, not Satan, revealed ancient Night to be a void profound. Fortunately, Rumrich and Danielson are too intelligent and sensitive to be blinded by their prejudices. Each sees where the other stumbles. Rumrich rightly insists that Chaos is eternal, and Danielson rightly recognizes that it is "without God." Together, these two insights militate against the view of Night that both critics would promote. "Satan's view" of the abyss reveals Milton's fear of what our universe might be. Milton does his best to confine Night to outer darkness, but she still casts her shadow over us and him. Milton's pale dominion only partly checks the Night.

NOTES

1. A. B. Chambers, "Chaos in *Paradise Lost*," *Journal of the History of Ideas* 24 (1963): 83. Chambers's observation has received surprisingly little attention from later critics.

2. Ibid., 83.

3. Edmund Spenser, *The Faerie Queene*, ed. Thomas P. Roche Jr., with the assistance of C. Patrick O'Donnell Jr. (London: Penguin, 1978).

4. John Milton, *Paradise Lost*, in *The Complete Poems*, ed. John Leonard (London: Penguin, 1998). All references to Milton's poetry are to this edition and are cited parenthetically in the text.

5. Chambers, "Chaos in *Paradise Lost*," 75.

6. Milton had certainly read Lucretius. He includes him in the syllabus of *Of Education*, he refers to him in *Areopagitica* as a versifier of "Epicurism," and he cites *De Rerum Natura* in his marginal annotations of Aratus. See John Milton, *Complete Prose Works of John Milton*, 8 vols., ed. Don M. Wolfe et al. (New Haven: Yale University Press, 1953–82), 2:395, 2:498. All subsequent references to Milton's prose are to this edition and are cited parenthetically in the text.

7. Ovid uses "chaos" many times in the *Metamorphoses*. See, for example, 1.7 and 2.299.

8. Titus Lucretius Carus, *De Rerum Natura* (Amsterdam, 1626). Unless otherwise noted, all references to Lucretius are to this edition and are cited parenthetically in the text.

9. For an exception, see Philip Hardie, "The Presence of Lucretius in *Paradise Lost*," *Milton Quarterly* 29 (1995): 13–24.

10. This is especially true of those seventeenth-century philosophers who tried to reconcile atomism with theism. Philosophers such as Pierre Gassendi, Walter Charleton, and the Cambridge Platonists felt a pressing need to dissociate themselves from pagan atomists. Charleton repudiated the eternity of the atoms as "this faeculent Doctrine of Epicurus." See Stephen M. Fallon, *Milton Among the Philosophers: Poetry and Materialism in Seventeenth-Century England* (Ithaca: Cornell University Press, 1991), 43.

11. *Lucy Hutchinson's Translation of Lucretius: "De rerum natura,"* ed. Hugh de Quehen (London: Duckworth, 1996), 82. Hutchinson's comment comes in her note to 2.1095, where Lucretius denies that any god could be powerful enough to govern the universe.

12. See Alexandre Koyré, *From the Closed World to the Infinite Universe* (Baltimore: Johns Hopkins University Press, 1957), 58.

13. Walter Clyde Curry, *Milton's Ontology, Cosmogony, and Physics* (Lexington: University Press of Kentucky, 1957), 77, 145.

14. Harris F. Fletcher cites various rabbinical sources in *Milton's Rabbinical Readings* (Urbana: University of Illinois Press, 1930), 133–36. A. H. Gilbert cites St. Thomas, and Harry F. Robins cites St. Augustine. See A. H. Gilbert, "The Outside Shell of Milton's World," *Studies in Philology* 20 (1923): 447, and Harry F. Robins, "The Crystalline Sphere and the Waters Above in *Paradise Lost*," *PMLA* 69 (1954): 908.

15. Henry More, *Conjectura Cabalistica, or a Conjectural Essay of Interpreting the Minde of Moses, according to a three-fold Cabala* (London: William Morden, 1653), 3.

16. Harinder Singh Marjara, *Contemplation of Created Things: Science in "Paradise Lost"* (Toronto: University of Toronto Press, 1992), 103.

17. Alastair Fowler, ed. *Paradise Lost*, by John Milton, 2d ed. (London: Longman, 1998), 213 n. iii.721.

18. John P. Rumrich, *Milton Unbound: Controversy and Reinterpretation* (Cambridge: Cambridge University Press, 1996), 118–46 (see esp. 130–31).

19. Dennis Danielson, *Milton's Good God: A Study in Literary Theodicy* (Cambridge: Cambridge University Press, 1982), 50.

20. John Evelyn, *An Essay on the First Book of T. Lucretius Carus, "de Rerum Natura": with the Text, Interpreted and made English Verse* (London, 1656), 77–79.

21. A discrepancy between Renaissance and modern editions of Lucretius has had the unfortunate effect of obscuring this Miltonic allusion. Modern editions read *"rerum,"* not *"terrae."* The two Renaissance editions I have consulted (those published at Frankfurt in 1583 and Amsterdam in 1626) both print *"terrae,"* which exactly corresponds to Milton's "centre" (meaning the earth).

22. Lucretius's phrase *"rerum . . . summam"* has an obvious connection with *Paradise Lost* 6.673, in which God, "Consulting on the sum of things," sends his Son into battle to prevent Heaven from turning into Chaos. Editors (myself included) have overlooked this source, even though Merritt Y. Hughes, ed. *John Milton: Complete Poems and Major Prose* (New York: Odyssey, 1957), 339 n., and Fowler, ed., *Paradise Lost*, 372 n. vi.673, cite *"summarum summa,"* which comes just six lines earlier in Lucretius (5.361).

23. Miner discussed this topos in a paper he presented on Milton and allu-

sion at the Fifth Internation Milton Symposium at Bangor, Wales, in 1995. He
is now preparing a variorum annotation of biblical and literary allusions in *Paradise Lost*.

24. Danielson, *Milton's Good God*, 49.

25. Rumrich, *Milton Unbound*, 145.

26. See Fallon, *Milton Among the Philosophers*, 41–49. Fallon avoids the
trap that other Miltonists have fallen into when he remarks: "[A] random, corporeal anomaly such as the atomic swerve is no more compatible with a libertarian conception of the will than is mechanist determinism" (43).

27. Catherine Gimelli Martin, " 'Pregnant Causes Mixt': The Wages of Sin
and the Laws of Entropy in Milton's Chaos," in *Arenas of Conflict: Milton and
the Unfettered Mind*, ed. Kristin Pruitt McColgan and Charles W. Durham
(Selinsgrove, Pa.: Susquehanna University Press, 1997), 168.

28. Rumrich cites the passage in *Milton Unbound*, 120. See also Danielson,
Milton's Good God, 41.

29. Danielson, *Milton's Good God*, 43.

30. Rumrich, *Milton Unbound*, 144.

31. John P. Rumrich, "Milton's God and the Matter of Chaos," *PMLA* 110
(1995): 1043.

32. Chambers, "Chaos in *Paradise Lost*," 76.

33. Ibid., 76–81.

34. The notion (common to Leucippus, Democritus, Epicurus, and Lucretius) that there can be a void—that "Nothing" can exist—has seemed an intolerable paradox to many philosophers. Bruno, Kepler, Descartes, and Leibnitz
rejected the idea; Henry More and Isaac Newton felt the need to argue for it.
See Koyré, *From the Closed World*, 46–48, 101–4, 207–8, 250–51.

35. Rumrich, *Milton Unbound*, 119.

36. Ibid., 127, 145.

37. Ibid., 130.

38. Edward Le Comte, *Milton and Sex* (London: Macmillan, 1978), 69.

39. George Chapman, "Hymnus in Noctem," from *The Shadow of Night*, in
The Poems of George Chapman, ed. Phyllis Brooks Bartlett (London: Oxford
University Press, 1941), 21.

40. Rumrich, *Milton Unbound*, 130.

41. Regina M. Schwartz, *Remembering and Repeating: Biblical Creation in
"Paradise Lost"* (Cambridge: Cambridge University Press, 1988), 19.

42. Le Comte, *Milton and Sex*, 69.

43. Schwartz, *Remembering and Repeating*, 19.

44. Robert M. Adams, "A Little Look into Chaos," in *Illustrious Evidence:
Approaches to English Literature of the Early Seventeenth Century*, ed. Earl
Miner (Berkeley and Los Angeles: University of California Press, 1975), 76–77.

45. Lucretius, *De Rerum Natura, with an English Translation by W. H. D.
Rouse*, rev. Martin Ferguson Smith (1924; reprint, Cambridge: Harvard University Press, 1992), 82. Renaissance texts read *"flumina"* [rivers] not *"fulmina"*
[lightning].

46. C. S. Lewis, *The Discarded Image: An Introduction to Medieval and Renaissance Literature* (Cambridge: Cambridge University Press, 1964), 111.

47. Ibid., 111–12.

48. Edward Harrison, *Darkness at Night: A Riddle of the Universe* (Cambridge: Harvard University Press, 1987), 42.

49. Ibid., 34, 63. Digges attached "A Pefit Description" as an appendix to
the revised edition of his father's *Prognostication Everlastinge* (London, 1576).

50. Lewis, *The Discarded Image*, 112.
51. Danielson, *Milton's Good God*, 51.
52. Rumrich, *Milton Unbound*, 141. Milton calls Chaos "the Anarch old" at 2.988.
53. Danielson, *Milton's Good God*, 50.

Of Chaos and Nightingales

JOHN RUMRICH

I agree with much of what John Leonard has to say in his essay on Chaos and Night in this volume. Even if I did not, devoting this response entirely to rejoinder would mean replying to a reply to a chapter in my book—a metacritical vortex further complicated by the fact that the chapter in question was itself conceived as a reply to scholars who have afforded Chaos a universal hiss for hostility to God. Rather than focus on Chaos alone, then, and at the risk of transforming this dialogue into a parody of one of Milton's college exercises (i.e., "Whether Day or Night is the More Excellent"), I will ultimately respond to Leonard's pregnant meditation on possibly infertile Night, limiting myself to a few remarks concerning his comments on my previous work on Chaos.

Leonard begins by saying that I have argued for the goodness of Chaos, which I have, and concludes by saying that although he finds the question of Chaos's goodness fascinating, he believes that the moral frame is irrelevant. I agree with him and, paradoxical as it may sound, will claim that this irrelevance is central to my claim for the goodness of Chaos. First, though, I'd like to indulge in a digression concerning method.

At one point, Leonard seems to suggest that bookish learning and theological background, at least as deployed by some, are not quite pertinent to a proper understanding of Milton's poetry. If he means that readers ought not backpedal in contextual circles so as to slip the impact of Milton's poetry, or worse, treat the poetry as a versification of intellectual history, we are again in agreement. Unfortunately, however, the characterization of learning, logic, or of Milton's own theological treatise as blind guides to his poetry has often preceded serious misreading. It is in my view the classic prelude in attempts to wrench Milton's poetry so that it will fit the version of Milton a given scholar would like to propagate.

Much as I admire C. S. Lewis, for example, his construction of *Paradise Lost* as a monument to "ordinary" Christianity follows from a description of Milton's theology as private and whimsical, rife with idiosyncrasies that the decorous Milton would never allow to intrude into his great epic.[1] The ongoing dispute over the authorship of *De Doctrina Christiana* (hereafter referred to as *Christian Doctrine*) looks to me like a variation on the same critical gambit, though the stakes have risen from, in Lewis's case, Milton's seriousness as a theologian, to, in the present case, Milton's authorship of the theological treatise long attributed to him. William B. Hunter has candidly admitted the advantage of divorcing Milton from the treatise—having done so, we can place the poet "closer to the great tradition of Christianity, no longer associated with a merely eccentric fringe."[2]

Contextual knowledge is instrumental to sound interpretation, and Milton's theological treatise is among the most relevant contexts for *Paradise Lost*. Appealing to it so as to amplify our understanding of a notably philosophical and theological epic is not a bookish evasion. These concerns I register on principle, since Leonard evidently follows his highly developed instincts as a reader of poetry without a preset agenda, and his insights seem to me acute and reliable. His opposition causes me to reconsider my own arguments, though I turn now to defend them.

Let me begin with a couple of isolated points. First, as Leonard observes, usually it is Night, not Chaos, whose name appears in connection with the word "womb." Oddly, the passage cited in Leonard's essay is one passage in which "the hoarie Deep"—that is, the realm of Chaos—is described as the womb that gave birth to Nature, rather than as a womb belonging to Night: "The Womb of Nature and perhaps her Grave" (2.911).[3] The realm of Chaos is definitely a womb, maybe a destined grave. Here the four elements are "in thir pregnant causes mixt"; here reside the "dark materials" that God would require if he were "to create more Worlds" (913, 916). In short, the state of Chaos is in Milton's epic often referred to as the womb of Night, a womb that requires God's intervention before giving birth to Nature. Such a limitation is not usually understood as infertility, however.

My second point overlaps the first and is somewhat more complicated. To begin with, I have never intended to suggest that the anarch Chaos—the allegorical personage—is female in gender. He is undeniably male. In my opinion, he represents the unorderly condition of God's uncreated material potency, from which creation proceeds *ex deo:* a "heterogeneous and substantial virtue . . . in a confused and disordered state," as Milton says in *Christian Doctrine* (6:308).[4] Night, on the other hand, is female. The realm of Chaos is hers, as Satan and the allegorical anarch himself imply (2.986, 1002). At this point, we need to ask ourselves just what Milton's allegory might mean by depicting a masculine anarch as spokesman for a substantially feminine place. My conclusion has been that Chaos speaks for God's *voluntary* absence from Night's realm. That is, the anarch represents the absence of God's goodness—his creative, ordering will—and the metaphysical consequence of that absence, that is, a state of material anarchy. The realm for which Chaos speaks is distinctively indeterminate, decidedly undecided. Observing that God nonetheless insists that he fills this state of being, I also argue that the realm of Chaos or the womb of Night is essential to him as creator *ex deo* of independent beings with free will. I first made this claim in 1982 and have repeated and elaborated it several times since.[5] Though various scholars have indicated that they do not accept my arguments concerning Chaos, none has addressed this claim, one central to my larger argument and I believe basic to a proper understanding of *Paradise Lost.*

Let me repeat the chief propositions constituting this claim: the realm of Chaos is God's undetermined material potency, essential and necessary to him as sovereign creator; the dimension of God absent from Chaos is the authority that in book 7 we see intervening in Chaos to produce creation. God calls this creative governing authority his goodness. It is the ultimate organizing cause of creation and the origin of the moral order. I acknowledge that Chaos lacks *this* goodness and claim that the precise function of the allegorical anarch within Milton's epic is to represent this absence.

Nevertheless, my main argument has long been, in a critical context roundly condemnatory of Chaos as hostile to God, that Chaos is not evil or God's enemy, that indeed, Chaos is, after its fashion, good. This argument apparently contradicts what I just admitted—that Chaos lacks God's creative and moral goodness. So, to be more exact, the realm of Chaos is good only in the sense that it is materially sufficient for God's creative purposes. I am using good here in much the same sense that Shylock uses it when asking if Antonio is "good" for the loan Bassanio has proposed.[6] Chaos supplies the raw material for God's creative will to shape. These materials are infinitely versatile and neither corrupt nor shoddy in quality; they are sufficient to answer an infinite God's creative purposes, whatever they might be. Substantiating God's moral goodness when he does choose to put it forth, Chaos is prior to the moral order. It is irrelevant to judge Chaos and Night in the moral terms that we would apply to created beings.

Milton did have alternatives available to him in his theological and poetic accounts of matter. He could have followed the example of Plato's theodical myth in the *Timaeus*, which describes the first matter as inherently unsuitable for answering the deity's great idea. Given the recalcitrance of the raw materials, the results can be justified only to a limited extent: "God made them as far as possible the fairest and best, out of things which were not fair and good."[7] Or Milton could have followed the example of thoroughgoing dualists who saw matter, or at least its transgressive, unorderly energy, as evil and something to be transcended by the rational discipline of creatures unfortunate enough to find their being so intimately involved with such stuff. Much scholarly work on Chaos in *Paradise Lost* suggests that Milton to one degree or another followed one or the other of these alternatives. A. B. Chambers, for example, argued that Milton's depiction owed to the Platonic scheme and concluded that Chaos and Night are second only to Satan in their enmity to God and divine creation.[8] And, appealing to dualistic antecedents, Regina M. Schwartz has claimed that at least at the regressive level of symbolic discourse, the boundary-violating realm of Chaos is even more of a threat than agents such as Satan; that is, Milton's depiction hearkens back to protobiblical mythologies of battle between a heroic divinity against the Chaos monster.[9] Most recently, John Rogers has similarly claimed that the presence in Chaos of "black tartareous cold infernal dregs," which he associates—like others before him—with Hell (7.238), and which Raphael describes as being purged from the first matter before creation of our world, represents "an intractable theological aporia"; "Milton, it can safely be said, has sabotaged his attempt to justify the ways of God to men."[10]

For readers unfamiliar with the commonplaces of Christian theology, the presence of these dregs does perhaps amount to an aporia. I doubt that the same held true for Milton, who had reconciled himself to a God who punishes disobedience by imposing conditions "Adverse to life" (7.239). Milton agrees with traditional Christian theology at least to the extent that he asserts that God's establishment of Hell to punish sinners is just.

Like Dante before him, he presents Hell as an edifice of divine justice. And for Milton, all creation is material creation. If Chaos is to be considered sufficient to an infinite God's purposes, there must be material in it that is appropriate to produce a place of punishment:

> A Universe of death, which God by curse
> Created evil, for evil onely good,
> Where all life dies, death lives, and Nature breeds
> Perverse, all monstrous, all prodigious things
> Abominable, inutterable, and worse
> Then Fables yet have feignd, or fear conceiv'd.
>
> (2.622–27)

Presumably, the infernal dregs described by Raphael as "Adverse to life" and so purged from the material mold of our world are the sort of material that went into God's creation of Hell. Whether or not Milton was comfortable with this doctrine, it is consistent both with his theology and his poetry. God's "heterogeneous and substantial virtue" contains material diverse enough to establish either a Heaven or a Hell; if it did not, his justice and his supreme power would be impaired.

It seems to me erroneous to identify Milton's epic with traditions in which matter is considered refractory or belligerent. Nor does it seem to me that our debates over Chaos stem from critics' heedless imposition of Milton's theological arguments on the sacred text of his poetry. Rather, I think that our confusion mostly owes to failures in reading his poetry—specifically his allegory of Chaos. When the allegorical anarch says that "Havock and spoil and ruin" are his gain, we take him at his word as if he were a psychologically real, actively willing character expressing hostility toward divine creation—and thus Satan's ally (2.1008). And assuredly from the perspective of already created beings, the prospect of a return to Chaos is undesirable. The confusion of Chaos can be used to symbolize all sorts of conditions that—in a realm that has already been created—would certainly be evil or a consequence of evil. Hence, the prospect of Chaos was commonly used by those, such as Hobbes, who during the 1640s and 1650s argued on behalf of strong central governmental authority and stern punishment of rebels.[11]

I therefore emphasize that Chaos is a state of *potency*, not of *privation*—the latter term being applicable only to phenomena that have already been created. Nor does privation itself always indicate *moral* evil. In itself the term signifies simply a lessening or loss of something that already is or was. In the created world, Night can be represented as "Privation meer of light and absent day" without ominous overtones (*Paradise Regained*, 4.400). Indeed, given the usual antipathy toward Night in Renaissance poetry, this description could be taken as a comforting reassurance: darkness in itself does not imply the positive evil of a bogeyman or woman; Night is only the absence of day. Even as created phenomena, Night and darkness are not evil. God himself calls them good after he establishes them. Thus far, I believe, Leonard and I are mostly in agreement.

From an Augustinian, ontological-moral perspective, privation has also a moral significance indicating something that ought to be a certain way but, to some degree, is not—a willful deviation from or perversion of what the maker has ordained. In a prelapsarian world, it can be difficult to distinguish the natural from the moral order. Moral goodness may be defined as goodness that one ought to choose regardless of one's natural inclination. But for an unfallen creature, everything that is natural to do is also moral to do. That is why humanity has the naturally opaque commandment about the otherwise desirable fruit and why Raphael goes to earth to explain that, yes, Adam and Eve could choose to eat it. As various Milton scholars have observed, God's announcement in book 5 is the angelic equivalent of the forbidden fruit. It provides the angels with a similar opportunity to distinguish moral from natural good. Adam and Eve, though in different ways, choose to disobey God and pursue what they believe is naturally best for themselves. Similarly, the rebel angels believe, despite Abdiel's objection, that submission to God's new law would violate their natural best interest, as beings "ordained to govern not to serve," and so refuse to obey God's command (5.802). The Son's merit, on the contrary, derives from the fact that he consistently chooses God's will over what appears to be his best interest, the most excruciating biblical instance occurring in the Garden of Gethsemane.

I dwell on these moral distinctions only to claim that such distinctions are obviated when it comes to Chaos and Night. Or ought to be. The state of Chaos is "unoriginal" (10.477), "uncreated" (2.150), "Eternal" (2.896). Because Chaos and Night have never been created, there is nothing that they "ought" to be. Moral privation—evil—is something that they are incapable of, unless we were to assume that they could resist God's decision to create out of their realm. We know from Raphael's history and

Uriel's eyewitness testimony, however, that when God chooses
to create, the realm of Chaos is immediately obedient to his will
(3.708–13, 7.216–21). Nor is there ever a hint that they could decline or resist, although in an allegorical register, the characters
representing this state of being insist that the divine building
program lies athwart their interest. They would like to preserve
the cosmic wetlands from further development. But the facti-
tious attitudes of allegorical characters do not qualify as ethical
lapses.

Much of what I have said so far is based on abstract theological
argument and logic, arguments that I derive from Milton's
poetry by reference to Milton's theological writings. I acknowledge that poetry is evocative of meaning in ways that theological
discourse is not and that what I have said so far does not come
near to replying to what Leonard registers as the scary freight of
Milton's representations of Night. And as Leonard shows, Night
can be terrifying.

Milton does not uniformly or predominantly present Night
and darkness as threatening, dreadful, or terrifying, however. In
tracing Night's poetic silhouette, Leonard neglects to mention
that Heaven, too, regularly witnesses the coming of Night and,
like the divine intention to show lapsed man mercy announced
in book 3, it smells good:

> when ambrosial Night with Clouds exhal'd
> From that high mount of God, whence light & shade
> Spring both.
>
> (5.642–44)

Night is quiet and peaceful; during the War in Heaven, Night,
"Inducing darkness, grateful truce impos'd / And silence on the
odious dinn of Warr" (6.407–8). In Raphael's telling, Night and
darkness are as intimately connected with God as day and light:

> There is a Cave
> Within the Mount of God, fast by his Throne,
> Where light and darkness in perpetual round
> Lodge and dislodge by turns, which makes through Heav'n
> Grateful vicissitude, like Day and Night;
> Light issues forth, and at the other door
> Obsequious darkness enters, till her houre
> To veile the Heav'n, though darkness there might well
> Seem twilight here.
>
> (6.4–12)

It might be objected that in Heaven the privation of light is far from "mere" in the old sense of "unadulerated," and this fact would seem to substantiate rather than qualify Leonard's case for Miltonic Night anxiety. In Heaven, Night has light mixed into it; it is not mere privation.

Certainly Milton wrote in a poetic culture with a strong antipathy to darkness and Night. Lewis counted fear and loathing of Night and darkness as one of Spenser's signature poetic traits.[12] Recall, for example, the bitter complaint of Prince Arthur at the close of day:

> Night thou foule Mother of annoyance sad,
> Sister of heavie death, and nourse of woe,
> Which wast begot in heaven, but for thy bad
> And brutish shape thrust downe to hell below,
> Where by the grim floud of Cocytus slow
> Thy dwelling is, in Herebus blacke house
> (Blacke Herebus thy husband is the fow
> Of all the Gods) where thou ungratious,
> Halfe of thy dayes does lead in horrour hideous.[13]

Night and darkness, like death, are in the Renaissance often imagined as having jaws; Milton's devils, especially Belial, fear them in this way. And Milton in his writings variously depicts Night as old, ugly, shrewish, frowning, jealous, envious, and lowering. I do not dispute any of this, just as I do not dispute that in Milton's poetry the anarchic disorder and transgressive energy we associate with Chaos can seem dreadful and related to horrible violence.

Yet, following Joseph Summers, I am drawn by the phrase "grateful vicissitude" in assessing Night and think Milton more remarkable for his deviation from than for his adherence to the cultural predisposition so vividly exemplified by his original, Spenser. While the fallen angels take darkness as their proprietary domain, they concede that God, preeminently dwelling in bright Heaven, often chooses to reside

> amidst
> Thick clouds and dark . . .
> his Glory unobscur'd,
> And with the Majesty of darkness round
> Covers his Throne.
>
> (2.263–67)

The good angels, too, suggest that in relation to the Deity, light and dark collide in something like a coincidence of opposites:

> when thou shad'st
> The full blaze of thy beams, and through a cloud
> Drawn round about thee like a radiant Shrine,
> Dark with excessive bright thy skirts appeer,
> Yet dazle Heav'n.
>
> (3.377–81)

When the triumphant Son rolls over his foes, moreover, he advances not like daylight scattering "the rear of darkness thin" ("L'Allegro," 50) but like Night: "Hee on his impious Foes right onward drove, / Gloomie as Night" (6.831–32). Again, it is the rebel angels who are the chief victims of Night terror.

We find a similar dialectic in Milton's earlier poetry. If Night is the preferred time for Comus's evil rites, as it is for Belial's, it is also the preferred time for Il Penseroso, who finds mere daylight garish, obvious, and loud. In *Paradise Lost*, Raphael's discussion of the design of our world similarly complicates the tendency to valorize light over dark:

> consider first, that Great
> Or Bright inferrs not Excellence: the Earth
> Though, in comparison of Heav'n, so small,
> Nor glistering, may of solid good containe
> More plenty then the Sun that barren shines.
>
> (8.90–94)

On Earth as in Heaven, a subterranean "dark Nativitie" houses the "materials dark and crude" of a burgeoning, beauteous creation (6.482, 478). And their "good," as opposed to the vigor of sunlight, is "solid." Finally, it seems crucial to recognize that, like his God, the blind poet is wrapped in "cloud . . . and ever-during dark" (3.45). For him, Night is day, the only time he can see ("Sonnet 19"). I will not argue that Milton presents his affliction as desirable, yet he does seem to register it as the condition of his epic inspiration. He thus compares himself to the Nightingale, making poetry "as the wakeful Bird / Sings darkling, and in shadiest Covert hid / Tunes her nocturnal Note" (3.38–40). And as Eve tells us, "sweet the coming on / Of grateful Eevning milde, then silent Night / With this her solemn Bird" (4.646–48). Perhaps darkness is the price to be paid for Nightingales.

NOTES

1. C. S. Lewis, *A Preface to "Paradise Lost"* (London: Oxford University Press, 1942), 91.

2. William B. Hunter, "Forum: Milton's *Christian Doctrine,*" *SEL* 32 (1992): 166.

3. John Milton, *Paradise Lost,* in *The Poetical Works of John Milton,* ed. Helen Darbishire (Oxford: Oxford University Press, 1958). All references to Milton's poetry are to this edition and are cited parenthetically in the text.

4. John Milton, *Christian Doctrine,* in *Complete Prose Works of John Milton,* 8 vols., ed. Don M. Wolfe et al. (New Haven: Yale University Press, 1953–82). All references to Milton's prose are to this edition and are cited parenthetically in the text.

5. John Peter Rumrich, "Milton's Concept of Substance," *English Language Notes* 19 (1982): 218–33; *Matter of Glory: A New Preface to "Paradise Lost"* (Pittsburgh: University of Pittsburgh Press, 1987), 53–69; "Milton's God and the Matter of Chaos," *PMLA* 110 (1995): 1035–46; *Milton Unbound* (Cambridge: Cambridge University Press, 1996), 118–46.

6. William Shakespeare, *The Merchant of Venice,* in *The Riverside Shakespeare,* ed. G. Blakemore Evans (Boston: Houghton Mifflin, 1974), 1.3.12–17.

7. Plato, *Timaeus,* in *The Collected Dialogues,* ed. Edith Hamilton and Huntington Cairns (Princeton: Princeton University Press, 1961), 53b.

8. A. B. Chambers, "Chaos in *Paradise Lost,*" *Journal of the History of Ideas* 24 (1963): 55–84.

9. Regina M. Schwartz, *Remembering and Repeating: Biblical Creation in "Paradise Lost"* (Cambridge: Cambridge University Press, 1988), 18–30.

10. John Rogers, *Matter of Revolution: Science, Poetry, and Politics in the Age of Milton* (Ithaca: Cornell University Press, 1996), 137.

11. Thomas Hobbes, *Leviathan,* ed. Richard Tuck (Cambridge: Cambridge University Press, 1991), 254, 299.

12. C. S. Lewis, *The Allegory of Love* (Oxford: Oxford University Press, 1936), 313.

13. Edmund Spenser, *The Faerie Queene,* in *Edmund Spenser's Poetry,* ed. Hugh Maclean and Anne Lake Prescott (New York: W. W. Norton, 1993), 3.4.55.

The Confounded Confusion of Chaos

WILLIAM B. HUNTER

A major subject to which the author, supposed to be John Milton, of *De Doctrina Christiana* [*Christian Doctrine*] bears witness is the denial of a dichotomized universe. Ever since Jack Adamson's essay "Milton and the Creation" appeared in 1962,[1] Milton's monism (argued from that treatise) has been a matter of near creedal acceptance. In brief, Adamson used *De Doctrina* to show that the substance of which God made the universe he did not create from nothing *(ex nihilo)* but from himself *(ex deo)*. "It is clear," the author of the treatise asserts, "that the world was made out of some sort of matter . . . [which] must either have always existed, independently of God, or else originated from God at some point in time" (6:307).[2] He proceeds to show that the latter alternative is the necessary choice and goes on to the logical extension that, derived from God as it was, it was necessarily good: "[T]his original matter was not an evil thing. . . . [I]t was good, and it contained the seeds of all subsequent good. . . . [I]t was in a confused and disordered state at first, but afterwards God made it ordered and beautiful" (6:308). Assuming, as everyone then did, that Milton was the author of these sentences, one would necessarily read their implications into the chaos of *Paradise Lost*, Raphael's description of the "Scale of Nature" that orders the universe, and the narration of its creation in book 7. Thus monism: matter underlies all being, including God, from whom it derives. But as Augustine pointed out, creation *ex deo* runs counter to the orthodox belief that only the Son was begotten (from eternity) from the divine substance: "You [God] created heaven and earth but you did not make them of your own substance. If you had done so, they would have been equal to your only begotten Son, and therefore to yourself."[3] Such problems do not, of course, arise for an Arian such as the author of *De Doctrina*.

I propose to reconsider the evidence that *Paradise Lost* affords.

228

(Milton never raises the issue of monism elsewhere. The *Art of Logic* discusses the material cause of things but does not consider the question of how matter originates.) It is clear that the material chaos in the poem must be equivalent to the original matter derived directly from God according to the treatise. But *De Doctrina* says unequivocally that "it was good," a fact that cannot be asserted of its ruler Chaos in the poem, who is certainly not good. He is lawless ("Anarch old," 2.988), and his realm consists of total disorder ("Confusion worse confounded," 996).[4] Satan's trip through it is one of unremitting violence. Chaos welcomes the evil visitor and helps him go on to the Earth, adding, "Havock and spoil and ruin are my gain" (1009), scarcely characteristics of goodness. He had opposed God's earlier creation of Hell, then of the visible universe, out of his dominions and obviously would like for them to be reduced again to chaos. The only sense in which his realm, the physical chaos, can be described as good is as providing the materials from which God founds creation. He would not create an evil Deep but one with the potential of becoming evil, as was true of his creation of the angel who would become the evil Satan and of Adam. I conclude with Michael Lieb that Chaos is neutral: "The Abyss is not inherently evil, although it can be put to evil use."[5] I see no way to identify the chaos described in the poem with the inherent goodness of the original matter as the treatise defines it. As to whether it derives *ex nihilo* or *ex deo*, the poem is simply silent; and Milton never raises the question elsewhere.

Believing that the same author was responsible for both treatise and poem, some of our most perceptive critics have wrestled with the reconciliation of this conflict between them. For example, A. S. P. Woodhouse rather unwillingly conceded that in contrast with the description of it in *De Doctrina*, chaos could indeed be evil in the poem.[6] Significantly, Regina M. Schwartz has devoted an entire chapter to some aspects of the problem, seeking "some resolution to the conflict between Milton's doctrine [in *De Doctrina*] and his depiction of it" in *Paradise Lost*, though she premised her discussion by giving up on its central problem: "I find the inference of an evil chaos so difficult to escape that it is not worth trying."[7] But if Milton did not author the chapter on creation in the treatise, the problem vanishes.

In order to understand clearly the significance of the contrast between the inherently good chaos of *De Doctrina* and the inherently neutral one of *Paradise Lost*, one must recognize that the latter exists in two distinct forms, all originally neutral, of which God transforms a part to good, the limited material upon which he will found his creation. This is the area that the Son encircles with the sweep of the golden compasses. At that action the "vast immeasurable Abyss / Outrageous as a Sea, dark, wasteful, wild" (7.211–12) changes with the concomitant command "Silence, ye troubl'd waves, and thou Deep, peace" (216), marking the emergence of the second, now good, stage of the existence of chaos, "purg'd" of its "black tartareous cold infernal dregs" (237–38). In his account of this same event viewed from a different perspective, Uriel, the angel of the Sun, saw how "at his [God's] Word the formless mass . . . came to a heap"— separated off from the rest—and the "Confusion [of Chaos] heard his voice" so that its "vast infinitude" would stand "rul'd [or] confin'd" (3.708–11). This limited area is the matrix of creation, which becomes the orbicular and illuminated universe that Satan sees from the darkness of chaos as he ends his long journey through it (2.1034–55).

Even before this event and before the Creation begins, the Father had directed and explained this transformation of a portion of the neutral chaos into one that provides the good matter for the universe: he directs his Son, the creative Word, to

> bid the Deep
> Within appointed bounds be Heav'n and Earth,
> Boundless the Deep, because I am who fill
> Infinitude, nor vacuous the space.
> Though I uncircumscrib'd my self retire,
> And put not forth my goodness, which is free
> To act or not, Necessitie and Chance
> Approach not mee, and what I will is Fate.
>
> (7.166–73)

Through the divine obscurity of this somewhat convoluted command, one perceives that the "Deep" is the original neutral chaos. It is "Boundless," as is God, but not identical with him. He claims responsibility for its origin and extent: infinite as he is, he has filled the Infinitude of a "Boundless . . . Deep." This has been interpreted in accord with the dogma of the treatise: it "originated from God." But it may mean merely that he "fill[ed] Infinitude" with this creation without any implication that this entity originated from himself.

He goes on in the next sentence to explain that he did not have to extend to this original Deep, or chaos, his "goodness, which is free / To act or not" and which thus is not necessarily good as the author of the *De Doctrina* insists that it is. In these lines, that is, Milton is taking an express stand against the moral (and physical) monism inherent in the Deep that the treatise supports. God's retirement from it is moral, not physical; for he is not in the least material: "Necessitie and Chance," he says, do not "approach" him in any way, but they do determine matter. In chaos, which certainly is material, "Chance governs all" (2.910), and Chance is a companion of Chaos's throne (965). Thus God expressly denies himself any materiality, which is subject to chance. In sharp contrast, the all-encompassing material monism that the author of *De Doctrina* postulates forbids such a distinction as Milton can make when he recognizes two stages in the existence of chaos.

Another account of the status of matter in the universe is Raphael's description (to Adam) of the Scale (ladder) of Nature (5.469–90) or Chain of Being that unifies the circumscribed matter "purg'd" of its adverse elements into which God extends his goodness. The angel elaborates the origin of beings that proceed from God (but he does not mention the earlier existence of matter derived from an undivided chaos—indeed, he does not mention chaos at all): "one Almightie is, from whom / All things proceed" and back to whom they may ultimately return. They all result from the impregnation of matter, common to everything, with the different forms that distinguish one being from another: this pre-existent matter has been "Indu'd with various forms" in "various degrees / Of substance" (469–74). At the beginning of the poem we learned that this impregnation happened when the "Spirit" (1.17) induced these forms into matter: there the narrator invokes that Spirit who

> from the first
> Wast present, and with mighty wings outspread,
> Dove-like satst brooding on the vast Abyss
> And mad'st it pregnant.
>
> (19–22)

This activity is restated when the "brooding wings" infused the matter with "vital vertue . . . and vital warmth" as the Creation begins in book 7 (235–36). But this matter, now constituting the "vast Abyss" or the matrix to be impregnated, is not the neutral original matter of chaos but that of its calmed and spatially restricted area to which God had extended his goodness with the sweep of the golden compasses.

The various levels of being that result from enduing matter with form, Raphael goes on to say, actively seek to rise to higher forms; thus the Scale of Nature results. "[B]ody [may] up to spirit work." The root becomes the stalk, which in turn becomes the leaves and fruit. They, "by gradual scale sublim'd," may "To vital Spirits aspire, to animal, / To intellectual." This last level, the human, may then seek to rise to the yet higher, angelic level (5.478–500). Thus the informed matter of food (body) may become a human being (spirit) or even an angel, who can find it nutritious as Raphael does. In this way the angel, as Milton's spokesman, tries to bridge the mind-body dichotomy that exercised many contemporaries such as Henry More, Ralph Cudworth, and René Descartes. The various levels of "spirits" that Raphael distinguishes determine the various levels of being; a single matter is common to everything.

I do not believe, however, that Raphael's declaration can withstand rigorous analysis. At its lower levels his "spirits" seem analogous to those postulated by contemporary science. According to Robert Burton, who is repeating the scientific commonplaces of the day, from digestion of food come the four humors, including blood. From blood, in turn, derives "Spirit . . . a most subtle vapour, which . . . is the instrument of the soul to perform all his actions; a common tie or *medium* betwixt the body and the soul, as some will have it."[8] According to him, there are three levels of such spirits, "Natural, vital, animal," which Raphael seems to be echoing in part with his "vital, animal, and intellectual" spirits. But Burton always defines his in the physiological terms of life processes. Thus his *animal spirits . . . give* sense and motion to the body." Such spirits he evidently considered to be corporeal substances, though highly refined ones. These are the physiological "animal spirits" derived from the blood, according to Burton, that Satan taints to produce Eve's dream in *Paradise Lost* (4.804–5).

Confusingly, Raphael skips Burton's "Natural" spirit but retains his "vital" and "animal" ones and adds the yet higher "intellectual," which provides "understanding, whence the Soul / Reason receives, and reason is her being" (5.485–87). But understanding and reason are not physiological spirits; they are psychological faculties, as Adam explains to Eve:

> But know that in the Soul
> Are many lesser Faculties that serve
> Reason as chief.
>
> (100–102)

Raphael thus must mean that reason is the identifying faculty or activity of the human soul, not identical with it as "her being." As Burton again observes, "The common division of the *soul* is into three principal faculties, *vegetal, sensitive,* and *rational.*"[9] For him, too, they are faculties, not spirits in the physiological sense; and they must be what Raphael is driving at with his "vital, animal, and intellectual" spirits.

Like Burton, but unlike Raphael, the treatise defines spirit in this context as faculty. First, *De Doctrina* observes that in the Bible the word "means nothing but the breath of life"—the incorporeal substance upon which Burton will elaborate in his long "Digression" upon spirits as demons and witches. But it can also mean "the vital or sensitive or rational faculty" (6:317)—this latter being identical with Burton's "three principal faculties" (not substances). The treatise is clear; Raphael's words are not—because of Milton's eagerness through Raphael as mouthpiece to unify the entire creation from the lowest to the highest informed matter into a single Chain of Being. Raphael's reason is not a substance but is rather the identifying ability or faculty possessed by one substance, the human soul. Satan accurately repeats this traditional series of faculties: "Growth, Sense, Reason, all summ'd up in Man" (9.113). Raphael confuses the physiological and corporeal meanings of "spirits" with the "spirits" that are synonymous with souls and yet higher forms of incorporeal substance.

De Doctrina appears superficially to be arguing the same monistic position: it asserts that matter "originated from God at some point in time," and thus "it was good, and it contained the seeds of all subsequent good." From the treatise's full-blown materialistic monism, Barbara Lewalski can argue that this same "principle underlies the epic's blurred distinction between matter and spirit, angels and humans, intuitive and discursive intellect"[10]—blurred distinctions that certainly exist in the poem. But as has been seen, it cannot account for its primitive neutral chaos. Furthermore, there is no evidence at all in *De Doctrina*'s chapter on creation to support the concept of a Scale of Nature or Chain of Being; nor does it give any indication that body may actively work its way up to higher forms as Raphael says it "aspires" to do.

One may posit against this last statement the importance that the treatise places in this chapter on the "power of matter." It asserts "that all form—and the human soul is a kind of form—is produced from [not by] the power of matter [*ex potentia mater-*

iae]'' (6:322). This may seem at first sight to be directly analogous to matter that can work its way, in Raphael's words, up to vital, animal, and intellectual spirits. Such, however, is a serious misunderstanding of the meaning of "power" as a translation of *potentia materiae.*[11] The concept derives from Aristotle, who viewed all being as composed of matter and form. Matter, in his view, had the capacity or potentiality (the true meaning here of *potentia*) to become a formed object. In itself matter is completely powerless, inert. Another being *educes* from it the object that it potentially can become. In no sense can it "aspire" to anything in Raphael's sense. The newly formed object educed from it (not induced into it) can in turn be the matter from which a yet higher form may be educed, and so on. A Chain of Being, that is, is implied in Aristotle's system, but its constituents do not, *qua* matter, seek such higher realization. Finally, the matter in Raphael's system is "indu'd" with externally derived forms. Milton in his poem and the author of the treatise, in conclusion, arrive at a monistic universe from quite different fundamentals. Milton's is spatially limited by the "golden Compasses," which "circumscribe / This Universe, and all created things" (7.225–27) but exclude the rest of chaos from which it derives, a separation never suggested in the treatise. It never alludes in any way to a Scale of Nature; Milton in turn never mentions the power of matter. In such attempted monism, neither satisfactorily resolved the mind-body dualism that troubled contemporaries. Through Raphael, Milton tries to achieve it at the expense of confusing two meanings of spirit. The treatise asserts monism with the concomitant failure to distinguish the created from the divine.

One should note that Raphael establishes the concept of the Scale of Nature to prove what may seem to be a rather minor point: that he can really eat and digest human food. The issue had been settled for all angelologists except Milton: angels merely seemed to eat.[12] But he insists that Adam, Eve, and Raphael sat down

> And to their viands fell, nor seemingly
> The Angel, nor in mist, the common gloss
> Of Theologians.
>
> (5.434–36)

This derives directly from Gen. 18.1–8, where Abraham entertains angels at a meal, the scriptural authority for Milton's views on this subject. Had he written *De Doctrina,* he could have found this passage a useful support for the argument presented there for creation *ex deo.* The author of the treatise was evidently not interested in angels' food nor in the fact that it might help document his position.

There is indeed no such biblical authority for angelic sexuality. John Donne's view in "The Relique" is the standard one, that angels are sexless: "Difference of sex no more wee knew, / Then our Guardian Angells doe" (25–26).[13] A basic reason for such a position is the belief that the primary reason for sexuality is the begetting of children; such, for example, has been the position of the Roman Catholic Church. Angelic sex would lead to the production of baby angels who would, I suppose, upset heaven's economy; and putti are useful only as decorative appendages to Renaissance pictures. The author of *De Doctrina* seems to have accepted some such dogma emphasizing the fertile aspect of sexuality in human beings. For him the "proper fruit" of marriage "is the procreation of children." "Since the fall of Adam, the relief of sexual desire has become" a kind of secondary end" (6:370). In contrast, in the poem before the fall of Adam, it obviously had been a primary end. Raphael rejoices, too, over God's great gift of sexuality to the angels. Companionship rather than procreation dominates the view of marriage in the divorce tracts. I do not see how the same man could classify sexuality as a "secondary end" in *De Doctrina* and also create the sexual speeches and scenes that he included in *Paradise Lost* (for what would Paradise be without sex?).

NOTES

"The Confounded Confusion of Chaos" originally appeared as chapter 8 in *Visitation Unimplor'd* (Pittsburgh: Duquesne University Press, 1998), 121–34. This revised version is reprinted by permission of the publisher.

1. Jack Adamson, "Milton and the Creation," *Journal of English and Germanic Philology* 61 (1962): 756–78.

2. *De Doctrina Christiana* [*Christian Doctrine*], in *Complete Prose Works of John Milton,* 8 vols., ed. Don M. Wolfe et al. (New Haven: Yale University Press, 1953–82). All references to the treatise are to this edition and are cited parenthetically in the text.

3. Augustine, *The Confessions,* trans. R. S. Pine-Coffin (London: Penguin, 1961), 12.7.

4. John Milton, *Paradise Lost,* in *The Complete Poetry of John Milton,* ed. John T. Shawcross, rev. ed. (Garden City, N.Y.: Doubleday, 1971). All references to Milton's poetry are to this edition and are cited parenthetically in the text.

5. Michael Lieb, *The Dialectics of Creation* (Amherst: University of Massachusetts Press, 1970), 16–17.

6. A. S. P. Woodhouse, "Notes on Milton's Views on the Creation: The Initial Phases," *Philological Quarterly* 28 (1949): 229 n. 30.

7. Regina M. Schwartz, *Remembering and Repeating: Biblical Creation in "Paradise Lost"* (Cambridge: Cambridge University Press, 1988), 11. Recent developments in chaos theory and in investigating Milton's depiction of chaos in its light have enlisted the interest of several perceptive critics. See especially the essays of Mary F. Norton, " 'The Rising World of Waters Dark and Deep': Chaos Theory and *Paradise Lost*," and Catherine Gimelli Martin, " 'Pregnant Causes Mixt': The Wages of Sin and the Laws of Entropy in Milton's Chaos," both in *Arenas of Conflict: Milton and the Unfettered Mind*, ed. Kristin Pruitt McColgan and Charles W. Durham (Selinsgrove, Pa.: Susquehanna University Press, 1997), 140–60 and 161–82; and John P. Rumrich, "Milton's God and the Matter of Chaos," *PMLA* 110 (1995): 1035–46.

8. Robert Burton, *The Anatomy of Melancholy*, 3 vols. (London: Dent, 1926), pt. 1, sec. 1, mem. 3, subsec. 2.

9. Ibid., subsec. 5.

10. Barbara Kiefer Lewalski, "Forum: Milton's *Christian Doctrine*," *SEL* 32 (1992): 149.

11. For further discussion of this concept, see William B. Hunter, "The Power of Matter," in *The Descent of Urania: Studies in Milton, 1946–1988* (Lewisburg, Pa.: Bucknell University Press, 1989), 137–48.

12. See Robert H. West, *Milton and the Angels* (Athens, Ga.: University of Georgia Press, 1955).

13. John Donne, "The Relique," in *The Complete Poetry of John Donne*, ed. John T. Shawcross (New York: New York University Press, 1968), 142.

"If Not Milton, Who Did Write the *DDC*?":
The Amyraldian Connection

PAUL R. SELLIN

> A proper account of the treatise must rest on the Latin text
> and must take appropriate account of the highly unusual
> character of the manuscript.
>
> Gordon Campbell, Thomas M. Corns, John K. Hale,
> David I. Holmes, and Fiona J. Tweedie

The natural challenge to Professor William B. Hunter's calling
into question the attribution of *De Doctrina Christiana* (hereafter designated *DDC*) to John Milton[1] is first, like Christopher
Hill, to demand, "if not Milton, who did write the *DDC*?" Then,
since identifying such an "unknown author" is supposedly
"fairly easy," authorial orthodoxy ridicules the endeavor when
there is no ready answer acceptable to pro-Miltonists.[2] Apart
from indulging in the obvious non sequitur that refuting Hunter
proves Milton's authorship, the method raises questions about
assumptions that we commonly use in clinging to the notion of
Milton's authorship.

To term the problem of identifying an alternative author a
light task betrays, first, some insouciance regarding prepposses-
sions. Many seem to think that as such a substitute author
ought to be someone in agreement with Milton's unorthodox
views, a simple-minded search for unusual ideas that he shares
will do. Thus, when a kindred advocate of divorce fails to turn
up, it follows that Milton authored the *DDC* and that other peculiar elements in the treatise are therefore his, too. But is the
premise sound? What happens if, now that the supposed cross-
reference to *Tetrachordon* in *DDC* has been discredited,[3] we
start with the equally tenable assumption that Milton was hostile to the treatise or an enemy of the author?

A second notion that should be questioned is single authorship of the sections of the treatise that have led, as Hunter puts

it, to religiously eccentric interpretations of Milton's work. That is, we have long known that substantial portions of the *DDC* are composite, deriving directly or indirectly not from Milton but other authors such as Johannes Wollebius and William Ames. Yet, Milton's sole authorship of the earlier parts of the treatise has until recently appeared too sacrosanct to call in question. However, as the independent labors of the Campbell-Corns-Hale-Holmes-Tweedie group in England and Hunter in America now suggest, much of this material may not be Milton's, either, albeit some sections still seem to be "accretions" or parts that do derive from him.[4] Whether one agrees with this (to me rather overly ingenious) manner of accounting for inconsistencies between the *DDC* and the rest of Milton's corpus, the point is that one can no longer be sure of what in the *DDC* is Miltonic. The sheer size of the problem becomes staggering because Campbell *cum suis* and Hunter have destabilized the text. They render it impossible to be absolutely certain that any specific dogma or controversial point necessarily represents Milton's thought. Anyone seeking to prove authorship is going to have to winnow through every issue separately and make that determination.

Thirdly, the theological colors under which the treatise has commonly been forced to march may be suspect. As I have pointed out elsewhere, the search for another author cannot be restricted to radical divines of Arminian or Socinian persuasion because the *DDC* exhibits an oddly conservative streak regarding predestination.[5] Subsequent research confirms that on the subject of predestination, the treatise is not a purely Remonstrant or "Arminian" document. It seems rather to be of Amyraldian origin, a controversial variant of Reformed divinity that,[6] with but a couple of exceptions,[7] Milton studies have completely overlooked,[8] partly because of its superficial resemblance to Arminianism,[9] partly because of Amyraut's royalist political philosophy.[10]

Let me elaborate. In his *Brief Traité de la Prédestination et de ses principales dépendances* of 1634, Moyse Amyraut, a leading divine at the Huguenot academy of Saumur, enunciated a striking theory of "hypothetical universalism," as it is frequently called.[11] Insisting that "it is necessary carefully to distinguish between the will to save mankind (which some, contrary to scriptural usage, call predestination to salvation) from election, or predestination to faith,"[12] his remarkably ecumenical spirit sought to reconcile conservative Calvinist dogma regarding double predestination with scriptural affirmations regarding the universality of redemption and the call to salvation.

According to the *Traité*, the term "predestination" is used with reference to three quite different things. The "word 'providence' being more often than not used for that which relates in general to management of the world, 'predestination' has been employed to denote not only that providence which keeps watch in general over human actions but the one in particular according to which God has directed human beings to their ends."[13] That is, God did not create the world haphazardly but according to a set plan that assigns an "end" [*but*] or final cause to each creature, and the organizing principle according to which God "predestined" mankind is conformity "à l'image de Son Fils." As God's chef d'oeuvre, created in his own image, mankind shared in the divine powers of intelligence, reasoning capable of comprehending the divine works, and choice. Adam's was a "condition naturelle" of perfect felicity; yet, owing to the special nature of his making, his state was "*muable*," contingent upon obedience.[14]

This leads to the second use of "predestination." As God had foreseen, man, deceived "par le diable," fell from "l'integrité en laquelle il avoit esté creé."[15] Because in between "the first creation of man and that end to which the Apostle says we have been directed in order to be adopted in Jesus Christ, sin intervened, the effects and consequences of which have been dreadful in the world, and which seems to have altered not only the entire face of the universe but even the whole design of his first creation," God was, "if one must so speak, induced" to make "new decisions."[16]

The first of these is a "decree" [*conseil*] or "[act of] will" [*volonté*][17] "by which God has arranged to carry out" his new plan.[18] That is, he decided to send his Son into the world as a "propitiation for their offences . . . and the salvation that he received from his Father in order to impart it to men in the sancification of the Spirit."[19] For "in the beginning," he had created us "both good and happy indeed, but in a natural condition nonetheless, and consequently mutable. That which is natural coming first and having corrupted itself, it befitted God's wisdom, since he wished to restore man, to place him in a supernatural condition . . . that far surpasses anything Adam ever had."[20] This *conseil* constitutes Amyraut's famous hypothetical act of "will" or general "decree" by which God bestowed salvation on fallen mankind. It is in the first place a "universal" decree: "The sacrifice that [Christ] made in propitiation of their offenses was for all, and the salvation that he received from his Father in order to pass it on to human beings in the sanctification of the Spirit and the glorification of the body, is intended for all, provided, I say, that the predisposition necessary for receiving it be in all men the same."[21]

It is also *not* an absolute decree, but an entirely conditional one:

Human misery being universal, and God's desire to deliver them by means of such a great Redeemer, proceeding from the compassion that he had for them as creatures of his fallen into such huge ruin; and as they are his creatures without preference, the grace of redemption which he has offered and procured for them had to be universal, provided they too were all predisposed to receive it. And in this, nor until then, there is no difference at all among them.[22]

The all-important "condition qui . . . est annexée" to this first decree of universal salvation[23] derives primarily from John 3.16. The words, "For God so loved the world, that he gave his only begotten Son, that whoever believes in him should not perish, but have eternal life," Amyraut tells us, "seem to arrange universal grace, as deriving from that love that God bore towards human kind, in such fashion that they nevertheless limit it to those who *believe,* and that it does not seem that those who have never heard of Christ are invited to believe in him, and yet they do NOT contradict what we have propounded above." [24]

In short, Christ died for all men, not just the elect; at the same time his death is not universally efficacious. If one considers

the care that God took in procuring salvation for humankind by sending his Son into the world and the things that he has done and suffered there to this end, grace is universal and offered to all men. But if you consider the condition that he of necessity attached to it, belief in his Son, you will find that although this care of his in providing a Redeemer for man proceeds from a marvellous love toward humankind, nevertheless this love does not go beyond the bound of bestowing salvation on men, provided that they do not turn it down; if they refuse it, he snatches hope of it away from them, and they through their unbelief worsen their condemnation. And therefore these words, "God wills the salvation of all men," necessarily incur this qualification, "provided that they believe." If they do NOT believe, it is not his will—his will to make the grace of salvation universal and common to all mankind being conditional to such an extent that unless the condition is fulfilled, it is entirely ineffectual.[25]

How does fallen mankind come to fulfill the condition of faith that God has laid down as necessary to salvation? This is the third thing to which the term "predestination" applies: Namely, the other postlapsarian *conseil* or *volonté* that establishes specific means for putting the general decree into effect. Unlike its predecessor, this decree is absolute, not conditional, and it is also particular, not universal. To Amyraut, this is the true "predestination de Dieu," properly denoted, for it is the means "by which he has arranged to fulfill the condition in some people and leave the others to themselves."[26] The power to believe is entirely dependent not on merit foreseen in the fallen creature subject to the decree but solely on the arbitrary pleasure and "la libre volonté de Dieu."[27] It is in effect a kind of irresistible "persuasion" that invades the minds and will of only the elect

in order that notwithstanding all the resistance that the darkness blinding the understanding and the perversity of the will bring about, [a human being] would nonetheless yield to the clarity of truth and acknowledge the necessity and the excellence of the Redeemer, and look to him for deliverance. It is, then, this decree that constitutes what one calls election, or predestination, in which [God] strives exceedingly to manifest both the abundantly excellent richness of his mercy towards those whom he has elected and predestined in order to bestow faith on them, and his sternness towards those whom he has forsaken, as well as his sovereign freedom in dispensing that worshipful mystery.[28]

As Brian G. Armstrong notes,[29] the scheme does in fact conform to Calvin and orthodox Reformed symbola, just as the *Eschantillon de la doctrine de Calvin, touchant la Predestination,* Amyraut's stout defense of Calvin against Roman Catholic attacks, in effect claims.[30] As the *Traité* explains,

Salvation and Christ's image, as we have shown above, is one and the same thing. And it is clear that the Apostle [Paul] speaks in that passage [Romans 8:28], not of all men equally and in general, but of those [specific persons] whom God *has foreknown,* that is to say, gave notice in every way of his mercy, and separated from the others for the sake of that inestimable privilege of Faith. But the reason is that the will of God pertaining to salvation, being conditional and concerned with all humankind alike, and humankind being universally corrupted by sin and incapable of fullfilling the condition on which salvation depends, it necessarily happens, not through any defect in the will of God, to consider it in itself, but through hardness of heart and obstinacy of the human mind that the first will of God, which some, as I have said, call predestination contrary to scriptural usage, is fruitless to those who have no share in the second, that is to say, in election.[31]

If election and predestination are conceived in this way, God cannot be accused of "favoring certain persons, nor of authoring sin," nor of being the cause of "the eternal perdition of human beings," standard objections to double-predestination.[32] No. If God "does not engender faith in them, it does not follow that he engenders the contrary."[33]

Such, then, is the core of Amyraut's doctrine of predestination, and it entails a number of salient features that distinguish it not only from standard orthodox views of the matter but also from Arminianism.[34] Among these are the following:

1. Terminology. It is evident from the above that Amyraut is reluctant to apply the term "predestination" to any element in the doctrine of salvation other than the absolute decree of election pertaining to particular individuals. The universal "decree" conditional on faith is but a *conseil* or *volonté*, and calling it "predestination" is, he says repeatedly, "contrary to scriptural usage." The very idea challenges the neoscholastic habits of early seventeenth-century Reformed orthodoxy.

2. The scope of the universal "will" to salvation. In Amyraut, God's plan for rescuing fallen man was highly controversial in that it encompasses all men universally, even pagans as well as peoples who have never been exposed to the gospel: "And although there may be many nations which lucid preaching of the Gospel has not yet reached through the mouth of the Apostles or their descendants, and which have no distinct knowledge of the Savior of the world, one must not, though, think that there is any people or even any man excluded by the will of God from the salvation with which he favored human kind, provided that he profit from the signs of grace that God bestows on him."[35]

3. Nature of the general decree. It presupposes no foreknowledge of differing acceptations of the word, since God gives faith only to the elect. In Arminius, the general decree is truly conditional in that it is human decision that determines salvation or perdition.

4. Nature of the second decree. In tune with Calvin and Re-

formed orthodoxy, true "predestination"—that is, the decree of election—is an absolute decree electing each individual to believe and persevere, not a conditional one, whereas for Arminians the antecedent general decree establishing salvation for fallen mankind and the subsequent decision to save or damn individuals specified in the divine mind are both contingent on human choice.

5. Efficacy of grace. In Arminian thinking, it is up to all human beings to accept or reject grace, whereas in Amyraut, grace may be hypothetically universal, but efficacious grace is extended only to the elect, the rest being totally excluded.

6. Human merit. According to Amyraut, particular election to grace is in no way founded on divine foreknowledge of merit, whereas in Arminius, predestination to reward or punishment is founded on foreknowledge of the uses ill or good to which individuals will put universal grace. Arminius does not admit the absolute character of predestination that Amyraut shares with Calvin.

7. The scope of redemption. The intention behind Christ's death is to save all men, but this cannot be realized in any except those individuals on whom election bestows faith. As in Calvin, God confers the power to believe on, Christ extends his merit to, the elect alone. According to Arminius, however, Christ died for all men, not only universally but also as individuals.

8. Reprobation. As Maurice Kelley observed, Arminius and his followers hold explicitly that fallen man is subject to a decree of reprobation as well as one of election to grace.[36] In Amyraut there is no absolute decree of reprobation whatever that consigns specific individuals to damnation whether before or after the Fall. The term "predestination" being colored with

> I know not how much bombast and seeming to have to be applied to decrees that take effect rather than to those which, because of unbelief and the absence of some preliminary condition, fail to be implemented, holy Scripture is not, on the one hand, in the habit of calling "predestined" people who, NOT having been elected to faith, render that other act of willing useless as far as they are concerned; and, on the other hand, it does speak of those who are elected to faith as if they had been predestined absolutely to salvation because, doubtless, the preliminary condition was met.[37]

In so doing, God manifests the richness of his mercy "towards those whom he has elected and predestined in order to bestow faith on them, and his sternness towards those whom he has abandoned to themselves, and his sovereign liberty in dispensing that worshipful mystery."[38] Damnation of individuals does not derive from a divine decree issued just for the "fun" and glory of it.[39] Perdition is but a consequence of original sin alone; one should never suffer from convictions of personal reprobation.[40]

Compare all this with the *DDC*. Chapter 3—the discussion of the nature of divine decreeing on which the argument of the rest of the treatise should turn if it is as systematic as it claims to be[41]—consists mainly of an endeavor, one "most wise, and in no respect unworthy of God," to defend precisely such a "non-absolute theory of decreeing."[42] Although the *DDC* is much more neo-scholastic in its method than Amyraut's *Traité*—the former proceeds by aphorism supported by exhaustive arrays of proof texts interlarded with commentary, whereas Amyraut unfolds in graceful, connected argument and with few, yet organically cogent proof texts—the common point of departure is the same desire to defend Reformed teachings on predestination against exactly such criticism by Roman Catholics as prompted Amyraut to compose the *Traité* in the first place.[43] That is, both arguments (as do those of the Remonstrants) insist the Fall was not the predetermined consequence of an absolute decree of predestination before creation but the result of disobedience on the part of creatures endowed with free will, in whose power it had been left for them to stand or to fall. Beginning with the notion that the supreme God "is not to be thought to have decreed anything absolutely that he left in the power of free agents"[44] ("neither God's decree nor his foreknowledge shackle free causes with any constraint whatever";[45] "that which was left to the power of the first man to make decisions could not have been decreed immutably or absolutely from eternity),"[46] the *DDC* insists again and again that "the decree [bestowing the gift of free will] itself was, beyond doubt, of the same nature qualitatively as the material, or object, of the divine decision (namely, angel or man on which free will had still to have to be bestowed [*impertiendus*], so either could fall or not fall), in order that all subsequent ills entailed could ensue, or not ensue."[47] God foreknows "all future things, but . . . he has not decreed them all absolutely, lest all sins be imputed to God, and devils and all ungodly go free of blame."[48] There is thus little doubt that Amyraut would have vigorously applauded the fillip against supralapsarianism that closes chapter 3: "There are some who, as they strive through right and wrong to oppose this [doctrine], do not hesitate even to assert God in and of himself to be the cause and author of sin; if I did not think that they say this out of error rather than wickedness, I would believe them the most flagitious of all blasphemers."[49]

So much for agreement between Amyraut and the *DDC* regarding divine decrees and mankind *before* the Fall. The crucial question is, what sorts of decrees emerged *after* the Fall? Do we find a distinction in the *DDC* between the divine will to save postlapsarian mankind in general and the decree of election, or "predestination to faith," that characterizes Amyraut's doctrine? Are the contingencies the same as those that Amyraut assigns to these decrees?

Similarities begin to appear in the very definition of predestination heading chapter 4, defined as "the principal special decree of God relating to [fallen] human beings" by which "God, before the foundations of the world were laid, in pity to humankind, though foreseeing that it was going to fall of its own will, predestined, in order to manifest the glory of his mercy, grace, and wisdom according to what he had appointed beforehand (or his plan) in Christ, those [persons] who were going to believe and continue in faith, to eternal salvation."[50] Accordingly, the argument proceeds *soigneusement,* exactly as Amyraut recommends, to work with a distinction between hypothetical predestination to salvation and particular election to faith very similar to the one that occurs in the *Traité.* That is, the general *decretum*—that is, the end of which is "the salvation of human beings"[51]—is both universal and conditional, just as in Amyraut. Assuming that "God has predestined to salvation, but under an imposed condition applying generally, all beings that have the power of deciding freely,"[52] the *DDC* states explicitly that there is "no individual predestination or election whatever, but only a general one—that is, of all those who believe in their heart and continue steadfast in their belief," that "no one is predestined or elected *qua* Peter or *qua* John except insofar as he believes and continues steadfast as a believer."[53]

The extent of this general predestination to salvation is every bit as universal as Amyraut's. According to the *DDC,* God "explicitly and frequently has declared that he desires the salvation of all, [wishes] the death of no one, as has been quoted above, hates nothing that he has made, left out nothing that might avail for the salvation of all."[54] Indeed, "God excludes no one from access to penitence and salvation until after grace—and that sufficient—has been refused and scorned (and that at a late hour), in order to manifest the glory of his forbearance and justice."[55] While the *DDC* does not go so far as expressly to include pagans, as Amyraut dared to do, in principle the net is wide enough:

> But, you say, not all have known Christ. I reply that this does not stand in the way of all persons being called in Christ alone, since if he had not been given to the world God would have called no one at all. Since, moreover, the price of redemption is in itself sufficient for all, all are called to share in that grace, although the reason for that grace may not be understood by all. . . . How much more [than Jews sacrificing for the unknown remainder of the ten tribes], then, ought we to believe that the most excellent sacrifice of Christ is in every way sufficient even for those believing only in God, although they never had heard his name.[56]

With respect to the contingent nature of this universal *voluntas* to save mankind, the "proclamation" of it in Scripture is "everywhere conditional."[57] More important, the condition is the same as Amyraut's too. If God "predestined 'in Christ,' " the *DDC* argues, it certainly must be on condition of "faith in Christ."[58] That is, "foreseeing that mankind would fall of its own accord," God "from eternity predestined" to salvation, as the treatise reiterates time and again, "all who should believe and persist in faith," "each [person] who believes and perseveres," "all persons who are going to believe."[59] Indeed, the *DDC* will even go so far as to maintain that "as often as the condition itself is not expressly added" in passages of Scripture dealing with the "covenant of grace,"[60] they should be so read, as the "basis of divine decree is in both [the New and the Old Testaments] the same,"[61] that is, conditional on faith. For if we imagine God long ago "in the act of predestining so" as "he that believeth and is baptized shall be saved; but he that believeth not shall be damned," what "endless controversies you will have put an end to" by means of "this one axiom" (Mark 16.16) or of—shades of Amyraut—"John 3.16 as well."[62]

What then of Amyraut's second *consilium* affecting postlapsarian predestination? This is, I think, what the *DDC* really means with the phrase "principal special decree of God relating to man."[63] Much as in Amyraut, it consists of the special election of particular individuals to salvation, and the terminology runs parallel to that of the Saumur divine. "It has been customary in [our Reformed] academies," the *DDC* observes right at the outset of chapter 4, to "misappropriate the word 'predestination,' not in order to denote election only but reprobation as well—most rashly in such a hard subject, since whenever scripture mentions this matter, the reference is clearly to election alone."[64] Indeed, wherever eternal "predestination is alluded to, it is always in the same sense of election alone;"[65] the term "always has to refer to election, and seems frequently to be taken as one and the same."[66] Thus, when speaking of election, the *DDC* understands "that special election which is almost the same thing as eternal predestination." Election is no more "a part of predestination" than it was for Amyraut but a term synonymous with it[67] that, if properly used, designates the special election that bestows faith. After all, "the 'elect' and 'believers' both are, and are termed, one and the same."[68]

Now such election seems to be particular, not general, contrary to what Kelley thought.[69] When belief and perseverance are present, the *DDC* states explicitly, "then indeed the general decree of election" gets "applied" not just to mankind in general but "to each particular believer individually." It also seems that such special election is absolute, not contingent on the "restored free will of man," as Kelley put it. For the *DDC* also claims openly in the same breath that this process at one and the same time "renders" election "unalterable [*ratum*] with respect to those who remain steadfast in faith."[70] While the treatise does not go on and further explore the ramifications of this statement, the word *ratum* (fixed as in the "fixed stars") hardly encourages one to think of such election and perseverance as any more resistible or reversible than Amyraut's out of Calvin.[71] At least, it too seems to manifest itself in a special vocation "by which God, whenever he chooses, invites some individuals rather than others, whether elect as they are called or reprobate, more clearly and more often"[72]—apparently a process in which God seems to induce not just a "natural basis for renovation"[73] but a "supernatural" one as well, one that restores "man's natural faculties of understanding correctly and of willing freely more fully than before, doubtless, but also makes especially the inner man like new, and by divine influence pours into the minds of those renewed in strength, new and supernatural faculties too."[74] There is also indication that such "saving faith" may derive, as it does in Amyraut, from a kind of *persuasio* that bends the mind and will of the elect in the right way. That is, the treatise defines it as "full persuasion engendered by the gift of God, by virtue of which we believe, on the authority itself of

God's promise, that all those things which God promised us in Christ are ours, and especially the grace of eternal life."[75]

In any event, the power to believe bestowed in election seems no more dependent than Amyraut's on merit foreseen in the creature subject to election. A gloss on Rom. 8.28–30 profiles the line of thought. First, God "foreknew those who were going to believe, that is, he decreed or allowed that it should be those alone upon whom in Christ he would look kindly, undoubtedly all men if they would believe. These he predestined to salvation, and to this end, he in various ways called all human beings that they might believe, that is, truly know God. Those actually thus believing he justified, and those persevering he at last glorified."[76] Election according to the foreknowledge of God (1 Pet. 1. 2), thus, is applicable to none but believers, "whom the Father elected according to his foreknowledge or allowance of them in the sanctification of the Spirit and in faith, without which the sprinkling of Christ's blood was going to profit them nothing."[77] Hence, although originally intended for all of fallen mankind, grace and redemption are efficacious only for the chosen. Christ died for everyone, but, as in Amyraut, fruition only applies to the elect.

Moreover, such faith and perseverance appear rooted solely in the unrestricted sovereignty of the divine will and pleasure, not in foreseen qualities or future behavior that qualify the fallen creature for election in grace. At one point, the *DDC* claims, St. Paul "defended God's lawful right over any kind of electing whatsoever, even of undeserving people, such as the gentiles then seemed to be";[78] at another, it states that "it is unnecessary to give any cause or reason for mercy, except [God's own] merciful will itself."[79] The clearest statement runs thus:

> If then God reject none but the disobedient and unbelieving, he un-
> doubtedly imparts grace to all (although not in equal measure) suf-
> ficient for arriving at perception of truth and salvation—[I said] "not
> in equal measure" because not even to the reprobate, as they are
> called, has he imparted uniformly the same decree of grace. . . . For
> God, like anyone else in his own affairs, lays claim to the right of
> deciding about them as he wills, nor is he obliged to render an ac-
> counting, although he could give a most upright one if he wished.
> . . . The reason why God does not hold all persons worthy of equal
> grace is his most high will; why he holds all worthy nonetheless of
> sufficient grace is his righteousness.[80]

But just exactly what "God looks for in those whom he elects" is impossible to know.[81] One argument the *DDC* expressly claims *not* to have made use of is the idea that in election, God paid "the slightest regard" to "righteousness."[82] As the treatise remarks earlier, though in a somewhat different context, "why should God have foreknown individual or specific human beings, or what could he have foreknown in them that should induce him to predestine those specific persons rather than all people in general, once the common condition of faith had been laid down? Suffice it in this matter to explore nothing else than that God, out of his mercy and most noble grace in Christ, has predestined all who are going to believe to salvation."[83] Such a stance is not, I believe, terribly removed from Amyraut's dismissal of what he considered vain attempts by the orthodox to pry into the secrets of God's arcane *consilia,* and on this point Arminius and his Remonstrant progenies come in, I think, for a frown as well:

> If you decide that God predestined human beings on the one condition that they believed and continued in their faith, predestination will not be altogether of grace but become dependent on human will and belief, the consequence being that the esteem proper to divine grace will not rest on something solid. . . . Because if the condition of the decree—the will, obviously, that he himself enfranchised and the faith that is required of human beings—is left to the power of human beings acting freely, this, since it is most fair, detracts not at all from grace, seeing that willing and believing either are a gift of God, or, to the extent they are situate in man, have nothing to do with good work or desert but are based only on a natural faculty. Nor does God thereby depend on human will, but he pursues his own will, in which he willed that in the love and worship of God, and chiefly in their own salvation, human beings always make use of their power to choose.[84]

If then election and its effects are viewed in this fashion, the objections that some urge so vehemently "against this way of thinking—that in this way, the repentance and faith of the predestined having been foreseen, predestination becomes subsequent to works; that it is rendered dependent on the will of human beings; that God is deprived of substantive glory of our salvation; that man is puffed up with pride; that Christian consolation in life and death is shaken to the foundation; that gratuitous justification is denied—" are utterly without merit.[85] The stance is patently redolent of Amyraut.

As for reprobation, it provides a touchstone that differentiates the *DDC* sharply from Arminius and his sectaries[86] and throws it into the Salmurian camp. Much of chapter 4 spends its energy in denying as vehemently as Amyraut that God from eternity ever issued a specific decree that absolutely relegates particular individuals to perdition. Not only does the treatise hold that the fall of Adam (though certain and foreknown) was "not necessary,"[87] but it emphatically proclaims that since God "has predestined from eternity all those who would believe and continue in their faith, it follows that there is no reprobation except of unbelievers and quitters, and even this rather as a consequence [consecutio] than a decree; hence there is no reprobation from eternity."[88] The rationale behind these assertions is not at all unfamiliar in light of the *Traité* and the *Eschantillon:*

> God in truth did not reprobate for one cause and condemn or sentence to death for another, according to the distinction commonly drawn, but those whom he condemned because of sin, he also reprobated because of sin, as in time so too from eternity. And this reprobation is based not so much on the divine will as on their own stubborn hearts; it is not so much a decree of God as a decree of the reprobates themselves because of their not repenting while they can. . . . Just as there is no condemnation except on account of unbelief or of sin . . . so from these texts [of Scripture] which are cited in order to sanction the decree of reprobation, we shall prove that no one is excluded by a decree of God from access to penitence and eternal salvation until after grace has been refused and scorned, and that at a late hour.[89]

On predestination, election, and reprobation, then, it would seem the *DDC* recapitulates, somewhat redundantly, a number of points that lie at the heart of Amyraut's doctrine. Of course, this is not to say that we have found the urtext behind the *DDC*. At best, Amyraut represents an ur-theology behind the notion of predestination advanced in the treatise.

However, the implications of this discovery are large. Unless, first, someone can show that Milton turned Amyraldian after 1634 (when Amyraut's work first appeared), he cannot be the author of chapters 3 and 4 of the *DDC*, at least not as presentation in good faith of "the several points of his religious belief, by the most careful perusal and meditation of the Holy Scriptures themselves."[90] That is, with respect to these two particular chapters, such earnest profession would be appropriate if the epistle were authored by a disciple of the school of Saumur—but not so for Milton, if he was indeed the Arminian he is usually taken for.

Secondly, if Milton should turn out not to be the author, we might better go looking for an Amyraldian alternative than an Arminian. However, the impulse to take up Hill's gauntlet and immediately throw oneself into a search for another author must be beaten down forthwith, lest we, too, prove guilty of ignoring another fundamental assumption *in re* the *DDC* that too often goes unchallenged. Those calling loudly for an alternative author or else evidently consider the work a systematic treatise made up of compatible theological ideas arranged according to an entelechy of consistent arguments based on principles of logical necessity or probability. However, comparison of the *DDC* with some of Amyraut's other writing casts doubt on this notion. For the sake of manageability, let us here treat only the parts of the treatise that even destabilizers of the text consider Miltonic.

I begin with the "insertion" on polygamy and divorce that Hunter believes may still represent authentic Milton. According to Amyraut's *Considerations sur les droits par lesquels la nature a reiglé les mariages* (1648), matrimony is "a natural relationship that makes man and woman one and the same flesh";[91] it entails the traditional ends, generation of children and a "remedy for incontinence."[92] Unlike the *DDC*, though, in *Considerations* marriage is indissoluble except for adultery;[93] it is also "un avec une"—"one man to one woman"[94]—and Amyraut's rejection of polygamy is total, absolute, and wholly unsympathetic.[95] Inasmuch as nothing in Amyraut's theory of either marriage or predestination as presented in the *Traité* and elsewhere seems to mandate the slightest heterodoxy in such matters, it would seem that the radical stances in the *DDC* do not have to flow from internal necessities or probabilities governing entelechy of argument. Others have suggested that these elements seem to be gratuitous insertions;[96] I concur, for they exhibit small logical interconnection with preceding argument.

Again, if we turn to book 1, chapters 1–6, the one part of the *DDC* that Campbell accepts as "certainly Miltonic,"[97] like suspicion arises even here with respect to the treatment of the Son and the Holy Spirit that follows upon predestination. A glance at Amyraut shows that while Christ as redeemer and object of faith is absolutely central to his thinking,[98] he leaves traditional conceptions of the Trinity undisturbed, and he does not put the ax to orthodox soteriology. The heterodox ratiocinations that chapter 5 in the *DDC* devotes to the Son are theologically provocative. But, in light of Amyraut (not to speak of Arminius), who dare maintain that they derive of necessity from the propositions regarding conditional predestination that preceded them in chapters 3 and 4, or that they are therefore uniquely organic to a single system of ideas that they subserve? As for the Holy Spirit, chapter 6 fares even worse. Whereas Amyraut does not use the idea that the Spirit is instrumental in bringing man to the faith and perseverance bestowed in election to threaten the Trinity, the *DDC* flatly denies participation of the Spirit in a triune Godhead.[99] I see no reason for thinking that the presence of this heresy bears any necessary relationship to the notions of predestination established in chapters 3 and 4. On the contrary, does it not rather tend to undermine them? Can one really say that uncoupling the Holy Spirit from the Trinity better serves the concept of election to faith on which the salvation of man depends?

Even within the scheme of hypothetical universalism that the *DDC* develops in chapters 3 and 4, absolute consistency may be questioned. In generating that very concept, to cite a telling instance or two, Amyraut uses as his point of departure Luther and Calvin's distinction between the revealed will of God and his hidden will,[100] universal conditional predestination to salvation deriving from the former, absolute particular election to faith from the latter. Yet in explicitly dismissing beforehand this fundamental idea of the Reformation as scholastic junk,[101] the *DDC* would seem potentially self-contradictory, undermining precisely that which provides a sound basis for the very kind of predestination that it purports to assert.

Similarly, whereas both Amyraut's universal decree of "predestination" to salvation and his particular decree of election (i.e., predestinating individuals to faith) seem to proceed from an infralapsarian position[102]—that is, God issues these decrees of predestination *after* both the Creation and the Fall—the *DDC* oddly predicates, as I have pointed out elsewhere,[103] an object of the decree—*homo creandus et lapsurus*—that is plainly supralapsarian (i.e., predestinated *before* the Creation and the Fall) rather than the fallen creature that at least Amyraut's second decree, the notion of particular election, would seem absolutely to require. It may be that the author of the *DDC* was making an irenic attempt to render Amyraut's scheme of predestination acceptable to supralapsarians as well as others by expanding it to include a supralapsarian basis for, say, the original prelapsarian *volonté*, or possibly even the universal one to save fallen man. If so, the *DDC* states no such intention explicitly, and the argument exhibits no sign whatever of seeking to resolve the potential contradiction. It may be just as likely that in this instance, too, the author was simply juxtaposing, as if in a commonplace book, contradictory ideas from differing sources without trying to reconcile the clash.

There is, then, some reason to ask, as did C. A. Patrides,[104] whether the *DDC* is in fact the "methodical," coherent "tractate" that Charles Sumner begot back in 1823.[105] Even though Arthur Sewell never did question whether the *DDC* was Milton's, much less raise the issue of plural authorship, surely he was not wholly wrong in calling the document "a patchwork thing, never conceived as a whole,"[106] for the entelechy this supposedly perfect system of divinity manifests seems to me dubious and anything but strong. Indeed, in light of Amyraut, can one really claim that it is anything more than a disproportionate collection of associated ideas, many of them appropriated, that are sometimes coherent and consistent, sometimes loosely related (if at all), sometimes misplaced, sometimes heterogeneous, and sometimes even self-contradictory? Might one see it as a composite rather along the lines of Jonson's *Discoveries* but arranged under borrowed orthodox headings, all strung together with sometimes organic but sometimes only superficially appropriate transitions? Indeed, given the way the document simply trails off at the end, have we the right even to call it a totality, much less a unified argument? Until such questions are settled, it is perhaps vain and certainly premature to ask, "if not Milton, who did write the *DDC*?"

NOTES

The indebtedness of this essay to Professors John Hale, Department of English, Otago University, New Zealand, and Margriet Lacy, Department of Modern Foreign Languages, Butler University, Indianapolis, Indiana, for their indispensable help in checking the French and Latin, correcting and suggesting translations, and for critiquing the essay cannot be overstated. However, this essay could not have been written without the many courtesies, including access to and copying rare Amyraut materials at the Bibliotheek, Vrije Universiteit, Amsterdam, that Dr. Willem Heijting, head, Department of Manuscripts and Early Printed Books/Study Centre for Protestant Book Culture, and his staff, especially Mr. Van Heel, kindly extended to me in the course of study. The epigraph is from Gordon Campbell et al., "The Provenance of *De Doctrina Christiana*," *Milton Quarterly* 31 (1997): 110.

1. William B. Hunter, "The Provenance of the *Christian Doctrine*," *SEL* 32 (1992): 129–42.

2. Christopher Hill, "Professor William B. Hunter, Bishop Burgess, and John Milton," *SEL* 34 (1994): 169.

3. Paul R. Sellin, "The Reference to John Milton's *Tetrachordon* in *De Doctrina Christiana*," *SEL* 37 (1997): 137–49; Sellin, "Further Responses," *Milton Quarterly* 33 (1999): 39–43.

4. Campbell et al., "The Provenance," 110; William B. Hunter, *Visitation Unimplor'd: Milton and the Authorship of "De Doctrina Christiana"* (Pittsburgh: Dusquesne University Press, 1998), 96–99.

5. Paul R. Sellin, "John Milton's *Paradise Lost* and *De Doctrina Christiana* on Predestination," *Milton Studies* 34 (1996): 50–51; Sellin, "Further Responses," 44–45.

6. See Frans P. van Stam, *The Controversy over the Theology of Saumur, 1635–1650* (Amsterdam: APA-Holland University Press, 1988), 29–409.

7. Joseph Moody McDill, *Milton and the Pattern of Calvinism* (Nashville, Tenn.: Private edition, 1942), 63–65, mentions Amyraut and sketches his theology but not in relation to the *DDC*. Dennis R. Danielson, *Milton's Good God: A Study in Literary Theodicy* (Cambridge: Cambridge University Press, 1982), 79 and notes 50–52, mentions two relevant texts by Amyraut but seems to have relied on Armstrong as he makes nothing of the Saumur divine in relation to Milton. McDill (326) finds the *DDC* "confused" about predestination but thinks Amyraut a possibility worth examining. As McDill does not list Amyraut in his bibliography (409), he was evidently unable to procure access to copies of these rare works and apparently never had a chance to read him.

8. There is no reference to Amyraut or Amyraldism in the indices to David Masson, *The Life of John Milton*, 7 vols. (London: 1859–94; reprint New York: Peter Smith, 1965); *The Works of John Milton*, 18 vols., ed. Frank Allen Patterson et al. (New York: Columbia University Press, 1931–38), hereafter designated *CM*; Maurice Kelley, *This Great Argument: A Study of Milton's "De Doctrina Christiana" as a Gloss upon "Paradise Lost"* (Princeton: Princeton University Press, 1941); or *Complete Prose Works of John Milton*, 8 vols., ed. Don M. Wolfe et al. (New Haven: Yale University Press, 1953–82), hereafter designated *YP*. For an outline of essential differences, see François Laplanche, *Orthodoxie et prédication: L'oeuvre d'Amyraut et la querelle de la grâce universelle* (Paris: Presses universitaires de France, 1965), 268–71. Hereafter, readings in the 1634 edition of Amyraut's *Traité* as cited and modernized by Laplanche that differ significantly from the revised edition of 1648 will be inserted between brackets within quotations from the 1648 text.

9. Nicely described in Francis Turretin, *Institutio Theologiae Elencticae*, in *Reformed Dogmatics*, trans. John W. Beardslee III (New York: Oxford University Press, 1965), question 17, item 4, 419–20.

10. Harmut Kretzer, *Calvinismus und französiche Monarchie im 17. Jahrhundert* (Berlin: Duncker and Humblot, 1975), 299–363.

11. See, for example, André Sabatier, *Étude historique sur l'universalisme hypothétique de Moïse Amyraut* (Toulouse: Imprimerie de A. Chauvin, 1867).

12. Moyse Amyraut, *Brief Traité de la Predestination avec l'Eschantillon de la doctrine de Calvin sur le mesme suiet. Et La Response a M. de L. M. sur la matiere de la grace et autres questions de Theologie. . . . Nouvelle edition reveuë et corrigée* (Saumur: Chés Isaac Desbordes, 1648), 138: "De ce que nous avons déduit cy-dessus, il a esté aisé de recueillir, qu'il faut soigneusement distinguer la volonté de sauver les hommes, laquelle quelques uns appellent, contre l'usage de l'Escriture, la predestination au salut, d'avec l'eslection ou la

predestination à la foy, qui est le moyen et la condition par l'accomplissement de laquelle nous y parvenons: dautant que celly-cy est absoluë, comme on parle, et ne depend d'aucune condition; celle-là ne peut avoit lieu quant à son effect que par la presupposition de cette condition prealable."

13. Ibid., 7: "[L]e mot de Providence estant plus souvent employé pour ce qui regarde en general la conduite du monde, celuy de Predestination a esté appliqué à denoter non pas seulement cette providence qui veille communement sur les actions des hommes, mais celle particulierement selon laquelle Dieu les a ordonnés à leur but."

14. Ibid., 6–7.

15. Ibid., 77.

16. Ibid., 7–8:

Et neantmoins pource qu'entre la premiere creation de l'homme, et ce but auquel l'Apostre dit que nous avons esté ordonnés pour estre adoptés en Iesus-Christ, est intervenu le peché duquel les effects et les suittes ont esté espouvantables au monde et qui semble avoir changé non seulement toute la face de l'Univers, mais mesmes tout le dessein de sa premiere creation, et s'il faut ainsi parler, induit Dieu à prendre de nouveaux conseils: pour bien demesler les plus importantes difficultés qui semblent se rencontrer en cette matiere à cause de ces changemens arrivés en la nature de l'homme et en ses dependances, il nous faut considerer ces choses separément et l'une apres l'autre, et parler en premier lieu du but auquel le monde avoit esté premierement ordonné en general; et puis apres de celuy auquel avoit esté particulierement destiné l'homme, afin de poursuivre puis apres chacune matiere en son ordre.

17. Ibid., 65.

18. Ibid.: "[P]ar laquelle Dieu a ordonné d'accomplir ce dessein, soit pour son estenduë, soit pour la condition qui y est annexée."

19. Ibid., 66: "[P]ropitiation de leurs offenses . . . et le salut qu'il a receu de son Pere pour le communiquer aux hommes en la sanctification de l'Esprit."

20. Ibid., 58: "[A]vec un merveilleux éclat la sapience de Dieu et sa misericorde. Car il nous avoit bien creés et bons et heureux au commencement à la verité, mais en une condition naturelle pourtant, et par consequent muable. Cela donc qui est naturel ayant precedé et s'estant corrompu, il estoit convenable à la sapience de Dieu, puis qu'il vouloit reparer l'homme, de le mettre en une condition surnaturelle . . . qui surpasse de bien loin ce que Adam en a iamais possedé."

21. Ibid., 66: "Le sacrifice qu'il a offert pour la propitiation de leurs offenses, a esté pour tous; et le salut qu'il a receu de son Pere pour le communiquer aux hommes en la sanctification de l'Esprit, et en la glorification du corps, est destiné à tous, pourveu, di-je [*sic*], que la disposition necessaire pour le recevoir soit en tous de mesmes." Again, 70: "C'est à dire que non seulement il n'en exclud aucun; mais il seroit bien aise que tout le monde s'en approchast, voire il y convie tout le monde, comme estant une grace laquelle il a destinée à tout le genre humain; s'il ne s'en monstre point indigne."

22. Ibid., 65: "La misere des hommes estant universelle, et le desir que Dieu a eu de les en delivrer par le moyen d'un si grand Redempteur, procedant de la compassion qu'il a euë d'eux, comme de ses creatures tombées en une si grande ruïne; puis qu'ils sont ses creatures indifferemment, la grace de la redemption qu'il leur a offerte et procurée a deu estre universelle, pourveu qu'aussi ils se trouvassent tous disposés à la recevoir. Et en cela, ny jusques là, il n'y a point de difference entr'eux." (Negative emphasis derives from *point*.)

23. Ibid.

24. Ibid., 70: "[S]emblent tellement faire cette grace universelle, comme procedante de l'amour que Dieu a porté au genre humain, que neantmoins ils la restraigent à ceux qui *croyent*, et qu'il ne semble pas que ceux soyent conviez à croire en Christ qui mesme n'ont pas ouy parler de luy, elles ne contredisent pourtant point aux choses que nous avons cy-dessus posées."

25. Ibid., 75–76:

Ainsi, si vous considerés le soin que Dieu a eu de procurer le salut au genre humain par l'envoy de son Fils au monde, et les choses qu'il y a faites et souffertes à cette fin, la grace est universelle et presentée à tous les hommes. Mais si vous regardés à la condition qu'il y a necessairement apposée, de croire en son Fils, vous trouverés qu'encore que ce soin de donner aux hommes un Redempteur procede d'une merveilleuse charité envers le genre humain, neantmoins cette charité ne passe pas cette mesure, de donner le salut aux hommes, pourveu qu'ils ne le refusent pas; s'ils le refusent, il leur en oste l'esperance, et eux par leur incredulité aggravent leur condemnation. Et partant, ces paroles: 'Dieu veut le salut de tous les hommes,' reçoivent necessairement cette limitation: 'pourveu qu'ils croyent.' S'ils ne croyent point, il ne le veut pas. Cette volonté de rendre la grace du salut universelle et commune à tous les humains, estant tellement conditionnelle, que, sans l'accomplissement de la condition, elle est entierement inefficacieuse. (Negative emphasis derives from *point*.)

26. Ibid., 87: "[P]ar laquelle il a ordonné d'accomplir en quelques uns cette condition, et laisser les autres à eux mesmes."

27. Ibid., 139.

28. Ibid., 88: "Afin que nonobstant toute la resistance qu'y apportent les tenebres de l'intellect et la perversité de la volunté, il [l'homme] cedast neanmoins à l'evidence de la verité, et reconnust la necessité et l'excellence du Redempteur, et cherchast en luy sa delivrance. C'est donc en ce conseil qu consiste ce que l'on appelle l'Eslection ou Predestination, où il monstre comme à l'envy et les abondamment excellentes richesses de sa misericorde envers ceux qu'il a éleus et predestinez pour leur donner la foy, et sa severité envers ceux qu'il a abandonnez, à eux mesmes, et sa souveraine liberté en la dispensation de cet [*sic*] adorable mystere."

29. Brian G. Armstrong, *Calvinism and the Amyraut Heresy: Protestant Scholasticism and Humanism in Seventeenth-Century France* (Madison: University of Wisconsin Press, 1969), 213–21, 269.

30. Amyraut, *Eschantillon*, in *Traité*, 167–228.

31. Ibid., 139–40:

Car le salut et l'image de Christ, comme nous avons monstré cy-dessus, est une mesme chose. Et il est clair que l'Apostre [Paul] parle en cet endroit [Romans 8.28], non de tous les hommes également et generalement, mais de ceux que Dieu *a preconnus*, c'est à dire, prevenus en toute maniere de sa misericorde, et separés d'entre les autres pour cette inestimable prerogative de la Foy. Mais la raison de cela est que la volonté de Dieu, qui concerne le salut, estant conditionelle, et regardant tout le genre humain, et le genre humain estant universellement corrumpu de peché et incapable d'accomplir cette condition dont le salut depend, il arrive necessairement, non par aucun vice de cette volonté de Dieu, à la considerer en elle mesme [1634: de la prédestination en elle-même], mais par la dureté du coeur et l'obstination de l'esprit humain, que cette premiere volonté [1634: predestination] de Dieu, que quelques uns, comme j'ay dit, appellent predestination, contre le stile de l'Escriture, est infructueuse [1634: frustratoire] pour ceux qui n'ont point de part en l'autre, c'est à dire en l'eslection.

32. Ibid., 101: "[Q]ue c'est imposer à Dieu qu'il ait égard à l'apparence des personnes, qu'il soit autheur de peché, et que par une cruauté indigne de l'excellence de sa nature, il ait voulu comme de gayeté de coeur tirer de la gloire de l'eternelle perditions des humains [1634: Que selon cette doctrine Dieu ne peut estre accusé d'acception de personnes, ny d'estre autheur de peché, ny cause de la perdition des hommes]."

33. Ibid., 105–7: "[I]l y a encore moins d'occasion de l'en accuser. Car de quel peché sera-ce? De celuy du premier homme? . . . Sera ce de la corruption qui en suitte a envahi tout le genre humain, et en la domination de laquelle nous sommes dés le ventre? Non plus. . . . Sera-ce de cet acte mesme de l'incredulité, comme on parle, par laquelle ils rejettent la grace laquelle il leur presente? Nenny encore. Car s'il ne leur donne pas d'y croire, ce n'est pas à dire pourcela qu'il leur donne de n'y croire pas. Si, di-je [sic], il n'engendre pas la foy en eux, il ne s'ensuit pas qu'il y engendre le contraire."

34. Points 2–7 below derive from Laplanche, *Orthodoxie*, 268–71.

35. Ibid., 68: "Et bien qu'il y ait plusiers nations vers lesquelles peut estre la claire predication de l'Evangile n'est point encore parvenuë par la bouche des Apostres, ny de leurs descendans, et qui n'ont aucune distincte connoissance du Sauveur du monde, il ne faut pas penser pourtant qu'il y ait ny aucun peuple, ny mesmes aucun homme exclus par la volonté de Dieu, du salut qu'il a acquis au genre humain, pourveu qu'il face son profit des tesmoinages de misericordes que Dieu luy donne."

36. Maurice Kelley, introduction to the *Christian Doctrine*, in *YP*, 6:84–85; see also Sellin, "John Milton's *Paradise Lost*," 54–55.

37. Amyraut, *Traité*, 140: "Le mot de predestination donc ayant je ne sçay quoy d'emphatique, et semblant devoir estre plustost donné aux conseils qui viennent à effect qu'à ceux dont l'incredulité et le defaut de quelque condition prealable empesche l'evenement, l'Escriture saincte d'un costé n'a pas accoustumé d'appeler predestinés ceux qui n'ayans point esté esleus à la foy, rendent cette autre volonté inutile à leur égard, et de l'autre elle parle de ceux qui sont esleus à la foy, comme s'ils avoient esté absolument predestinés au salut, à cause de l'indubitable évenement de la condition prealable." (Negative emphasis derives from *point*.)

38. Ibid., 88.

39. Ibid., 101: "Ces choses expliquées en cette maniere, je ne pense pas qu'il y ait aucun qui voulust crier alencontre, comme on a accoustumé de faire contre le poinct de la Predestination, que c'est imposer à Dieu qu'il ait égard à l'apparence de personnes, qu'il soit autheur de peché, et que par une cruauté indigne de l'excellence de sa nature, il ait voulu comme de gayeté de coeur tirer de la gloire de l'eternelle perdition des humains."

40. Sabatier, *Étude historique*, 22–25.

41. *YP*, 6:120; see *De Doctrina Christiana*, trans. Charles R. Sumner, *CM*, 14:6–7.

42. *De Doctrina Christiana*, Public Records Office, London, S P. 9/61, 20 (hereafter referred to as *DDC* PRO): "Sin ad humanam rationem divina exigere decreta fas est, quoniam de ijs multi multa in utramque partem subtilius ferè quam solidius disputant, defendi haec non absoluta decernendi ratio, ut sapentissima Deoque nullo modo indigna, humanis etiam argumentis breviter potest."

43. See also Amyraut, *Eschantillon*, in *Traité*, 167–68.

44. *DDC* PRO, 19: "Nihil itaque Deus decrevisse absolute censendus est,

quod in potestate libere agentium reliquit: id quod scripturae totius series ostendit."

45. Ibid., 24: "[E]x his omnibus quae dicta sunt satis tandem liquet neque decretum Dei neque praescientiam causas liberas necessitate ulla praepedire."

46. Ibid., 22: "Quod itaque primo homini arbitrium erat, id ab aeterno immutabile aut decretum absolutè esse non poterat. et certè in potestate hominis aut nihil fuit aut si fuit quicquam, de eo simpliciter statuisse Deum non est dicendum."

47. Ibid., 22: "Qualis itaque materia sive obiectum divini consilii erat, nempe angelus vel homo libera voluntate impertiendus, qui posset labi, vel non labi, tale procul dubio decretum ipsum erat, ut omnia quae exinde consecuta sunt mala, potuissent sequi, vel non sequi: si steteris, manebis; non steteris, eijciere: si non comederis, vives; comedens, moriere."

48. Ibid., 23: "Ut aliquando succinctè finiamus tenendum est, Deum praescire quidem futura omnia, non autem omnia absolute decrevisse, ne peccata omnia Deo imputentur, Daemonesque, et quicunque impij culpa eximantur."

49. Ibid., 24: "Quod tamen nonnulli dum per fas nefasque oppugnare moliuntur, non dubitant Deum asseverare causam per se peccati et authorem: hos equidem nisi per errorem non malitiose hoc dicere putarem blasphemorum omnium perditissimos crederem."

50. Ibid., 25: "Decretum Dei speciale de hominibus praecipuum, Praedestinatio nominatur: qua Deus, ante jacta mundi fundamenta, generis humani, quamvis sua sponte lapsuri, misertus, ad gloriam misericordiae, gratiae, sapientiaeque suae patefaciendam, juxta praestitutum, sive propositum suum in Christo, eos qui credituri essent atque in fide permansuri, ad salutem aeternam praedestinavit."

51. Ibid., 28: "Praedestinavit. i.e. designavit, elegit. et quasi scopum et finem salutem hominum sibi proposuit."

52. Ibid., 38–39: "Cum itaque tam perspicuum sit praedestinasse Deum omnes ab aeterno qui credidissent atque in fide permansissent, sequitur, nisi non credentium aut non permanentium reprobationem esse nullam, eamque potius consecutione quàm decreto esse; nullam deinde ab aeterno esse hominum singulorum. Deus enim omnes libero arbitrio utentes communi conditione proposita, ad salutem praedestinavit; ad interitum neminem, nisi sua culpa et quodammodo per accidens; quemadmodum et Evangelium offendiculo esse et exitio quibusdam dicitur."

53. Ibid., 29: "Praedestinatio itaque et electio videtur nulla esse singularis, sed duntaxat generalis; id est, eorum omnium qui ex animo credunt et credere persistunt; praedestinari neminem aut eligi qua Petrus est aut Joannes, sed quatenus credit credensque perseverat: atque tum demum generale electionis decretum credenti unicuique singulatim applicari et perseverantibus ratum fieri."

54. Ibid., 28: "Atque hinc praeteritionis ab aeterno, derelictionisque commenta illa redarguuntur; quod contrà planè idque saepè testatus est Deus velle se omnium salutem, nullius interitum, ut supra citatum est, nihil odisse quod fecit, nihil omisisse quod ad salutem omnium sufficeret." See also: "Quod si Deus neminem nisi non obedientem, non credentem reijcit, certè gratiam etsi non parem attamen sufficentem omnibus impertit, qua possint ad agnitionem veritatis et salutem pervenire" (40).

55. Ibid., 42: "Teneatur hoc itaque firmumque maneat: Deus neminem nisi

post gratiam, eamque sufficientem, repudiatam ac spretam, idque sero, ad gloriam longanimitatis [*sic*] atque justitiae suae patefaciendam, poenitentiae ac
salutis aeternae aditu excludit."

56. Ibid., 225–26:

> At inquis, omnes Christum non norunt. Respondeo, id non obstare quo minus in
> Christo solo omnes vocentur, cum nisi is mundo datus fuisset, Deus omninò nemi-
> nem vocasset: cumque pretium redemptionis in se quidem omnibus sufficiat, ad illam
> gratiam participandam omnes vocantur, tametsi non ab omnibus intellecta ratio illius
> gratiae sit. Si enim sacrificia sua Jobus credidit valere pro liberis suis etiam non assis-
> tentibus, etiam fortasse nihil tale cogitantibus, cap. 1.5, si reduces Judaei se pro tribu-
> bus decem reliquis, tum quidem longissime remotis, et quid ageretur Hierosolymae
> nescientibus, non frustra sacrificare crediderunt, quanto magis perfectissimam
> Christi hostiam pro ijs etiam qui nomen Christi nunquam audiverunt, Deo solum
> credentibus a[bun]dè satisfacere credamus?

57. Ibid., 30: "Promulgatio autem decreti, quod alterum est probandum,
passim conditionalis est."

58. Ibid., 32: "Porro, si in Christo, ut iam supra demonstratum est, praedestinavit Deus, certe per fidem in Christo."

59. Ibid., 38: "Cum itaque tam perspicuum sit praedestinasse Deum
omnes ab aeterno qui credidissent atque in fide permansissent." See also:
"[O]mnis qui credit ac perseverat, eum praedestinavit atque elegit Deus" and
"Deum ex misericordia summàque sua gratia in Christo, omnes credituros, ad
salutem praedestinasse" (34).

60. Ibid., 31: "Idem attendendum est in foedere gratiae sicubi conditio non
adjungitur, sed ferè adjungitur."

61. Ibid., 30–31: "[D]ivini tamen decreti ratio utrobique eadem est."

62. Ibid., 31: "Idem attendendum est in foedere gratiae, sicubi conditio non
adjungitur, sed fere adjungitur. . . . cogitate audire sic olim praedestinantem
Deum; controversias infinitas hac una sententia sustuleris."

63. Ibid., 25: "Decretum Dei speciale de hominibus praecipuum, Praedestinatio nominatur."

64. Ibid., 25: "Solet quidem vox praedestinationis non ad electionem
solùm, sed etiam ad reprobationem significandam in scholis usurpari: temerè
nimis in re tam ardua, cum scriptura disertè ad unam electionem referat, quot-
ies hac de re verba facit."

65. Ibid., 25: "Alijs loquendi modis eodem sensu praedestinatio electionem semper unam spectat."

66. Ibid., 26: "Praedestinatio itaque ad electionem referenda semper est, et
pro eodem [*sic*] saepè sumi videtur."

67. Ibid., 27: "[S]ed illam hic specialem electionem intelligimus, quae cum
aeterna praedestinatione idem ferè est. electio igitur pars praedestinationis non
est multoque minus Reprobatio."

68. Ibid., 32: "[U]nde electos et credentes ubique eosdem et esse et dici
crediderim."

69. Kelley, introduction, in *YP*, 6:84.

70. *DDC* PRO, 29: "[P]raedestinari neminem aut eligi qua Petrus est aut
Joannes, sed quatenus credit credensque perseverat: atque tum demum generale electionis decretum credenti unicuique singulatim applicari et perseverantibus ratum fieri."

71. Amyraut, *Eschantillon*, in *Traité*, 223–25.

72. *DDC* PRO, 226: "Vocatio specialis est qua D[eus] hos quam illos, sive electos quos vocant sive reprobos, c[la]rius ac saepius, quandocunque vult invitat."

73. Ibid., 234–35: "Vocatio itaque eamque sequens in natur[li] homine alteratio cùm de naturali tantum ratione renovationis sint, citra regenerationem non conferrunt salutem."

74. Ibid., 236: "Supernaturalis renovationis ratio, non solum naturales hominis facultates rectè nimirum intelligendi liberèque volendi plenius adhuc restituit, sed etiam internum praesertim hominem quasi novum creat, novasque etiam facultates supernaturales, renovatorum mentibus divinitus infundit, estque estque [sic] regeneratio et insitio in Christum."

75. Ibid., 248: "Effectum regenerationis alterum est salvifica fides. Ea est dono Dei ingenita nobis plena persuasio, qua, propter ipsam promittentis Dei authoritatem, credimus, ea omnia esse nostra, quae Deus nobis in Christo promisit, gratiam praesertim vitae aeternae."

76. Ibid., 33: "[P]rimum Deus credituros praenovit, i, e, decrevit vel approbavit eos fore duntaxat quos in Christo respiceret, omnes utique si credidissent; eos ad salutem predestinavit; adeoque omnes varijs modis vocavit, ut crederent, i, e, Deum verè agnoscerent; ita credentes justificavit, perseverantes demum glorificavit." See also his further commentary on the same page.

77. Ibid., 33–34: "Quid est hoc totum nisi credentibus? quos elegit pater juxta praenotionem sive approbationem eorum in sanctificatione spiritus et fide, sine qua aspersio sanguinis Christi nihil erat ijs profutura."

78. Ibid., 44: "Sic asseruit jus Dei Paulus in electione quacunque etiam immerentium; quales videbantur tunc esse gentes."

79. Ibid., 42: "Nam misericordiae causam ullam aut rationem reddi necesse non est, nisi ipsam voluntatem misericordem."

80. Ibid., 40: "Quod si Deus neminem nisi non obedientem, non credentem reijcit, certè gratiam etsi non parem attamen sufficientem omnibus impertit, qua possint ad agnitionem veritatis et salutem pervenire. . . . hoc enim juris vendicat sibi Deus, ut quivis alius in res suas, ut statuat de ijs pro arbitrio suo, nec rationem reddere cogatur, quamvis justissimam reddere, si velit, possit. . . . Causa igitur cur Deus non omnes pari gratia dignetur, est suprema ipsius voluntas; quod sufficienti tamen omnes, est justitia ejus." See also 35–36.

81. Ibid., 36: "Respondeo, neque posse statui ex his locis quid spectet Deus in ijs quos eligit."

82. Ibid.: "[P]rimum enim justitiam spectasse vel minimam non disputavimus."

83. Ibid., 34: "Cur enim singulos aut certos homines praenosceret Deus, aut quid in ijs praenosse potuit quod eum induceret ad certos illos potius quam omnes praedestinandos, communi conditione fidei sancita? Satis sit nobis hac in re nihil aliud indagare, quàm Deum ex misericordia summaque sua gratia in Christo, omnes credituros, ad salutem praedestinasse."

84. Ibid., 37–38:

Verum adhuc fortassis obijcietur [sic], si sic statuis Deum praedestinasse homines, hac nempe conditione duntaxat, si credidissent atque in fide permansissent, praedestinatio non erit [sic] tota gratiae; ex voluntate ac fide hominum pendebit: unde gratiae divinae sua laus in solidum non constabit. . . . Quod si conditio decreti, voluntas nempe ab ipso liberata, et fides, quae ab hominibus postulatur, in potestate hominum liberè agentium relinquitur, id, cum aequissimum est, tum gratiae nihil derogat: quandoquidem velle et credere aut donum Dei est, aut, quantum ejus est in homine situm, nullam boni operis aut meriti, sed facultatis duntaxat naturalis rationem habet. Neque idcirco Deus voluntate pendet humana, sed voluntatem ipse exequitur suam, qua voluit homines in amore atque cultu Dei, adeoque in salute sua, suo semper uti arbitrio.

85. Ibid., 38: "Quae itaque toties declamitant nonnulli et queruntur, hoc modo praedestinationem operibus, poenitentia fideque praevisa poni ordine posteriorem; ab hominibus voluntate suspendi; Deum solida salutis nostrae gloria spoliari; hominem superbia inflari; consolationem Christianam in vita et morte labefactari; iustificationem gratuitam abnegari; nihil horum huic sententiae obijci merito potest: ratio interim, adeoque laus divinae non solum gratiae, verum etiam sapientiae ac justitiae aliquanto clariùs elucet; quem finem pradestinationis Deus proposuit sibi primarium."

86. See Laplanche, *Orthodoxie*, 268; Sellin, "John Milton's *Paradise Lost*," table 1, 49, 54–55.

87. *DDC* PRO, 23–24: "[Q]uod igitur contingenter et liberè futurum est, non ex praescientia Dei tandem producitur, sed ex causis suis libere agentibus quae Deum non latent quam in partem sponte sua inclinaturae sint; sic novit Adamum sua sponte lapsurum; certo igitur lapsurus erat; non necessario, quia sponte sua, contraria enim hae duo sunt."

88. Ibid., 38–39: "Cum itaque tam perspicuum sit praedestinasse Deum omnes ab aeterno qui credidissent atque in fide permansissent, sequitur, nisi non credentium aut non permanentium reprobationem esse nullam, eamque potius consecutione quàm decreto esse; nullam deinde ab aeterno esse."

89. Ibid., 42:

Neque vero ob aliam causam reprobavit Deus, ob aliam condemnavit mortiqueaddixit, ut vulgo distinguunt; sed quos propter peccatum condemnavit, eos propter peccatum quemadmodum in tempore, ita etiam ab aeterno reprobavit. Atque haec non tam in voluntate divina, quam in ipsorum obstinato animo reprobatio est posita; non tam est decretum Dei quàm ipsorum decretum reproborum de non agenda paenitentia dum licet. . . . Neque enim minus injustum esset reprobationem decernere nisi propter peccatum quàm condemnare. Quemadmodum igitur nulla condemnatio est nisi propter incredulitatem aut peccatum; . . . ita ex omnibus ijs locis quae ad sanciendum reprobationis decretum afferuntur, demonstrabimus neminem Dei decreto, nisi post gratiam repudiatam [ac spretam, idque sero, poenitentiae ac salutis aeternae aditu excludi].

90. Ibid., 2: "[S]tatui divinis in rebus, non aliorum niti vel fide vel iudicio, sed quid credendum in religione est, id fide non aliunde quàm divinitus accepta, et quod mearum erat partium non omisso, ex ipsa Dei scriptura quam diligentissime perlecta atque perpensa, unumquodque habere mihimet ipsi, meaque ipsius opera exploratum atque cognitum."

91. Moyse Amyraut, *Considerations sur les droits par lesquels la nature a reiglé les mariages* (Saumur: Chés Isaac Desbordes, 1648), 162: "[U]ne communication naturelle, qui fait l'homme et la femme une mesme chair."

92. Ibid., 119–20: "[L]e remede à l'incontinence."

93. Ibid., 160–61, 187.

94. Ibid., 187.

95. Ibid., 164–87.

96. John T. Shawcross, according to Hunter, *Visitation Unimplor'd*, 140.

97. Gordon Campbell, e-mail to author, 2 July 1997.

98. See notes 9, 12 above.

99. *DDC* PRO, 110.

100. See Armstrong, *Calvinism and the Amyraut Heresy*, 187–221.

101. *DDC* PRO, 29.

102. Amyraut, *Eschantillon*, in *Traité*, 203, is most explicit on Amyraut's infralapsarian posture: "Mais Dieu ne peut plus considerer l'homme en cet estat [la premiere integrité] puis qu'il en est decheu: il faut necessairement qu'il le considere comme pecheur. . . . Dieu Donc [*sic*] ayant pour object devant les yeux les hommes en cet estat, estoit en pleine et absoluë liberté de le punir selon sa justice s'il vouloit. . . . Mais neatmoins . . . une certaine inclination à aimer les hommes . . . ayant prevalu, il a resolu d'user envers luy de misericorde. Et partant c'est en la dispensation de cette misericorde qu'il faut considerer la Predestination."

103. Sellin, "John Milton's *Paradise Lost*," 50–51; Sellin, "Further Responses," 44–45. While the latter essay prevenes many of Stephen M. Fallon's arguments in "Milton's Arminianism and the Authorship of *De doctrina Christiana*," *Texas Studies in Literature and Language* 41 (1999): 103–27, the discussion on pp. 117–18 of the language that the *DDC* actually uses in this passage needs separate comment. He attempts to elude the thrust of the Latin grammar by shifting the point of view regarding the promulgation of the decree of predestination from the temporal or human to the divine and eternal, in which of course predestination, creation, election, and reprobation constitute for God but one pure, simple, simultaneous act. While such procedure enables one to insist on *DDC* as Arminian against the clear sense of the Latin text, the same tactic in reasoning also can be used, if one wishes, to prove Arminius a supralapsarian. Not a very helpful exercise if determining theological positions is one's end, and certainly not the point of view St. Augustine adopted in the very treatises on predestination that begot Protestant discussion of the whole question to begin with. Secondly, Fallon wholly ignores the fact that the *DDC* apparently derives this very terminology, as I point out on p. 44, straight from Wollebius—a hard-lining Calvinist, not an Arminian—and then modifies the statement in such a way as to make it even more supralapsarian than Wollebius's original expression. Thirdly, Fallon's statements seem inexplicably unaware of why around mid-century or shortly thereafter certain supralapsarian Reformed found a need to substitute *creandus* in lieu of *creabilis*. The problem was that in addition to human beings that God decided actually to create, he could also have had an infinite number of souls in mind on which he might not decide to impose creation. Obviously, as the decree of predestination could hardly take as its object beings that might not or would never be created, it properly applies only to beings that are definitely going to be created. Hence for a supralapsarian, the object of the decree would have to be a human being that was going actually to be created (*homo creandus*) as distinct from a potential being that was only capable of being created (*creabilis*) and might not be. Use of the form *creandus* is thus clearly supralapsarian, not Arminian as Fallon's dialectic tries to maintain, since for infralapsarian Calvinists (the mainstream predestinarians whom he completely ignores), Arminian Remonstrants, or Amyraldians—all of whom presuppose *homo creatus*, not *creandus*, as the object of the decree—the problem is irrelevant and the distinction superfluous.

104. C. A. Patrides, "*Paradise Lost* and the Language of Theology," in *Language and Style in Milton: A Symposium in Honor of the Tercentenary of*

"Paradise Lost," ed. Ronald D. Emma and John T. Shawcross (New York: Frederick Ungar, 1967), 104–8.

105. His translation for "aliquam doctrinae Christianae methodicam institutionem, aut saltem disquisitionem," *DDC* PRO, 226, 2.

106. Arthur Sewell, *A Study in Milton's "Christian Doctrine"* (London: Oxford University Press, 1939), 10; see also 160.

Milton's Heterodoxy of the Incarnation and Subjectivity in *De Doctrina Christiana* and *Paradise Lost*

KENNETH BORRIS

In *De Doctrina Christiana* [*Christian Doctrine*], Milton defines and promotes a unique and highly unorthodox theory of the Incarnation. Even though William B. Hunter, Hugh MacCallum, Barbara Kiefer Lewalski, and Marshall Grossman have demonstrated the relevance of the Miltonic Incarnation to the portrayal of Christ and Christian heroism in *Paradise Regained*, it has been generally considered irrelevant to *Paradise Lost*. Most recently, for example, MacCallum claims that Milton's distinctive doctrine profoundly affects *Paradise Regained* yet "is not found at all in the Christology of *Paradise Lost*." But exclusion of this doctrine from *Paradise Lost* is oddly inconsistent with arguments for its relevance to *Paradise Regained*. As MacCallum points out, Milton's "rejection of the orthodox view" of the Incarnation "is clearly of primary significance in his treatment of the humanity of Christ." Though MacCallum restricts the force of this observation to *Paradise Regained*, it applies also to *Paradise Lost* because, as he himself declares, that poem also "repeatedly anticipates and reflects upon the Incarnation." Accordingly, unless Milton would wholly compromise his own beliefs on an issue so basic for his Christianity, his unique understanding of the Incarnation has major importance for *Paradise Lost* as well as *Paradise Regained*, however much concerns about potential censorship and the requirements of poetry precluded any explicit treatment of his doctrine in them. The way in which the Son comes to assume human characteristics determines also the way in which he can serve humanity as a model for Christian heroism, and that is indeed the central subject of both poems. Reflecting shifts in the cultural circumstances and possibilities of subjectivity, this major writer's heterodoxy of the

Incarnation is a significant part of the seventeenth-century history of the subject.[1]

We must first consider how *De Doctrina Christiana* relates to *Paradise Lost*. Though Hunter and some others have recently denied any Miltonic authorship of the treatise, the evidence points clearly enough to Milton's serious authorial commitment, as most concur, and so I have argued for the relevance of its christological heterodoxy to Milton's later poems partly on that basis. But those of Hunter's persuasion should note that Milton's authorial relation to *De Doctrina Christiana* is not a necessary premise of my argument. Even if Milton contributed nothing to *De Doctrina*, he certainly had some substantial and continuing interest in its contents, according to Hunter's account, and it thus remains a potentially significant Miltonic source, influence, and intertext. In that case, since the conventional elements of the treatise could be found in many more readily accessible printed texts, Milton would presumably have been most interested in the distinctive aspects of the manuscript: its heterodoxies such as the special doctrine of the Incarnation. I provide various kinds of textual and conceptual evidence from *Paradise Lost* and *Paradise Regained* that both poems reflect and engage this particular heterodoxy, and so those who accept Hunter's reattribution of *De Doctrina* need only modify my premise of Milton's authorship to accept my argument.[2]

However, my findings nonetheless remove one of Hunter's main objections to the standard Miltonic provenance. Despite his own former work relating *Paradise Regained* to *De Doctrina* on the Incarnation, and Lewalski's, Hunter now claims that Milton's writings aside from the disputed treatise evince no internal evidence of its heterodox theory of the Incarnation. The textual aspect of my argument shows the contrary. Moreover, because the theory of the Incarnation in the treatise is highly distinctive, its reflection in Milton's later poetry tends to indicate a joint author.[3]

Of course, Milton's production of the treatise does not mean it glosses the poem, for their genres and purposes differ vastly. There is clearly some hermeneutic distance between the poem's theology and the treatise's, as Balachandra Rajan observes, for *De Doctrina* omits any direct angelic exaltation of the Son, for example. However, when *Paradise Lost* was taking shape in the early 1660s, *De Doctrina* had apparently reached a fairly advanced stage of development, and producing it afforded Milton means to think his theology through in some conjunction with the poem. Stylometric analysis has recently verified that the introductory epistle is highly Miltonic, and it advertises the treatise as the author's "dearest and best possession" (*YP*, 6:121).[4] So the main theological positions of the treatise, especially original ones such as its doctrine of the Incarnation, should be accorded some provisional importance in assessments of Milton's mature writings. Though the relation of *De Doctrina* to *Paradise Lost* is complex and indirect, their thematic and chronological interconnections are nevertheless both close and extensive, so their contexts can be appropriately compared in a pragmatic way cognizant of diverse possibilities, including contradiction and local irrelevance. Milton's poetics would require certain differences, and the fact that *Paradise Lost* could be published, unlike *De Doctrina*, shows that the poem approaches heterodoxy with much circumspection. Whereas the Latin *De Doctrina* restricts its heterodoxies to learned audiences, *Paradise Lost* addresses readers broadly in a more ecumenical way by blurring its doctrinal positions, yet Milton thereby secures some latitude for encoding controversial meanings. Through equivocation in his theological epic, Milton avoids hypocritically effacing the hard-won religious views explored in *De Doctrina*.[5]

Milton's account of the Incarnation in *De Doctrina* repudiates both Protestant and Roman Catholic orthodoxy and largely follows from the significance of the person in his thought. In *Contra Eutychen et Nestorium*, an attack on early heresies about the Incarnation, Boethius had seminally defined "person" as an "individual substance of a rational nature," and Milton explains it similarly: *"Person* is a theatrical term which has been adopted by scholastic theologians to mean any one individual being, as the logicians put it: any intelligent ens, numerically one, whether it be one God or one angel or one man" (*YP*, 6:423).[6]

But Milton proceeds to condemn "the sheer vacuity of the orthodox view" that Christ assumed only a generalized human nature subsisting in the Logos and devoid of any particular or personal human identity. For Milton, so much of what it is to be human is contingent on having a distinctive personal identity, with all the attendant responsibilities of choice, that the Son's assumption of human nature in the Incarnation must necessarily entail his union with a specific human person:

There is . . . in Christ a mutual hypostatic union of two natures or, in other words, of two essences, of two substances and consequently of two persons [i.e., human and divine]. And there is nothing to stop the properties of each from remaining individually distinct. It is quite certain that this is so. We do not know how it is so, and it is best for us to be ignorant of things which God wishes to remain secret. . . . How much better for us, then, to know only that the Son of God, our Mediator, was made flesh and that he is called and is in fact both God and man. The Greeks express this concept very neatly by the single word θεάνθρωπο;ζυ. . . . The fact that Christ had a body shows that he was a real man.

(YP, 6:424, 426)

Indeed, Christ mediates for humanity only "as θεάνθρωπο;ζυ." In Miltonic theology, this oxymoron defines Christ's incarnate being as a profound crux: a single person produced through union of human and divine natures and persons and thus physically incorporated at a specific point within human history. While Milton does not seek to force anyone's conscience on this or the antitrinitarian issue in *Paradise Lost*, or at least ingeniously endeavors to avoid being censored, the poem nevertheless tends to privilege his special theory of the Incarnation.

If we compare passages on the Incarnation in *Paradise Lost* with the positions and terminology of *De Doctrina*, plenty of scope for allusion to Milton's unorthodox Christology appears. The Father's initial pronouncement on the subject in book 3, addressed to the Son, might seem most problematic:

> Thou therefore whom thou only canst redeem,
> Their nature also to thy nature join
> And be thy self man among men on earth,
> Made flesh, when time shall be, of virgin seed,
> By wondrous birth: be thou in Adam's room
> The head of all mankind, though Adam's son.
>
> (3.281–86)[7]

Hunter claims, as would MacCallum, that this passage confirms "the incarnate Christ will join two natures," as in the orthodox view, "not two persons."[8] But the passage also readily accommodates the Miltonic doctrine of united natures and persons because, in that view, the term "nature" implies "person" in this connection: once again, Christ is "a mutual hypostatic union of two natures or, *in other words . . . consequently of two* persons" (emphasis mine). For Milton, human nature is inseparable from and includes the human person, and so he dismisses the orthodox theory, in which the Son assumes only a generalized humanity: "But what a[n] absurd idea, that someone should take human nature upon himself without taking manhood [*homi-nem*; i.e., a specific individuality] as well! For human nature, that is the form of man contained in flesh, must, at the very moment when it comes into existence, bring a man into existence too, and a whole man, with no part of his essence or his subsistence . . . or his personality missing" (*YP*, 6:422). As "the fact that Christ had a body shows that he was a real man," so he thus united with a human person rather than a generalized human nature.[9] From that viewpoint, at least, Milton's Father's dictum in *Paradise Lost*, "*be thy self man . . . Made flesh*," amounts to a proof text for Milton's special theory of the Incarnation (3.283–84).

De Doctrina further declares that if "Christ's human nature never had its own separate subsistence [i.e., as a person], or supposing the Son did not take that subsistence upon himself: it would follow that he could not have been a real man, and that he could not have taken upon himself the true and perfect substance or essence of man" (*YP*, 6:423). According to the treatise, then, the orthodox view of the Incarnation compromises the fundamentals of Christianity so that correction is theologically imperative.[10]

Not only does the Father's vocabulary at least accommodate this crucial Miltonic doctrine, but his speech subtly promotes it by indicating that Christ will in some sense become a particular human being within the collective mass of humanity: "[B]e *thy self man* among *men*." That is precisely where the Miltonic Incarnation differs most radically from orthodox Reformed accounts in which Christ assumed a generalized human nature that possessed hypostatic subsistence only through union with the Logos, and thus assumed manhood in an absolutely unprecedented way not to be casually subsumed "among men," as in Milton's Father's wording. The role of "man" and the status of particular human identity in Richard Hooker's and Johannes Wolleb's orthodox Christology help reveal the contrary impulses of Milton's wording throughout *Paradise Lost*. For Hooker, the Word "built her house of that *nature* which is common unto all, she made not *this* or that man her habitation, but dwelt *in us*."[11] Likewise for Wolleb, "Christ assumed *not man*, but the humanity; *not the person, but the nature*. . . . Christs humane nature hath no other, or particular Hypostasis or subsistence, then that of the Word. . . . In this point, Christ differs from all other men; because every man hath a peculiar Hypostasis or subsistence, by

which he differs from other Persons . . . : but Christs humane
nature wanting a proper subsistence, is assumed into the fellowship of the Hypostasis of the divine nature.''[12] Milton brusquely
dismisses such views in the treatise: "Obviously the Logos became what it assumed, and if it assumed human nature, but not
manhood [*non hominem*], then it became an example of human
nature, *not a man* [*non homo*]. But, of course, the two things are
really inseparable" (*YP*, 6:422–23, emphasis mine; see also *CM*,
15:268).

Interpreted according to the Christology of *De Doctrina*, the
Father's prophecy of the Incarnation comes to seem all the more
"wondrous," for the Son thus partakes as fully as possible of
what it is to be a human being and becomes head of humankind
in terms of that specific human identity. This way of conceiving
the event envisions a most full and concretely realized union between divine and human agencies in which the human person is
united, in a saving apotheosis, with the divinely endowed person
of Milton's Son. Thus acutely uniting the divine and human orders, the Incarnation crystallizes their potential for dynamic in-
teraction and underwrites the poem's epic synthesis.

In the Father's prophecy and elsewhere in *Paradise Lost*, the
poet strategically reverses the expository technique of the treatise, which carefully defines the main terms involved, to express
his special doctrine of the Incarnation. To accommodate this
theory, the poem instead exploits the potential ambiguity of the
word "man," which can mean a certain human being, person, or
male; yet also humanity in general. Among various possibilities,
then, the Father's comment "man, as is most just, / Shall satisfy
for man" (3.294–95) can sequentially oppose the particular sense
to the general one so that the Son may thus assume a certain
human individuality to effect a general satisfaction. In the
Father's assurance of the God-man's full exaltation, Milton can
again play on the particular and general senses of "man":

> thy humiliation shall exalt
> With thee thy manhood also to this throne,
> Here shalt thou sit incarnate, here shalt reign
> Both God and man, Son both of God and man.
>
> (3.313–16)

Because *De Doctrina* emphasizes that there is no such thing as
a generalized humanity with which the Son could have united,
its definitions, at least, would construe every such reference to

"man," including Adam's awestruck recognition near the end of *Paradise Lost*, "so God with man unites" (12.382), in an individualistic sense implying no lack whatsoever in any part of essence or person.

Even when Milton's Son first proposes his saving intervention, Milton's association of him with "man" invites the humanly personal interpretation:

> Behold *me* then, *me* for him, *life* for *life*
> I offer, *on me* let thine anger fall;
> Account *me man*; *I* for his sake will leave
> Thy bosom, and this glory next to thee
> Freely put off, and for him *lastly die*
> Well pleased, *on me* let Death wreak *all* his rage.
>
> (3.236–41; emphasis mine)

While this passage, like the others, accommodates orthodox christological reading, its urgent specification of a certain sacrificial identity most befits the Miltonic Incarnation, which urges the irreducible integrity and significance of the person.

That emphasis and Milton's further heightening of the union that constitutes Jesus Christ involve him in another heterodoxy in *De Doctrina:* even the divine aspect of the incarnate Christ was subject to suffering and died, so that "Christ . . . was totally killed" (*YP*, 6:440). In the lines just quoted from *Paradise Lost*, Milton's insistence on the personal impact of the Son's offer befits this special extremity that his unique Christology entails. Contrary to various critics such as Hunter and Lewalski, the Son's subsequent statement "now to Death I yield, and am his due / All that of me can die" (3.245–46) does not really contradict the total death of Christ in *De Doctrina* but hedges as elsewhere in the poem to admit heterodoxy indirectly. Milton's Christ evades any clear endorsement of the orthodox view that his divine aspect cannot die and instead anticipates the death of *all* of him that *can* die. This wording accommodates both orthodoxy and the position of *De Doctrina* while signaling Milton's heterodoxy through its periphrastic circumlocution, in which the very Word here equivocates about itself. In effect, the poem exploits some ambiguities within *De Doctrina*: "Even the Son . . . does not know absolutely everything, for there are some secrets which the Father has kept to himself alone"; and as for the Son's "divine nature, it is more questionable whether that also succumbed to death" (*YP*, 6:265, 439).[13]

Considered from a christological standpoint, even the epic proposition at the outset of *Paradise Lost* appears to signal and promulgate the Miltonic doctrine of the Incarnation. Over against the generality of *"man's"* first disobedience, Milton specifies that *"one* greater *man"* will restore humankind:

> Of man's first disobedience, and the fruit
> Of that forbidden tree, whose mortal taste
> Brought death into the world, and all our woe,
> With loss of Eden, till one greater man
> Restore us, and regain the blissful seat,
> Sing heavenly Muse.
>
> (1.1–6)

In contrast to the previously cited formulations of Hooker and Wolleb, which stress Christ's generalized humanity, and qualify usage of "man" to preclude connotations of singularity and specificity, Milton emphatically hails *one man,* just as his Christ assumed manhood only in terms of *one particular man.* Insofar as it relates to Christology, the epic proposition of *Paradise Lost* most readily reads as a proclamation of the Miltonic heterodoxy.[14]

Milton insists on this formulation of the human aspect of Jesus Christ by repeating it in the proposition of *Paradise Regained:*

> I who erewhile the happy garden sung,
> By one man's disobedience lost, now sing
> Recovered Paradise to all mankind,
> By one man's firm obedience fully tried
> Through all temptation, and the tempter foiled.
>
> (1.1–5)

Again over against a generalized humanity, "all mankind," Milton stresses that restoration occurs through *one* particularized *man.* In this case, the poet clearly echoes Rom. 5.19: "For as by one man's disobedience many were made sinners, so by the obedience of one shall many be made righteous."[15] Whereas the biblical obedient "one" is relatively vague as a means of designating Jesus Christ, broadly meaning "a certain person" whose characteristics are indefinite aside from obedience, Milton juxtaposes "all mankind" with "one man" and intensively combines "one" and "man" to produce a pointedly more specific definition that is, according to the terminological norms of seventeenth-century Christology, again most consistent with Milton's special theory of the Incarnation. The poet would certainly have been cognizant of the nuances of christological language, just as his account of the Incarnation in his early poem "On the Morning of Christ's Nativity" is orthodox. In that text, he twice uses the generalizing phrase "with us," reminiscent of orthodox formulations, to describe the mode of Christ's earthly presence, and his treatment of the humanity of Jesus is purely general: the Son assumes "with us a darksome house of mortal clay" (14), which could be anyone's body, rather than the distinctive human individuality implied by "one man." Although previous advocates of the relevance of the Miltonic Incarnation to *Paradise Regained* miss the christological implications of the proposition and do not relate the doctrine to *Paradise Lost*, these complementary major poems seem jointly framed to evoke that doctrine from the outset as the common focus of their salvific narratives.[16]

Contrary to former critical assumptions that the Miltonic Incarnation is irrelevant to *Paradise Lost*, the poem not only leaves the being of Jesus Christ provisionally open to both that and the orthodox interpretation but also tends subtly to promote the former. Milton's conscientiously developed position on this subject has major significance in his thought, as MacCallum concedes, so it should have important applications to *Paradise Lost*. Further, it is much more consistent with various basic metaphysical, moral, and psychological assumptions of that poem. Within the special universe of *Paradise Lost*, Reformed orthodoxy on the Incarnation seems theologically erroneous, for it does not accord as well with the phenomena and focuses their analogical relations and collective divine telos far less sharply.

In *Artis Logicae* and *Paradise Lost*, Milton reverses the typical conceptions of matter and form: rather than matter being individual and form common, Milton considers matter what creatures have in common and form what individuates them (*YP*, 8:228–35). Clearly analogous, Milton's heterodoxy of the Incarnation in *De Doctrina* seems partly to stem from that conception. To have assumed the form of man, Milton argues, the Son must have assumed an individuated manhood and thus united with a specific human person as well as a generalized human nature. According to *Artis Logicae*, form is *"the cause through which a thing is what it is," "distinguished from all other things"*; *"if the form is taken away the thing is taken away."* Though Milton distinguishes "common" or generic forms from

"proper" forms, so that "the rational soul is the form of man ge-
nerically," and "the soul of Socrates is the proper form of Socrates," proper form is necessary for anything to be *"that which it
is."* Also, Milton insists that *"the form is generated within a
thing simultaneously with the thing itself"* (*YP*, 8:232, 234;
trans. Walter J. Ong and Charles J. Ermatinger). Likewise, contrary to christological orthodoxy, Milton, as was mentioned earlier, insists in *De Doctrina* that "human nature, that is, the form
of man contained in flesh, must, at the very moment when it
comes into existence, bring a man into existence too, and a
whole man, with no part of his essence or his subsistence . . . or
his personality missing." Just as *Paradise Lost* reflects Milton's
special conceptions of matter and form, as John Rumrich has
shown, so those same metaphysical assumptions, I would add,
imply the Miltonic doctrine of the Incarnation within the
poem.[17]

Moreover, because Milton's particularized Incarnation unites
divine and human persons radically unequal in essence but considered analogous in their potential to be united, it seems to
epitomize and guarantee his cherished doctrine of the continu-
ity of matter and spirit and the prospects of individual human
involvement in the evolving transformation of the lower into
the higher, to become all in all in God, as *Paradise Lost* repeatedly insists. If human and divine persons so unite in the God-
man, then these other claims seem fitting and easy, as if her-
alded by that stunning, paradoxical union thought concretely
manifested to public view within the course of an overarching,
teleological providence.

However, most fundamental for Milton's concept of the Incarnation is his characteristic emphasis on the person as a freely
choosing center of intelligence characterized by the jointly operative faculties of reason and will. For Milton, that is so definitively what it means to be human that his doctrine of the
Incarnation follows as a logical consequence, and orthodox
Christology, in which Christ only assumed generalized human
properties, seems absurd. Of course, the orthodox view maintained that Christ's human nature included the power of choice;
but for Milton volition is proper to and defines the person, not
any generalized nature, so that a Christ who assumed only
human nature would nonsensically lack effectual human powers and responsibilities of exercising choice. In *Areopagitica*,
Milton considers complaints against Providence for allowing
Adam's transgression similarly "foolish": "[W]hen God gave

him reason, he gave him freedom to choose, for reason is but choosing; he had bin else but a meer artificiall Adam. . . . We our selves esteem not of that obedience, or love, or gift, which is of force: God therefore left him free, set before him a provoking object. . . . [H]erein consisted his merit, herein . . . the praise of his abstinence" (*YP*, 2:527). If the Son did not assume the full personal extent and responsibilities of these powers in becoming incarnate, he would have been a mere artificial Jesus, in Milton's view, devoid of the very capacities that constitute meaningful humanity. In that sense, the human person *is* Miltonic human nature, and they cannot exist independently, so that Milton must reformulate the Incarnation accordingly.

Likewise, Milton's Father stresses that "Freely they stood who stood, and fell who fell" (3.102), as the power of choice is essential for independently rational beings:

> will and reason (reason also is choice)
> Useless and vain, of freedom both despoiled,
> Made passive both, had served necessity,
> Not me. They therefore as to right belonged,
> So were created.
>
> (3.108–12)

Or as Raphael explains God's purposes to Adam:

> good he made thee, but to persevere
> He left it in thy power, ordained thy will
> By nature free, not over-ruled by fate
> Inextricable, or strict necessity;
> Our voluntary service he requires,
> Not our necessitated, such with him
> Finds no acceptance, nor can find, for how
> Can hearts, not free, be tried?
>
> (5.525–32)

So "freely we serve, / Because we freely love, as in our will / To love or not; in this we stand or fall" (538–40). From Milton's viewpoint, the Christian significance of the Incarnation requires that, in Christ's earthly life, the human condition must have been fully assumed and at stake so that the Son must have united with a human person.[18]

The logic of this Miltonic theory is certainly integral to *Paradise Lost* because Milton's portrayal of human relations with God crucially depends on personal capacities of rational choice.

In effect, the poem's initial reference to Christ as "one greater man" and its overall context tilt its ambiguities about the Incarnation toward Milton's own view explicitly presented in *De Doctrina* while avoiding an outspoken challenge to orthodoxy that could have jeopardized the poem's chances of reaching, establishing, and maintaining a readership. In *Paradise Regained*, the Miltonic doctrine of the Incarnation affects Christ's personal encounter with temptation and the meaning of Christian heroism in that sense. But in *Paradise Lost*, which does not deal directly with the earthly life of Christ, it more broadly underwrites the coherence of Milton's morally significant cosmic system and focuses the role and condition of the Christian hero in that context. As Hunter formerly commented on *Paradise Regained*, Milton's theory that the Son assumed humanity in a certain personal mode stresses that, insofar as regeneration involves human agency, "the union of the elect with the Son is accomplished by each individual rather than by the common human nature of each."[19] Just so, *Paradise Lost* accents the responsibilities of personal endeavor in its Arminian treatment of heroic potential, as in Michael's examples of singular individuals distinct from a perverse world, such as Noah and Enoch, who freely stand firm in their fidelity to God.

Milton further stresses that Jesus Christ attained to the fullest possible expression of the divine image within the ambit of a particular human awareness: thus "the entire person of Christ, both human and divine, expresses the image of God through actions of service and self-sacrifice."[20] Moreover, as mediator, Milton's Christ not only provides satisfaction of the Father's justice, but he is also internally realized within the regenerate so that they come to conform to his image. In these ways, too, Milton's concept of the Incarnation makes the God-man an exemplar for spiritual endeavor that can most strongly affirm and realize the distinctive identity, value, and potential of each human person while also establishing a definitive standard for all such efforts.

The chapter of *De Doctrina* in which Milton presents his unique theory of the Incarnation is entitled *"De Hominis et Christo Redemptore"*: Milton's special Christology underwrites restoration to humanity as he conceives it and thus seeks to accent the significance and freedom of the human person. As Dennis Danielson says of Milton's theodicy, the poet grounds significant relations between individuals, such as love, faith, and allegiance, upon his concept of the person as a free agency capable of rational choice.[21] Raphael, we have seen, says as much to Adam. Moreover, in *De Doctrina* the union of believers with Christ seems somewhat analogous to that of the divine and human persons in Christ as Milton understands it, for he uses the same vocabulary of "union" and "coalescence" to define both. Engrafting in Christ, for example, is a process through which believers are made "sharers in Christ" and rendered "fit to join [*coalescant*], eventually, in one body with Christ"; likewise, a human person and the Son "coalesced [*coalescere*]" in the incarnate Christ (*YP*, 6:477, 425).[22] On account of the mortalism of *De Doctrina*, the very continuation of human identity after the general resurrection depends upon the significance of the Incarnation: "[E]ach man will rise with the same identity as he had before. . . . If this were not so we should not be like Christ. He entered into glory with that . . . very same flesh and blood, with which he had died and risen again" (*YP*, 6:620–21). In *Paradise Lost*, the Miltonic Incarnation is the ultimate exemplar for the relations of human heroes to God and to divinely authorized community and their principle of validation.

Though Milton's unique theory of Jesus Christ's identity is clearly bound up with his conceptions of human individual agency and responsibility, Miltonists have yet to confront the full implications of that linkage. It implies that Milton's later poems, including *Paradise Lost*, tend to assume that particular Christology whenever they deal with individual choices and commitments in any relation to Christ, just as Milton's thought, unlike Spenser's, is strongly systematic. Moreover, the Miltonic Incarnation is not merely speculative, as if Milton would casually propound a radical heresy, but it provides the centerpiece of his strenuous endeavor to construct his own Christian system of the universe. His distinctive Christology affords him means to finesse a besetting cultural difficulty in which his own thought was deeply implicated. Until Milton's time, "individual" was an adjective broadly meaning "indivisible," but then it began to develop its current substantive meaning, which implies a socially atomic concept of personal identity. Concepts of the self were undergoing significant shifts in the seventeenth century, from previous tendencies to ground identity in collective social wholes and standards of good located beyond the self in some cosmic order, to enhanced possibilities for self-recognized personal autonomy and "individuality." Among the diverse factors contributing to this change, the Puritan emphasis on a personal relation to God, rather than one mediated by any church, would have been especially crucial for Milton. He himself was eagerly exploring ideas of freedom of conscience, individual liberty, and greater scope for human agency.[23]

Milton's special doctrine of the Incarnation provides his system an exemplary guarantee of the status, heroic potential, and unique identity of the human person while also furnishing means of incorporation into ideal Christian community under Christ's headship and a perfect, humanly accommodated external criterion of value. Recuperating older collective conceptions of personality in a new form, Milton's Christology reconciles them with a heightened sense of discrete selfhood. At the same time, his theory seeks to anchor such self-consciousness securely in commitment to Jesus Christ himself as the ultimate paradigm for a fully realized human identity so that it does not threaten to become satanically self-involved or skeptically relativisitic. Only by rejecting orthodox Christology could Milton reconcile his concerns with freedom of conscience, liberty, and individual choice with his Christian principles and with contemporary reconsiderations of the self.

To find the Incarnation so much at stake in Milton's encounter with the self and in the seventeenth-century history of the subject is not surprising. Ideas of what constitutes a person in Western culture are substantially rooted in early Christian attempts to define the Incarnation and the Trinity because those efforts forced intensely critical attention upon that question, as never before. In keeping with interest in reformulating notions of the self and personal identity in the sixteenth and seventeenth centuries, such doctrinal questions were reopened to disputation with renewed force and topicality, as Milton's contemporary John Owen observes, and we find Milton himself energetically intervening in those debates according to his own particular standpoint on the condition of humanity. Milton's view of individuals in relation to society apparently endeavors to build on the Pauline promise that the God-man assures a paradoxically collective fulfillment of participants who each remain distinctively capable: "[A]s we have many members in one body, and all members have not the same office: So we, being many, are one body in Christ, and every one members one of another"; yet each with "gifts differing according to the grace that is given to us" (Rom. 12.4–6).[24]

Paradise Lost grounds godly human relations, identity, and heroic potential in Milton's unique conception of its "greater man": the Son thus unites with a specific and complete human person, not a generalized human nature as in orthodox accounts.

Incorporating this doctrine into the poem's vision of life, Milton endeavors to realize a new Christian synthesis that can accommodate the increasing dignity, responsibility, and autonomy attributed to human individuals in seventeenth-century thought without sacrificing former notions of collective support for personal identity and the dependence of the self on ideal external standards of good. Though many assume that "in Milton's epics we see the 'abstract—*isolated*—human individual' for the first time," as if Milton is the prototypical bourgeois individualist, his texts are transitional. *Paradise Lost* strives to save the older appearances by restructuring them in ways that promise some recuperation.[25]

Notes

1. Important previous discussions of the Miltonic Incarnation and its influence on *Paradise Regained* are William B. Hunter, "Milton on the Incarnation," in *Bright Essence: Studies in Milton's Theology*, ed. William B. Hunter, C. A. Patrides, and J. H. Adamson (Salt Lake City: University of Utah Press, 1971), 131–48; Hugh MacCallum, *Milton and the Sons of God: The Divine Image in Milton's Epic Poetry* (Toronto: University of Toronto Press, 1986), 214–15, 210; Barbara Kiefer Lewalski, *Milton's Brief Epic: The Genre, Meaning, and Art of "Paradise Regained"* (Providence: Brown University Press, 1966), chap. 6; and Marshall Grossman, " 'In Pensive trance, and anguish, and ecstatic fit': Milton on the Passion," in *A Fine Tuning: Studies of the Religious Poetry of Herbert and Milton*, ed. Mary A. Maleski (Binghamton, N.Y.: Medieval and Renaissance Texts and Studies, 1989), 205–10. Hunter, MacCallum, and Lewalski also debate possible relationships of Milton's theory to Nestorian, Eutychian, and other early Christian heterodoxies. In *This Great Argument: A Study of Milton's "De Doctrina Christiana" as a Gloss upon "Paradise Lost"* (Princeton: Princeton University Press, 1941), 159, Maurice Kelley briefly draws very general parallels between *De Doctrina* on the Incarnation and *Paradise Lost*, but he does not indicate or explain the theological implications and poetic relevance of Milton's doctrine on this point.

2. The manuscript of *De Doctrina* was most likely produced by persons specifically acting for Milton as amanuenses; Hunter grants that Milton clearly had and retained the manuscript and that it remained among the poet's papers until his death. The controversy about attribution began with Hunter's "The Provenance of the *Christian Doctrine*," *SEL* 32 (1992): 129–42, and the subsequent "Forum: Milton's *Christian Doctrine*," in that issue, featuring rebuttals by Lewalski and John T. Shawcross and Hunter's reply (143–66). The most important recent contribution to this debate is Gordon Campbell, Thomas M. Corns, John K. Hale, David I. Holmes, and Fiona J. Tweedie, "The Provenance of *De Doctrina Christiana*," *Milton Quarterly* 31 (1997): 67–121. While indicating that the treatise seems a palimpsest of a varyingly Miltonic character, like his *Artis Logicae* [*Art of Logic*], their stylometric analysis shows it was indeed "a working manuscript under revision by Milton" and that he

"had not yet finished it for the press" (110). For other contributions, most of which argue for Miltonic authorship, see their bibliography (112–17). Aside from the numerous correspondences between *De Doctrina* and the rest of Milton's later canon, the hypothesis of Milton's authorial involvement provides a much more direct and thus logically more credible account of the known facts of provenance and documentation, by Occam's criteria, than Hunter's most recent alternative, which must propose a relatively convoluted and unverifiable rationale involving unknown authorship, unknown contacts, hypothetical transmissions and transcriptions, and suppositiously fraudulent misrepresentations by Milton's contemporaries, to account for the same facts.

3. For Hunter's complaint that we lack textual evidence in the poems for Milton's heterodox understanding of the Incarnation as in *De Doctrina*, see his "Animadversions upon the Remonstrants' Defenses against Burgess and Hunter," *SEL* 32 (1994): 197–98.

4. Balachandra Rajan's insight appears in *"Paradise Lost" and the Seventeenth Century Reader* (London: Chatto and Windus, 1947), 31–33. On the Miltonic authorship of the epistle for *De Doctrina*, see Campbell et al., "Provenance," 108; I quote Milton's epistle from *De Doctrina*, trans. John Carey, in *Complete Prose Works of John Milton*, 8 vols., ed. Don M. Wolfe et al. (New Haven: Yale University Press, 1953–82), hereafter designated *YP*. Unless otherwise noted, all references to Milton's prose and to Carey's translation of *De Doctrina* are to this edition and are cited parenthetically in the text.

5. Christopher Hill (*Milton and the English Revolution* [London: Faber and Faber, 1977], 233–39) observes that, by 1658, "Milton could announce that he was 'hoping and planning still greater things' than the *Defence of the People of England*, for 'all Christian men . . . of every land.' No work other than *De Doctrina* answers to that description"; see *YP*, 4:537. Just so, it is written in Latin, the contemporary lingua franca, and addressed "To All the Churches of Christ and to All in any part of the world who profess the Christian Faith" (*YP*, 6:117). On the dating of Milton's texts, see John M. Steadman, *"De Doctrina Christiana,"* in *A Milton Encyclopedia*, 9 vols., ed. William B. Hunter et al. (Lewisburg, Pa.: Bucknell University Press, 1978–80). For cogent discussion of the interpretively important constraints of censorship on Milton's writing, see Hill, index, s. v. "censorship." On reservation of difficult doctrinal questions for the learned, see Milton's *Commonplace Book:* "That the profound questions concerning God, which the human reason explains or comprehends with considerable difficulty, should either not be thought about or should be suppressed in silence lest they be proclaimed to the people and from this source a cause of schisms be given in the Church, Constantine very wisely admonishes" (*YP*, 1:380).

6. Boethius, *Theological Tractates*, ed. and trans. H. F. Stewart and E. K. Rand III. Elsewhere in *De Doctrina*, Milton defines "person" likewise as "any individual thing gifted with intelligence" or "any intelligent substance" (*YP*, 6:142, 285). See also Aquinas, *Summa Theologiae*, Ia.29. "Person" in this sense is to be distinguished from current associations of "character," "personality," and "self"; so, even though the theologians sometimes used "personality" as a variant of the term "person," I avoid those words in this connection.

7. John Milton, *Paradise Lost*, in *The Poems of John Milton*, ed. John Carey and Alastair Fowler (London: Longman, 1968). All references to Milton's poetry are to this edition and are cited parenthetically in the text.

8. Hunter, "Incarnation," 133.

9. On the Miltonic synonomy of "nature" and "person," see also *YP*, 6:423. MacCallum (*Milton and the Sons of God*, 214–15) surmises that since Milton subsequently "reverts to referring to the two *natures* rather than the two *persons* of Christ" in his ensuing argument in *De Doctrina*, "some of the language through which he states the doctrine is of only passing interest to him." However, after clearly stating that natures and persons are equivalent in this application (after defining his terms, in other words), Milton can properly use "natures" in his sense incorporating "persons." Rather than erratically losing interest in this important and heterodox definition (which would indicate intellectual incompetence), Milton proceeds to assume and enforce it in *De Doctrina*.

10. For Milton's Latin text, see *De Doctrina Christiana*, in *The Works of John Milton*, 18 vols., ed. Frank Allen Patterson et al. (New York: Columbia University Press, 1933–38), 15:266, hereafter designated *CM* and cited parenthetically in the text. As Lewalski observes in *Milton's Brief Epic*, Milton's Incarnation and his antitrinitarianism both "stem from the same logical quarrel with the orthodox formulas distinguishing the concepts 'nature' and 'person' " (138; see also 152). So these doctrines would reasonably have a linked importance and influence in Milton's later thought and poetry: both follow from the same root perception, which meant so much to Milton that he staked these major heterodoxies upon it. *Paradise Lost* has been exhaustively studied in relation to antitrinitarianism yet not at all in relation to Milton's theory of the Incarnation.

11. Richard Hooker, *Of the Laws of Ecclesiastical Polity*, V.lii.3, in *Works*, ed. Rev. John Keble, 7th rev. ed., 3 vols. (Oxford, 1888), 2:224, with Hooker's italics; for general discussion of the Incarnation, highly instructive for grasping the different implications of Milton's diction in *Paradise Lost*, see chap. li–liv.

12. Johannes Wolleb, *Abridgement of Christian Divinity*, trans. Alexander Ross (London, 1656), 199–200; emphasis mine. Or as John W. Beardslee III translates Wolleb in his anthology *Reformed Dogmatics* (New York: Oxford University Press, 1965), 91: "The human nature of Christ has no individuality other than the hypostasis or subsistence of the Logos; that is, of the Son of God."

13. On the mode and extent of the union of humanity and divinity in Milton's Christology, see Hunter, "Incarnation," 144–45; Lewalski, *Milton's Brief Epic*, 155–56; and MacCallum, *Milton and the Sons of God*, 216–25. They concur that this union is intimately permanent but dispute whether it amounts to Monophysite fusion. Hunter and Lewalski assume that *De Doctrina* and *Paradise Lost* necessarily diverge on the death of Christ, first (1992) in Hunter's "Provenance of the *Christian Doctrine*," 131, and then in Lewalski's immediately appended response in "Forum: Milton's *Christian Doctrine*," 151–52. Hunter uses this supposed divergence between poem and treatise as "clear" proof that the latter is incompatible with the poem and thus not by Milton; Lewalski's rejoinder unfortunately accepts Hunter's assumption that this is a "real discrepancy between the treatise and the late poems." *Paradise Lost* comprehends this position of *De Doctrina* in a way appropriate to its different genre and purposes.

14. On the divergence of orthodox christological language from Milton's in *Paradise Lost*, compare also, e.g., Hooker, *Laws*, V.lii.3:

"The Word (saith St. John) was made flesh and dwelt *in us.*" The Evangelist useth the plural number, men for manhood, *us* for the nature whereof we consist. . . . *It pleased not the Word or Wisdom of God to take to itself some one person* amongst men, for then should that *one* have been advanced which was assumed *and no more*. . . . Nestorius imagined in Christ as well a personal human subsistence as a divine, the Church acknowledging a substance both divine and human, but no other personal subsistence than divine, because the Son of God took not to himself a man's person, but the nature only of a man.

(2:224; emphasis mine, aside from Hooker's biblical quotation)

Conversely, *Paradise Lost* denominates Jesus Christ *"one* greater *man"* from the outset, pointedly eschewing plural or general constructions through emphatic specification of singularity, and *Paradise Regained* follows suit.

15. All biblical references are to the King James Version and are cited parenthetically in the text.

16. I am thankful to J. Martin Evans for referring me to "On the Morning of Christ's Nativity."

17. John Peter Rumrich, *Matter of Glory: A New Preface to "Paradise Lost"* (Pittsburgh: University of Pittsburgh Press, 1987), chap. 4. I am thankful to Rumrich for having advised me of the relationship between Milton's concepts of matter and form and his heterodoxy of the Incarnation.

18. A statement on love and free will closely analogous to Raphael's appears in *De Doctrina, YP,* 6:189:

[T]his condition . . . is absolutely in keeping with justice and does not detract at all from the importance of divine grace. For the power to will and believe is either the gift of God or, insofar as it is inherent in man at all, has no relation to good work or merit but only to the natural faculties. God does not then . . . depend upon the will of man, but accomplishes his own will, and in doing so has willed that in the love and worship of God, and thus in their own salvation, men should always use their free will. If we do not, whatever worship or love we men offer to God is worthless and of no account. The will which is threatened or overshadowed by any external decree cannot be free, and once force is imposed all esteem for services rendered . . . vanishes altogether.

19. Hunter, "Incarnation," 140.

20. MacCallum, *Milton and the Sons of God,* 220; see also 57–58, 171–72.

21. Dennis Danielson, *Milton's Good God: A Study in Literary Theodicy* (Cambridge: Cambridge University Press, 1982), 97–125.

22. I quote the interpolated Latin terms from *De Doctrina, CM,* 16:1, 15:272. I follow Hunter's observation of the terminological similarity of Milton's accounts of the ecclesiological and christological unions in "Incarnation," 140.

23. On "individual," see Jim Swan, "Difference and Silence: John Milton and the Question of Gender," in *The (M)other Tongue: Essays in Feminist Psychoanalytic Interpretation,* ed. Shirley Nelson Garner, Claire Kahane, and Madelon Sprengnether (Ithaca: Cornell University Press, 1985), 158–60. On the Western history of the subject, see David Aers, "A Whisper in the Ear of Early Modernists; or, Reflections on Literary Critics Writing the 'History of the Subject,' " in *Culture and History 1350–1600: Essays on English Communities, Identities, and Writing,* ed., David Aers (Detroit: Wayne State University Press, 1992), 177–202; *Reconstructing Individualism: Autonomy, Individuality, and the Self in Western Thought,* ed. Thomas C. Heller et al. (Stanford, Calif.: Stanford University Press, 1986); Charles Taylor, *Sources of the Self: The Making of the Modern Identity* (Cambridge: Harvard University Press, 1989).

24. According to Hooker (*Laws*, V.lii.1 , in *Works*, 2:222–23), for example, the way in which God and man unite in Jesus Christ is so problematic for human understanding that for "the space of vie hundred years after Christ, the Church was almost troubled with nothing else saving only with care and travail to preserve this article from the sinister construction of heretics." On the seventeenth-century topicality of reformulating the Incarnation, see John Owen (*Christologia* [London, 1679], sig. C3v), defending orthodoxy: "[T]he oppositions unto this sacred Truth, the fundamental Article of the Church and the Christian Religion, concerning his Divine Person, its constitution and use, as the Human Nature conjoyned substantially unto it, and subsisteth in it, are in this last Age encreases . . . managed under so great variety of forms . . . [and] promoted with more subtilty and specious pretences than in former Ages."

25. Carrol B. Cox, "Citizen Angels: Civil Society and the Abstract Individual in *Paradise Lost*," *Milton Studies* 23 (1988): 166. On Milton's supposedly untrammeled individualism, see also David Aers and Bob Hodge, " 'Rational Burning': Milton on Sex and Marriage," *Milton Studies* 13 (1979): 12–14; and Christopher Kendrick, *Milton: A Study in Ideology and Form* (New York: Methuen, 1986), 13–16. Alternatively, for Milton's treatment of individualism as "means to a communal end," see Joan Malory Webber, "The Politics of Poetry: Feminism and *Paradise Lost*," *Milton Studies* 14 (1980): 3–24.

Belial, Popery, and True Religion: Milton's *Of True Religion* and Antipapist Sentiment

HONG WON SUH

1

On 15 March 1672, Charles II issued the Declaration of Indulgence, the second of many attempts at promoting toleration, not only for Nonconformists—those Protestants who refused to take the Anglican sacraments—but also for Roman Catholics. Two days later, the third Anglo-Dutch War was declared. Charles had signed a secret treaty with France in 1670, now called the Treaty of Dover, in which he promised Louis XIV the reestablishment of the rights of Roman Catholics in England and military support for France against the Dutch in return for a substantial sum of money that would ease his financial troubles. He was also to announce his conversion to Catholicism and to receive further stipends for the purpose of financing an army of six thousand provided by the French king, which was to deal with the reaction of English Protestants following the announcement. The nature of the pact was such that, were the terms to leak out, England would have been plunged into utter chaos. Even without the knowledge of the Treaty of Dover, the reaction of English Protestants against the Declaration of Indulgence was immediate and vehement. The fact that Charles sided with a Catholic nation against what was so recently a Protestant ally was enough to raise the suspicion that the Declaration was part of a broader Catholic conspiracy, which it was in a way, although Charles's real motives are not very clear.[1] Scores of pamphlets poured out against toleration of Roman Catholics, and Parliament, when it convened in February and March 1673, swiftly passed the Test Act, which enforced penal laws against Roman Catholics and threw out their priests, and also prohibited non-Anglicans from holding public offices. The speed and decisiveness of the Act would have been impossible had Anglicans and Nonconformists not been able to unite against their common enemy, the Papists. The king, alarmed at the vehemence of the reaction, had to capitulate and to issue a Royal Proclamation and praise Parliament's efforts "for the preservation of True Religion."[2] To reward those Nonconformists who joined in the outcry against the Declaration of Indulgence, the House of Commons "gratefully passed a Bill for the 'Ease of Protestant Dissenters' " before the sessions ended on 29 March.[3] Two things stand out in the events surrounding the Declaration of Indulgence. The first is that the fear of popery was strong enough to unite Anglicans with the Nonconformists against toleration of Roman Catholics. The second is that this fear was prompted even without the revelation of Charles's frightening secret treaty with France, testifying further to the intensity of the English Protestants' fear of Rome.

The title of Milton's *Of True Religion* contains an ironic allusion to Charles's insincere praise of Parliament, calling attention to the fluidity of terms and the need to reestablish the meaning of true religion. The arrangement of the title on the cover page may give us some insight into what Milton intended when he published this pamphlet. The title is divided into three parts: the first has, as a group, "True Religion, HÆRESIE, SCHISM, TOLERATION"; the second is in small print connecting the first and the third parts with, "And what best means may be us'd against the growth of"; and the third part contains the single word "POPERY" in the largest type size. The effect of dividing the title thus is to oppose the first group of words against "POPERY," in effect bringing together widely incompatible terms under one rubric (8:416).[4] How can true religion be aligned with schism and heresies? More urgently, what is the role of toleration in true religion? The purpose of the pamphlet appears to be twofold. The more visible purpose is the suppression of popery—Roman Catholicism, after all, is the true heresy. Milton also stresses the need for toleration, however, so much so that this second purpose potentially conflicts with the first. Has Milton forced himself into an impossible position?

William Riley Parker believes that Milton sought this opportunity to convey his long-held convictions against Roman Catholicism and for religious toleration, all in one simple package, expecting the House of Lords to pass the Bill of ease for Nonconformist Protestants in its next session in October.[5] Christopher

Hill argues that, while he does inveigh against popery, Milton's real purpose is to express his support for broad tolerance under the guise of antipapist writing. "What is remarkable about *Of True Religion*," he says, "is the daring breadth of its tolerance," more inclusive than the one intended by the Commons when it passed the Bill.[6] Hill further points out that Milton, like some of his contemporaries, did not seriously consider the "popish danger as a main issue, . . . but the political advantages of attacking Stuart absolutist aspirations through traditional popular hostility to popery seemed clear."[7] Mary Ann Radzinowicz sees *Of True Religion* as a more nuanced work. Radzinowicz argues that Milton, rather than taking advantage of the fear of popery for political purposes, as Hill suggests, tries to channel the fear of popery into something more positive by making the public see the real issue, which is toleration:

> The occasion of the work was Milton's discovery that popular support existed for his own profoundest convictions, although that support arose not from pure confidence in toleration but rather was triggered by the public fears of popery. Milton therefore spoke as carefully as he could to strengthen and broaden the possible common ground between himself and Parliament. . . . To all men of good will Milton offered to draw out the implication of their anti-popish uneasiness. That implication was simply the need for toleration of all Protestants by all Protestants.[8]

If Radzinowicz sees Milton's argument in the pamphlet as subtle and "canny,"[9] Reuben Marquez Sánchez Jr. sees it as downright "devious," arguing for toleration so radically inclusive that it seems to include toleration even for Roman Catholics.[10] Sánchez is not very clear on whether Milton is arguing for or against toleration of Roman Catholics. Despite Milton's statement that Roman Catholicism must not be tolerated (8:430), Sánchez argues that he also permits it back in by an "appeal for tolerating and testing of all beliefs," including "false religions as well."[11] Although Sánchez has a good grasp on what Milton means by "true religion," which is foremost a tolerant religion, he unfortunately does not have an equal understanding of the opposite of "true religion," which is "Popery . . . the only or the greatest Heresie" (8:421). We need to look more closely at how Milton views popery and Roman Catholicism, terms that do not always converge in meaning. As I will elaborate later, it may be best to keep in mind John T. Shawcross's observation that "popery" is a word both understood and used politically.[12]

In this paper, I propose that Milton wrote *Of True Religion* as a critique of the Test Act and more broadly of the use of civil power in ecclesiastical matters. This latter had been a problem for Milton not only before the Civil War and after the Restoration but even during the Presbyterian-dominated Interregnum. The Restoration and the Anglican church's revival made matters only worse. The pamphlet, in other words, is a severe critique of Anglican policies toward Nonconformists. To support my argument, I examine first the figure of Belial. Milton and his contemporaries frequently talk about Belial or the sons of Belial when they describe the popish practices of the Anglican church; in Milton's case, he even compares the Presbyterians to the sons of Belial. The easy transference of the figure of Belial to describe first the corruption in Roman Catholicism, then in episcopacy, and yet again in Presbyterianism suggests not only the corrupting power of the pagan god but also the vulnerability of such religious institutions. Next, I look at the English fear of popish plots throughout the Stuart age; my emphasis will be on the overblown nature of the fear. It is the Belial-like insidiousness of popery more than any overt or perceptible threat that feeds the English imagination. But the real danger is that, in the frenzy to eradicate popery, one faces the possibility of becoming that which one fears and hates. Finally, I examine the argument in *Of True Religion*, focusing on Milton's definition of true religion and its opposite, popery, and his views on toleration based on these definitions. I compare these views with those found in his other writings and focus eventually on the split between the institutionalized church and the individual conscience.

2

Of all the fallen angels who have acquired an earthly name, Belial has a special distinction: "a Spirit more lewd / Fell not from Heaven, or more gross to love / Vice for itself" (1.490–92).[13] He is a god without a temple to his honor, which is a sign that he is unworthy of his place among the "prime in order and in might" of these angels (506). Yet in the council in Hell, Milton puts him in the limelight by making him perform a most brilliant speech against Moloch, third in might among the devils. What is it about Belial that merits special attention? Next to Satan, he is the most multifaceted. He does not have the many names of Baal, nor his or her dual sexuality, but Belial's identity is the most difficult to fix. Because he loves vice for itself, as against the other gods who are vicious for a purpose, he is like a chameleon, shifting identities and allegiances in the pursuit of vice:

> To him no Temple stood
> Or Altar smok'd; yet who more oft than hee
> In Temples and at Altars, when the Priest
> Turns Atheist, as did Ely's Sons, who fill'd
> With lust and violence the house of God.
> In Courts and Palaces he also Reigns
> And in luxurious Cities, where the noise
> Of riot ascends above thir loftiest Tow'rs,
> And injury and outrage: And when Night
> Darkens the Streets, then wander forth the Sons
> Of Belial, flown with insolence and wine.
> Witness the Streets of Sodom, and that night
> In Gibeah, when the hospitable door
> Expos'd a Matron to avoid worse rape.
>
> (492–505)

Belial's kind of sexual corruption has violent overtones; witness in the passage above the alarming union of sex, rape, and murder (which, by the way, was the fate of the "matron" exposed in Gibeah).[14] In him are concentrated all the various vices of the devils "prime in order and in might." In the roll call of the devils, the more notorious of them are given certain identifiable qualities. Moloch personifies hatred, and Baal-Peor stands for sexual corruption; and their temples erected on the Mount of Olives give testimony to their activities. Thus, the sight of Baal-Peor's temple next to the temple of Moloch is described by Milton as a juxtaposition of lust and hate: "lust hard by hate" (417). Belial, the devil of hateful lust, embodies the qualities of both Moloch and Baal-Peor, and in his power to corrupt he is as gifted as Satan, who fails in direct confrontation and succeeds only by policy. He is perhaps the more insidious because, though he has no temple to his name, he insinuates himself into the temples of other gods, turning the worshiper against her goddess or a priest to corruption; it may be Belial who creates all the frenzy inside Moloch's, and Baal-Peor's, and Astoreth's temples on "th' offensive Mountain [the Mount of Olives]" (443). He also triumphs whenever a court or a city falls into luxury and riot.

In the minds of the Puritan writers before the revolution, Belial was thriving in England, both in the church and in the court.

In 1633, Thomas Welde, a Nonconformist minister who had been driven out of England by Bishop William Laud (made archbishop in August that year), sent a letter to his friends in his hometown of Terling, Essex, describing his new home in Massachusetts: "Here are none of the men of Gibea the sonnes of Belial knocking at our doors disturbing our sweet peace or threatening violence. Here blessed by the Lord God for euer Our eares are not beaten nor the aire filled with Oathes. Swearers nor Railers, Nor our eyes and eares vexed with the vnclea [sic] Conversation of the wicked" (130–31).[15] Welde describes the riots of prerevolutionary England as a literal assault upon the eyes and ears of the godly; how happy he is in the New World, without the disturbance of peace or the threat of violence. What is interesting is that the riots are, in Welde's mind, not differentiated from religious oppression, the "knocking at our doors" that struck terror in the hearts of Nonconformists. There was great hope for them in 1640, when Laud and his minions were removed from their seats both in church and in the House of Lords, but those who hoped for a swift removal of all corruption in the Church of England were disappointed. They had succeeded only in removing the worst of the offenders and, with episcopacy so far intact, the sons of Belial were far from being extirpated.

The reformers were equally disappointed with Charles I. When war was declared between Charles and Parliament, an anonymous pamphlet *The Late Covenant Asserted* justified the Parliamentary cause by equating the king's resistance to reform with the Benjaminites' refusal to give up the members of their tribe, those "children of Belial" who had raped the concubine at Gibeah. Among the sons of Belial under the protection of Charles were the Anglican bishops, largely blamed for the corruption of the Church of England, and the Irish Catholic rebels, whose insurrection in October 1641 fed the rumor mills with reports of atrocities fit for hell. The Oxford "treaty" or "covenant," the subject matter of *The Late Covenant Asserted*, had brought together the two groups most hated by English Protestants:[16] "So they [the eleven tribes of Israel, excluding the Benjaminites] require their Brother *Benjamin* to deliver-up those children of *Belial*, which are in *Gibeah*, that wee may put them to death (as we have resolved in our Parliament) and put away evill from Israel. *Benjamin* are stout, they will not hearken, they will maintaine the true Religion, according to Covenant, that shall be their prime worke still. And they will maintaine those *Children of Belial* too; All this will agree together (as Christ and

Belial) so they are resolved."[17] This work is particularly interesting because of the sarcasm in the use of the words "true Religion." The anonymous author scathingly attacks the claims
made by Charles and his Cavaliers that they were preserving
"true Religion" when all the while they were protecting those
very people who threatened the true Church of England.

Ironically, when Milton uses the words "son of Belial" for the
first time, it is to refute a characterization of himself as a drunk-
ard, a swearer, and a frequenter of brothels, made by the modest
confuter of the *Animadversions*. Milton counters that the modest confuter's characterization is based on his firsthand experience of the vices he so vividly describes. Though Milton would
like to enter a pleasing conversation with his readers on the
value of true love, it is impossible right now, he says, "not in
these noises, the adversary as ye know, barking at the doore; or
searching for me at the Burdello's where it may be he has lost
himselfe" (1:892). The modest confuter's "barking at the doore,"
and his propensity to lose himself in the bordellos sets him up
as the real son of Belial: "And [. . .] like a son of Belial without
the hire of *Iesabel* charges me *of blaspheming God and the King,*
as ordnarily as he imagines *me to drink Sack and sweare,*
meerely because this was a shred in his common place-book, and
seem'd to come off roundly, as if he were some Empirick of false
accusations to try his poysons upon me whether they would
work or no" (1:893).[18]

Just to be sure that he has covered all possibilities, Milton
even suggests that the descriptions of the vices may have come
from a commonplace book. Milton himself had such a book,
from which he gained valuable experience, albeit vicariously.[19]
What should be underscored is the fact that Milton is acutely
aware of the way images circulate. Certain tropes, like "sons of
Belial," have a way of penetrating speech and writing without
the aid of actual events or experience to give credence to their
existence. They feed on the imagination and spread like conta-
gion, but because they have little or no association with reality,
they tend to attach to widely divergent subjects. Milton himself
uses the phrase "brood of Belial" to describe at one time certain
people who wish to use his arguments for divorce to justify their
licentiousness (2:225) and then at another time to attack the avarice of Presbyterian ministers who try to maintain tithing
(7:296). What is nearly universal, however, is that the words
"sons of Belial" are used in association with popery. When Milton attacks the Presbyterians for collecting tithes, for instance,

he is arguing that tithing is popish because it is a vestige of
Roman Catholicism, passed down through episcopacy.

3

The circulation of the word "popery" is as interesting as that
of "sons of Belial." The definition of "popery" is clear
enough—it points to anything relating to or resembling the practices of and adherency to the Pope—but what is not so clear is
the application of the word in English society. As we shall soon
see, "popery" or "papist" and like epithets were used with
plenty of feeling and little discretion.

Catholic conspiracies were uncovered frequently during the
Stuart Age, beginning with the Gunpowder Plot. Annual celebrations of the discovery of this Plot—Milton participated in the
celebrations with some Latin exercises—symbolized the Protestant resolve against the encroachments of Rome. The threat of
Roman Catholicism seemed very real in England. When war between Charles and Parliament was declared and Queen Henrietta Maria brought in royalist supporters from the Continent,
and when Charles signed a pact with the Irish rebels, suspicions
of the king's papist leanings seemed quite justified. With the
shocking details of the carnage in Ireland still quite fresh in the
memory, the country was once again jolted by a report of the
Cavaliers' sacking of the towns of Abington and Alisbury. Not
only were the houses and household goods destroyed but also
livestock were cut down or shot and the women raped.[20] Although writers like Milton were more willing to talk about the
evils of popery in terms of implicit faith and custom, and (when
they felt more adventurous) of corruption that "gives a Vomit to
GOD himselfe" (1:537), those who had an ear for propaganda
seized upon the lurid details of the rapine in Ireland and in the
beleaguered towns of Abington and Alisbury to visualize for the
English Protestants the consequences of Roman Catholic rule in
England.[21]

Even as the Roundheads won and prepared to launch the Re-
public, it appeared that they would be sailing in a sea of Roman
Catholicism, which was enjoying a renewed expansion of power
throughout the Continent. One of the bloodiest events that occurred during the Roman Catholic resurgence was the massacre,
in April 1655, of the Waldensians by the Duke of Savoy's men.
Soon after, the details of the massacre reached England, and a

pamphlet called *A Collection of Several Papers Sent to his Highness the Lord Protector . . . Concerning the Bloody and Barbarous Massacres, Murthers, and Other Cruelties, Committed on Many Thousands . . . Dwelling in the Vallies of Piedmont* was printed in June 1655 by Jean Baptiste Stouppe, giving official testimony to the rumors that were circulating. The graphic images of violence in the pamphlet would have been familiar to the English because of the accounts of what had reportedly happened in Ireland during the rebellion and in the English towns run over by the Cavaliers, but the massacre at Piedmont touched the nerve of the English in a very strange way. Cromwell himself took up the cause, and Milton left a vehement, apocalyptic sonnet on the subject. The acts of popery, the dashing of babies on the rocks and the rape of virgins, were etched indelibly in the minds of the English. Using these images, Samuel Morland delivered a speech on behalf of Cromwell to the Duke of Savoy, the first Latin draft of which was presumably written by Milton. The following is a translation of the revised version that Morland delivered, in which the atrocities committed by Savoy's men were depicted more graphically than in the first draft:

> Oh the fired houses which are yet smoking, the torn limbs, and ground defiled with bloud! Virgins being ravished, have afterwards had their wombs stuffed up with gravel and Rubbish, and in that miserable manner breathed out their last. Some men an hundred years old, decrepit with age, and bed-rid, have been burnt in their beds. Some infants have been dashed against the Rocks, others their throats cut, whose brains have with more than Cyclopsean cruelty, being boiled and eaten by the Murtherers! What need I mention more? although I could reckon up very many cruelties of the like kinde, if I were not astonished at the very thought of them.[22]

No rule of decency applied to papists' treatment of the innocent victims. Notably lacking among the victims were men who could fight; there was no possibility of a legitimate battle between Savoy's men and the Piedmontese. The slaughter of old men and infants, and the rape of virgins take on the appearance of a gruesome ritual performed by the Sons of Belial.

The fear of popery intensified after the Restoration because, as Milton had pointed out in *The Readie and Easie Way*, England was not only getting back a monarch but also his papist family (7:425).[23] People grew increasingly mistrustful of Charles's presumed Catholic leanings, and in the late 1670s, there were (yet again) widespread rumors of a papist invasion, accompanied by the suspicion that the king was raising an army against Parliament. James, his brother and heir, refused to take the Anglican sacrament, as all public figures were required to do in accordance with the Test Act (1673), in effect declaring himself a Roman Catholic. The Exclusion Crisis of the late 1670s was fueled by a fear that, once he became king, James would open the doors of England to Rome. Henry Care, a fierce antipapist, drew up a lurid picture of England being sacked by Roman Catholics:

> Yourselves forced to fly destitute of bread and harbour, your wives prostituted to the lust of every savage bog-trotter, your daughters ravished by goatish monks, your smaller children tossed upon pikes, or torn limb from limb, whilst you have your own bowels ripped up . . . or else murdered with some other exquisite tortures and holy candles made of your grease (which was done within our memory of Ireland), your dearest friends flaming in Smithfield, foreigners rendering your poor babes that can escape everlasting slaves, never more to see a Bible, nor hear again the joyful sounds of Liberty and Property. This, this gentlemen is Popery.[24]

Care's details and those in Morland's address to Savoy are remarkably similar, and they appear to be sharing the same stock images of the papists. The English Catholics in reality had neither the power nor the unity of purpose to unsettle the State, but this fact hardly mattered. In any case, a Catholic king in combination with the threat across the channel would have been enough to persuade the people that Care was right. The English saw papists lurking in every corner of the streets, their vivid imagination fueled by propagandists such as Care.[25]

Fear often turned to paranoia, even among the otherwise most sensible of religious leaders. No one provides a more striking example of this than one of the most celebrated Presbyterian ministers, William Prynne. His case against Bishop Laud was based on a suspicion that there was a "Popish Plot" to corrupt the king, the evidence of which he promised but was never able to produce. Once the bishops were removed, however, and the Anglican ministers ousted from their seats, Prynne turned his eyes on the Independents in the army and saw in their actions a similar papist plot. The army, he believed, had been infiltrated by Jesuits, and it was by their prodding that Pride's Purge and the most heinous execution of Charles I had been committed. In 1671, Peter du Moulin recalls a correspondence with Prynne, in which Prynne told him that the captured king had secretly agreed to pass strict measures against the Catholics and that "the Jesuites in France, at a general meeting there, presently resolved to bring him to Justice and take off his head, by the power of their Friends in the Army."[26] Richard Baxter also, otherwise a level-headed minister, believed Prynne's theory that Henrietta Maria's chaplain had disguised himself as a soldier attending the execution and had also exulted in the king's death. The Restoration had not diminished Prynne's zeal. It was his fierce contention that the Quakers were Catholics in disguise, despite all appearances to the contrary, and that the Great Fire of London (1666) was yet another Jesuit plot.[27]

One of the most ludicrous, but hardly laughable, products of such paranoia was a "discovery" of a popish plot by one Titus Oates in 1678. There was in reality no plot, popish or otherwise; it was a fiction created by Oates himself, a mercenary as John Miller describes him, ready to sell his story to the highest bidder. At first he attempted to sell it to the king, touting a plot to murder the king's own person, after which twenty thousand Catholics were to rise in London alone and cut one hundred thousand Protestant throats. The king did not bite, and Oates then went to the king's enemies in Parliament and found them more willing to buy his story. England was plunged in such paranoia that they did not see through Oates's complete rehashing of images and plotlines from a long tradition of antipapist writings. The stock images and notions, based largely on Prynne's conspiracy theory, in which even the dead Milton was implicated—he was to have frequented a popish club—merely confirmed the worst for the imaginative English.[28] In his greed, Oates had driven the whole country into a renewed frenzy of anti-Catholic sentiment, which Care took advantage of. As a result, Charles had to pass one of the strictest measures in his time against Roman Catholics, in order to appease the bloodthirstiness of his political opponents, as he had reluctantly done many times before, including 1673.

4

Milton's own hatred of Roman Catholicism feeds upon his Puritan contempt for forms—idols, ceremony, and the Sacrament. In *Of Reformation*, he says that because the Roman Catholic priests cannot "make themselves *heavenly*," they turn all heavenly things "earthly, and fleshly," making "the very shape of *God* himselfe, into an exterior, and bodily forme" (1:520). Once the exterior is formed, it is lavishly decorated and codified, until "all the inward acts of *worship* issuing from the native strength of the SOULE, run out lavishly to the upper skin, and there harden into a crust of Formallitie" (1:522). One of the most appalling results of this love of exterior forms is the Sacrament, the body of Christ, that "is supposed to be made out of bread at the moment when the priest murmurs the four words, *this is my body*, and to be broken as soon as it is made" (6:559). The Holy Communion has become a "cannibal feast" (6:554) that, taken literally, does the Savior the worst service: "It [the Catholic Mass] drags it [Christ's holy body] back to the earth, though it has suffered every pain and hardship already, to a state of humiliation even more wretched and degrading than before: to be broken once more and crushed and ground, even by the fangs of brutes. Then, when it has been driven through all the stomach's filthy channels, it shoots it out—one shudders even to mention it—into the latrine" (6:560). An earlier description of the "Table of Communion" as a "Table of Separation" emphasizes the purpose behind all this formality. The table is

> fortifi'd with bulwark, and barricado, to keep off the profane touch of the Laicks, whilst the obscene, and surfeted Priest scruples not to paw, and mammock the sacramentall bread, as familiarly as his Tavern Bisket. And thus the people vilifi'd and rejected by them, give over the earnest study of vertue, and godlinesse as a thing of greater purity then they need, and the search of divine knowledge as a mystery too high for their capacity's, and only for Churchmen to meddle with, which is that the Prelates desire, that . . . we might commit to their dispose the whole managing of our salvation.
>
> (1:548)

The prelates perform the Sacrament not to hold communion but to monopolize access to God, and toward this aim they also encourage implicit faith in the lay person. This last quotation, however, is not an attack on the Roman Catholic Mass but on the Anglican worship. In 1633, five parishioners at St. Gregory's appealed that the placing of the table of communion at the east end of the chancel, with rails around it, deprived the people of the right to communicate. Not only did Laud dismiss this appeal but also two years later he "ordered all communion tables to be removed to the east end of the chancel and railed in."[29] It was no secret among reform-minded Protestants that popery lived on in the Anglican church.

How is it, then, that Milton seems to be making overtures to the Anglicans in *Of True Religion*? He even refers to the Anglican Thirty-nine Articles to arrive at a definition of true religion, as if to concede the superiority of Anglican doctrine:

> True Religion is the true Worship and Service of God, learnt and believed from the Word of God only. . . . With good and Religious Reason therefore all Protestant Churches with one consent, and particularly the Church of *England* in Her thirty nine Articles, Artic. *6th, 19th, 20th, 21st,* and elsewhere, maintain these two points, as the main Principles of True Religion: that the Rule of true Religion is the Word of God only: and that their Faith ought not to be an implicit faith, that is, to believe, though as the Church believes, against or without express authority of the Scripture.
>
> (8:418–19)

The appeal to the Anglican articles of faith, however, is not a conciliatory gesture. On the contrary, as he has often done in the past, he shows how far Anglican discipline has strayed from its own doctrine.[30]

The opposite of true religion is heresy, which "is Religion taken up and believ'd from the traditions of men and additions to the word of God," from which definition Milton asserts that "of all known Sects or pretended Religions at this day in Christendom, Popery is the only or the greatest Heresie" (8:421). Therefore, anyone who charges other people of heresy is "the obstinate Papist, the only Heretick" (8:421). This view agrees with the curious layout of the title page that aligns "True Religion, HÆRESIE, SCHISM, TOLERATION" against "Popery." A true religion is one that is tolerant and may very well be a religion attacked by papists as a heresy or a schism;[31] opposed to this is popery, "the only or the greatest heresy." By this definition of heresy, it would not be too difficult to see that Anglicanism, or the kind of Anglicanism that was being practiced then, was popery, for the Anglican Church of the 1670s was no different from that of the 1630s.

When the Cavalier Parliament came to power in 1661, one of the first things it did was to reinstate the Anglican bishops to their seats. Subsequently, Parliament, with the blessing of the bishops, passed act upon act to restrict the freedom of all Nonconformists. The most notorious of these was the Act of Uniformity in 1662 that ejected all ministers who refused to pledge allegiance to the new Book of Common Prayer. Many Nonconformist ministers refused to comply with the Act of Uniformity, but, more importantly, many more *did* swear allegiance to the

Prayer Book and retained their seats. The Anglicans were now caught in a double bind. They needed a public declaration of allegiance from the ministers in order to cleanse the church of dissent and bring back the stray sheep, but having allowed some of these sheep into their fold, they could not help wondering whether these were wolves in sheep clothing.[32]

The Anglicans were compelled to push for increasingly stricter measures and urge vigilance. The first Conventicle Act of 1664 was intended to clamp down on secret meetings among those who appeared to conform and yet performed private services not sanctioned by the church. Various attempts were made to uncover such meeting places, in most cases unsuccessfully, because those who hosted conventicles were powerful people. The more they persecuted, the more invisible their enemies seemed to become, but no less potent. Because their efforts had been misdirected, the Anglicans had achieved nothing by their actions, or worse than nothing—they had helped the enemy spawn more sons, within their own ranks. The Anglicans could have benefited from a reading of *Areopagitica*, for Milton's argument about the futility of censorship applies equally to the futile attempts by the Anglican Church to shut out the Nonconformists: "[T]hose corruptions which it seeks to prevent, break in faster at other dores which cannot be shut" (2:537). The Anglicans were trying to expose those who had infiltrated their ranks, in the belief that the church can be purified by shutting their doors on them. While they were terrorizing the Nonconformists with the threat of expulsion, Charles was holding a court "of vast expence and luxurie, masks and revels, to the debaushing of our prime gentry both male and female" (7:425). The Anglicans had transformed themselves and their allies into the very enemy they were desperately trying to expel; they had become the sons of Belial, knocking at the doors and looking out for acts of popery everywhere—everywhere but in the mirror.

This is what Milton is suggesting in *Of True Religion*. If to be a *Roman* Catholic is to be a contradiction, "For Catholic in Greek signifies universal" (8:422) and therefore cannot be applied to a specific place, then the Anglican claim that it is the true Catholic church is not only insular but also contradictory.[33] Step by step, Milton criticizes Anglican attempts to monopolize religion. The principles that prompt a predominantly Anglican Parliament not to tolerate Roman Catholics also make it intolerant of fellow Protestants, those Lutherans and Calvinists, along with those of the so-called sects and schism—Anabaptists,

Socinians, and Arminians—who "are no Hereticks" (8:423).[34] Milton distinguishes between *error* and *heresy:* on the one hand, error is against the will, and is something that may happen despite all earnest attempts to know Scripture aright; heresy, on the other hand, is willful distortion of Scripture. Error is not conducive to implicit faith, whereas heresy encourages it. What the so-called sects proclaim and practice are no more than errors that hardly call for the kind of persecutions they are suffering under Anglican leadership; a true church should by principle be more charitable to such errors. Milton asks, calling to mind the Thirty-nine Articles he had cited earlier: "What Protestant then who himself maintains the same Principles, and disavowes all implicit Faith, would persecute, and not rather charitably tolerate such men as these unless he mean to abjure the Principles of his own Religion?" (8:426). Because Anglicans "brand all others for Hereticks" (8:421) in spite of their professed doctrine, it follows that they have become the very papists they abhor. Milton's attack on the Anglicans is driven by his desire to promote toleration, which he achieves by reexamining the definition of "popery" that operates without rhyme or reason against all manner of dissent.

In contradistinction to his recommendations for toleration of Protestant religions, Milton's advice against Roman Catholicism is adamantly for nontoleration. The way he leads to this conclusion deserves some attention. "Popery," he says "is a double thing to deal with, and claims a twofold Power, Ecclesiastical, and Political, both usurpt, and the one supporting the other." But ecclesiastical power, he argues further, "is ever pretended to Political" (8:429). "Pretend" is an interesting word, as it signifies deceit as well as aspiration to a seat of power. Thus, the pope "pretends right to Kingdoms and States, and especially to this of England, Thrones and Unthrones Kings, and absolves the people from their obedience to them" (8:429). More significantly, Roman Catholicism is a pretended religion—pretended, that is, for political gain—and therefore no religion at all. In *A Treatise of Civil Power*, Milton argues in such a vein: "Their religion [Roman Catholicism] the more considerd, the less can be acknowledgd a religion; but a Roman principalitie rather, endevouring to keep up her old universal dominion under a new name and meer shaddow of a catholic religion; being indeed more rightly nam'd a catholic heresie against the scripture; supported mainly by a civil, and, except in *Rome*, by a forein power: justly therfore to be suspected, not tolerated by the magistrate of another countrey" (7:254). All the while, Milton is arguing why English ministers (Presbyterians in this case) should avoid repeating acts of popery that they claim so loudly to abhor.

Milton's recommendations against popery further support my point that *Of True Religion* is in large part an argument against Anglicanism. The first recommendation is for the removal of idols, which cannot be conducted without some degree of force: "[F]irst we must remove their Idolatry, and all the furniture thereof, whether Idols, or the Mass wherein they adore their God under Bread and Wine" (8:431–32). The violence involved here is justified because Roman Catholicism is not a religion but a "meer shaddow of" a true religion. Milton has a ready answer for those who would argue that such violence is against the principles of toleration: "If they say that by removing their Idols we violate their Consciences, we have no warrant to regard Conscience which is not grounded on Scripture" (8:432). The overall emphasis of Milton's recommendations, however, is on nonviolence. Even when he discusses the removal of idols, Milton's emphasis is not on retaliation but on denying the grounds that make a papist sin. What is this, if not an oblique but firm critique of Anglican intolerance, that relies heavily on violence to repress conscience grounded on Scripture? Moreover, the attack on "the Mass wherein they adore their God under Bread and Wine" is two pronged, indicting Anglicans as well as Roman Catholics. Milton's other recommendations include "constant reading of Scripture" and mutual toleration, that is, not "dissent[ing] in matters not essential to belief," which will deprive the papist of the "advantage of our several [i.e., dissenting] opinions" (8:435–36). And who gives the papist this advantage, other than Anglicans, who try their utmost to "impose things indifferent without Scripture" (8:428)?

During the course of investigating and prescribing against popery, Milton's argument shifts from Parliament's and the Anglicans' concern with *How to overcome popery, which is an external threat,* to what he sees as the real problem: *How do we avoid the corruption of popery, which is internal?* This cannot be more clearly expressed than in the last of his recommendations against popery, which he calls *avoiding* popery: "The last means to avoid Popery, is to amend our lives: it is a general complaint that this Nation of late years, is grown more numerously and excessively vitious then heretofore; Pride, Luxury, Drunkenness, Whoredom, Cursing, Swearing, bold and open Atheism every where abounding: Where these grow, no wonder if Popery also grow a pace" (8:438–39). The apparent justification of Parliament's actions with which this pamphlet began turns in the end into a warning to repent: "[L]east through impenitency we run into that stupidly, which we now seek all means so warily to avoid, the worst of superstitions, and the heaviest of all Gods Judgements, Popery" (8:440). The Test Act of March 1673 was for Milton little more than a popish act against popery. The rejection of "popery" was only superficial, and real popery, the one that corrupts from within with the power of Belial, was still running rampant in the Church of England.

NOTES

1. On the details of the events surrounding the Declaration of Indulgence and the third Anglo-Dutch War, see Barry Coward, *The Stuart Age: England 1603–1714*, 2d ed. (London: Longman, 1994), 305–12. According to Coward, Charles's motives, first for the triple alliance against the French and then for the *volte-face* alliance with the French, are difficult to pin down. He does strongly suggest, however, that religion did not factor largely in the king's decisions.

2. From the Royal Proclamation, dated 13 March 1673, quoted in Keith W. F. Stavely, preface and notes, in *Complete Prose Works of John Milton*, 8 vols., ed. Don M. Wolfe et al. (New Haven: Yale University Press, 1982), 8:417 n. 1.

3. William Riley Parker, *Milton: A Biography*, 2d ed., 2 vols., ed. Gordon Campbell (Oxford: Clarendon Press, 1996), 1:623. The Bill, unfortunately, was stalled in the House of Lords. Parker confuses the dating somewhat and narrates the events as if Charles proclaimed the Declaration while the parliamentary session of early 1673 was already in full swing. The Declaration came a year before, and there was almost a full year of heated debate over the issue of toleration before Parliament passed the Test Act.

4. John Milton, *Of True Religion*, in *Complete Prose Works*. All references to Milton's prose works are to this edition and are cited parenthetically in the text. Milton's own title pages, especially those of the pamphlets, yield interesting details about how he aligns himself in a cause or how he conceives of the issue at hand. That Milton paid special attention to title pages may be seen by his lengthy analysis of the decorum of the modest confuter's title page, which he ridicules as a "toling signe-post to call passengers" in *An Apology against a Pamphlet Call'd a Modest Confutation*, in *Complete Prose Works*, 1:875.

5. Parker, *Milton: A Biography*, 1:624. See also Stavely, preface and notes, in *Complete Prose Works*, 8:413.

6. Christopher Hill, *Milton and the English Revolution* (New York: Viking, 1978), 219.

7. Ibid., 220.

8. Mary Ann Radzinowicz, *Toward "Samson Agonistes": The Growth of Milton's Mind* (Princeton: Princeton University Press, 1978), 165.

9. Ibid.

10. Reuben Marquez Sánchez Jr., " 'The Worst of Superstitions': Milton's *Of*

True Religion and the Issue of Religious Tolerance," *Prose Studies* 9.3 (1986): 26, 32–35.

11. Ibid., 36.

12. John T. Shawcross, *John Milton: The Self and the World* (Lexington: University Press of Kentucky, 1993), 240–41.

13. John Milton, *Paradise Lost,* in *John Milton: Complete Poems and Major Prose,* ed. Merritt Y. Hughes (New York: Odyssey, 1957). All references to Milton's poetry are to this edition and are cited parenthetically in the text.

14. Michael Lieb provides a thoroughly useful account of the biblical sources of the sons of Belial in *Milton and the Culture of Violence* (Ithaca: Cornell University Press, 1994), 114–34. For allusions by Milton's contemporaries to Belial and the sons of Belial, see George Wesley Whiting, *Milton's Literary Milieu* (Chapel Hill: University of North Carolina Press, 1939), 218–31.

15. Thomas Welde, "A Letter of Master Wells from New England to Old England to His People at Tarling in Essex," *Transactions* [of the Colonial Society of Massachusetts] 13 (1910–11): 130–31. Another reference to Gibeah (and also Sodom) is made by John Winthrop in a sermon that holds the famous passage on the "city upon a hill." With regard to charity, he takes as examples "Abraham and Lot in entertaining the angels and the old man of Gibeah" (John Winthrop, "A Model of Christian Charity," in *The Puritans in America: A Narrative Anthology,* ed. Alan Heimert and Andrew Delbanco [Cambridge: Harvard University Press, 1985], 84). The violence at Sodom and Gibeah is not mentioned, but it is all too well understood by Winthrop and his audience; thus, the need for love even in situations (probably their sufferings in England) where it is difficult for them to feel charity: "[T]he Gospel commands love to an enemy" (84).

16. The Oxford "treaty" resulted in the Cessation Treaty between Charles and the Irish rebels in September 1643. Charles continued to alienate himself from the Protestants in both Scotland and in England. For a more detailed account of the Protestant suspicion of Charles, see Coward, *Stuart England,* 204–9.

17. *The Late Covenant Asserted* (London, 1643), 14; quoted in Whiting, *Milton's Literary Milieu,* 226.

18. I thank John T. Shawcross for pointing out to me the error in the Yale prose edition of inserting the pronoun "I" before "like a son of Belial."

19. In fact, the passage I have quoted is part of a broader discussion of the value of chastity, in which Milton discusses how he has learned the virtues of chastity from none other than books. Milton's bookish experience of the world may be seen, for instance, in "Elegy I," in which the young poet's description of life in London appears suspiciously like purloined scenes from the classics. As Shawcross notes of the girls Milton sees in the groves, "it is only observance from afar; he has not communed with any of these young women of Britain" (*John Milton,* 43). The girls might as well be moving statues or portraits or, to take the allusion to Ovid's *Heroides* seriously ("Elegy I," 63), figures in an Ovidian narrative. Coming back to *An Apology,* one of Milton's strategies in the pamphlet is to attack the modest confuter as a novice who has no experience whatsoever of the things he talks about. Whether the modest confuter has gained his knowledge of the brothels from personal experience or whether he has gained it vicariously does not matter to Milton; he wins either way.

20. G. H., *Abingtons and Alisburies Present Miseries. Both Which Towns Being Lately Lamentably Plundered by Prince Robert and His Cavaliers. Ex-*

pressly Related as It Was Certified to Some of the Honourable the High Court of Parliament. And Therefore Published (London, 1642), 61. Summarized in Whiting, Milton's Literary Milieu, 228–29.

21. John Temple, a propagandist for the Parliamentary cause, made more than judicious use of such images in The Irish Rebellion: Or, An History of the Beginnings and First Progress of the General Rebellion Raised Within the Kingdom of Ireland, upon the Three and Twentieth Day of October, in the Year 1641. Together with the Barbarous Cruelties and Bloody Massacres Which Ensued Thereupon (London, 1646).

22. Printed in John Milton, The Works of John Milton, 18 vols., ed. Frank A. Patterson et al. (New York: Columbia University Press, 1931–38), 13:485, 87. Morland had included this translation alongside the original Latin in his History of the Evangelical Churches of the Valleys of Piedmont (London, 1658). On the discussion of the massacre, see Lieb, Milton and the Culture of Violence, 29–37. Robert Fallon offers a complete account of the flurry of activities in the Protectorate government in response, first to reports of oppression, and then the massacre of the Piedmontese, in Milton in Government (University Park, Pa.: Pennsylvania State University Press, 1993), 139–51.

23. Charles II actually married after the Restoration.

24. Henry Care, The Weekly Pacquet of Advice from Rome, or the History of Popery, 4 vols. (London, 1679–82), 3:160, quoted in John Miller, Popery and Politics in England 1660–1688 (Cambridge: Cambridge University Press, 1973), 75. On Care's war against papists and censors alike, see Richard L. Greaves, Secrets of the Kingdom: British Radicals from the Popish Plot to the Revolution of 1688–1689 (Stanford, Calif.: Stanford University Press, 1992), 15–16.

25. See Coward, Stuart England, 304–29. A more detailed examination of the actual strength of the Catholics in England in the seventeenth century and its irrelevance to the antipapist sentiment is provided by Miller, Popery and Politics in England, 3–27.

26. Peter du Moulin, A Vindication of the Sincerity of the Protestant Religion (London, 1671), 65, quoted in William M. Lamont, Marginal Prynne, 1600–1669 (London: Routledge, 1963), 139.

27. See Lamont, Marginal Prynne, 119–48. A short summary of Prynne's paranoia is in William M. Lamont, Puritanism and the Historical Controversy (Montreal: McGill–Queen's University Press, 1996), 22–25. Baxter did not believe that the king's execution was a Roman Catholic plot. Rather, he held to a "Grotian" belief that French Catholics (who wanted Catholicism without Rome's influence) had aimed to set English Protestants against each other. See Lamont, Puritanism and Historical Controversy, 50–52. Baxter's view actually made more sense because the threat of Catholic France was more tangible than that of Rome. Charles's attempts to form an alliance with France and his frequent Declarations of Indulgence, in the aid of both Protestant dissenters and Catholics, continued to fuel the English fear of popery.

28. Miller, Popery and Politics in England, 155–59. On Milton's supposed visits to a popish club, see J. Milton French, The Life Records of John Milton, 5 vols. (New York: Gordian, 1966), 5:118–22.

29. Don M. Wolfe and William Alfred, preface and notes, in Complete Prose Works, 1:547–48 n. 109.

30. In Of Reformation, Milton defines "discipline" as "the execution and applying of Doctrine home, and laying the salve to the very Orifice of the

wound; yea tenting and searching to the *Core,* without which *Pulpit Preaching* is but shooting at Rovers" (1:526).

31. It appears that more than one denomination meets the definition of true religion set earlier by Milton—adherence to the Scriptures and rejection of implicit faith. Each denomination may qualify as *a* true religion, although differing in degrees of truth according to its proximity to the one True Religion, the completely reformed Church.

32. See John Trevor Cliffe's lucid account in *Puritan Gentry Besieged, 1650–1700* (London: Routledge, 1993), chap. 7, 9, and 10. See also Coward, *Stuart England,* 287–88; and Paul Seaward, *The Cavalier Parliament and the Reconstruction of the Old Regime, 1661–1667* (Cambridge: Cambridge University Press, 1989), 162–95.

33. When Bishop Hall calls the Church of England mother, Milton retorts in *Animadversions:* "Wee acknowledge, and beleeve the Catholick reformed Church, and if any man be dispos'd to use a trope or figure, as Saint *Paul* once did in calling her the common Mother of us all, let him doe as his owne rhethorick shall perswade him. If therefore we must needs have a mother, and if the Catholick Church onely be, and must be she, let all Genealogie tell us if it can, what we must call the Church of *England,* unless we shall make every English Protestant a kind of poeticall *Bacchus,* to have two Mothers" (1:727). Clearly, as in *Of True Religion,* Milton plays with the Greek meaning of the word "Catholic" as "universal."

34. Here Milton mixes the Lutherans and Calvinists with those denominations that are not tolerated, trying to demonstrate the "errors" of the latter are hardly more egregious than those of the former. Strangely, he leaves the most persecuted Quakers out of the list.

Contributors

KENNETH BORRIS is associate professor of English at McGill University. The recipient of two major research grants, he was awarded the Isabel MacCaffrey Prize for the best Spenser essay published internationally in 1990, is author of *Spenser's Poetics of Prophecy in "The Faerie Queene" V*, and has published numerous articles on Spenser and Milton.

CHARLES W. DURHAM, professor emeritus of English at Middle Tennessee State University, is codirector of the biennial Conference on John Milton and coeditor of *Spokesperson Milton: Voices in Contemporary Criticism, Arenas of Conflict: Milton and the Unfettered Mind* (winner of the Irene Samuel Award for the most distinguished collection on Milton published in 1997), and *"All in All": Unity, Diversity, and the Miltonic Perspective*. He is also a member of the executive committee of the Milton Society of America.

J. MARTIN EVANS, professor of English at Stanford University, is author of *"Paradise Lost" and the Genesis Tradition, Milton's Imperial Epic: "Paradise Lost" and the Discourse of Colonialism*, and *The Miltonic Moment*.

RAPHAEL FALCO is associate professor of English at the University of Maryland, Baltimore County. His publications include *Conceived Presences: Literary Genealogy in Renaissance England* and *Charismatic Authority in Early Modern English Tragedy*.

CHERYL H. FRESCH, associate professor of English at the University of New Mexico, is currently serving as contributing editor for book 4 of *Paradise Lost* for the Milton Variorum Project. Her essay "Milton and Blake: Visualizing the Explusion" appeared in *"All in All": Unity, Diversity, and the Miltonic Perspective*.

LYNNE GREENBERG is a doctoral candidate at The City University of New York, specializing in the works of John Milton. She

303

has a J.D. from the University of Chicago Law School, has published on copyright and First Amendment issues in law journals, and has an article forthcoming in a volume on *Samson Agonistes* edited by Joseph Wittreich and Mark Kelley. She is also editing and writing introductions to two volumes of a series entitled *The Early Modern Englishwoman: A Facsimile Library of Essential Works.*

WILLIAM B. HUNTER, who in retirement claims no academic connection, has for nearly a decade been questioning the assignment to John Milton of the religiously eccentric treatise, *De Doctrina Christiana,* his position being most fully stated in *Visitation Unimplor'd.* He is also currently engaged in establishing the date and occasion for John Donne's "Lamentations of Jeremy."

JOHN LEONARD is professor of English at the University of Western Ontario. He has edited the Penguin Classics edition of Milton's *Complete Poems* (1998), and his book *Naming in Paradise* was a cowinner of the James Holly Hanford Award in 1990. He is currently preparing a Penguin edition of Milton's selected prose and writing a book about Milton's allusions.

MICHAEL LIEB is professor of English and research professor of humanities at the University of Illinois at Chicago. His interests include Milton and the early modern period, on the one hand, and the Bible and culture, on the other. Most recently, he has published *Children of Ezekiel: Aliens, UFOs, the Crisis of Race, and the Advent of End Time.* Among his other books are *Milton and the Culture of Violence* and *The Visionary Mode: Biblical Prophecy, Hermeneutics, and Cultural Change.* Lieb is Honored Scholar of the Milton Society of America, and his books are the recipients of the James Holly Hanford and Irene Samuel Awards.

SUSAN MCDONALD is a SSHRC doctoral fellow in the Department of English at the University of Western Ontario. Her thesis research investigates the commercial and legal options and obligations of publishing authors in seventeenth-century English.

SARAH R. MORRISON is associate professor of English at Morehead State University in Morehead, Kentucky. Her essay "Of Woman Borne: Male Experience and Feminine Truth in Jane Austen's Novels" appeared in *Studies in the Novel,* and her essay " 'Toil, Envy, Want, the reader, and the Jail': Reader Entrapment in Samuel Johnson's *Life of Savage*" appeared in *The Age of Johnson*.

ANNA K. NARDO, alumni professor of English literature at Louisiana State University, is author of *Milton's Sonnets and the Ideal Community, The Ludic Self in Seventeenth-Century English Literature*, "Academic Interludes in *Paradise Lost*" (winner of the James Holly Hanford Award from the Milton Society of America) in *Milton Studies*, and "*Romola* and Milton: A Cultural History of Rewriting" in *Nineteenth-Century Literature*.

KRISTIN A. PRUITT, professor of English and dean of the School of Arts at Christian Brothers University, is codirector of the biennial Conference on John Milton and coeditor of *Spokesperson Milton: Voices in Contemporary Criticism, Arenas of Conflict: Milton and the Unfettered Mind* (winner of the Irene Samuel Award for the most distinguished collection on Milton published in 1997), and "*All in All*": *Unity, Diversity, and the Miltonic Perspective*.

JOHN RUMRICH is professor of English at the University of Texas, Austin, and coeditor of *Texas Studies in Literature and Language*. His work on Milton includes *Matter of Glory: A New Preface to "Paradise Lost"* and *Milton Unbound*, and he is coeditor of *Milton and Heresy*.

PEGGY SAMUELS is assistant professor of English at Drew University in Madison, New Jersey. Her most recent publications are "Labor in the Chambers: *Paradise Regained* and the Discourse of Quiet" in *Milton Studies* and "Duelling Erasers: Milton and Scripture" in *Studies in Philology*.

PAUL R. SELLIN is professor emeritus of English and ex-chair, Netherlandic Studies Program, International and Overseas Programs, at the University of California, Los Angeles; Oudhoogleraar, Engelse letterkunde na 1500, Vrije Universiteit, Amsterdam; and advisory editor for the Netherlands section of the forthcoming *Oxford Companion to the Renaissance*. He has published a number of books, translations, and scholarly articles on seventeenth-century literary criticism, Anglo-Dutch relations, Daniel Heinsius, Donne, Marvell, Milton, Morus, and (currently) Michel le Blon and related matters involving art, literary, and Anglo-Continental diplomatic history.

CLAUDE N. STULTING JR., assistant professor of English and religion at Furman University, is author of *"Difference* and the *Deus Absconditus:* The Satanic Predicament in *Paradise Lost,"* published in *"All in All": Unity, Diversity, and the Miltonic Perspective.*

HONG WON SUH recently completed his dissertation, "They Also Serve: Haste and Delay in the Works of John Milton," under the direction of Stephen M. Fallon at the University of Notre Dame and is presently teaching at Yonsei University, South Korea, and expanding his dissertation into a book on Milton and ethics.

Index

Abelard, Peter, 55 n. 13
Achinstein, Sharon, 176 n. 12
Adams, Robert, 208
Adamson, Jack, 228
Addison, Joseph, 178, 194 n. 1
Aers, David, 281 n. 23, 282 n. 24
Alfred, William, 301 n. 29
Allen, Don Cameron, 162
Ames, William, 238
Amyraut, Moyse, 17, 238–53, 254 nn. 7 and 8, 254–55 n. 12, 255 nn. 13–22, 256 nn. 23–28, 31, 257 nn. 32 and 33, 37, 38, and 39, 43, 259 n. 71, 261 nn. 92–95, 262 n. 102
Aquinas, Thomas, Saint, 160 n. 42, 200, 215 n. 14, 279 n. 6
Aratus, 214 n. 6
Aristotle, 132, 200, 234
Arminius, Jacobus, 242–43, 249, 251, 262 n. 103
Armstrong, Brian G., 241, 254 n. 7, 262 n. 100
Armstrong, John, 45 n. 20
Ascensius, 142 n. 9
Athanasius, 144
Augustine, Saint, 23, 44 n. 7, 182, 200, 215 n. 14, 228, 262 n. 103
Austin, R. G., 141–42 n. 8

Bacon, Francis, 124
Baker, J. H., 115 nn. 13, 14, and 15
Baroni, Leonora, 58, 62
Baxter, Richard, 293, 301 n. 27
Bayne, Peter, 66
Beardslee, John W. III, 280 n. 12
Beier, Lucinda McCray, 97 nn. 20 and 24
Bell, Millicent, 53
Bell, Robert H., 43 n. 2
Bembo, Pietro, 142 n. 9
Bentley, Richard, 212

Beroaldo, Filippo, 142 n. 9
Berres, T., 141–42 n. 8
Bible: 1 Chronicles, 46 n. 32, 195 n. 16; 1 Corinthians, 181; 2 Corinthians, 45 n. 20, 158 n. 14; Daniel, 36, 172–73; Exodus, 31–32; Ephesians, 46–47 n. 32; Ezekiel, 172, 173, 182; Genesis, 21–22, 26, 29, 33–36, 38, 40–41, 43 n. 5, 46 n. 31–32, 49–51, 81, 91, 95, 99, 102–4, 150, 168, 170, 172, 174, 176 n. 10, 181–82, 191–93, 197 n. 43, 201, 234; Isaiah, 36; Jeremiah, 168–69; Job, 36–37; John, 29, 96 n. 14, 240, 246; Judges, 46 n. 32; 1 Kings, 172–73; 2 Kings, 172–73; Luke, 45 n. 20; Malachi, 169; Mark, 246; 1 Peter, 248; Psalms, 168–69; Revelation, 45 n. 20; Romans, 147, 241, 248, 271, 277; Ruth, 46 n. 32; 1 Samuel, 46 n. 32, 172–73; 2 Samuel, 46–47 n. 32; Song of Solomon, 170
Blackstone, William, 114 n. 4, 115 n. 16
Blessington, Francis C., 43 n. 2
Blumenfeld-Kosinski, Renate, 90, 97 n. 33, 98 nn. 39 and 46
Boethius, 266
Borris, Kenneth, 178–79, 186
Boyle, Robert, 163, 195 n. 12
Briggs, Charles A., 176 n. 9
Broadbent, J. B., 154
Brodwin, Leonora Leet, 187, 196 n. 38
Brown, Francis, 176 n. 9
Browning, Robert, 57
Bruno, Giordano, 200, 210, 216 n. 34
Buber, Martin, 176 n. 10
Bulwer-Lytton, Edward, 58–61, 63–64, 66, 68–69, 77, 79 n. 14
Bunyan, John, 23, 44 n. 7
Burden, Dennis, 159 n. 29
Burnett, Stephen G., 175 n. 2

307